Works Of Martin Luther With Introductions And Notes Volume I

Martin Luther

TABLE OF CONTENTS

INTRODUCTION

No historical study of current issues—politics or social science or theology—can far proceed without bringing the student face to face with the principles asserted by the Reformation of the Sixteenth Century and its great leader, Martin Luther. He has had many critics and many champions, but neither his critics nor his champions feel that the last word concerning him has been spoken, for scarcely a year passes that does not witness the publication of a new biography.

Had Luther been nothing more than a man of his own time and his own nation the task of estimating him would long since have been completed. A few exhaustive treatises would have answered all demands. But the Catalogue of the British Museum, published in 1894, contains over two hundred folio pages, averaging about thirty-five titles to the page, of books and pamphlets written either by or about him, that have been gathered into this single collection, in a land foreign to the sphere of his labors, and this list has been greatly augmented since 1894. Above all other historical characters that have appeared since the first years of Christianity, he is a man of the present day no less than of the day in which he lived.

But Luther can be properly known and estimated only when he is allowed to speak for himself. He should be seen not through the eyes of others, but through our own. In order to judge the man we must know all sides of the man, and read the heaviest as well as the lightest of his works, the more scientific and theological as well as the more practical and popular, his informal letters as well as his formal treatises. We must take account of the time of each writing and the circumstances under which it was composed, of the adversaries against whom he was contending, and of the progress which he made in his opinions as time went on. The great fund of primary sources which the historical methods of the last generation have made available should also be laid under contribution to shed light upon his statements and his attitude toward the various questions involved in his life-struggles.

As long as a writer can be read only in the language or languages in which he wrote, this necessary closer contact with his personality can be enjoyed only by a very limited circle of advanced scholars. But many of these will be grateful for a translation into their vernacular for more rapid reading, from which they may turn to the standard text when a question of more minute criticism is at stake. Even advanced students appreciate accurately rendered and scholarly annotated translations, by which the range of the leaders of human thought, with whom it is possible for them to be occupied, may be greatly enlarged. Such series of translations as those comprised in the well-edited Ante-Nicene, Nicene and Post-Nicene Libraries of the Fathers have served a most excellent purpose.

In the series introduced by this volume the attempt is made to render a similar service with respect to Luther. This is no ambitious project to reproduce in English all that he wrote or that fell from his lips in the lecture-room or in the pulpit. The plan has been to furnish

1

within the space of ten volumes a selection of such treatises as are either of most permanent value, or supply the best means for obtaining a true view of his many-sided literary activity and the sources of his abiding influence. The aim is not to popularize the writer, but to make the English, as far as possible, a faithful reproduction of the German or Latin. The work has been done by a small group of scholarly Lutheran pastors, residing near each other, and jointly preparing the copy for the printer. The first draft of each translation was thoroughly discussed and revised in a joint conference of the translators before final approval. Representative scholars, who have given more or less special study to Luther, have been called in to prepare some of the introductions. While the part contributed by each individual is credited at the proper place, it must yet be added that my former colleague, the late Rev. Prof. Adolph Spaeth, D. D., LL. D. (died June 25, 1910), was actively engaged as the Chairman of the Committee that organized the work, determined the plan, and, with the undersigned, made the first selection of the material to be included.

The other members of the Committee are the Rev. T. E. Schmauk,

D. D., LL. D., the Rev. L. D. Reed, D. D., the Rev. W. A. Lambert,

J. J. Schindel, A. Steimle, A. T. W. Steinhaeuser, and C. M.

Jacobs, D. D.; upon the five last named the burden of preparing

the translations and notes has rested.

Their work has been laborious and difficult. Luther's complaints concerning the seriousness of his task in attempting to teach the patriarch Job to speak idiomatic German might doubtless have found an echo in the experience of this corps of scholars in forcing Luther into idiomatic English. We are confident, however, that, as in Luther's case, so also here, the general verdict of readers will be that they have been eminently successful. It should also be known that it has been purely a labor of love, performed in the midst of the exacting duties of large pastorates, and to serve the Church, to whose ministry they have consecrated their lives.

The approaching jubilee of the Reformation in 1917 will call renewed attention to the author of these treatises. These volumes have been prepared with especial reference to the discussions which, we have every reason to believe, will then occur.

Henry Eyster Jacobs.

Luther Theological Seminary,

Mt. Airy, Philadelphia.

TRANSLATORS' NOTE

The languages from which the following translations have been made are the Latin and the German,—the Latin of the German Universities, the German of the people, and both distinctively Luther's. In the Latin there is added to the imperfection of the form, when measured by classical standards, the difficulty of expressing in an old language the new thoughts of the Reformation. German was regarded even by Gibbon, two hundred and fifty years later, as a barbarous idiom. Luther, especially in his earlier writings, struggled to give form to a language and to express the highest thoughts in it. Where Luther thus struggled with two languages, it is evident that they have no easy task who attempt to reproduce the two in a third.

Modern Germans find it convenient to read Luther's German in a modernized text, sometimes rather hastily and uncritically constructed, and altogether unsafe as a basis for translation. Where the Germans have had to modify, a translator meets double difficulties. It may be puzzling for him to know Luther's exact meaning; it is even more puzzling to find the exact English equivalent.

In order to overcome these difficulties, in part at least, and present a translation both accurate and readable, the present group of translators have not simply distributed the work among themselves, but have together revised each translation as it was made. The original translator, at a meeting of the group, has submitted his work to the rest for criticism and correction, amounting at times to retranslation. No doubtful point, whether in sense or in sound, has been passed by unchallenged.

Even with such care, the translation is not perfect. In places a variant reading is possible, a variant interpretation plausible. We can only claim that an honest effort has been made to be both accurate and clear, and submit the result of our labors to a fair and scholarly criticism. Critics can hardly be more severe than we have been to one another. If they find errors, it may be that we have seen them, and preferred the seeming error to the suggested correction; if not, we can accept criticism from others as gracefully as from each other.

The sources from which our translations have been made are the best texts available in each case. In general, these are found in the Weimar Edition (D. Martin Luthers Werke. Kritische Gesammtausgabe. Weimar. Hermann Böhlaus Nachfolger, 1883 ff.), so far as this is completed. A more complete and fairly satisfactory edition is that known as the Erlangen Edition, in which the German and Latin works are published in separate series, 1826 ff. The text of the Berlin Edition (Luthers Werke, herausgegeben von Pfarrer D. Dr. Buchwald, etc., Berlin, C. A. Schwetschke und Sohn, third edition, 1905, ten volumes) is modernized, and where it has been used it has been carefully compared with the more critical texts. The two editions of Walch—the original, published 1740-1753, in twenty-four volumes, at Halle, and the modern edition, known as the St. Louis, Mo., edition, 1880 ff.—are entirely German, and somewhat modernized. For our purpose they could be used only as helps in the interpretation, and not as standard texts for translation. A very convenient and satisfactory critical text of selected treatises is to be found in Otto Clemen, Luthers Werke in Auswahl, Bonn, 4 vols., of which two volumes appeared in 1912.

WORKS OF MARTIN LUTHER

SELECTIONS FROM LUTHER'S PREFACES TO HIS WORKS 1539 and 1545

I

LUTHER'S PREFACE TO THE FIRST PART OF HIS GERMAN WORKS[1]

EDITION OF 1539

I would gladly have seen all my books forgotten and destroyed; if only for the reason that I am afraid of the example.[2] For I see what benefit it has brought to the churches, that men have begun to collect many books and great libraries, outside and alongside of the Holy Scriptures; and have begun especially to scramble together, without any distinction, all sorts of "Fathers," "Councils," and "Doctors." Not only has good time been wasted, and the study of the Scriptures neglected; but the pure understanding of the divine Word is lost, until at last the Bible has come to lie forgotten in the dust under the bench.

Although it is both useful and necessary that the writings of some of the Fathers and the decrees of some of the Councils should be preserved as witnesses and records, nevertheless, I think, est modus in rebus,[3] and it is no pity that the books of many of the Fathers and Councils have, by God's grace, been lost. If they had all remained, one could scarce go in or out for books, and we should still have nothing better than we find in the Holy Scriptures.

Then, too, it was our intention and our hope, when we began to put the Bible into German, that there would be less writing, and more studying and reading of the Scriptures. For all other writings should point to the Scriptures, as John pointed to Christ; when he said, "He must increase, but I must decrease." [John 3:30] In this way every one may drink for himself from the fresh spring, as all the Fathers have had to do when they wished to produce anything worth while. Neither Fathers nor Councils nor we ourselves will do so well, even when our very best is done, as the Holy Scriptures have done; that is to say, we shall never do so well as God Himself. Even though for our salvation we need to have the Holy Spirit and faith and divine language and divine works, nevertheless we must let the Prophets and Apostles sit at the desk, while we sit at their feet and listen to what they say. It is not for us to say what they must hear.

Since, however, I cannot prevent it, and, without my wish, they are now bent on collecting and printing my books—small honor to me—I shall have to let them put their energy and labor on the venture. I comfort myself with the thought that my books will yet be forgotten in the dust, especially when, by God's grace, I have written something good. Non ero melior patribus meis.[4][1 Kings 19:4] The other kind will be more likely to endure. For when the Bible can be left lying under the bench, and when it is true of the Fathers and Councils that the better they were, the more completely they have been forgotten; there is good hope that, when the curiosity of this age has been satisfied, my books too will not long remain; the more so, since it has begun to rain and snow books and "Doctors," of which many are already forgotten and gone to dust, so that one no longer remembers even their names. They themselves had hoped, to be sure, that they would always be in the market, and play schoolmaster to the churches.

Well, then, let it go, in God's Name. I only ask in all kindness that the man who wishes at this time to have my books will by no means let them be a hindrance to his own study of the Scriptures, but read them as I read the orders and the ordures of the pope[5] and the books of the sophists. I look now and then to see what they have done, or learn from them the history and thought of their time, but I do not study them, or feel myself bound to conform to them. I do not treat the Fathers and the Councils very differently. In this I follow the example of St. Augustine, who is one of the first, and almost the only one of them to subject himself to the Holy Scriptures alone, uninfluenced by the books of all the Fathers and the Saints. This brought him into a hard fray with St. Jerome, who cast up to him the writings of his predecessors; but he did not care for that. If this example of St. Augustine had been followed, the pope would not have become Antichrist, the countless vermin, the swarming, parasitic mass of books would not have come into the Church, and the Bible would have kept its place in the pulpit.

FOOTNOTES

[1] Text as given in the Berlin Edition of the Buchwald and others, Vol. I pp. ix ff.

[2] I. e. The example set by preserving and collecting them.

[3] "There is moderation in all things."

[4] "I shall not be better than my fathers." Cf. 1 Kings 19:4

[5] Des Pabats Drecet and Drecketal. Luther makes a pun on decreta and decretalia—the official names for the decrees of the Pope.

II DR. MARTIN LUTHER TO THE CHRISTIAN READER[1] EDITION OF 1545

Above all things I beseech the Christian reader and beg him for the sake of our Lord Jesus Christ, to read my earliest books very circumspectly and with much pity, knowing that before now I too was a monk, and one of the right frantic and raving papists. When I took up this matter against Indulgences, I was so full and drunken, yea, so besotted in papal doctrine that, out of my great zeal, I would have been ready to do murder—at least, I would have been glad to see and help that murder should be done—on all who would not be obedient and subject to the pope, even to his smallest word.

Such a Saul was I at that time; and I meant it right earnestly; and there are still many such today. In a word, I was not such a frozen and ice-cold[2] champion of the papacy as Eck and others of his kind have been and still are. They defend the Roman See more for the sake of the shameful belly, which is their god, than because they are really attached to its cause. Indeed I am wholly of the opinion that like latter-day Epicureans,[3] they only laugh at the pope. But I verily espoused this cause in deepest earnest and in all fidelity; the more so because I shrank from the Last Day with great anxiety and fear and terror, and yet from the depths of my heart desired to be saved.

Therefore, Christian reader, thou wilt find in my earliest books and writings how many points of faith I then, with all humility, yielded and conceded to the pope, which since then I have held and condemned for the most horrible blasphemy and abomination, and which I would have to be so held and so condemned forever. Amen.

Thou wilt therefore ascribe this my error, or as my opponents venomously call it, this inconsistency of mine,[4] to the time, and to my ignorance and inexperience. At the beginning I was quite alone and without any helpers, and moreover, to tell the truth, unskilled in all these things, and far too unlearned to discuss such high and weighty matters. For it was without any intention, purpose, or will of mine that I fell, quite unexpectedly, into this wrangling and contention. This I take God, the Searcher of hearts, to witness.

I tell these things to the end that, if thou shalt read my books, thou mayest know and remember that I am one of those who, as St. Augustine says of himself, have grown by writing and by teaching others, and not one of those who, starting with nothing, have in a trice become the most exalted and most learned doctors. We find, alas! many of these self-grown doctors; who in truth are nothing, do nothing and accomplish nothing, are moreover untried and inexperienced, and yet, after a single took at the Scriptures, think themselves able wholly to exhaust its spirit.

Farewell, dear reader, in the Lord. Pray that the Word may be further spread abroad, and may be strong against the miserable devil. For he is mighty and wicked, and just now is raving everywhere and raging cruelly, like one who well knows and feels that his time is short, and that the kingdom of his Vicar, the Antichrist in Rome,[5] is sore beset. But may the God of all grace and mercy strengthen and complete in us the work He has begun, to His honor and to the comfort of His little flock. Amen.

FOOTNOTES

[1] From the Preface to the Complete Works (1545). Text according to the Berlin Edition of the Buchwald and others, Vol. I, pp. xi ff.

[2] Evidently a play on the Latin frigidus, often used in the sense of "trivial" or "silly"; so Luther refers to the "frigida decreta Paperum" in his Propositions for the Leipzipg Disputation (1519).

[3] i. e. Frivolous mockers at holy things.

[4] See Prefatory Note to the Fourteen of Consolation, below, p.109.

[5] Long before this Luther had repeatedly expressed the conviction that the Pope was the Antichrist foretold in 2 Thess. 2:3 f., and Rev. 13 and 17.

THE DISPUTATION OF DOCTOR MARTIN LUTHER

ON THE POWER AND EFFICACY OF INDULGENCES

(THE NINETY-FIVE THESES)

1517

TOGETHER WITH THREE LETTERS EXPLANATORY OF THE THESES

INTRODUCTION

"A Disputation of the Power and Efficacy of Indulgences" [1] is the full title of the document commonly called "The Ninety-five Theses." The form of the document was determined by the academic practice of the Middle Ages. In all the Mediæval Universities the "disputation" was a well-established institution. It was a debate, conducted according to accepted rules, on any subject which the chief disputant might elect, and no student's education was thought to be complete until he had shown his ability to defend himself in discussions of this kind. It was customary to set forth the subject which was to be discussed, in a series of "theses," which were statements of opinion tentatively advanced as the basis of argument. The author, or some other person he might designate, announced himself ready to defend these statements against all comers, and invited all who might wish to debate with him to a part in the discussion. Such an academic document, one out of many hundreds, exhaling the atmosphere of the Mediæval University, is the Disputation, which by its historical importance has earned the name "The XCV Theses."

The Theses were published on the Eve of All Saints (Oct 31), 1517. They were not intended for any other public than that of the University,[2] and Luther did not even have them printed at first, though copies were forwarded to the Archbishop of Mainz, and to Luther's own diocesan, the Bishop of Brandenburg. The manner of their publication too was academic. They were simply posted on the door of the Church of All Saints—called the "Castle-church," to distinguish it from its neighbor, the "Town-church"—not because more people would see them there than elsewhere, but because that church-door was the customary place for posting such announcements, the predecessor of the "black-board" in the modern German University. It was not night, but mid-day[3] when the Theses were nailed up, and the Eve of All Saints was chosen, not that the crowds who would frequent the next day's festival might read them, for they were written in Latin, but because it was the customary day for the posting of theses. Moreover, the Feast of All Saints was the time when the precious relics, which earned the man who "adored" them, long years of indulgence,[4] were exhibited to worshipers, and the approach of this high feast-day put the thought of indulgences uppermost in the minds of everybody in Wittenberg, including the author of the Theses.[5]

But neither the Theses nor the results which followed them could be confined to Wittenberg. Contrary to Luther's expectation and to his great surprise,[6] they circulated all through Germany with a rapidity that was startling. Within two months, before the end of 1517, three editions of the Latin text had been printed, one at Wittenberg, one at Nürnberg, and one as far away as Basel, and copies of the Theses had been sent to Rome. Numerous editions, both Latin and German, quickly followed. Luther's contemporaries saw in the publication of the Theses "the beginning of the Reformation," [7] and the judgment of modern times has confirmed their verdict, but the Protestant of to-day, and especially the Protestant layman, is almost certain to be surprised, possibly deeply disappointed, at their contents. They are not "a trumpet-blast of reform"; that title must be reserved for the great works of 1520.[8] The word "faith," destined to become the watchword of the Reformation, does not once occur in them; the validity of the Sacrament of Penance is not disputed; the right of the pope to forgive sins, especially in "reserved cases," is not denied; even the virtue of indulgences is admitted, within limits, and the question at issue is simply "What is that virtue?"

To read the Theses, therefore, with a fair degree of comprehension we must know something of the time that produced them, and we must bear two facts continually in mind. We must remember that at this time Luther was a devoted son of the Church and servant of the pope, perhaps not quite the "right frantic and raving papist" [9] he afterwards called himself, but as yet entirely without suspicion of the extent to which he had inwardly diverged from the teachings of Roman theology. We must also remember that the Theses were no attempt at a searching examination of the whole structure and content of Roman teaching, but were directed against what Luther conceived to be merely abuses which had sprung up around a single group of doctrines centering in the Sacrament of Penance. He sincerely thought that the teaching of the Theses was in full agreement with the best traditions of the Church,[10] and his surprise that they should have caused so much excitement is undoubtedly genuine and not feigned. He shows himself both hurt and astonished that he should be assailed as a heretic and schismatic, and "called by six hundred other names of ignominy." [11] On the other hand, we are compelled to admit that from the outset Luther's opponents had grasped far more completely than he himself the true significance of his "purely academic protest."

2. Penance and Indulgence.—The purpose of the disputation which Luther proposed to hold was to clear up the subject of the virtue of "indulgences," and the indulgences were the most striking and characteristic feature of the religious life of the Church in the last three Centuries of the Middle Ages.[12] We meet them everywhere—indulgences for the adoration of relics, indulgences for worship at certain shrines, indulgences for pilgrimages here or there, indulgences for contributions to this or that special object of charity. Luther roundly charges the indulgence-vendors with teaching the people that the indulgences as a means to the remission of sins. What are these indulgences?

Their history is connected, on the one hand, with the history of the Sacrament of Penance, on the other with the history of the development of papal power. The Sacrament of Penance developed out of the administration of Church discipline. In the earliest days of the Church, the Christian who fell into sin was punished by exclusion from the communion of the Church. This excommunication was not, however, permanent, and the sinner could be restored to the privileges of Church-fellowship after he had confessed his sin, professed penitence, and performed certain penitential acts, chief among which were alms-giving, fasting and prayer, and, somewhat later, pilgrimage. These acts of penitence came to have the name of "satisfactions," and were a condition precedent to the reception of absolution. They varied in duration and severity, according to the enormity of the offence, end for the guidance of those who administered the discipline of the Church, sets of rules were formulated by which the "satisfactions" or "penances" were imposed. These codes are the "Penitential Canons." [13] The first step in the development of the indulgences may be found in the practice which gradually arose, of remitting some part of the enjoined "penances" on consideration of the performance of certain acts which could be regarded as meritorious.

The indulgences received a new form, however, and became a part of the regular Church administration, when the popes discovered the possibilities which lay in this institution for the advancement of their own power and the furtherance of their own interests. This discovery seems to date from the time of the Crusades. The crusading-indulgences, granted at first only to those who actually went to the Holy War, subsequently to those also who contributed to the expense of the expedition, were virtually the acceptance of this work as a substitute for any penance which the Church might otherwise require. As zeal for the Crusades began to wane, the indulgences were used more and more freely to stimulate lagging interest; their number was greatly increased, and those who purchased the

9

indulgences with money far outnumbered those who actually took the Cross. Failing in their purpose as an incentive to enlistment in the crusading armies, they showed their value as a source of income, and from the beginning of the XIV. Century the sale of indulgences became a regular business.

About the same time a new kind of indulgence arose to take the place of the now somewhat antiquated crusading-indulgence. This was the Jubilee-indulgence, and had its origin in the Jubilee of 1300. By the Bull Antiquorum Habet Fide, Boniface VIII. granted to all who would visit the shrines of the Apostles in Rome during the year 1300 and during each succeeding centennial year, a plenary indulgence.[14] Little by little it became the custom to increase the number of these Jubilee-indulgences. Once in a hundred years was not often enough for Christians to have a chance for plenary forgiveness, and at last, unwilling to deprive of the privileges of the Jubilee those who were kept away from Rome, the popes came to grant the same plenary indulgence to all who would make certain contributions to the papal treasury.[15]

Meanwhile the Sacrament of Penance had become an integral part of the Roman sacramental system, and had replaced the earlier penitential discipline as the means by which the Church granted Christians forgiveness for sins committed after baptism. The scholastic theologians had busied themselves with the theory of this Sacrament. They distinguished between its "material," its "form" and its "effect." The "form" of the Sacrament was the absolution: its "effect," the forgiveness of sins; Its "material," three acts of the penitent: "confession," "contrition," and "satisfaction." "Confession" must be by word of mouth, and must include all the sins which the sinner could remember to have committed; "contrition" must be sincere sorrow of the heart, and must include the purpose henceforth to avoid sin; "satisfaction" must be made by works prescribed by the priest who heard confession. In the administration of the Sacrament, however, the absolution preceded "satisfaction" instead of following it, as it had done in the discipline of the early Church.[16] To justify this apparent inconsistency, the Doctors further distinguished between the "guilt" and the "penalty" of sin.[17] Sins were classified as "mortal" and "venial." [18] Mortal sins for which the offender had not received absolution were punished eternally, while venial sins were those which merited only some smaller penalty; but when a mortal sin was confessed and absolution granted, the guilt of the sin was done away, and with it the eternal penalty. And yet the absolution did not open the gate of heaven, though it closed the door of hell; the eternal penalty was not to be exacted, but there was a temporal penalty to be paid. The "satisfaction" was the temporal penalty, and if satisfaction was in arrears at death, the arrearage must be paid in purgatory, a place of punishment for mortal sins confessed and repented, but "unsatisfied," and for venial sins, which were not serious enough to bring eternal condemnation. The penalties of purgatory were "temporal," viz., they stopped somewhere this side of eternity, and their duration could be measured in days and years, though the number of the years might mount high into the thousands and tens of thousands.

It was at this point that the practice of indulgences united with the theory of the Sacrament of Penance. The indulgences had to do with the "satisfaction." [19] They might be "partial," remitting only a portion of the penalties, measured by days or years of purgatory; or they might be "plenary," remitting all penalties due in this world or the next. In theory, however, no indulgence could remit the guilt or the eternal penalty of sin,[20] and the purchaser of an indulgence was not only expected to confess and be absolved, but he was also supposed to be corde contritus, i. e., "truly penitent." [21] A rigid insistence on the fulfilment of these conditions would have greatly restricted the value of the indulgences as a means of gain, for the right to hear confession and grant absolution belonged to the parish-priests. Consequently, it became the custom to endow the indulgence-vendors with extraordinary powers. They were given the authority to hear confession and grant absolution wherever they might be, and to absolve even from the sins which were normally "reserved" for the absolution of the higher Church authorities.

The demand for contrition was somewhat more difficult to meet. But here too there was a way out. Complete contrition included love to God as its motive, and the truly contrite man was not always easy to find; but some of the scholastic Doctors had discovered a substitute for contrition in what they called "attrition." viz., incomplete contrition, which might have fear for a motive, and which the Sacrament of Penance could transform into contrition. When, therefore, a man was afraid of hell or of purgatory, he could make his confession to the indulgence-seller or his agent, receive from him the absolution which gave his imperfect repentance the value of true contrition, released him from the guilt of sin, and changed its eternal penalty to a temporal penalty; then he could purchase the plenary indulgence, which remitted the temporal penalty, and so in one transaction, in which all the demands of the Church were formally met, he could become sure of heaven. Thus the indulgence robbed the Sacrament of Penance of its ethical content.

Furthermore, indulgences were made available for souls already in purgatory. This kind of indulgence seems to have been granted for the first time in 1476. It had long been been that the prayers of the living availed to shorten the pains of the departed, and the institution of masses for the dead was of long standing; but it was not without some difficulty that the Popes succeeded in establishing their claim to power over purgatory. Their power over the souls of the living was not disputed. The "Power of the Keys" had been given to Peter and transmitted to his successors; the "Treasury of the Church," [22] i. e., the merits of Christ and of the Saints, was believed to be at their disposal, and it was this treasury which they employed in the granting of indulgences;[23] but it seemed reasonable to suppose that their jurisdiction ended with death. Accordingly, Pope Sixtus IV, in 1477, declared that the power of the Pope over purgatory, while genuine, was exercised only per modum sufiragii, "by way of intercession." [24] The distinction was thought dogmatically important, but to the layman, who looked more to results than to methods, the difference between intercession and jurisdiction was trifling. To him the important thing was that the Pope, whether by jurisdiction or intercession, was able to release the soul of a departed Christian from the penalties of purgatory. It is needless to say that these indulgences for the dead were eagerly purchased. In filial love and natural affection the indulgence vendor had powerful allies.

3. The Indulgence of 1515.—The XCV Theses were called forth by the preaching of the "Jubilee Indulgence" [25] of 1510, which was not placed on sale in central Germany until 1515. The financial needs of the papacy were never greater than in the last years of the XV. and the first years of the XVI. Century, and they were further increased by the resolve of Julius II. to erect a new church of St. Peter, which should surpass in magnificence all the churches of the world. The indulgence of 1510 was an extraordinary financial measure, the proceeds of which were to pay for the erection of the new Basilica, but when Julius died in 1513, the church was not completed, and the money had not been raised. The double task was bequeathed to his successor, Leo X. On the 31st of March, 1515, Leo proclaimed a plenary indulgence for the Archbishops of Magdeburg and Mainz, and appointed Albrecht, of Brandenburg, who was the incumbent of both sees and of the bishopric of Halberstadt as well, Commissioner for the sale of this indulgence. By a secret agreement, of which Luther was, of course, entirely ignorant, one-half of the proceeds was to be paid to the Fuggers of Ausburg on account of money advanced to the Archbishop for the payment of the fees to Rome, and of the sums demanded in consideration of a dispensation allowing him to occupy three sees at the same time; the other half of the proceeds was to go to the papal treasury to be applied to the building of the new church. The period during which the indulgence was to be on sale was eight years.

The actual work of organizing the "indulgence-campaign" was put into the hands of John Tetzel, whose large experience in the selling of indulgences fitted him excellently for the post of Sub-commissioner. The indulgence-sellers acted under the commission of the Archbishop and the directions of Tetzel, who took personal charge of the enterprise. The preachers went from city to city, and during the time that they were preaching the indulgence in any given place, all other preaching was required to cease.[26] They held out the usual inducements to prospective buyers. The plenary nature of the indulgence was made especially prominent, and the people were eloquently exhorted that the purchase of indulgence-letters was better than all good works, that they were an insurance against the pains of hell and of purgatory, that they availed for all satisfactions, even in the case of the most heinous sins that could be conceived.[27] "Confessional letters" [28] were one of the forms of this indulgence. They gave their possessor permission to choose his own confessor, and entitled him to plenary remission once in his life, to absolution from sins normally reserved, etc. The indulgences for the dead were zealously proclaimed, and the duty of purchasing for departed souls release from the pains of purgatory was most urgently enjoined. So great was the power of the indulgence to alleviate the pains of purgatory, that the souls of the departed were said to pass into heaven the instant that the coins of the indulgence-buyer jinked in the money-box.[29]

4. Luther's Protest—The Theses were Luther's protest against the manner in which this indulgence was preached, and against the Use conception of the efficacy of indulgences which the people obtained from such preaching. They were not his first protest, however. In a sermon, preached July 37th, 1516,[30] he had issued a warning against the false idea that a man who had bought an indulgence was sure of salvation, and had declared the

12

assertion that souls could be bought out of purgatory to be "a piece of temerity." His warnings were repeated in other sermons, preached October 31st, 1516, and February 14th, 1517.[31] The burden of these warnings is always the same: the indulgences lead men astray; they incite to fear of God's penalties and not to fear of sin; they encourage false hopes of salvation, and make light of the true condition of forgiveness, vis., sincere and genuine repentance.

These warnings are repeated in the Theses. The preaching of indulgences has concealed the true nature of repentance; the first thing to consider is what "our Lord and Master Jesus Christ means," when He says, "Repent." [32] Without denying the pope's right to the power of the keys, Luther wishes to come into the clear about the extent of the pope's jurisdiction, which does not reach as far as purgatory. He believes that the pope has the right to remit "penalties," but these penalties are of the same sort as those which were imposed in the early Church as a condition precedent to the absolution; they are ecclesiastical penalties merely, and do not extend beyond the grave; the true penalty of sin is hatred of self, which continues until entrance into the kingdom of heaven.[33]

The Theses are formulated with continual reference to the statements of the indulgence-preachers, and of the Instruction to the Commissaries issued under the name of the Archbishop of Mainz. [34] For this reason there is little logical sequence in the arrangement of the Theses, and none of the attempts to discover a plan or scheme underlying them has been successful.[35] In a general way it may be said that for the positive views of Luther on the subjects discussed, Theses 30-37 and 41-51 are the most vital, while Theses 92-95 are sufficient evidence of the motive which led Luther to make his protest.

5. Conclusion—The editors of this Translation present herewith a new translation of the Theses, together with three letters, which will help the reader to understand the mind of Luther at the time of their composition and his motive in preparing them. The first of these letters is that which was sent, with a copy of the Theses, to Albrecht of Mainz. The second and third are addressed respectively to Staupitz and Leo X., and were written to accompany the "Resolutions," [36] an exhaustive explanation and defense of the Theses, published in 1518, after the controversy had become bitter.

6. Literature—(a) Sources. The source material for history of indulgences is naturally widely scattered. The most convenient collection is found in Koehler, Dokumente zum Ablassstreit, Tübingen, 1900. For the indulgences against which Luther protested, see, beside the Editions of Luther's Works, Kapp, Schauplatz des Tetselischen Ablass-Krams, Leipzig, 1720; Sammlung einiger zum päbstlichen Ablass gehörigen Schriften, Leipzig, 1721; Kleine Nachlese zur Erläuterung der Reformationsgeschicte, Leipzig, 1730 and 1733; also Loescher, Vollständige Reformationsacta, I, Leipzig, 1720

(b) Secondary Works. Beside the general works in Church History and History of Doctrine, see the Lives of Luther, in German especially those of Köstlin-Kawerau, Kolde, Berger and Hausrath; in English those of Beard, Jacobs, Lindsay, Smith and McGiffert; also Boehmer, Luther im Lichte der neueren Forschung, ad ed., Leipzig, 1910.

On the indulgences in their relation to the Sacrament of Penance, H, C. Lea, History of Confession and Indulgence, especially Vol. III, Philadelphia, 1896; Brieger, Das Wesen des Ablasses am Ausgang des Mittelalters, Leizig, 1897, and Article Indulgenzen in PRE.3 IX, pp. 76 ff. (Eng. in Schaff-Herzog v., pp. 485-88); Gottlob, Kreuzablass und Almosenablass, Stuttgart, 1906 (especially valuable for the origin of indulgences).

On the indulgences and the XCV Theses, Koestlin, Luther's

Theologie, Leipzig, 1883 (Eng. Trans, by Hay, The Theology of

Luther, Philadelphia, 1897); Bratke, Luther's XCV Thesen und

ihre dogmengeschictlichen Voraussetzungen, Göttingen, 1884;

Dieckhoff, Der Ablassstreit dogmengeschichtlich dargestellt,

Gotha, 1886; Lindsay, History of the Reformation, I, New York,

1906; Tschackert, Entstehung der lutherischen und reformierten

Kirchenlehre, Göttingen, 1910.

On the financial aspects of the indulgence-traffic, Schulte, Die

Fugger in Rom, 2 vols., Leipzig, 1904.

CHARLES M. JACOBS.

Allentown, PA.

FOOTNOTES

[1] Disputato pro declaratione virutis indulgentiarum.

[2] Luther says, Apud nostros et propter nostros editae aunt. Weimar Ed., I. 528. On the whole subject see Letters to Staupitz and the Pope, below.

[3] Cf. Weimar Ed., I, 229.

[4] The Church of All Saints at Wittenberg was the repository of the great collection of relics which Frederick the Wise had gathered. A catalogue of the collection, with

illustrations by Lucas Cranach, was published in 1509. The collection contained 5005 sacred objects, including a bit of the crown of thorns and some of the Virgin Mother's milk. Adoration of these relics on All Saints' Day (Nov. 1st) was rewarded with indulgence for more than 500,000 years. So, Vol Bezold, Die deutsche Reformation (1890), p. 100; see also Barge, Karlstadt, I, 39ff.

[5] Luther had preached a sermon warning against the danger of indulgences on the Eve of All Saints (1516). See below.

[6] See below, Letter to Leo X.

[7] Weimar Ed., I, 230.

[8] The Address to the Christian Nobility and the Babylonian Captivity of the Church.

[9] Introduction to the Complete Works (1545); above p.10.

[10] See Letter to Staupitz, below.

[11] See Letter to Leo X, below.

[12] Cf. Gottlob, Kreuzablass und Almosenblass, p. I.

[13] See Theses 5, 8, 85.

[14] Non solam plenam et largiorem, imo plenissimam omnium suorum concedemus et concedimus veniam peccatorum. Mirbt, Quellen, 2d ed., No. 243.

[15] This custom of putting the Jubilee-indulgences on sale seems to date from the year 1390. Cf. Lea, Hist. of Conf. and Indulg., III, 206.

No mention is here made of the indulgences attached to adoration of the relics, etc. On the development of this form of indulgence see Lea, Hist. of Conf. and Indulg., III, 131-194, 234-195, and Gottlog, Kreuzablass und Almosenablass, pp. 195-254.

[16] See Thesis 12.

[17] See Theses 4-6, Note 2.

[18] For Luther's opinion of this distinction, see the Discourse Concerning Confession elsewhere in the present volume.

[19] "Not even the poorest part of the penance which is called 'satisfaction,' but the remission of the poorest part of penance." Letter to Staupitz, below.

[20] There is ample proof that in practice the indulgences were preached as sufficient to secure the purchaser the entire remission of sin, and the form a culpa et poena was officially employed in many cases (Cf. Brieger, Das Wesen des Abiases am Ausgang des M A. and PRE3 IX. 83 ff., and Lea, History of Confession, etc., III, 54 ff.). "It is difficult to withstand the conclution that even in theory indulgences had been declared to be efficacious for the removal of the guilt of sin in the presence of God," Lindsay, History of the Reformation, I, 226.

[21] It is the basis of this theory that Roman Catholic writers on indulgences declare them to be "extra-sacramental," i. e., outside the Sacrament of Penance. So, e.g., Kent, in The Catholic Encyclopedia, Art. Indulgence.

[22] See Theses 56-58.

[23] The doctrine of the "Treasury of the Church" grew up as a result of the indulgences. It was an attempt to answer the question, How can a "satisfaction," which God demands, be waived? The answer is, By the application of merits earned by Christ and by the Saints who did more than God requires. These merits form the Treasury of the Church. Cf. Seeberg, PRE3 XV, 417; Lea, Hist. of Confession, etc., III, 14-28.

[24] See Theses 26.

[25] i. e. A plenary indulgence similar to those granted for pilgrimage to Rome in Jubilee-years. See above, p.18.

[26] See Theses 53-55.

[27] See Thesis 75.

[28] See Thesis 35.

[29] See Thesis 27.

[30] Weimar Ed., I, 63 ff.; Erl. Ed., I, 101 ff.

[31] Weimar Ed., I, 94 ff,; Erl. Ed., I, 171 ff., 177 ff.

[32] See Thesis 1.

[33] See Thesis 4.

[34] See Letter to Archbishop, below. The text of this Instruction in Kapp, Sammlung, etc. (1721), pp. 117-206. Tschackert has surmised that even the number of the Theses was determined by the number of the paragraphs in this Instruction. There were 94 of these paragraphs, and of the Theses 94 + 1. Enstehung d. luth. u. ref. Kirchenlehre (1910), p. 16, note 1.

[35] The following, based on an unpublished manuscript of Th.

Brieger, is an interesting analysis of the contents and subject

matter of the Theses. For the sake of brevity the minor

subdivisions are omitted:

Introduction. The ideas fundamentally involved in the concept of poenitentia (Th. 1-7).

I. Indulgences for souls in purgatory (Th. 8-29).

    1. Canonical Penalties and the pains of purgatory (Th. 8-19).

    2. The relation of the Pope to purgatory (Th. 8-19).

II. Indulgences for the living (Th. 30-80).

    1. The content and nature of the preaching of indulgences
    (Th. 30-55).

    2. The treasury of the Church (Th. 56-66).

    3. The duty of the regular church-authorities on the
    matter (Th. 67-80).

Conclusion (Th. 81-95).

    1. The objections of the laity of the indulgence-traffic
    (Th. 81-91).

    2. The evil motive of the traffic in indulgences, with
    special references to the statements of Th. 1-4 (Th.
    91-95). H. Hermelink in Krüger's Handbuch der
    Kirchengeschicte (1911), III, 66.

[36] Weimar Ed., I, pp. 525 ff.

I

LETTER TO THE ARCHBISHOP ALBRECHT OF MAINZ

OCTOBER 31, 1517

To the Most Reverend Father in Christ and Most Illustrious Lord,
Albrecht of Magdeburg and Mainz, Archbishop and Primate of the
Church, Margrave of Brandenburg, etc., his own lord and pastor in
Christ, worthy of reverence and fear, and most gracious.

JESUS[1]

The grace of God be with you in all its fulness and power! Spare me. Most Reverend Father
in Christ and Most Illustrious Prince, that I, the dregs of humanity, have so much boldness
that I have dared to think of a letter to the height of your Sublimity. The Lord Jesus is my

witness that, conscious of my smallness and baseness, I have long deferred what I am now shameless enough to do,—moved thereto most of all by the duty of fidelity which I acknowledge that I owe to your most Reverend Fatherhood in Christ. Meanwhile, therefore, may your Highness deign to cast an eye upon one speck of dust, and for the sake of your pontifical clemency to heed my prayer.

Papal indulgences for the building of St. Peter's are circulating under your most distinguished name, and as regards them, I do not bring accusation against the outcries of the preachers, which I have not heard, so much as I grieve over the wholly false impressions which the people have conceived from them; to wit,—the unhappy souls believe that if they have purchased letters of indulgence they are sure of their salvation;[2] again, that so soon as they cast their contributions into the money-box, souls fly out of purgatory;[3] furthermore, that these graces [i. e., the graces conferred in the indulgences] are so great that there is no sin too great to be absolved, even, as they say—though the thing is impossible—if one had violated the Mother of God;[4] again, that a man is free, through these indulgences, from all penalty and guilt.[5]

O God, most good! Thus souls committed to your care, good Father, are taught to their death, and the strict account, which you must render for all such, grows and increases. For this reason I have no longer been able to keep quiet about this matter, for it is by no gift of a bishop that man becomes sure of salvation, since he gains this certainty not even by the "inpoured grace" [6] of God, but the Apostle bids us always "work out our own salvation in fear and trembling," [Phil. 2:12] and Peter says, "the righteous scarcely shall be saved." [1 Pet. 4:18, Matt] Finally, so narrow is the way that leads to life, that the Lord, through the prophets Amos and Zechariah, calls those who shall be saved "brands plucked from the burning," [Amos 4:11, Zech. 3:2] and everywhere declares the difficulty of salvation.

Why, then, do the preachers of pardons, by these false fables and promises, make the people careless and fearless? Whereas indulgences confer on us no good gift, either for salvation or for sanctity, but only take away the external penalty, which it was formerly the custom to impose according to the canons.[7]

Finally, works of piety and love are infinitely better than indulgences,[8] and yet these are not preached with such ceremony or such zeal; nay, for the sake of preaching the indulgences they are kept quiet, though it is the first and the sole duty of all bishops that the people should learn the Gospel and the love of Christ, for Christ never taught that indulgences should be preached. How great then is the horror, how great the peril of a bishop, if he permits the Gospel to be kept quiet, and nothing but the noise of indulgences to be spread among his people![9] Will not Christ say to them, "straining at a gnat and swallowing a camel"? [Matt. 23:34][10]

In addition to this, Most Reverend Father in the Lord, it is said in the Instruction to the Commissaries[11] which is issued under your name, Most Reverend Father (doubtless without your knowledge and consent), that one of the chief graces of indulgence is that inestimable gift of God by which man is reconciled to God, and all the penalties of purgatory are destroyed.[12] Again, it is said that contrition is not necessary in those who purchase souls [out of purgatory] or buy confessionalia.[13]

But what can I do, good Primate and Most Illustrious Prince, except pray your Most Reverend Fatherhood by the Lord Jesus Christ that you would deign to look [on this matter] with the eye of fatherly care, and do away entirely with that treatise[14] and impose upon the preachers of pardons another form of preaching; lest, perchance, one may some time arise, who will publish writings in which he will confute both them and that treatise, to the shame of your Most Illustrious Sublimity. I shrink very much from thinking that this will be done, and yet I fear that it will come to pass, unless there is some speedy remedy.

These faithful offices of my insignificance I beg that your Most Illustrious Grace may deign to accept in the spirit of a Prince and a Bishop, i. e., with the greatest clemency, as I offer them out of a faithful heart, altogether devoted to you, Most Reverend Father, since I too am a part of your flock.

May the Lord Jesus have your Most Reverend Fatherhood eternally in His keeping. Amen.

From Wittenberg on the Vigil of All Saints, MDXVII.

If it please the Most Reverend Father he may see these my Disputations, and learn how doubtful a thing is the opinion of indulgences which those men spread as though it were most certain.

To the Most Reverend Father,

Brother Martin Luther.

FOOTNOTES

[1] In the original editions the word Jesus appears at the head of the works, and the present editors have retained the use, which was apparently an act of obedience to the command, "Whatsoever ye do, in word or in deed, do all in the name of the Lord Jesus" (Col. 3:17).

[2] See Theses 18-24, 32, 52.

[3] See Thesis 27.

[4] See Thesis 75.

[5] See Theses 5, 6, 20, 21.

[6] Gratia infusa, meaning the working of God upon the hearts of men, by means of which their lives become pleasing to God. Cf. Loors' Dogmengeschicte, 4th ed., pp. 562 ff.

[7] See Thesis 5.

[8] See Theses 41-47.

[9] See Theses 52-55.

[10] See Thesis 80.

[11] See above, Introduction, p. 22 f.

[12] See Theses 21, 33.

[13] See Thesis 55, and Introduction, p.22.

[15] viz., The Instruction to the Commissaries.

II

DISPUTATION OF DOCTOR MARTIN LUTHER ON THE POWER AND EFFICACY OF INDULGENCES

OCTOBER 31, 1517

Out of love for the truth and the desire to bring it to light, the following propositions will be discussed at Wittenberg, under the presidency of the Reverend Father Martin Luther, Master of Arts and of Sacred Theology, and Lecturer in Ordinary on the same at that place. Wherefore he requests that those who are unable to be present and debate orally with us, may do so by letter.

In the Name our Lord Jesus Christ. Amen.

1. Our Lord and Master Jesus Christ, when He said Poenitentiam agite,[1] willed that the whole life of believers should be repentance. [Matt. 4:17]

2. This word cannot be understood to mean sacramental penance, i. e., confession and satisfaction, which is administered by the priests.

3. Yet it means not inward repentance only; nay, there is no inward repentance which does not outwardly work divers mortifications of the flesh.

4. The penalty[2] [of sin], therefore, continues so long as hatred of self continues; for this is the true inward repentance, and continues until our entrance into the kingdom of heaven.

5. The pope does not intend to remit, and cannot remit any penalties other than those which he has imposed either by his own authority or by that of the Canons.[3]

6. The pope cannot remit any guilt, except by declaring that it has been remitted by God and by assenting to God's remission; though, to be sure, he may grant remission in cases reserved to his judgment. If his right to grant remission in such cases were despised, the guilt would remain entirely unforgiven.

7. God remits guilt to no one whom He does not, at the same time, humble in all things and bring into subjection to His vicar, the priest.

8. The penitential canons are imposed only on the living, and, according to them, nothing should be imposed on the dying.

9. Therefore the Holy Spirit in the pope is kind to us, because in his decrees he always makes exception of the article of death and of necessity.[4]

10. Ignorant and wicked are the doings of those priests who, in the case of the dying, reserve canonical penances for purgatory.

11. This changing of the canonical penalty to the penalty of purgatory is quite evidently one of the tares that were sown while the bishops slept. [Matt. 13:25]

13. In former times the canonical penalties were imposed not after, but before absolution, as tests of true contrition.

13. The dying are freed by death from all penalties; they are already dead to canonical rules, and have a right to be released from them.

14. The imperfect health [of soul], that is to say, the imperfect love, of the dying brings with it, of necessity, great fear; and the smaller the love, the greater is the fear.

15. This fear and horror is sufficient of itself alone (to say nothing of other things) to constitute the penalty of purgatory, since it is very near to the horror of despair.

16. Hell, purgatory, and heaven seem to differ as do despair, almost-despair, and the assurance of safety.

17. With souls in purgatory it seems necessary that horror would grow less and love increase.

18. It seems unproved, either by reason or Scripture, that they are outside the state of merit, that is to say, of increasing love.

19. Again, it seems unproved that they, or at least that all of them, are certain or assured of their own blessedness, though we may be quite certain of it.

20. Therefore by "full remission of all penalties" the pope means not actually "of all," but only of those imposed by himself.

21. Therefore those preachers of indulgences are in error, who say that by the pope's indulgences a man is freed from every penalty, and saved;

22. Whereas he remits to souls in purgatory no penalty which, according to the canons, they would have had to pay in this life.

23. If it is at all possible to grant to any one the remission of all penalties whatsoever, it is certain that this remission can be granted only to the most perfect, that is, to the very fewest.

24. It must needs be, therefore, that the greater part of the people are deceived by that indiscriminate and high-sounding promise of release from penalty.

25. The power which the pope has, in a general way, over purgatory, is just like the power which any bishop or curate has, in a special way, within his own diocese or parish.

36. The pope does well when he grants remission to souls [in purgatory], not by the power of the keys (which he does not possess),[5] but by way of intercession.

27. They preach man[6] who say that so soon as the penny jingles into the money-box, the soul flies out [of purgatory]. [7]

28. It is certain that when the penny jingles into the money-box, gain and avarice can be increased, but the result of the intercession of the Church is in the power of God alone.

29. Who knows whether all the souls in purgatory wish to be bought out of it, as in the legend of Sts. Severinus and Paschal.[8]

30. No one is sure that his own contrition is sincere; much less that he has attained full remission.

31. Rare as is the man that is truly penitent, so rare is also the man who truly buys indulgences, i. e., such men are most rare.

32. They will be condemned eternally, together with their teachers, who believe themselves sure of their salvation because they have letters of pardon.[9]

33. Men must be on their guard against those who say that the pope's pardons are that inestimable gift of God by which man is reconciled to Him;

34. For these "graces of pardon" concern only the penalties of sacramental satisfaction, and these are appointed by man.[10]

35. They preach no Christian doctrine who teach that contrition is not necessary in those who intend to buy souls out of purgatory or to buy confessionalia.[11]

36. Every truly repentant Christian has a right to full remission of penalty and guilt, even without letters of pardon.

37. Every true Christian, whether living or dead, has part in all the blessings of Christ and the Church; and this is granted him by God, even without letters of pardon.

38. Nevertheless, the remission and participation [in the blessings of the Church] which are granted by the pope are in no way to be despised, for they are, as I have said,[12] the declaration of divine remission.

39. It is most difficult, even for the very keenest theologians, at one and the same time to commend to the people the abundance of pardons and [the need of] true contrition.

40. True contrition seeks and loves penalties, but liberal pardons only relax penalties and cause them to be hated, or at least, furnish an occasion [for hating them].

41. Apostolic[13] pardons are to be preached with caution, lest the people may falsely think them preferable to other good works of love.

42. Christians are to be taught that the pope does not intend the buying of pardons to be compared in any way to works of mercy.

43. Christians are to be taught that he who gives to the poor or lends to the needy does a better work than buying pardons;

44. Because love grows by works of love, and man becomes better; but by pardons man does not grow better, only more free from penalty.

45. Christians are to be taught that he who sees a man in need, and passes him by, and gives [his money] for pardons, purchases not the indulgences of the pope, but the indignation of God.

46. Christians are to be taught that unless they have more than they need, they are bound to keep back what is necessary for their own families, and by no means to squander it on pardons.

47. Christians are to be taught that the buying of pardons is a matter of free will, and not of commandment.

48. Christians are to be taught that the pope, in granting pardons, needs, and therefore desires, their devout prayer for him more than the money they bring.

49. Christians are to be taught that the pope's pardons are useful, if they do not put their trust in them; but altogether harmful, if through them they lose their fear of God.[14]

50. Christians are to be taught that if the pope knew the exactions of the pardon-preachers, he would rather that St. Peter's church should go to ashes, than that it should be built up with the skin, flesh and bones of his sheep.

51. Christians are to be taught that it would be the pope's wish, as it is his duty, to give of his own money to very many of those from whom certain hawkers of pardons cajole money, even though the church of St. Peter might have to be sold.

53. The assurance of salvation by letters of pardon is vain, even though the commissary,[15] nay, even though the pope himself, were to stake his soul upon it.

53. They are enemies of Christ and of the pope, who bid the Word of God be altogether silent in some Churches, in order that pardons may be preached in others.

54. Injury is done the Word of God when, in the same sermon, an equal or a longer time is spent on pardons than on this Word.[16]

55. It must be the intention of the pope that if pardons, which are a very small thing, are celebrated with one bell, with single processions and ceremonies, then the Gospel, which is the very greatest thing, should be preached with a hundred bells, a hundred processions, a hundred ceremonies.

56. The "treasures of the Church," [17] out of which the pope grants indulgences, are not sufficiently named or known among the people of Christ.

57. That they are not temporal treasures is certainly evident, for many of the vendors do not pour out such treasures so easily, but only gather them.

58. Not are they the merits of Christ and the Saints, for even without the pope, these always work grace for the inner man, and the cross, death, and hell for the outward man.

59. St. Lawrence said that the treasures of the Church were the Church's poor, but he spoke according to the usage of the word in his own time.

60. Without rashness we say that the keys of the Church, given by Christ's merit, are that treasure;

61. For it is clear that for the remission of penalties and of reserved cases, the power of the pope is of itself sufficient.

62. The true treasure of the Church is the Most Holy Gospel of the glory and the grace of God.

63. But this treasure is naturally most odious, for it makes the first to be last.

64. On the other hand, the treasure of indulgences is naturally most acceptable, for it makes the last to be first.

65. Therefore the treasures of the Gospel are nets with which they formerly were wont to fish for men of riches.

66. The treasures of the indulgences are nets with which they now fish for the riches of men.

67. The indulgences which the preachers cry as the "greatest graces" are known to be truly such, in so far as they promote gain.

68. Yet they are in truth the very smallest graces compared with the grace of God and the piety of the Cross.

69. Bishops and curates are bound to admit the commissaries of apostolic pardons, with all reverence.

70. But still more are they bound to strain all their eyes and attend with all their ears, lest these men preach their own dreams instead of the commission of the pope.

71. He who speaks against the truth of apostolic pardons, let him be anathema and accursed!

73. But he who guards against the lust and license of the pardon-preachers, let him be blessed!

73. The pope justly thunders[18] against those who, by any art, contrive the injury of the traffic in pardons.

74. But much more does he intend to thunder against those who use the pretext of pardons to contrive the injury of holy love and truth.

75. To think the papal pardons so great that they could absolve a man even if he had committed an impossible sin and violated the Mother of God—this is madness.[19]

76. We say, on the contrary, that the papal pardons are not able to remove the very least of venial sins, so far as its guilt is concerned.[20]

77. It is said that even St. Peter, if he were now Pope, could not bestow greater graces; this is blasphemy against St. Peter and against the pope.

78. We say, on the contrary, that even the present pope, and any pope at all, has greater graces at his disposal; to wit, the Gospel, powers, gifts of healing, etc., as it is written in I. Corinthians xii.

79. To say that the cross, emblazoned with the papal arms, which is set up [by the preachers of indulgences], is of equal worth with the Cross of Christ, is blasphemy.

80. The bishops, curates and theologians who allow such talk to be spread among the people, will have an account to render.

81. This unbridled preaching of pardons makes it no easy matter, even for learned men, to rescue the reverence due to the pope from slander, or even from the shrewd questionings of the laity.

82. To wit:—"Why does not the pope empty purgatory, for the sake of holy love and of the dire need of the souls that are there, if he redeems an infinite number of souls for the sake of miserable money with which to build a Church? The former reasons would be most just; the latter is most trivial."

83. Again:—"Why are mortuary and anniversary masses for the dead continued, and why does he not return or permit the withdrawal of the endowments founded on their behalf, since it is wrong to pray for the redeemed?"

84. Again:—"What is this new piety of God and the pope, that for money they allow a man who is impious and their enemy to buy out of purgatory the pious soul of a friend of God, and do not rather, because of that pious and beloved soul's own need, free it for pure love's sake?"

85. Again:—"Why are the penitential canons,[21] long since in actual fact and through disuse abrogated and dead, now satisfied by the granting of indulgences, as though they were still alive and in force?"

86. Again:—"Why does not the pope, whose wealth is to-day greater than the riches of the richest, build just this one church of St. Peter with his own money, rather than with the money of poor believers?"

87. Again:—"What is it that the pope remits, and what participation[22] does he grant to those who, by perfect contrition, have a right to full remission and participation?"

88. Again:—"What greater blessing could come to the Church than if the pope were to do a hundred times a day what he now does once,[23] and bestow on every believer these remissions and participations?"

89. "Since the pope, by his pardons, seeks the salvation of souls rather than money, why does he suspend the indulgences and pardons granted heretofore, since these have equal efficacy?" [24]

90. To repress these arguments and scruples of the laity by force alone, and not to resolve them by giving reasons, is to expose the Church and the pope to the ridicule of their enemies, and to make Christians unhappy.

91. If, therefore, pardons were preached according to the spirit and mind of the pope, all these doubts would be readily resolved; nay, they would not exist.

92. Away, then, with all those prophets who say to the people of Christ, "Peace, peace," and there is no peace! [Ezek. 13:10]

93. Blessed be all those prophets who say to the people of Christ, "Cross, cross," and there is no cross![25]

30

94. Christians are to be exhorted that they be diligent in following Christ, their Head, through penalties, deaths, and hell;

95. And thus be confident of altering into heaven rather through many tribulations, than through the assurance of peace. [Acts 14:22]

FOOTNOTES

[1] Matt. 4:17. Greek, μετα??e?te; English "repent"; German Bussetun. The Latin and German versions may also be rendered, "Do penance"; the Greek, on the other hand, can only mean "Repent."

[2] The Roman theology distinguishes between the "guilt" and the "penalty" of sin. See Introduction, p.19.

[3] Decrees of the Church, having the force of law. The canons referred to here and below (Cf. Theses 8, 85) are the so-called penitential Canons. See Introduction, p.17.

[4] Commenting on this Thesis in the Resolutions, Luther distinguishes between "temporal" and "eternal" necessity. "Necessity knows no law." "Death is the necessity of necessities" (Weimar Ed., I, 549; Erl. Ed. op. var. arg., II, 166).

[5] This is not a denial of the power of the keys, i. e., the power to forgive and retain sin, but merely that the power of the keys extends to purgatory.

[6] i. e., Merely human doctrine.

[7] An alleged statement of indulgence-vendors. See Letter to Mainz and Introduction.

[8] Luther refers again to this story in the Resolutions (Weimar Ed., I, p.586). The story is that these saints preferred to remain longer in purgatory that they might have greater glory in heaven. Luther adds, "Whoever will, may believe in these stories; it is no concern of mine."

[9] Luther uses the terms "pardon" and "indulgence" interchangeably.

[10] For meaning of the term "satisfaction," see Introduction, p. 19f.

[11] Privileges entitling their holder to choose his own confessor and relieving him of certain satisfactions. See Introduction, p. 22.

[12] See above, Thesis 6.

[13] i. e., "Papal."

[14] Cf. Thesis 32.

[15] The commissioner who sold the letters of indulgence.

[16] The best texts read illi, "on it," i. e., the Word of God. The Erl. Ed. has a variant verbis evangelics, "the words of the Gospel" (op. var. arg., I, 289).

[17] See Introduction, p. 20, note 2.

[18] i. e., Threatens with "thunder-bolt" of excommunication.

[19] See Letter to Mainz, above p. 26. For repetition and defense of the statement against which Luther here protests, see Disp. I. Jo Tetzelii, Th. 99-101; Loescher. I, 513.

[20] Cf. Thesis 6.

[21] Cf. Thesis 5 and note.

[22] Cf. Theses 36, 37.

[23] The letter of indulgence entitled its possessor to absolution "once in life and in the article of death."

[24] During the time when the Jubilee-indulgences were preached, other Indulgences were suspended.

[25] In a letter to Michael Dressel, 22 June, 1516, Luther had written: "It is not that man, therefore whom no one disturbs who has peace—which is indeed, the peace of the world— but he whom all men and all things harass and who bears all quietly with joy. You say with Israel: 'Peace, peace,' and there is no peace; say rather with Christ, 'Cross, cross' and there is no cross. For the cross ceases to be a cross as soon as you say joyfully: 'Blessed cross, there is no tree like you'" (Preserved Smith, Luther, p. 32).

III

LETTER TO JOHN STAUPITZ ACCOMPANYING THE "RESOLUTIONS" TO THE XCV THESES

1518

To his Reverend and Dear Father

JOHN STAUPITZ,

Professor of Sacred Theology, Vicar of the Augustinian Order,

Brother Martin Luther,

his pupil,

sendeth greeting.

I remember, dear Father, that once, among those pleasant and wholesome talks of thine, with which the Lord Jesus ofttimes gives me wondrous consolation, the word poenitentia[1] was mentioned. We were moved with pity for many consciences, and for those tormentors

33

who teach, with rules innumerable and unbearable, what they call a modus confitendi.[2] Then we heard thee say as with a voice from heaven, that there is no true penitence which does not begin with love of righteousness and of God, and that this love, which others think to be the end and the completion of penitence, is rather its beginning.

This word of thine stuck in me like a sharp arrow of the mighty, [Ps. 120:4] and from that time forth I began to compare it with the texts of Scripture which teach penitence. Lo, there began a joyous game! The words frollicked with me everywhere! They laughed and gamboled around this saying. Before that there was scarcely a word in all the Scriptures more bitter to me than "penitence," though I was busy making pretences to God and trying to produce a forced, feigned love; but now there is no word which has for me a sweeter or more pleasing sound than "penitence." For God's commands are sweet, when we find that they are to be read not in books alone, but in the wounds of our sweet Saviour.

After this it came about that, by the grace of the learned men who dutifully teach us Greek and Hebrew, I learned that this word is in Greek metanoia and is derived from meta and noun, i. e., post and mentem,[3] so that poenitentia or metanoia is a "coming to one's senses," and is a knowledge of one's own evil, gained after punishment has been accepted and error acknowledged; and this cannot possibly happen without a change in our heart and our love. All this answers so aptly to the theology of Paul, that nothing, at least in my judgment, can so aptly illustrate St. Paul.

Then I went on and saw that metanoia can be derived, though not without violence, not only from post and mentem, but also from trans and mentem, [4] so that metanoia signifies a changing[5] of the mind and heart, because it seemed to indicate not only a change of the heart, but also a manner of changing it, i. e., the grace of God. For that "passing over of the mind," [6] which is true repentance, is of very frequent mention in the Scriptures. Christ has displayed the true significance of that old word "Passover"; and long before the Passover, [Ex. 19:11] Abraham was a type of it, when he was called a "pilgrim," [1 Cor. 5:7] i. e., a "Hebrew," [7] that is to say, one who "passed over" into Mesopotamia, as the Doctor of Bourgos[8] learnedly explains. With this accords, too, the title of the Psalm [Ps. 39] in which Jeduthun, i. e., "the pilgrim," [9] is introduced as the singer.

Depending on these things, I ventured to think those men false teachers who ascribed so much to works of penitence that they left us scarcely anything of penitence itself except trivial satisfactions[10] and laborious confession, because, forsooth, they had derived their idea from the Latin words poenitentiam agere,[11] which indicate an action, rather than a change of heart, and are in no way an equivalent for the Greek metanoia.

While this thought was boiling in my mind, suddenly new trumpets of indulgences and bugles of remissions began to peal and to bray all about us; but they were not intended to arouse us to keen eagerness for battle. In a word, the doctrine of true penitence was passed by, and they presumed to praise not even that poorest part of penitence which is called "satisfaction," [12] but the remission of that poorest part of penitence; and they praised it so highly that such praise was never heard before. Then, too, they taught impious and false and heretical doctrines with such authority (I wished to say "with such assurance") that he who even muttered anything to the contrary under his breath, would straightway be consigned to the flames as a heretic, and condemned to eternal malediction.

Unable to meet their rage half-way, I determined to enter a modest dissent, and to call their teaching into question, relying on the opinion of all the doctors and of the whole Church, that to render satisfaction is better than to secure the remission of satisfaction, i. e., to buy indulgences. Nor is there anybody who ever taught otherwise. Therefore, I published my Disputation;[13] in other words, I brought upon my head all the curses, high, middle and low, which these lovers of money (I should say "of souls") are able to send or to have sent upon me. For these most courteous men, armed, as they are, with very dense acumen, since they cannot deny what I have said, now pretend that in my Disputation I have spoken against the power of the Supreme Pontiff.[14]

That is the reason. Reverend Father, why I now regretfully come out in public. For I have ever been a lover of my corner, and prefer to look upon the beauteous passing show of the great minds of our age, rather than to be looked upon and laughed at. But I see that the bean must appear among the cabbages,[15] and the black must be put with the white, for the sake of seemliness and loveliness.

I ask, therefore, that thou wilt take this foolish work of mine and forward it, if possible, to the most Excellent Pontiff, Leo X, where it may plead my cause against the designs of those who hate me. Not that I wish thee to share my danger! Nay, I wish this to be done at my peril only. Christ will see whether what I have said is His or my own; and without His permission there is not a word in the Supreme Pontiff's tongue, nor is the heart of the king in his own hand. [Ps. 138:4 (Vulgate), Prov. 21:1] He is the Judge whose verdict I await from the Roman See.

As for those threatening friends of mine, I have no answer for them but that word of Reuchlin's—"He who is poor fears nothing; he has nothing to lose." Fortune I neither have nor desire; if I have had reputation and honor, he who destroys them is always at work; there remains only one poor body, weak and wearied with constant hardships, and if by force or wile they do away with that (as a service to God), they will but make me poorer by perhaps an hour or two of life. [John 16:2] Enough for me is the most sweet Saviour and Redeemer, my Lord Jesus Christ, to Whom I shall always sing my song; [Ps. 104:33] if any one is unwilling to sing with me, what is that to me? Let him howl, if he likes, by himself.

The Lord Jesus keep thee eternally, my gracious Father!

Wittenberg, Day of the Holy Trinity, MDXVIII

FOOTNOTES

[1] "Penitence," "repentance," "penance," are all translations of this word. See above, p.29, note 1.

[2] The modus confitendi, or "way of confession" is the teaching of what sins are to be confessed to the priest and how they are to be confessed. The subject is discussed fully by Luther in his Discussion of Confession, below, pp. 81-102.

[3] Gr. μετ?, Lat., post. Eng., "after"; Gr. ????, Lat., mens, Eng., "mind."

[4] The Greek μετ? can also be translated by the Latin trans, which, in compounds, denotes movement from one place, or thing, or condition, to another.

[5] Lat. transmutatio, "the act or process of changing," not simply "a change" (mutatio).

[6] Transitus mentis.

[7] The derivative of the term "Hebrew" is still disputed (v. PRE3 VII, p.507). Luther conceives it to mean transitor, "one who passes through tor across the land," "a pilgrim." Cf. Genesis 12:6.

[8] Burgenesis, i. e. Paul of Bourgos (1353-1435).

[9] Another bit of Mediæval philology.

[10] See Introduction, p. 19.

[11] Cf. Thesis 1, and foot-note.

[12] Here again, as above, we have the double sense of poentitentia. Satisfaction is a part of sacramental penance. Luther's charge is that in preaching the remission of this part of the Sacrament the doctrine of true penitence (cf. Thesis 1) is passed by.

[13] The Ninety-five Theses.

[14] Tetzel's reply to the Theses (Disputatio II, Jo. Tetzelli), 1517. Loescher, I, pp. 517 ff.

[15] A Latin adage, chorcorus inter olern.

IV

LETTER TO POPE LEO X, ACCOMPANYING THE "RESOLUTIONS" TO THE XCV THESES 1518

To the

Most Blessed Father,

LEO X.

Martin Luther,

Augustinian Friar,

wisheth everlasting welfare.

I have heard evil reports about myself, most blessed Father, by which I know that certain friends have put my name in very bad odor with you and yours, saying that I have attempted to belittle the power of the keys and of the Supreme Pontiff. Therefore I am accused of heresy, apostasy, and perfidy, and am called by six hundred other names of ignominy. My ears shudder and my eyes are astounded. But the one thing in which I put my confidence remains unshaken—my clear and quiet conscience. Moreover, what I hear is nothing new. With such like decorations I have been adorned in my own country by those same honorable and truthful men, i. e., by the men whose own conscience convicts them of wrong-doing, and who are trying to put their own monstrous doings off on me, and to glorify their own shame by bringing shame to me. But you will deign, blessed Father, to hear the true case from me, though I am but an uncouth child. [Jer. 2:6]

It is not long ago that the preaching of the Jubilee indulgences[1] was begun in our country, and matters went so far that the preachers of indulgences, thinking that the protection of your name made anything permissible, ventured openly to teach the most impious and heretical doctrines, which threatened to make the power of the Church a scandal and a laughing-stock as if the decretals De abusionibus quaestorum[2] did not apply to them.

Not content with spreading this poison of theirs by word of mouth, they published tracts and scattered them among the people. In these books—to say nothing of the insatiable and unheard of avarice of which almost every letter in them vilely smells—they laid down those same impious and heretical doctrines, and laid them down in such wise that confessors were bound by their oath to be faithful and insistent in urging them upon the people. I speak the truth, and none of them can hide himself from the heat thereof [Ps. 19:6]. The tracts are extant and they cannot disown them. These teachings were so successfully carried on, and the people, with their false hopes, were sucked so dry that, as the Prophet says, "they plucked their flesh from off their bones"; [Mic. 3:2] but they themselves meanwhile were fed most pleasantly on the fat of the land.

There was just one means which they used to quiet opposition, to wit, the protection of your name, the threat of burning at the stake, and the disgrace of the name "heretic." It is incredible how ready they are to threaten, even, at times, when they perceive that it is only their own mere silly opinions which are contradicted. As though this were to quiet opposition, and not rather to arouse schisms and seditions by sheer tyranny!

None the less, however, stories about the avarice of the priests were bruited in the taverns, and evil was spoken of the power of the keys and of the Supreme Pontiff, and as evidence of this, I could cite the common talk of this whole land. I truly confess that I was on fire with zeal for Christ, as I thought, or with the heat of youth, if you prefer to have it so; and yet I saw that it was not in place for me to make any decrees or to do anything in these matters. Therefore I privately admonished some of the prelates of the Church. By some of them I was kindly received, to others I seemed ridiculous, to still others something worse; for the terror of your name and the threat of Church censures prevailed. At last, since I could do nothing else, it seemed good that I should offer at least a gentle resistance to them, i. e., question and discuss their teachings. Therefore I published a set of theses, inviting only the more learned to dispute with me if they wished; as should be evident, even to my adversaries, from the Preface to the Disputation.[3]

Lo, this is the fire with which they complain that all the world is now ablaze! Perhaps it is because they are indignant that I, who by your own apostolic authority am a Master of Theology, have the right to conduct public disputations, according to the custom of all the Universities and of the whole Church, not only about indulgences, but also about God's power and remission and mercy, which are incomparably greater subjects. I am not much moved, however, by the fact that they envy me the privilege granted me by the power of your Holiness, since I am unwillingly compelled to yield to them in things of far greater moment, viz., when they mix the dreams of Aristotle with theological matters, and conduct nonsensical disputations about the majesty of God, beyond and against the privilege granted them.

It is a miracle to me by what fate it has come about that this single Disputation of mine should, more than any other, of mine or of any of the teachers, have gone out into very nearly the whole land. It was made public at our University and for our University only, and it was made public in such wise that I cannot believe it has become known to all men. For it is a set of theses, not doctrines or dogmas, and they are put, according to custom, in an obscure and enigmatic way. Otherwise, if I had been able to foresee what was coming, I should have taken care, for my part, that they would be easier to understand.

Now what shall I do? I cannot recant them; and yet I see that marvelous enmity is inflamed against me because of their dissemination. It is unwillingly that I incur the public and perilous and various judgment of men, especially since I am unlearned, dull of brain, empty of scholarship; and that too in this brilliant age of ours, which by its achievements in letters and learning can force even Cicero into the corner, though he was no base follower of the public light. But necessity compels me to be the goose that squawks among the swans.

And so, to soften my enemies and to fulfil the desires of many, I herewith send forth these trifling explanations of my Disputation; I send them forth in order, too, that I may be more safe under the defense of your name and the shadow of your protection. In them all may see, who will, how purely and amply I have sought after and cherished the power of the Church and reverence for the keys; and, at the same rime, how unjustly and falsely my adversaries have befouled me with so many names. For if I had been such a one as they wish to make me out, and if I had not, on the contrary, done everything correctly, according to my academic privilege, the Most Illustrious Prince Frederick, Duke of Saxony, Imperial Elector, etc., would never have tolerated such a pest in his University, for he most dearly loves the Catholic and Apostolic truth, nor could I have been tolerated by the keen and learned men of our University. But what has been done, I do because those most courteous men do not fear openly to involve both the Prince and the University in the same disgrace with myself.[4]

Wherefore, most blessed Father, I cast myself at the feet of your Holiness, with all that I have and all that I am. Quicken, kill, call, recall, approve, reprove, as you will. In your voice

I shall recognize the voice of Christ directing you and speaking in you. If I have deserved death, I shall not refuse to die. For the earth is the Lord's and the fulness thereof. [Ps. 24:1] He is blessed forever. Amen.

May He have you too forever in His keeping. Amen.

ANNO MDXVIII.

FOOTNOTES

[1] See Introduction, pp. 18, 21.

[2] i. e. The papal laws regulating the methods of collectors of church-funds.

[3] The Ninety-five Theses.

[4] See Tetzel's II. Disputation, Theses 47, 48. Loescher, I, p. 522.

A TREATISE ON THE HOLY SACRAMENT OF BAPTISM 1529

INTRODUCTION

This treatise is not a sermon in the ordinary acceptation of the term. It was not preached, but, according to the Latin usage of the word "sermo," was rather "a discourse," "a discussion," "a disputation" concerning baptism. Even in popular usage, the term "sermon" implies careful preparation and the orderly arrangement of thought. Here, therefore, we have a carefully prepared statement of Luther's opinion of the real significance of baptism. Published in November, 1519, and shortly afterward in a Latin translation,[1] it shows that the leading features of his doctrine on this subject were already fixed. With it should be read the chapter in the Large Catechism (1519), and the treatise Von der Wiedertaufe (1538).[2] The treatment is not polemical, but objective and practical. The Anabaptist controversy was still in the future. No objections against Infant Baptism or problems that it suggested were pressing for attention. Nothing more is attempted than to explain in a very plain and practical way how every one who has been baptised should regard his baptism. It commits to writing in an entirely impersonal way a problem of Luther's own inner life, for the instruction of others similarly perplexed.

He is confronted with a rite universally found in Christendom and nowhere else, the one distinctive mark of a Christian, the seal of a divine covenant. What it means is proclaimed by its very external form. But it is more than a mere object-lesson pictorially representing a great truth. With Luther, Word and Spirit, sign and that which is signified, belong together. Wherever the one is present, there also is the efficacy of the other. The sign is not limited to the moment of administration, and that which is signified is not projected far into the distant future of adult years.

The emphatic preference here shown for immersion may surprise those not familiar with Luther's writings. He prefers it as a matter of choice between non-essentials. To quote only his treatise of the next year on the Babylonian Captivity: "I wish that those to be baptised were entirely sunken in the water; not that I think it necessary, but that of so perfect and complete a thing, there should be also an equally complete and perfect sign." [3] It was a form that was granted as permissible in current Orders approved by the Roman Church, and was continued in succeeding Orders.[4] Even when immersion was not used, the copious application of the water was a prominent feature of the ceremony. No one is better qualified to speak on this subject than Prof. Rietschel, himself formerly a Wittenberger: "The form of baptism at Wittenberg is manifest from the picture by L. Cranach on the altar of the Wittenberg Pfarrkirche, in which Melanchthon is administering baptism. At Melanchthon's left hand lies the completely naked child over the foot. With his right hand he is pouring water upon the child's head, from which the water is copiously flowing." [5]

Nor should it be forgotten that the immersion which Luther had in mind was not that of adults, almost unknown at the time, and as he himself says, practically unknown for about a thousand years,[6] but that of infants. In the immersion of infants, he finds two things: first, the sinking of the child beneath the water, and, then, its being raised out, the one signifying death to sin and all its consequences, and the other, the new life into which the child is introduced. Four years later Luther introduced into the revised Order of Baptism which he prepared, the Collect of ancient form, but which the most diligent search of liturgical scholars has thus far been unable to discover in any of the prayers of the Ancient or Mediæval Church, expressing in condensed form this thought. We quote the introduction, as freely rendered by Cranmer in the First Prayer Book of Edward VI: "Almighty and Everlasting God, Which, of Thy justice, didst destroy by floods of water the whole world for sin, except eight persons, whom of Thy mercy Thou didst save, the same time, in the ark; and when Thou didst drown in the Red Sea wicked King Pharaoh with all his army, yet, the same time, Thou didst lead Thy people, the children of Israel, safely through the midst thereof; whereby Thou didst figure the washing of Thy holy baptism, and by the baptism of Thy well-beloved Son, Jesus Christ, didst sanctify the flood of Jordan, and all other waters, to the mystical washing away of sin," etc.[7]

The figure is to him not that of an act, but of a process extending throughout the entire earthly life of the one baptised. Sin is not drowned at once, or its consequences escaped in a moment. It is a graphic presentation in epitome of the entire work of grace with this subject.[8] Life, therefore, in the language of this treatise, is "a perpetual baptism." As the mark of our Christian profession, as the sacramental oath of the soldier of the cross, it is the solemn declaration of relentless warfare against sin, and of life-long devotion to Christ our Leader. As the true bride is responsive to no other love than that of her husband, so one faithful to his baptism is dead to all else. It is as though all else had been sunk beneath the sea.

In the distinction drawn between the sacramental sign and the sacramental efficacy in paragraphs seven and eight, the Protestant distinction between justification and sanctification is involved. The one baptised, becomes in his baptism, wholly dead to the condemning power of sin; but so far as the presence of sin is concerned, the work of deliverance has just begun. This is in glaring contrast with the scholastic doctrine that original sin itself is entirely eradicated in baptism.[9] For baptism but begins the constant struggle against sin that ends only with the close of life. Hence the warning against making of baptism a ground for presumption, and against relaxing the earnestness of the struggle upon the assumption that one has been baptised. For unless baptism be the beginning of a new life, it is without meaning.

Nor is the error less fatal which resorts to satisfactions, self-chosen or ecclesiastically appointed, for the forgiveness of sin committed after baptism. For as every sin committed after baptism is a falling away from baptism, all repentance is a return to baptism. No forgiveness is to be found except upon the terms of our baptism. Never changing is God's covenant. If broken on our part, no new covenant is to be sought. We must return to the faith of our childhood or be lost. The Mediæval Church had devised a sacrament of penance to supplement and repair the alleged broken down and inoperative sacrament of baptism. Baptism, so ran the teaching, blotted out the past and put one on a plane to make a new beginning; but, then, when he fell, there was this new sacrament, to which resort could be taken. It was the "second plank," wrote Jerome, "by which one could swim out of the sea of his sins." "No," exclaimed Luther, in the Large Catechism, "the ship of our baptism never goes down. If we fall out of the ship, there it is, ready for our return." [10]

There are, then, no vows whatever that can be substitutes for our baptism, or can supplement it. The baptismal vow comprehends everything. Only one distinction is admissible. While the vow made in baptism is universal, binding all alike to complete obedience to God, there are particular spheres in which this general vow is to be exercised and fulfilled. Not all Christians have the same office at the same calling. When one answers a divine call directing him to some specific form of Christian service, the vow made in response to such call is only the re-affirmation and application to a peculiar relation of the one obligatory vow of baptism.[11]

While the divine institution and Word of God in baptism are of prime importance, the office of faith must also be made prominent. Faith is the third element in baptism. Faith does not make the sacrament; but faith appropriates and applies to self what the sacrament offers. Non sacramentum, sed fides sacramenti justificat. Nor are we left in doubt as to what is here meant by the term "faith." In paragraph fourteen it is explicitly described. Faith, we are then taught, is nothing else than to look away from self to the mercy of God, as He offers it in the word of His grace, whereof baptism is the seal to every child baptised.

Luther's purpose, in this discussion, being to guard against the Mediæval theory of any opus operatum[12] efficacy in the sacrament, he would have wandered from his subject, if he had entered at this place into any extended discussion of the nature of the faith that is required. A few years later (1528), the Anabaptist reaction, which over-emphasised the subjective, and depreciated the objective side of the sacraments, necessitated a much fuller treatment of the peculiar office of faith with respect to baptism. To complete the discussion, the citation of a few sentences from his treatise, Von der Wiedertaufe, may, therefore, not be without use. Insisting that, important as faith is, the divine Word, and not faith, is the basis of baptism, he shows how one who regards faith, on the part of the candidate for baptism, essential to its validity, can never, if consistent, administer baptism; since there is no case in which he can have absolute certainty that faith is present. Or if one should have doubts as to the validity of his baptism in infancy, because he has no evidence that he then believed, and, for this reason, should ask to be baptised in adult years, then if Satan should again trouble him as to whether, even when baptised the second time, he really had faith, he would have to be baptised a third, and a fourth time, and so on ad infinitum, as long as such doubts recurred.[13] "For it often happens that one who thinks that he has faith, has none whatever, and that one who thinks that he has no faith but only doubts, actually believes. We are not told: 'He who knows that he believes,' or 'If you know that you believe,' but: 'He that believeth shall be saved.' [14] In other words, it is not faith in our faith that is asked, but faith in the Word and institution of God. Again: "Tell me: Which is the greater, the Word of God or faith? Is not the Word of God the greater? For the Word does not depend upon faith, but it is faith that is dependent on God's Word. Faith wavers and changes; but the Word of God abides forever."[15] "The man who bases his baptism on his faith, is not only uncertain, but he is a godless and hypocritical Christian; for he puts his trust in what is not his own, viz., in a gift which God has given him, and not alone in the Word of God; just as another builds upon his strength, wisdom, power, holiness, which, nevertheless, are gifts which God has given us." [16] Even though at the time of baptism there be no faith, the baptism, nevertheless, is valid. For if at the time of marriage, a maiden be without love to the man whom she marries, when, two years later, she has learned to love her husband, there is no need of a new betrothal and a new marriage; the covenant previously made is sufficient.[17]

In harmony with the stress laid in this treatise upon the fact that baptism is a treasury of consolation offered to the faith of every individual baptised, is the great emphasis which Luther, in other places, was constrained to lay upon personal as distinguished from vicarious faith. Neither the faith of the sponsors, nor that of the Church, for which, according to Augustine, the sponsors speak, avails more than simply to bring the child to baptism, where it becomes an independent agent, with whom God now deals directly. Thus the Large Catechism declares: "We bring the child in the purpose and hope that it may believe, and we pray God to grant it faith, but we do not baptise it upon that, but solely

43

upon the command of God." [18] Still more explicit is a sermon on the Third Sunday after Epiphany; "The words, Mark 16:16, Romans 1:17, and John 3:16, 18 are clear, to the effect that every one must believe for himself, and no one can be helped by the faith of any me else, but only by his own faith." "It is just as in the natural life, no one can be born for me, but I must be born myself. My mother may bring me to birth, but it is I who am born, and no me else." "Thus no one is saved by the faith of another, but solely by his own faith." [19]

The treatise is found in Weimar Ed., II, 724-737; Erlangen

Ed., XXI, 229-244; St. Louis Ed., X, 2113-2116; Clemen and

Leitzmann, Luthers Werke, I, (1912), 185-195.

HENRY E. JACOBS.

Mount Airy, Philadelphia.

FOOTNOTES

[1] Erl. Ed., op. var. arg., III, 394-410.

[2] Erl. Ed., XXVI, 256-294.

[3] Erl. Ed., op. var. arg., V. 66. For an exhaustive treatment of Luther's attitude to immersion, sprinkling, and pouring, see Krauth, Conservative Reformation, 519-544.

[4] For formulas, see Höfling, Das Sacrament der Taufe, II. 40.

[5] Riechschel, Lehrbuch der Liturgik, II, 67 f.

[6] "If Infant Baptism were not right, then for one thousand years there was no baptism and no Christian Church," Erl. Ed., XXVI, 287.

[7] More literally, but with no great difference, in the Lutheran Church Book, p. 323. The Book of Common Prayer, following the II. Prayerbook of Edward VI, has abbreviated it.

[8] Small Catechism: "Baptism signifies that the old Adam in us is to be drowned and destroyed by daily sorrow and repentance, together with all sins and evil lusts; and that

again the new man should daily come forth and rise, that shall live in the presence of God, in righteousness and purity for ever."

[9] Decrees of Trent, Session V, 5: "If any one asserts that the whole of that which has the proper nature of sin is not taken away, but only evaded or not imputed, let him be accursed."

[10] Book of Concord, Eng. Trans., p. 475.

[11] Luther recurs to this subject in a subsequent treatise, the Confitendi Ratio, below pp. 81 ff.

[12] i. e. The theory of the Roman Church that even without the faith of a recipient, the blessing of the sacrament is bestowed.

[13] Erl. Ed., XXVI, 268.

[14] Ibid., 269.

[15] Erl. Ed., XXVI, 292.

[16] Ibid., 275.

[17] Ibid., 275.

[18] Book of Concord, English Translation, p. 473.

[19] Erl. Ed., XI, 63, 48, 2d Ed., XI, 65, 61. See discussion by writer in Lutheran Church Review, XVIII, 598-657, where passages cited may be found with full context translated, together with other statements of Luther and those who followed him, on the same subject.

A TREATISE ON BAPTISM

I. Baptism [German, die Taufe] is called in the Greek language baptismos, in Latin mersio, which means to plunge something entirely into the water, so that the water closes over it. And although in many places it is the custom no longer to thrust and plunge children into the font of baptism, but only to pour the baptismal water upon them out of the font, nevertheless the former is what should be done; and it would be right, according to the meaning of the word Taufe, that the child, or whoever is baptised, should be sunk entirely into the water, and then drawn out again; for even in the German tongue the word Taufe comes undoubtedly from the word tief, and means that what is baptised is sunk deep into the water. This usage is also demanded by the significance of baptism, for baptism signifies that the old man and the sinful birth of flesh and blood are to be wholly drowned by the grace of God, as we shall hear. We should, therefore, do justice to its meaning and make baptism a true and complete sign of the thing it signifies.

II. Baptism is an external sign or token, which so divides us from all men not baptised, that thereby we are known as a people of Christ, [Heb. 2:10] our Captain, under Whose banner (i. e., the Holy Cross) we continually fight against sin. Therefore in this Holy Sacrament we must have regard to three things—the sign, the significance thereof, and the faith. The sign consists in this, that we are thrust into the water in the Name of the Father and of the Son and of the Holy Ghost; but we are not left there, for we are drawn out again. Hence the saying, Aus der Taufe gehoben.[1] The sign must, therefore, have both its parts, the putting in and the drawing out.

III. The significance of baptism is a blessed dying unto sin and a resurrection in the grace of God, so that the old man, which is conceived and born in sin, is there drowned, and a new man, born in grace, comes forth and rises. Thus St. Paul, in Titus iii, calls baptism a "washing of regeneration," [Tit. 3:5] since in this washing man is born again and made new. As Christ also says, in John iii, "Except ye be born again of water and the Spirit of grace, ye shall not enter into the Kingdom of Heaven." [John 3:5] For just as a child is drawn out of its mother's womb and born, and through this fleshly birth is a sinful man and a child of wrath, [Eph. 2:3] so man is drawn out of baptism and spiritually born, and through this spiritual birth is a child of grace and a justified man. Therefore sins are drowned in baptism, and in place of sin, righteousness comes forth.

IV. This significance of baptism, viz., the dying or drowning of sin, is not fulfilled completely in this life, nay, not until man passes through bodily death also, and utterly decays to dust. The sacrament, or sign, of baptism is quickly over, as we plainly see. But the thing it signifies, viz., the spiritual baptism, the drowning of sin, lasts so long as we live, and is completed only in death. Then it is that man is completely sunk in baptism, and that thing comes to pass which baptism signifies. Therefore this life is nothing else than a spiritual baptism which does not cease till death, and he who is baptised is condemned to die; as though the priest, when he baptises, were to say, "Lo, thou art sinful flesh; therefore I drown thee in God's Name, and in His Name condemn thee to thy death, that with thee all thy sins may die and be destroyed." Wherefore St. Paul says, in Romans vi, "We are buried with Christ by baptism into death"; [Rom. 6:4] and the sooner after baptism a man dies, the sooner is his baptism completed; for sin never entirely ceases while this body lives, which is so wholly conceived in sin that sin is its very nature, as saith the Prophet, "Behold I was conceived in sin, and in iniquity did my mother bear me"; [Ps. 51:5] and there is no help for the sinful nature unless it dies and is destroyed with all its sin. So, then, the life of a Christian, from baptism to the grave, is nothing else than the beginning of a blessed death, for at the Last Day God will make him altogether new.

[Sidenote: Its Completion]

V. In like manner the lifting up out of baptism is quickly done, but the thing it signifies, the spiritual birth, the increase of grace and righteousness, though it begins indeed in baptism, lasts until death, nay, even until the Last Day. Only then will that be finished which the lifting up out of baptism signifies. Then shall we arise from death, from sins and from all evil, pure in body and in soul, and then shall we live forever. Then shall we be truly lifted up out of baptism and completely born, and we shall put on the true baptismal garment of immortal life in heaven. As though the sponsors when they lift the child up out of baptism,[2] were to say, "Lo, now thy sins are drowned; we receive thee in God's Name into an eternal life of innocence." For so will the angels at the Last Day raise up all Christians, all pious baptised men, and will there fulfil what baptism and the sponsors signify; as Christ says in Matthew xxiv, "He shall send forth His angels, and they shall gather unto Him His elect from the four places of the winds, and from the rising to the setting of the sun." [Matt 24:31]

VI. Baptism was presaged of old in Noah's flood, when the whole world was drowned, save Noah with three sons and their wives, eight souls, who were kept in the ark. That the people of the world were drowned, signifies that in baptism sins are drowned; but that the eight in the ark, with beasts of every sort, were preserved, signifies that through baptism man is saved, as St. Peter explains, [1 Pet. 3:20 f.] Now baptism is by far a greater flood than was that of Noah. For that flood drowned men during no more than one year, but baptism drowns all sorts of men throughout the world, from the birth of Christ even till the Day of Judgment. Moreover, it is a flood of grace, as that was a flood of wrath, as is declared in Psalm xxviii, "God will make a continual new flood." [3] [Ps. 29:10] For without doubt many more people are baptised than were drowned in the flood.

[Sidenote: The Continuance of Sin]

VII. From this it follows that when a man comes forth out of baptism, he is pure and without sin, wholly guiltless. But there are many who do not rightly understand this, and think that sin is no more present, and so they become slothful and negligent in the killing of their sinful nature, even as some do when they have gone to Confession. For this reason, as I said above,[4] it should be rightly understood, and it should be known that our flesh, so long as it lives here, is by nature wicked and sinful. To correct this wickedness God has devised the plan of making it altogether new, even as Jeremiah shows. The potter, when the pot "was marred in his hand," thrust it again into the lump of clay, and kneaded it, and afterwards made another pot, as it seemed good to him. "So," says God, "are ye in My hands." [Jer. 18:4 f.] In the first birth we are marred; therefore He thrusts us into the earth again by death, and makes us over at the Last Day, that then we may be perfect and without sin.

This plan He begins in baptism, which signifies death and the resurrection at the Last Day, as has been said.[5] Therefore, so far as the sign of the sacrament and its significance are concerned, sins and the man are both already dead, and he has risen again, and so the sacrament has taken place; but the work of the sacrament has not yet been fully done, that is to say, death and the resurrection at the Last Day are yet before us.

[Sidenote: Sins after Baptism]

VII. Man, therefore, is altogether pure and guiltless, but sacramentally, which means nothing else than that he has the sign of God, i. e., baptism, by which it is shown that his signs are all to be dead, and that he too is to die in grace, and at the Last Day to rise again, pure, sinless, guiltless, to everlasting life. Because of the sacrament, then, it is true that he is without sin and guilt; but because this is not yet completed, and he still lives in sinful flesh, he is not without sin, and not in all things pure, but has begun to grow into purity and innocence.

Therefore when a man comes to mature age, the natural, sinful appetites—wrath, impurity, lust, avarice, pride, and the like—begin to stir, whereas there would be none of these if all sins were drowned in the sacrament and were dead. But the sacrament only signifies that they are to be drowned through death and the resurrection at the Last Day. [Rom. 7:18] So St. Paul, in Romans vii, and all saints with him, lament that they are sinners and have sin in their nature, although they were baptised and were holy; and they so lament because the natural, sinful appetites are always active so long as we live.

[Sidenote: Baptism a Covenant]

IX. But you ask, "How does baptism help me, if it does not altogether blot out and put away sin?" This is the place for the right understanding of the sacrament of baptism. The holy sacrament of baptism helps you, because in it God allies Himself with you, and becomes one with you in a gracious covenant of comfort.

[Sidenote: Man's Pledge]

First of all, you give yourself up to the sacrament of baptism and what it signifies, i. e., you desire to die, together with your sins, and to be made new at the Last Day, as the sacrament declares, and as has been said.[6] This God accepts at your hands, and grants you baptism, and from that hour begins to make you a new man, pours into you His grace and Holy Spirit, Who begins to slay nature and sin, and to prepare you for death and the resurrection at the Last Day.

Again, you pledge yourself to continue in this, and more and more to slay your sin as long as you live, even until your death. This too God accepts, and trains and tries you all your life long, with many good works and manifold sufferings; whereby He effects what you in baptism have desired, viz., that you may become free from sin, may die and rise again at the Last Day, and so fulfil your baptism. Therefore, we read and see how bitterly He has let His saints be tortured, and how much He has let them suffer, to the end that they might be quickly slain, might fulfil their baptism, die and be made new. For when this does not happen, and we suffer not and are not tried, then the evil nature overcomes a man, so that he makes his baptism of none effect, falls into sin, and remains the same old man as before.

[Sidenote: God's Pledge]

X. So long, now, as you keep your pledge to God, He, in turn, gives you His grace, and pledges Himself not to count against you the sins which remain in your nature after baptism, and not to regard them or to condemn you because of them. He is satisfied and well-pleased if you are constantly striving and desiring to slay these sins and to be rid of them by your death. For this cause, although the evil thoughts and appetites may be at work, nay, even although you may sin and fall at times, these sins are already done away by the power of the sacrament and covenant, if only you rise again and enter into the covenant, as St. Paul says in Romans viii. No one who believes in Christ is condemned by the evil, sinful inclination of his nature, if only he does not follow it and consent to it; [Rom. 8:1] and St. John, in his Epistle, writes, "If any man sin, we have an Advocate with God, even Jesus Christ, Who has become the forgiveness of our sins." [1 John 2:2 f.] All this takes place in baptism, where Christ is given us, as we shall hear in the remainder of the treatise.

[Sidenote: The Comfort of the Covenant]

XI. Now if this covenant did not exist, and God were not so merciful as to wink at our sins, there could be no sin so so small but it would condemn us. For the judgment of God can endure no sin. Therefore there is on earth no greater comfort than baptism, for through it we come under the judgment of grace and mercy, which does not condemn our sins, but drives them out by many trials. There is a fine sentence of St. Augustine, which says, "Sin is altogether forgiven in baptism; not in such wise that it is no longer present, but in such wise that it is not taken into account." As though he were to say, "Sin remains in our flesh even until death, and works without ceasing; but so long as we do not consent thereto or remain therein, it is so overruled by our baptism that it does not condemn us and is not harmful to us, but is daily more and more destroyed until our death."

For this reason no one should be terrified if he feel evil lust or love, nor should he despair even if he fall, but he should remember his baptism, and comfort himself joyfully with it, since God has there bound Himself to slay his sin for him, and not to count it a cause for condemnation, if only he does not consent to sin or remain in sin. Moreover, these wild thoughts and appetites, and even a fall into sin, should not be regarded as an occasion for despair, but rather as a warning from God that man should remember his baptism and what was there spoken, that he should call upon God's mercy, and exercise himself in striving against sin, that he should even be desirous of death in order that he may be rid of sin.

[Sidenote: The Office of Faith]

XII. Here, then, is the place to discuss the third thing in the sacrament, i. e., faith, to wit, that a man should firmly believe all this; viz., that this sacrament not only signifies death and the resurrection at the Last Day, by which man is made new for an everlasting, sinless life; but also that it assuredly begins and effects this, and unites us with God, so that we have the will to slay sin, even till the time of our death, and to fight against it; on the other hand, that it is His will to be merciful to us, to deal graciously with us, and not to judge us with severity, because we are not sinless in this life until purified through death. Thus you understand how a man becomes in baptism guiltless, pure and sinless, and yet continues full of evil inclinations, that he is called pure only because he has begun to be pure, and has a sign and covenant of this purity, and is always to become more pure. Because of this God will not count against him the impurity which still cleaves to him, and, therefore, he is pure

50

rather through the gracious imputation of God than through anything in his own nature; as the Prophet says in Psalm xxxii, "Blessed is he whose transgression is forgiven; blessed is the man unto whom the Lord imputeth not iniquity." [Ps. 52:1 f.]

This faith is of all things the most necessary, for it is the ground of all comfort. He who has not this faith must despair in his sins. For the sin which remains after baptism makes it impossible for any good works to be pure before God. For this reason we must hold boldly and fearlessly to our baptism, and hold it up against all sins and terrors of conscience, and humbly say, "I know full well that I have not a single work which is pure, but I am baptised, and through my baptism God, Who cannot lie, has bound Himself in a covenant with me, not to count my sin against me, but to slay it and blot it out."

XIII. So, then, we understand that the innocence which is ours by baptism is so called simply and solely because of the mercy of God, which has begun this work in us, bears patiently with sin, and regards us as though we were sinless, This also explains why Christians are called in the Scriptures the children of mercy, a people of grace, and men of God's good-will. [Eph. 5:1, 9] It is because in baptism they have begun to become pure, [Luke 2:14] and by God's mercy are not condemned with their sins that still remain, until, through death and at the Last Day, they become wholly pure, as the sign of baptism shows.

Therefore they greatly err who think that through baptism they have become wholly pure. They go about in their unwisdom, and do not slay their sin; they will not admit that it is sin; they persist in it, and so they make their baptism of no effect; they remain entangled in certain outward works, and meanwhile pride, hatred, and other evils of their nature are disregarded and grow worse and worse. Nay, not so! Sin and evil inclination must be recognized as truly sin; that it does not harm us is to be ascribed to the grace of God, Who will not count it against us if only we strive against it in many trials, works, and sufferings, and slay it at last in death. To them who do this not, God will not forgive their sins, because they do not live according to their baptism and covenant, and hinder the work which God and their baptism have begun.

[Sidenote: Baptism and Repentance]

XIV. Of this sort are they also who think to blot out and put away their sin by "satisfaction," [7] and even regard their baptism lightly, as though they had no more need of it after they had been baptised,[8] and do not know that it is in force all through life, even until death, nay, even at the Last Day, as was said above.[9] For this cause they think to find some other way of blotting out sin, viz., their own works; and so they make, for themselves and for all others, evil, terrified, uncertain consciences, and despair in the hour of death; and they know not how they stand with God, thinking that by sin they have lost their baptism and that it profits them no more.

51

Guard yourself, by all means, against this error. For, as has been said, if any one has fallen into sin, he should the more remember his baptism, and how God has there made a covenant with him to forgive all his sins, if only he has the will to fight against them, even until death. Upon this truth, upon this alliance with God, a man must joyfully dare to rely, and then baptism goes again into operation and effect, his heart becomes again peaceful and glad, not in his own work or "satisfaction," but in God's mercy, promised him in baptism, and to be held fast forever. This faith a man must hold so firmly that he would cling to it even though all creatures and all sins attacked him, since he who lets himself be forced away from it makes God a liar in His covenant, the sacrament of baptism.

[Sidenote: Baptism and Penance]

XV. It is this faith that the devil most attacks. If he overthrows it, he has won the battle. For the sacrament of penance also (of which we have already spoken)[10] has its foundation in this sacrament, since sins are forgiven only to those who are baptised, i. e., to those whose sins God has promised to forgive. The sacrament of penance thus renews and points out again the sacrament of baptism, as though the priest, in the absolution, were to say, "Lo, God hath now forgiven thee thy sin, as He long since hath promised thee in baptism, and as He hath now commanded me, by the power of the keys,[11] and now thou comest again into that which thy baptism does and is. Believe, and thou hast it; doubt, and thou art lost." So we find that through sin baptism is, indeed, hindered in its work, i. e., in the forgiveness and the slaying of sin; yet only by unbelief in its operation is baptism brought to naught. Faith, in turn, removes the hindrance to the operation of baptism. So much depends on faith.

[Sidenote: Forgiveness and Sanctification]

To speak quite plainly, it is one thing to forgive sins, and another thing to put them away or drive them out. The forgiveness of sins is obtained by faith, even though they are not entirely driven out; but to drive out sins is to exercise ourselves against them, and at last it is to die; for in death sin perishes utterly. But both the forgiveness and the driving out of sins are the work of baptism. Thus the Apostle writes to the Hebrews, [Heb. 12:1] who were baptised, and whose sins were forgiven, that they shall lay aside the sin which doth beset them. For so long as I believe that God is willing not to count my sins against me, my baptism is in force and my sins are forgiven, though they may still, in a great measure, remain. After that follows the driving out of my sins through sufferings, death, etc. This is what we confess in the article [of the Creed], "I believe in the Holy Ghost, the forgiveness of sins, etc." Here there is special reference to baptism, for in it the forgiveness takes place through God's covenant with us; therefore we must not doubt this forgiveness.

XVI. It follows, therefore, that baptism makes all sufferings and especially death, profitable and helpful, since these things can only serve baptism in the doing of its work, i. e., in the slaying of sin. For he who would fulfil the work and purpose of his baptism and be rid of sin, must die. It cannot be otherwise. Sin, however, does not like to die, and for this reason it makes death so bitter and so horrible. Such is the grace and power of God that sin, which has brought death, is driven out again by its own work, viz., by death.[12]

You find many people who wish to live in order that they may become righteous, and who say that they would like to be righteous. Now there is no shorter way or manner than through baptism and the work of baptism, i. e., through suffering and death, and so long as they are not willing to take this way, it is a sign that they do not rightly intend or know how to become righteous. Therefore God has instituted many estates in life in which men are to learn to exercise themselves and to suffer. To some He has commanded the estate of matrimony, to others the estate of the clergy, to others, again, the estate of the rulers, and to all He has commanded that they shall toil and labor to kill the flesh and accustom it to death, because for all such as are baptised their baptism has made the repose, the ease, the plenty of this life a very poison, and a hindrance to its work. For in these things no one learns to suffer, to die with gladness, to get rid of sin, and to live in accordance with baptism; but instead of these things there grows love of this life and horror of eternal life, fear of death and unwillingness to blot out sin.

[Sidenote: Baptism and Good Works]

XVII. Now behold the lives of men. Many there are who fast and pray and go on pilgrimage and exercise themselves in such things, thinking thereby only to heap up merit, and to sit down in the high places of heaven. But fasting and all such exercises should be directed toward holding down the old Adam, the sinful nature, and accustoming it to do without all that is pleasing for this life, and thus daily preparing it more and more for death, so that the work and purpose of baptism may be fulfilled. And all these exercises and toils are to be measured, not by their number or their greatness, but by the demands of baptism; that is to say, each man is to take upon him so much of these works as is good and profitable for the suppressing of his sinful nature and for fitting it for death, and is to increase or diminish them according as he sees that sin increases or decreases. As it is, they go their heedless way, take upon themselves this, that, and the other task, do now this, now that, according to the appearance or the reputation of the work, and again quickly leave off, and thus become altogether inconstant, till in the end they amount to nothing; nay, some of them so rack their brains over the whole thing, and so abuse nature, that they are of no use either to themselves or others.

All this is the fruit of that doctrine with which we have been so possessed as to think that after repentance or baptism we are without sin, and that our good works are to be heaped up, not for the blotting out of sin, but for their own sake, or as a satisfaction for sins already done. This is encouraged by those preachers who preach unwisely the legends and works of the blessed Saints, and make of them examples for all. The ignorant fall eagerly upon these things, and work their own destruction out of the examples of the Saints. God has given every saint a special way and a special grace by which to live according to his baptism. But baptism and its significance He has set as a common standard for all men, so that every man is to examine himself according to his station in life, to find what is the best way for him to fulfil the work and purpose of his baptism, i. e., to slay sin and to die. Then Christ's burden grows light and easy, [Matt. 11:30] and it is not carried with worry and care, as Solomon says of it, "The labor of the foolish wearieth every one of them, because he knoweth not how to go to the city." [Eccl. 10:15] For even as they are worried who wish to go to the city and cannot find the way, so it is with these men; all their life and labor is a burden to them, and yet they accomplish nothing.

[Sidenote: The Vow of Baptism and Other Vows]

XVIII. In this place, then, belongs the question whether baptism and the vow which we there make to God, is something more or something greater than the vows of chastity, of the priesthood, of the clergy, since baptism is common to all Christians, and it is thought that the clergy have taken a special and a higher vow. I answer: From what has been said, this is an easy question to answer. For in baptism we all make one and the same vow, viz., to slay sin and to become holy through the work and grace of God, to Whom we yield and offer ourselves, as clay to the potter [13] and in this no one is better than another. But for a life in accordance with baptism, i. e., for slaying sin, there can be no one method and no special estate in life. Therefore I have said[14] that each man must prove himself, that he may know in what estate he may best slay sin and put a check upon his nature. It is true, then, that there is no vow higher, better, or greater than the vow of baptism. What more can we promise than to drive out an, to die, to hate this life, and to become holy?

Over and above this vow, a man may, indeed, bind himself to some special estate, if it seems to him to be suitable and helpful for the completion of his baptism. It is just as though two men went to the same city, and the one went by the foot-path, the other by the high-way, according as each thought best. So he who binds himself to the estate of matrimony, walks in the toils and sufferings which belong to that estate and lays upon himself its burdens, in order that he may grow used to pleasure and sorrow, avoid sin, and prepare himself for death better than he could do outside of that estate. But he who seeks more suffering, and by much exercise would speedily prepare himself for death and soon attain the work of baptism, let him bind himself to chastity, or the spiritual order; for the spiritual estate,[15] if it is as it ought to be, should be full of torment and suffering, in order that he who belongs to it may have more exercise in the work of his baptism than the man who is in the estate of matrimony, and through such torment quickly grow used to welcome death with joy, and so attain the purpose of his baptism. Now above this estate there is another and a higher, that which rules in the spiritual order, viz., the estate of bishop, priest, etc. And these men should be well practised in sufferings and works, and ready at every hour for death, not only for their own sake, but for the sake of those who are their subjects.

Yet in all these estates the standard, of which we spoke above, should never be forgotten, viz., that a man should so exercise himself only to the end that sin may be driven out, and should not be guided by the number or the greatness of works. But, alas how we have forgotten our baptism and what it means, and what vows we made there, and that we are to walk in its works and attain its purpose! So, too, we have forgotten about the ways to that goal, and about the estates, and do not know to what end these estates were instituted, and how we are in them to keep at the fulfilling of our baptism. They have been made a gorgeous show, and little more remains of them than worldly display, as Isaiah says, "Thy silver is become dross, thy wine mixed with water." [Isa. 1:22] On this may God have mercy! Amen.

[Sidenote: The Joy of Baptism]

XIX. If, then, the holy sacrament of baptism is a thing so great, so gracious and full of comfort, we should pay earnest heed to thank God for it ceaselessly, joyfully, and from the heart, and to give Him praise and honor. For I fear that by our thanklessness we have deserved our blindness and become unworthy to behold such grace, though the whole world was, and still is, full of baptism and the grace of God. But we have been led astray in our own anxious works, afterwards in indulgences and such like false comforts, and have thought that we are not to trust God until we are righteous and have made satisfaction for our sin, as though we would buy His grace from Him or pay Him for it. In truth, he who does not see in God's grace how it bears with him as a sinner, and will make him blessed, and who looks forward only to God's judgment, that man will never be joyful in God, and can neither love nor praise Him. But if we hear and firmly believe that He receives us sinners in the covenant of baptism, spares us, and makes us pure from day to day, then our heart must be joyful, and love and praise God. So He says in the Prophet, "I will spare them, as a man spareth his own son." [Mal. 3:17] Wherefore it is needful that we give thanks to the Blessed Majesty, Who shows Himself so gracious and merciful toward us poor condemned worms, and magnify and acknowledge His work.

[Sidenote: The Danger of False Confidence]

XX. At the same time, however, we must have a care that no false security creeps in and says to itself: "Baptism is so gracious and so great a thing that God will not count our sins against us, and as soon as we turn again from sin, everything is right, by virtue of baptism; meanwhile, therefore, I will live and do my own will, and afterwards, or when about to die, will remember my baptism and remind God of His covenant, and then fulfil the work and purpose of my baptism."

Baptism is, indeed, so great a thing that if you turn again from sins and appeal to the covenant of baptism, your sins are forgiven. Only see to it, if you thus wickedly and wantonly sin, presuming on God's grace, that the judgment does not lay hold upon you and anticipate your turning back; and beware lest, even if you then desired to believe or to trust in your baptism, your trial be, by God's decree, so great that your faith is not able to stand. If they scarcely remain who do do sin or who fall because of sheer weakness, where shall your wickedness remain, which has tempted and mocked God's grace? [1 Pet. 4:18]

Let us, therefore, walk with carefulness and fear, that with a firm faith we may hold fast the riches of God's grace, and joyfully give thanks to His mercy forever and ever. Amen. [Eph. 5:15]

FOOTNOTES

[1] Literally, "lifted or raised out of baptism"; in common usage simply "baptised." Cf. "aus der Taufe beben," "to stand sponsor."

[2] See above, p.56, note 1.

[3] Luther habitually quoted the Vulgate and quoted from memory; hence the many variations from the familiar test of Scripture.

[4] See above, p. 58.

[5] See above, p. 57.

[6] See above, p. 57.

[7] Good works prescribed as "penances" upon confession to the priest.

[8] Literally, "lifted up out of it." See above, p. 57, note 1.

[9] See above, p.58.

[10] Luther here refers to his Treatise on the Sacrament of Penance, which was published just before the present treatise on baptism, in 1519. See Weimar Ed., II, pp. 709 ff and p. 724.

[11] The power to forgive and retain sin, belonging, according to Roman teaching, to the priest, and normally exercised in the sacrament of penance.

[12] Cf. Fourteen of Consolation, Part II, ch. II; below, pp. 146 ff.

[13] See above, p. 59.

[14] See above, p. 67.

[15] The "spiritual estate" or "spiritual order" includes all those who have deserted the world and worldly pursuits for the religious life. It includes monks and friars and nuns, as well as priests, etc.

A DISCUSSION OF CONFESSION (CONFITENDI RATIO) 1520

The Confitendi Ratio is the culmination of a series of tracts published by Luther after the memorable October 31st, 1517, and before his final breach with Rome.[1] In them is clearly traceable the progress that he was making in dealing with the practical problems offered by the confessional, and which had started the mighty conflict in which he was engaged. They open to us an insight into his own conscientious efforts during the period, when, as a penitent, he was himself endeavoring to meet every requirement which the Church imposed, In order to secure the assurance of the forgiveness of sins, as well as to present the questions which as a father confessor and spiritual adviser he asked those who were under his pastoral care. First of all, we find, therefore, tables of duties and sins, reminding us of the lists of cardinal sins and cardinal virtues in which Roman Catholic books abound. The main effort here is to promote the most searching self-examination and the most complete enumeration of the details of sins, since, from the Medieval standpoint, the completeness of the absolution is proportioned to the exhaustiveness of the confession. Although the first of these briefer tracts closes with its note of warning that the value of the confession is not to be estimated by the enumeration of details, but that it rests solely in the resort that is had to the Grace of God and the word of His promise, the transition from the one mode of thought to the other is very apparent.

In the Kurze Untetweisung wie man beichten soll of 1519, of which this is a Latin re-elaboration, and, therefore, intended more for the educated man than as a popular presentation, he has advanced so far as to warn against the attempt to make an exhaustive enumeration of sins. He advises that the confession be made in the most general terms, covering sins both known and unknown. "If one would confess all mortal sins, it may be done in the following words; 'Yea, my whole life, and all that I do, act, speak, and think, is such as to be deadly and condemnable.' For if one regard himself as being without mortal sin, this is of all mortal sins the most mortal." [2] According to this maturer view, the purpose of the most searching self-examination is to exhibit the utter impossibility of ever fathoming the depth of corruption that lies beneath the surface. The reader of the Tessaradecas will recall Luther's statement there, that it is of God's great mercy that man is able to see but a very small portion of the sin within him, for were he to see it in its full extent, he would perish at the sight. The physician need not count every pustule on the body to diagnose the disease as small-pox. A glance is enough to determine the case. The sins that are discovered are the symptoms of the one radical sin that lies beneath them all.[3] The cry is no longer "Mea peccata, mea peccata," as though these recognized sins were the exception to a life otherwise without a flaw, but rather, overwhelmed with confusion, the penitent finds in himself nothing but sin, except for what he has by God's grace alone. Most clearly does Luther enforce this in his exposition of the Fifty-first Psalm, of 1531, a treatise we most earnestly commend to those who desire fuller information concerning Luther's doctrine of sin, and his conception of the value of confession and absolution. He shows that it is not by committing a particular sin that we become sinners, but that the sin is committed because our nature is still sinful, and that the poisonous tree has grown from roots deeply imbedded in the soil. We are sinners not because particular acts of sin have been devised and carried to completion, but before the acts are committed we are sinners; otherwise such fruits would not have been borne. A bad tree can grow from nothing but a bad root.[4]

In his Sermon on Confession and the Sacrament of 1524, he discourages habits of morbid self-introspection, and exposes the perplexities produced by the extractions of the confessional in constantly sinking the probe deeper and deeper into the heart of the already crushed and quivering penitent. He shows how one need not look far to find enough to prompt the confession of utter helplessness and the casting of self unreservedly upon God's mercy. "Bring to the confession only those sins that occur to thee, and say: I am so frail and fallen that I need consolation and good counsel. For the confession should be brief....No one, therefore, should be troubled, even though he have forgotten his sins. If they be forgotten, they are none the less forgiven. For what God considers, is not how thou hast confessed, but His Word and how thou hast believed." [5]

In this is made prominent the radical difference between the Roman Catholic and the Lutheran conception of confession. In the former, it is a part of penance, the second of the three elements of "contrition," "confession," and "satisfaction," an absolute condition of the forgiveness of every sin. In the Roman confessional, sins are treated atomistically. Some are forgiven, while others are still to be forgiven. Every sin stands by itself, and requires separate treatment. No unconfessed sin is forgiven. To be forgiven, a sin must be known and lamented, and confessed in all its details and circumstances to the priest, who, as a spiritual judge, proportions the amount of the satisfaction to be rendered by the penitent to the degree of guilt of the offence, as judged from the facts before him. Thus the debt has to be painfully and punctiliously worked off, sin by sin, as in the financial world a note may be extinguished by successive payments, dollar by dollar. Everything, therefore, is made to depend upon the fulness and completeness of the confession. It becomes a work, on account of which one is forgiven. The absolution becomes simply the stamp of approval that is placed upon the confession.

The Lutheran conception is centered upon the person of the sinner, rather than on his sins. It is the person who is forgiven his sins. Where the person is forgiven but one sin, all his sins are forgiven; where the least sin is retained, all sins are retained, and none forgiven, for "there is no condemnation to them that are in Christ Jesus" (Rom. 8:1). The value of the confession lies not in the confession itself, but in that, through this confession, we turn to Christ and the word of His promise.[6]

In Luther's opinion, there are three species of confession.[7] One to God, in one's own heart, which is of absolute necessity, and which the true believer is always making; a second to our neighbor, when we have done him a wrong, which is also of divine command; and, a third to a "brother," "wherein we receive from the mouth of that brother the word of consolation sent from God." [8] This last species, the verbum solatii ex ore fratris, while not commanded in Holy Scripture, is commended because of the great value which it has for those who fed the need of consolation, and the instruction for which it affords the opportunity. It is only by the individualizing of the confession that the comfort to be derived by the individualizing of the promise can be obtained. Hence, as the Augsburg Confession declares (Article XI.): "Private" [i. e., personal] "confession is retained because of the absolution."[9] Not that, without the absolution, there is not forgiveness, but that, through it, the one absolved rejoices all the more in the possession of that which he possessed even before the absolution, and goes forth from it strengthened to meet temptation because of the new assurance that he has of God's love. This form of confession, therefore, instead of being a condition of forgiveness, as is our inner confession to God, is a privilege of the justified man, who, before he has made such confession, has been forgiven, and whose sins that lie still concealed from his knowledge are just as truly forgiven as those over which he grieves.

The confession, therefore, being entirely voluntary and a privilege, penitents are not to be tormented with "the ocean of distinctions" hitherto urged, such, e.g., as those between mortal and venial sins, whereof he says that "there is no doctor so learned as to draw accurately the distinction";[10] and between the inner impulses that may arise without the least consent of the will resulting from than, and those to which the will, in varying measure, may actually consent. On the contrary, it is not well to look too deeply into the abyss. When Peter began to count the waves, he was lost; when he looked away from them to Jesus, he was saved. Thus, while "the good purpose" to amend the life must be insisted upon as an indispensable accompaniment of every sincere confession, tender consciences may search within for such purpose, and be distressed because they cannot find satisfactory evidence of its presence. How excellent then the advice of this experienced pastor, that those thus troubled should pray for this "purpose" which they cannot detect; for no one can actually pray for such purpose without, in the prayer, having the very object he is seeking.

So also he rules out of the sphere of the confession the violation of matters of purely ecclesiastical regulation. Nothing is to be regarded a sin except that which is a violation of one of the Ten Commandments. To make that a sin which God's law does not make sin, is only the next step to ecclesiastical regulations to the level of divine commands, we lower divine commands to the level of ecclesiastical regulations. Even Private Confession, therefore, useful as it is, when properly understood and practised, since it rests after all upon ecclesiastical rule, is so little to be urged as a matter of necessity that Luther here defends the suggestion of Gerson, that occasionally one should go to the Lord's Supper without having made confession, in order thereby to testify that it is in God's mercy and His promise that we trust, rather than in the value of any particular outward observance.

The treatment of "Reserved Cases," with which this tract ends, shows the moderation and caution with which Luther is moving, but, at the same time, how the new wine is working in the old bottles, which soon must break. The principle of "the reservation of cases" he discusses in his Address to the German Nobility.[11] It is critical also in Augsburg Confession, Article XXVIII, 2, 41; Apology of the Augsburg Confession, English Translation, pp. 181, 212. The Roman Catholic dogma is officially presented in the Decrees of Trent, Session XIV, Chapter 7,[12] viz., "that certain more atrocious and more heinous crimes be absolved not by all priests, but only by the highest priests." Thus the power is centralized in the pope, and is delegated for exercise in ordinary cases to each particular parish-priest within the limits by which he is circumscribed, but no farther.[13] The contrast is between delegated and reserved rights. The Protestant principle is that all the power of the Church is in the Word of God which it administers; that wherever all the Word is, there also is all the power of the Church; and hence that, according to divine tight, all pastors have equal authority. For this reason, Luther here declares that in regard to secret sins, i. e., those known only to God and the penitent, no reservation whatever is to be admitted. But there is still a distinction which he is ready to concede. It has to do with public offences where scandal has been given. As "the more flagrant and more heinous crimes," If public, have to do with a wider circle than the members of a particular parish, the reparation for the offence should be as extensive as the scandal which it has created. In the Apology, Melanchthon claims that such reservation should be limited to the ecclesiastical penalties to be inflicted, but that it had not been Intended to comprise also the guilt involved; it was a reservatio poenae, but not a reservatio culpae.[14] Luther suggests the same here, but with more than usual caution.

In the same spirit as in his Treatise on Baptism, he protests against the numerous vows, the binding force of which was a constant subject of treatment in pastoral dealing with souls. The multiplication of vows had caused a depredation of the one all-embracing vow of baptism. Nevertheless the pope's right to give a dispensation he regards as limited entirely to such matters as those concerning which God's Word has given no command. With matters which concern only the relation of the individual to God, the Pope's authority is of no avail.

Literature.—Chemnitz, Martin, Examin Concilii Tridentini, 1578

(Preuss edition), 441-456. Steitz, G. E., Die Privatbeichte und

Privatabsolution d. luth. Kirche aus d. Quellen des XVI. Jahrh.,

1854. Pfeisterrer, G. F. Luthers Lehre von der Beichte, 1857.

Klieftoth, Th. Lit. Abhandlungen, 2: Die Beichte und

Absolution, 1856. Fischer, E., Zur Geschichte der evangelischen

Beichte, 2 vols., 1902-1903. Rietschel, G., Lehrbuch der

Liturgik, vol 2, particularly secs. 44, 45, Luthers Affassung

der Beichte and Luthers Auffassung von der Absolution.

Koestlin, Julius, Luther's Theology (English Translation),

I:357, 360, 400. See also Smalcald Articles, Book of Concord

(English Translation), 326, 899.

Henry E. Jacobs.

Mount Airy, Philadelphia.

FOOTNOTES

[1] 1. Decem Praecepta Wittebergenai praedicata populo, 1518, Erl. Ed., op. ex. lat., I, 218. A series of sermons entering into almost minute analyses of sins.

2. Die zehen Gebote Gottes mit einer kurzen Auslegung ihre Erfüllung und Uebertretung, Weimar Ed., I, 247 ff; Erl. Ed., XXXVI, 145-154. Reduces contents of the sermons to a few pages. A brief handbook for use in the confessional first printed in tabular form, giving a very condensed exposition of each commandment, followed by a catalogue of sins prohibited and virtues enjoined. Written a month before the publication of the Theses, and published the next year.

3. Instructio pro confessione peccatorum abbrevianda secundum decalogum. Latin form of the above, published shortly after the original. Erl. Ed., op. ex. lat., XII, 229-230.

4. Kurze Unterweisung wie man beichten soll. Weimar Ed., II, 57 ff.; Erl. Ed., XXI, 245-253 prepared by request of Spalatin, first in Latin, and then translated, Köstlin thinks by Spalatin, into German. Published 1518. Contains eight introductory propositions, followed by lists of sins against each commandment.

5. Confitendi Ratio, published in 1520, a re-elaboration by Luther of the preceding German treatise. Weimar Ed., VI, 159-169; Erl. Ed., IV, 152-170; St. Louis Ed., XIX, 786-806.

[2] "Ja, mein ganzes Leben, und alles, das ich thu, handel, red und gedenk, ist also gethan, das es todlich und vordammlich ist." These are almost the words of the public confessional prayer in the Kirchenbuch of the General Council of the Lutheran Church in America: "Also dans alle meine Natur und Wesensträflich und verdammlich ist."

[3] Erl. Ed., op. var. arg., IV, 89 aq. "Si enim suum malum sentiret, infernum sentiret, nam infernum in se ipso habet." See this volume, p. 115f.

[4] Erl. Ed., op. ex. lat., XIX, 1-154.

[5] Erl. Ed. (2d ed.), XI, 173.

[6] See the opening paragraph of this treatise.

[7] Erl. Ed., XI, 166, XXIX, 352-359. Cf. with this, the still fuller treatment by Chemnitz, Examin Concilii Tridentini (Preuss edition), 441-453.

[8] Babylonian Captivity, Erl. Ed., op. var. arg., V, 82.

[9] Cf. Augsburg Confession, Art. XXV; Apology in Book of Concord, English Translation, pp. 133, 173, 185, 188, 196; Smalcald Articles, 330-339; Small Catechism, 371.

[10] Sermon vom Sacrament der Busse, Erl. Ed., XX, 190. For definition of "mortal and venial," see Introduction to XCV Theses, above, p. 19.

[11] See Vol. II. of this edition.

[12] Deninger, Enchridion Symbolorum, soc. 782; Sceaff's Creeds of Christendom.

[13] "As though the Word of God cannot forgive sins, except where power derived from the Pope assist it." Chemnitz, Examen Concilii Tridentini (Preuss ed.), p. 456.

[14] Apology, p. 212; "There is a reservation of canonical punishments; there is not a reservation of guilt before God in those who are truly converted."

A DISCUSSION OF CONFESSION

(CONFITENDI RATIO)

1520

FIRST

[Sidenote: Need of Faith]

In this our age, the consciences of almost all have been led astray by human doctrines into a false trust in their own righteousness and their own works, and knowledge about faith and trust in God has almost ceased. Therefore, for him who is about to go to confession, it is before all things necessary that he should not place his trust in his confession—either the confession which he is about to make or the confession which he has made—but that, with complete fulness of faith, he put his trust only in the most gracious promise of God; to wit, he must be altogether certain that He, Who has promised pardon to the man who shall confess his sins, will most faithfully fulfil His promise. For we are to glory, not because we confess, but because He has promised pardon to those who do confess; that is, not because of the worthiness or sufficiency of our confession (for there is no such worthiness or sufficiency), but because of the truth and certitude of His promise, as says the xxiv. Psalm: "For Thy Name's sake, O Lord, pardon mine iniquity." [Ps. 25:35] It does not say, "for my sake," or "for my worthiness' sake," or "for my name's sake," but "for Thy Name's sake." So it is evident that the work of confession is nothing else than an occasion by which God is called to the fulfilment of His own promise, or by which we are trained to believe that we shall without doubt obtain the promise. It is just as if we were to say: "Not unto us, O Lord, but unto Thy Name give glory, [Ps. 115:1] and rejoice, not because we have blessed

63

Thee, but because Thou hast blessed us, as Thou sayest by Ezekiel." [Ezek. 20:44] Let this be the manner of our confession, that he who glories may glory in the Lord, and may not commend himself, but may glorify the grace of God; and it shall come to pass that "confession and majesty shall be the work of God." [1] Psalm cxi [Ps. 111:3].

SECOND

[Sidenote: God's Promises]

But God, for the glory of His grace and mercy, has promised pardon. And this can be proved from Scripture. First from Psalm xxxii, "I said, I will confess my transgressions unto the Lord, and Thou forgavest the iniquity of my sin." [Ps. 32:5] Then from II. Samuel xii, from which this Psalm is taken. David first said, "I have sinned against the Lord," and Nathan straightway said, "The Lord also hath put away thy sin; thou shalt not die." [2 Sam. 12:13] Again, from Jeremiah xviii, "If that nation turn away from their evil, I will repent of the evil that I thought to do." [Jer. 18:8] Once more from I. John i, "If we confess our sins, He is faithful and just to forgive us our sins, and to cleanse us from all unrighteousness." [1 John 1:9] The true definition of the righteous man is found in Proverbs xviii, "The righteous man is his own first accuser," [2] [Prov.18:17] that is to say, he is righteous because he accuses himself. The verse goes on to say, "His neighbor (i. e., Christ) cometh and searcheth him," that is, He seeketh him, and suffereth him not to perish; He will even find him and bring him back from the depths of hell. Hence Joshua vii. also calls the confessing of sin the glorifying of God, saying to Achan, "My son, give glory to God, and confess, and tell me what thou hast done." [Josh. 7:19] St. Jerome comments on this passage, "Confession of sin is praise of God." No wonder! For he who confesses his own sins speaks truth; but God is truth; therefore he also confesses God. Thus Manasseh, King of Judah, says in his most beautiful Prayer,[3] which is most excellently suited for one who goes to confession, "But Thou, Lord, according to Thy goodness hast promised repentance for the remission of sins, etc." [Prayer of Manasseh, 7] Truly, "according to Thy goodness Thou hast promised," for our confession is nothing unless the promise of God is sure, and it is altogether of His divine goodness that He has promised remission, which could not be obtained by any righteousness, unless He had given the promise. Thus faith in that promise is the first and supreme necessity for one who is about to go to confession, lest, perchance, he may presumptuously think that by his own diligence, his own memory, his own strength, he is provoking God to forgive his sins. Nay, rather it is God Himself Who, with ready forgiveness, will anticipate his confession, and allure and provoke him, by the goodness of His sweet promise, to accept remission and to make confession.

THIRD

[Sidenote: The Purpose of a Better Life—Its Necessity]

Before a man confesses to the priest, who is the vicar, he ought first to confess to God, Who is the Principal. But he should regard this matter seriously, since nothing escapes and nothing deceives the eye of God. Wherefore he ought here, without pretence, to ponder his purpose to lead a better life and his hatred of sin. For there is scarcely anything which deceives more penitents than that subtle and profound dissimulation by which they oftentime pretend, even to themselves, a violent hatred of sin and a purpose to lead a better life. The unhappy outcome proves their insincerity, for after confession they quickly return to their natural bent, and, as though relieved of the great burden of confession, they live again at ease, careless and unmindful of their purpose; by which one fact they can be convicted of their sad pretending. Wherefore a man ought in this matter to be altogether frank, and to speak of himself within himself just as he feels himself moved to speak, just as he could wish to speak if there were do punishment, no God, no commandment, and just as he would speak in the ear of some familiar friend, to whom he would not be ashamed to reveal everything about himself. As he could wish to speak quite freely to such a one about his faults, so let him speak to God, Who loves us far more than we love ourselves.

For if there is any one who does not find himself seriously inclined toward a good life, I know not whether it is safe for him to make confession. This I do know, that it were better for him to stay away from confession. For in this matter he need not care for the commandment of the Church, whether it excommunicate him or inflict some lesser punishment. It is better for him not to listen to the Church, than, at his own peril, to come to God with a false heart. In the latter case he sins against God, in the former case only against the Church; if, indeed, he sin at all in such a case by not listening to the Church, seeing that the Church has no right to command anything in which there is peril to the soul, and a case of this kind is always excepted from the commandments of the Church. For whatever the Church commands, she commands for God and for the soul's salvation, presuming that a man is capable of receiving her commandment and able to fulfil it. If this presumption falls, the precept does not hold, since nothing can be decreed contrary to the commandments of God, which bind the conscience.

[Sidenote: The purpose of a Better Life—Its Difficulty]

It is certainly to be feared that many come to confession out of fear of the commandment of the Church, who in their hearts are still pleased with their former evil life. If, however, a man is entangled in these difficulties, fearing to stay away from confession, and yet perceiving (if the truth were told) that he lacks the disposition toward a better life, let him lay hold of the one thing that remains, and hear the counsel of the Prophet, "Pour out your heart before Him"; [Ps. 62:8] and let him abase himself, and openly confess to God the whole evil of his heart, and pray for and desire a good purpose. Who, indeed, is so proud as to think he does not need this counsel? There is no one whose good purpose is as great as it ought to be. Let a man, therefore, fearlessly seek from God what he knows he cannot find in himself, until the thought of a better life begin seriously and truly to please him, and his own life to displease him. For the doctrines about the forming of a good purpose, which have been handed down to us and are everywhere taught, are not to be understood in the sense that a man should of himself form and work out this good purpose. Such an understanding is death and perdition; as one says, "There is death in the pot, O man of God." [2 Kings 4:40] And yet very many are grievously tormented by this idea, because they are taught to strive after the impossible. But in very despair, and pouring out his heart before God, a man should say, "Lord God, I have not what I ought to have, and cannot do what I ought to do. Give what Thou commandest, and command what Thou wilt." For thus St. Augustine prays in his Confessions. [4]

FIFTH

[Sidenote: The Purpose of a Better Life—Its Nature]

But what has been said about a good purpose, I wish to have understood with caution. For a good purpose ought to be twofold. First, a purpose with regard to open, mortal sins, such as adultery, homicide, fornication, theft, robbery, usury, slander, etc. The purpose to avoid these sins belongs properly to sacramental Confession, and to confession before God it belongs at any moment after the sins have been committed; according to the word of Ecclesiasticus, "My son, hast thou sinned? Do so no more, but ask pardon for thy former sins," [Ecclus. 21:1] and again, "Make no tarrying to turn to the Lord." [Ecclus. 5:8] In the second place, however, as regards all the sins they call "venial" (of which more below), it is entirely vain to labor after the forming of a good purpose, because if one rightly considers himself, he will find such a purpose altogether impossible, if he wishes henceforth to live in the flesh; since (as Augustine says) this life cannot be lived without such sins as unnecessary and thoughtless laughter, language, imaginations, sights, sounds, etc. As regards such things it is uncertain whether they are sins, or temptations by which merit is increased. And yet it is marvelous how a patent is vexed and worried in these matters by the present wordy manner of confessing. A purpose ought to be certain, and directed toward things which are certain and which can be shunned in common living, like the aforesaid open, mortal sins.

SIXTH

[Sidenote: Hidden Sins—Are They to be Confessed?]

Whether the hidden sins of the heart, which are known only to God and the man who commits them, belong to sacramental confession or not, is more than I can say. I should prefer to say that they do not. For the need of confessing these sins can in no way be proved, either by reason or by Scripture, and I have often suspected that it was all an invention of avaricious or curious or tyrannical prelates, who took this way of bringing the people of Christ to fear them. This is, in my opinion, laying hands on the judgment of God and is a violation of the rights of God, especially if men are forced to it.[5]

Here comes in that whole sea of laws and impossible questions about "cases of sin," [6] etc., since it is impossible for a man to know when he has in his heart committed the mortal sins of pride, lust, or envy. Nay, how can the priest know this, when he is set in judgment upon mortal sins alone? Can he know another's heart who does not thoroughly know his own? Hence it comes that many people confess many things, not knowing whether they are sins or not; and to this they are driven by that sentence of Gregory, "A good mind will confess guilt even where there is no guilt." They [i. e., the priests] wish that what is offered to God shall be offered to themselves—so immense is the arrogance of priests and pontiffs, and so haughty the pride of the Pharisees—and they do not see, meanwhile, that if this offering were made to man, the whole of life would be nothing else than confession, and that even this confession would have to be confessed in another confession by the man who fears guilt where there is no guilt, since even good works are not without guilt, and Job is afraid of all his works. [Job 9:28]

SEVENTH

[Sidenote: Hidden Sins—What Hidden Sins Should be Confessed?]

Let some one else, then, explain this. I am content with this, that not all the sins of the heart are to be confessed. But if some are to be confessed, I say that it is only those which a man clearly knows that he has purposed in his heart against the commandments of God;[7] not, therefore, mere thoughts about a virgin or a woman, nor, on the other hand, the thoughts of a woman about a youth, nor the affections or ardor of lust, that is to say, the inclinations of the one sex toward the other, however unseemly, nor, I would add, even passions of this sort; for these thoughts are frequently passions inspired by the flesh, the world, or the devil, which the soul is compelled unwillingly to bear, sometimes for a long while, even for a whole day, or a week; as the apostle Paul confesses of his thorn in the flesh. [2 Cor. 12:7]

The consequence of all this is that a purpose to avoid these things is impossible and vain and deceitful, for the inclinations and desires of the sexes for one another do not cease so long as occasion is given them, and the devil is not quiet, and out whole nature is sin. But those who wish to be without sin and who believe that man is sound and whole, erect these crosses for us that we may not cease to confess (even to the priest) what things soever tickle us never so little. Therefore, if these hidden things of the heart ought to be confessed at all, only those things should be confessed which involve full consent to the deed; and such things happen very rarely or never to those who wish to lead pious lives, even though they are constantly harassed by desires and passions.

EIGHT

[Sidenote: Mortal and Venial Sins]

At this place we should also speak of that race of audacious theologians who are born to the end that the true fear of God may be extinguished in human hearts, and that they may smite the whole world with false terrors. It might seem that Christ was speaking of them when he told of "terrors from heaven." [Luke 21:11 Vulg.] These are the men who have undertaken to distinguish for us between mortal and venial sin. When men have heard that a certain sin is venial, they are careless and wholly leave off fearing God, as if He counted a venial sin for naught; again, if they have heard that the consent of the heart is a mortal sin, and if they have failed to listen to the precepts of the Church, or have committed some other trifling offence, there is no place in their hearts for Christ, because of the confusion made by the roaring sea of a troubled conscience.

Against these teachers it should be known that a man ought to give up in despair the idea that he can ever confess all his mortal sins, and that the doctrine which is contained in the Decretals[8] and is current in the Church, to wit, that every Christian should once in a year make confession of all his sins (so the words run), is either a devilish and most murderous doctrine, or else is sorely in need of a loose interpretation.

Not all sins, I say, either mortal or venial, are to be confessed, but it should be known that after a man has used all diligence in confessing, he has yet confessed only the smaller part of his sins. How do we know this? Because the Scripture says, "Cleanse Thou me from hidden sins, O Lord." [Ps. 19:12] These hidden sins God alone knows. And again it says, "Create in me a clean heart, O God." [Ps. 51:10] Even this holy prophet confesses that his heart is unclean. And all the holy Church prays, "Thy will be done"; [Matt. 6:10] and thus confesses that she does not do the will of God, and is herself a sinner.

[Sidenote: Should All Mortal Sins be Confessed?]

Furthermore, we are so far from being able to know or confess all the mortal sins that even our good works are damnable and mortal, if God were to judge with strictness, and not to receive them with forgiving mercy. If, therefore, all mortal sins are to be confessed, it can be done in a brief word, by saying at once, "Behold, all that I am, my life, all that I do and say, is such that it is mortal and damnable"; according to what is written in the cxliii. Psalm, "Enter not into judgment with Thy servant, for in Thy sight shall no flesh living be justified" [Ps. 143:2]; and in the Epistle to the Romans, Chapter vii, "But I am carnal, sold under sin; I know that in my flesh dwelleth no good thing; the evil that I would not, that I do, etc." [Rom. 7:14, 18, 19]

But of all mortal sins, this is the most mortal, not to believe that we are hateful in the sight of God because of damnable and mortal sin. To such madness these theologians, with this rule of theirs, strive zealously and perniciously to drag the consciences of men, by teaching that venial sins are to be distinguished from mortal sins, and that according to their own

68

fashion. For we read in Augustine, Cyprian, and other Fathers that those things which are bound and loosed are not mortal sins, but criminal offences, i. e., those acts of which men can be accused and convicted.

Therefore, by the term "all sins" in the Decretal we should understand those things of which a man is accused, either by others or by his own conscience. By "conscience" I mean a right conscience, not a conscience seared and deformed by human traditions, but a conscience which is expert in the commandments of God, and which knows that much more is to be left solely to the goodness of God than is to be committed to its own diligence.

But what if the devil, when a man is dying, raises the obstacle of sins which have not been confessed, as we read in many of the stories?[9] I answer. Let these sins go long with those of which it is said, "Who can understand his faults?" [Ps. 19:12] and with those others of which it is written, "Enter not into judgment with Thy servant." [Ps. 143:2] Whatever stories have been made up contrary to these sayings, have either been invented under some devilish delusion, or are not rightly understood. It is enough that thou hast had the will to confess all things, if thou hadst known them or hadst been able. God wills that His mercy be glorified. But how? In our righteousness? Nay, in our sins and miseries. The Scriptures should be esteemed more highly than any stories.

NINTH

[Sidenote: Distinction between Sins]

By thus getting down to the thing itself,[10] the penitent, of whom I have so often spoken, does away entirely with that riot of distinctions; to wit, whether he has committed sin by fear humbling him to evil, or by love inflaming him to evil; what sins he has committed against the three theological virtues of faith, hope, and charity; what sins against the four cardinal virtues; what sins by the five senses; what of the seven mortal sins, what against the seven sacraments, what against the seven gifts of the Holy Spirit, what against the eight beatitudes, what of the nine peccata aliena, what against the twelve Articles of Faith, what of the silent sins, what of the sins crying to heaven; or whether he has sinned by or against anything else.[11] That hateful and wearisome catalogue of distinctions is altogether useless, nay, it is altogether harmful. Some have added to these evils a most troublesome business of "circumstances."

By all this they have produced two results. First, the penitent makes so much of these trifles that he is not able really to give heed to the thing of chief importance, namely, the desire for a better life. He is compelled to tax his memory with such a mass of details, and so to fill his heart with the business of rightly expressing his cares and anxieties, while seeking out forgotten sins or a way of confessing them, that he entirely loses the present pangs of

69

conscience, and the whole profit and salutary effect of confession. When he is absolved, therefore, he rejoices not so much because he is absolved, as because he has freed himself once for all from the wretched worry of confession; for what he has been seeking has been not the absolution, but rather the end of the laborious nuisance of confessing. Thus, while we sleep secure, everything is upset again. In the second place, such penitents weary the confessor, stealing his time, and standing in the way of other penitents.

[Sidenote: The Commandments a Guide to Confession]

We ought, therefore, to look briefly at the Commandments of God, in which, if they are rightly understood, all sins are, without doubt, contained.[12] And not even all of these are to be considered, but the last two Commandments are to be excluded entirely from confession. Confession should be brief, and should be a confession chiefly of those sins which cause pain at the time of confession, and, as they say, "move to confession." For the sacrament of confession was instituted for the quieting, not for the disturbing, of the conscience.

For example, as regards the Commandment, "Thou shalt not commit adultery," let the penitent quickly say in what manner he has given place to lust, either in act or word, or by consent, just as though he were describing himself entirely, with all his limbs and senses, in that Commandment. Why, then, should he uselessly bring in the five senses, the mortal sins, and the rest of that ocean of distinctions? So in the case of the Commandment, "Thou shalt not kill." Let him quickly say by what kind of wrath he has sinned, whether by hatred, slander or cursing, or by the act of murder itself. And so with the rest; as I have tried to show in my Preceptorium and my writings on the Decalogue.[13]

Let it not disturb anyone that in the Decretals on Penance and in the IV. Book of the Sentences[14] this matter is differently treated. For they all are full of human inventions; and no wonder! They have taken everything they say out of a certain apocryphal and unlearned book called De vera et falsa poenitentia,[15] which is widely circulated, and ascribed, by a lying title, to St. Augustine.

TENTH

[Sidenote: Commandments of God and of Man]

In making confession diligence should be used to distinguish with great care between sins committed against the Commandments of God and sins committed against the statutes of men. I say this because of the mad opinion, which is now prevalent, that sins which are

70

committed against the decretals of the popes are to be noted with wondrous care, but sins committed against God, with little or none.

Let me give you some illustrations:

You will find priests and monks who are horrified, as at some prodigy, if they stammer, or repeat even a syllable in the Canon of the Mass,[16] though this may be a natural defect of the tongue, or an accident, and is not a sin. Again, there is no priest who does not confess that he was distracted, or failed to read his Preparatoria, or other old-womanish trifles of the kind. There was one who, even when he was at the altar celebrating, called a priest three times and confessed that something had happened. Indeed, I have seen these endless jests of the devil taken by many so seriously that they almost lost their minds. And yet the fact that they cherished hatred or envy in their hearts, that they had cursed before or after Mass, that they had intentionally lied or slandered, all this moved them not at all. Whence this perversity? From the "traditions of men who turn from the truth," [Tit. 1:14] as the Apostle says. Because we have neglected to offer God a confession of true sins, He has given us up to our reprobate sense, [Rom. 1:24] so that we delude ourselves with fictitious sins and deprive ourselves of the benefit of the sacrament,[17] and the more we seem to seek it, the more this is true.

[Sidenote: They Tyranny of Ordinances]

Of this stuff are those who make the neglect of the canonical hours[18] an almost irremissible sin, while they easily remit fornication, which is against the commandments of God, or the neglect of duty toward our neighbor. These are they who so approve of that dream or story about St. Severinus[19] that they think they cannot read their Hours in advance, or afterward make them up without sin, even if they have been hindered at the proper time by the most just cause, such as ministering to the necessities of a neighbor, which is of six hundred times more merit than their worthless and all but damnable prayers. So far do they go in their failure to observe that the commandment of God, in the service of one's neighbor, should be preferred to the commandment of men, in the thoughtless mumbling of the words of the Hours. To this class too belong those who think it a crime to speak or to call a boy during the Canon of the Mass even in case of the greatest necessity or danger. Finally, these men make the fasting of nature one thing, and the fasting of the Church another thing, and if one has thoughtlessly swallowed some drops of liquid, or has taken some medicine, they exclude him utterly from the sacrament, and make it a sin, even the very greatest sin. I wonder whence these men have the authority to set up such laws as these and to trouble consciences with sins of their own invention. By these illustrations other, similar cases may be judged.

71

Of the laity, one confesses that he has tasted sweets, another that he has listened to jests, smelted perfumes, touched things that were soft.

Let us come to greater things! The common people are persuaded that to eat butter or eggs on fast-days is heretical; so cruelly do the laws of men rave in the Church of God! And we unconcernedly profit by this superstition of the people, nay, by this tyranny of ours, caring nothing that the commandments of God are taken in jest, so long as men tremble and turn pale at our laws. No one calls an adulterer a heretic; fornication is a light sin; schisms and discords, inspired, preserved and increased by the authority and in the name of the Church, are merits; but to eat meat on Friday is the sum of all heresies. Thus we teach the people of Christ, and permit them to be taught! But I am disgusted, wearied, shamed, distressed at the endless chaos of superstitions which has been inflicted upon this most salutary sacrament of confession by the ignorance of true theology, which has been its own tyrant ever since the time that men have been making its laws.

ELEVENTH

[Sidenote: Communion Without Confession]

I advise, therefore, as John Gerson[20] used to advise, that a man shall now and then go to the altar or to the Sacrament "with a scruple of conscience," that is, without confession, even if he has been immoderate in drinking, talking, or sleeping, or has done something else that is wrong, or has not prayed a single one of the Hours. Would you know why this advice is given? Listen! It is in order that a man may learn to trust more in the mercy of God than in his own confession or in his own diligence. For enough cannot be done toward shaking that accursed trust in our own works. It should be done for this reason, too, that if a man is assailed by some necessity, whether temptation or death, and those hidden sins begin to appear which he has never been able to see or to confess, then he may have, ready and prepared, a practice of trusting in the mercy which God offers to the unworthy; according to the word, "His heart is prepared to trust in the Lord." [21] [Ps. 57:7] How shall a man hope, in the face of the sudden inroads of such a great mass of sins, if he has not learned in this life, while there was time, to hope in the Lord against the smallest, nay, against even an imagined sin? If you say, "What if this were despising the sacrament and tempting God?" I answer, It will not be tempting God if it is done for the glory of God; that is, if you do it, not because you despise God's sacrament nor because you want to tempt Him (since you are ready to make the fullest confession), but only in order that you may accustom a troubled conscience to trust in God and not to tremble at the rustling of every falling leaf. Do not doubt that everything pleases God which is done to the end that you may have trust in Him, since it is all His glory that we trust with our whole heart in His mercy.

I do not wish, however, that a man should always go to the altar without confession; but I say that it should be done sometimes, and then only for the arousing of trust in God and the destroying of trust in our own act of confession. For a man will hardly go to mass without guilt, if he thinks his forgiveness sure because he has confessed, rather than because God is merciful; nay, this is altogether an impiety. The summa summarum[22] is, "Blessed are all they that put their trust in the Lord." [Ps. 2:12] When you hear this word, "in the Lord," know that he is unblessed who puts his trust in anything whatsoever that is not the Lord Himself. And such a man those "artists of confession" make; for what has the "art of confession" done except to destroy the art and practice of confiding, until at last we have learned to confess a great deal, to confide not at all.

TWELFTH

[Sidenote: Reserved Cases—No Hidden Sins can be Reserved]

In the matter of reserved cases,[23] many are troubled. For my own part, because I know that the laws of men to be subject to mercy, and be applied with mildness rather than with severity, I follow the custom and advice of those who think that in hidden sins no case is to be reserved, and therefore all penitents are to be absolved whose sins are hidden, as are the sins of the flesh, that is to say, every form of lust, the procuring of abortion, and the like. For it should not be presumed that any pope would be willing, in matters of hidden sin, to set so many snares and dangers for men's souls. But when a sin has been public, an open reserved case, it should be left entirely to the authorities of the Church, no matter whether they are just or unjust. In such case, however, the confessor may so moderate the power of the keys[24] as not to let the penitent depart without absolution, for those sins at least which he knows to be not reserved. Just now, to be sure, I am in doubt, and have not yet found a place for the proper discussion of it, whether any sin can be reserved, or ever is reserved, so far as the remission of guilt[25] is concerned; that the penalty can be reserved is not doubted; but of this let others judge. But even in the remission of the penalty, neither the confessor nor the penitent should be too much troubled by scruples. The penalty I have especially in mind is excommunication, or any other censure of the Church—what they call their lightnings and thunders. Since excommunication is only penalty and not guilt, and can be laid upon the innocent and allowed to remain upon the man who has returned to his senses, and, furthermore, since it is sometimes necessary to put off satisfaction, because of the length of the journey required or because of poverty; therefore the penitent who is excommunicated or under censure should be absolved from all his sins, if he seeks absolution, and be dismissed to the higher authorities to be loosed from excommunication and to make satisfaction. Thus he should be absolved in the judgment of God and of conscience from guilt and sins, and sent to the judgment of the Church to be freed from the penalty. This is what is meant when it is said that the desire to make satisfaction[26] suffices for the absolving of a sinner.

LAST

[Sidenote: Vows]

The subject of vows should also have consideration, for it is almost the greatest question involved in this whole matter, and gives rise to much more confusion than does the reservation of cases, though this, too, rules its Babylon with great tyranny. If one would wish to speak freely on this subject, "the land would not be able to bear all his words," [Amos 7:10] as the impious Amaziah says of Amos.

[Sidenote: Their Abuse]

The first and best plan would be for the pontiffs and preachers to dissuade and deter the people from their proneness to the making of vows, to show them how the visiting of the Holy Land, Rome, Compostella,[27] and other holy places, as well as zeal in fastings, prayers, and works chosen by themselves, are nothing when compared with the works commanded by God and the vows which we have taken in baptism.[28] These vows every one can keep in his own home by doing his duty toward his neighbors, his wife, his children, his servants, his masters, and thereby gain incomparably greater merit than he can find by fulfilling vows to do works chosen by himself and not commanded by God. The foolish opinion of the common people and the ostentation of the Bulls[29] have brought it to pass that these vows of pilgrimages, fastings, prayers, and other works of the kind far outweigh in importance the works of God's Law, although we never have sufficient strength to do these last works. For my part, I could wish that there should not henceforth be any vows among Christian people except those which we take in baptism, and this, indeed, seems formerly to have been the case; and I would wish all to understand what is required of them, namely, that they be obedient to the commandments of God. For the vows of baptism seem to have been altogether cheapened by the too great practice, parade, dispensation, and redemption of these other vows. Let us put all our strength to the task, I say, and we shall find that we have vowed in baptism more than we are ever able to perform.

Some vows, including oaths, are made to men, others to God. Those made to men are admitted to be binding, so far and so long as he may desire, to whom the vow is made. Accordingly, it should be known that, as Gerson correctly thinks, the oaths and vows usually taken in the Universities or to worldly lords[30] ought not to be so rigorously regarded that every violation of them should be regarded as the breaking of a vow or an act of perjury. It is more just not to consider vows of this kind broken unless they are violated out of contempt and obstinate malice. It is otherwise in things that are vowed to God.

[Sidenote: Vows Made to God]

In vows made to God, I see dispensation granted by the pontiffs, but I shall never be persuaded that he is safe to whom such a dispensation is granted. For such a vow is of divine law, and no pontiff, either mediate or supreme, has any more authority in this matter than any Christian brother, though I know that certain of the Decretals and the Glosses on the Decretals venture many statements about it which I do not believe.

This, however, I would readily believe, that a vow of chastity given before puberty, neither holds nor binds, because he who made the vow was ignorant of what he was promising, since he had not yet felt the "thorn of the flesh." [2 Cor. 12:7] It is my pious opinion that such a vow is counted by God as foolish and void, and that the fathers of the monasteries should be forbidden by a general edict of the Church to receive a man before his twentieth, or at least his eighteenth, year, and girls before their fifteenth or sixteenth, if we are really concerned about the care of souls.

[Sidenote: Commutation of Vows]

It is also a great piece of boldness, in commuting or remitting vows, to impose what they call "a better work." In the eyes of God there is no difference in works, and He judges works not according to their number or greatness, but according to the disposition of the doer; moreover, "the Lord is the weigher of spirits," [Rom. 8:27] as the Scripture says, and He often prefers the manual labor of the poor artisan to the fasting and prayer of the priest, of which we find an illustration in St. Anthony and the shoemaker of Alexandria.[31] Since these things are so, who shall be so bold and presumptuous as to commute a vow into some "better work"? But these things will have to be spoken of elsewhere, for here we have undertaken to speak of confession only as it concerns the Commandments of God, for the quieting and composing of consciences which are troubled by scruples.

[Sidenote: Abuses of Penance]

I shall add but one thing. There are many who set perilous snares for married folk, especially in case of incest; and when any one (for these things can happen, nay, alas! they do happen) has defiled the sister of his wife, or his mother-in-law, or one related to him in any degree of consanguinity, they at once deprive him of the right to pay the debt of matrimony, and nevertheless they suffer him not, nay, they forbid him, to desert his wife's bed. What monstrous thing is this? What new remedy for sin? What sort of satisfaction for sin? Does it not show how these tyrants make laws for other men's infirmity and indulge their own? Show me the law-giver, however penitent and chaste, who would allow such a law to be made for himself. They put dry wood on the fire and say, Do not burn; they put a man in a woman's arms and forbid him to touch her or know her; and they do this on their own authority and without the command of God. What madness! My advice is that the confessor beware of tyrannical decrees or laws, and confidently sentence a sinner to some other penance, or totally abstain from punishing, leaving free to him the right of matrimony which has been given him not by man, but by God. For no angel in heaven, still less any man on earth, has the power to enjoin this penance, which is the burning occasion of continual sin. Wherefore they are not to be heeded who wish such things to be done, and the penitent is to be freed from this scruple and peril.

But who may recount all the tyrannies with which the troubled consciences of penitent and confessing Christians are daily disturbed, by means of death-bringing "constitutions" and customs, administered by silly manikins, who only know how to bind and place on the shoulders of men burdens grievous and heavy to be borne, which they themselves are not willing to move with a finger? [Matt. 23:4] So this most salutary sacrament of penance has become nothing else than a mere tyranny of the great, then a disease, and a means to the increase of sins. Thus in the end it signifies one thing and works another thing for miserable sinners, because priestlings, impious and unlearned in the law of the Lord, administer the Church of God, which they have filled with their laws and their dreams.

Here follows, in the original, a paraphrase of the apocryphal Prayer of Manasseh.

FOOTNOTES

[1] Luther quotes from the Vulgate and frequently from memory, a fact which should always be remembered in comparing his quotations from the text of Scripture.

[2] Vulgate, Justus prior est accusator.

[3] The apocryphal Prayer of Manasseh was included by Luther as an appendix to this treatise.

[4] Augustine Conf., X, 29.

[5] i. e., Forced to confess hidden sins.

[6] The so-called "science of casuistry," by which the moral value of an act is determined and the exact degree of guilt attaching to a given sin is estinated.

[7] Cf. Small Catechism, "Of Confession," Ques. "What sins ought we to confess?"

[8] The decrees of the Popes collected in the Canon Law. The decretal here referred to is C. Omnis Utriusque, X. de poententiis et remissionibus.

[9] Anecdotes illustrating the doctrines of the Church were favorite contents of the sermons in Luther's day. Various collections of these edifying legends are still extant. Cf. p. 224, and note.

[10] i. e., By thinking of the nature of confession.

[11] The reader of this minute classification of sins, which could be duplicated out of almost any manual of casuistry, may judge for himself whether Luther was correct in calling it a "riot of distinctions."

[12] Luther steadily maintained that the Ten Commandments were a complete guide to holy living and that every possible sin his prohibited somewhere in the Decalogue. See, beside the various smaller treatises (Kurze Unterweisung wie man beichten soll (1518), Kurze Form des zehn Gobte (1520), etc.), the large Discourse on Good Works, below, pp. 184 ff.

[13] The writings mentioned are found in the Weimar Ed., Vol I, pp. 250 ff, 258 ff, 398 ff. See above, p. 75, note 1.

[14] The Sentences of Peter the Lombard was the standard text-book of Medieval theology.

[15] "On True and False Penitence," now universally admitted not to have been written by St. Augustine, but passing under his name till after the Reformation.

[16] That part of the liturgy of the Mass in which the miraculous transformation of the elements into the Body and Blood of Christ is believed to take place.

[17] i. e., Of the sacrament of confession.

[18] The fixed hours of daily prayer observed in the monasteries, afterward applied to the liturgy for these services, viz., the Breviary. The daily reading of this breviary at the appointed hours is required of all clergy.

[19] An Italian saint, d. 482, noted for the strictness and severity of his ascetic practices.

[20] Professor of the University of Paris; one of the most popular and famous of the later Scholastics. He died 1429.

[21] Vulgate, "Cor ejus paratus est."

[22] We would say, "the whole thing in a nutshell."

[23] i. e., Sins for which the confessor was not allowed to grant absolution without reference to some higher Church authority, to whose absolution they were "reserved." See Introduction, p. 79.

[24] The power to "bind and loose" (Matt. 16:19), i. e., to forgive and to retain sins (John 20:23).

[25] The Roman Church distinguished between the "guilt" and the "penalty" of sin. It was thought possible to forgive the former and retain the latter. Submission to the penalty is "satisfaction." See Introduction to XCV. Theses, p. 19.

[26] Votum satisfactionis. It was and is the teaching of the Roman Church that, where the actual reception of any sacrament is impossible, the earnest desire to receive it suffices for salvation. The desire is known as the votum sacramenti.

[27] In Spain. The shrine of St. James at that place was a famous resort for pilgrims. Cf. below, p. 191, and note.

[28] See the Treatise on the Sacrament of Baptism, above, pp. 68 ff.

[29] Luther doubtless refers to the decrees of the popes by which special rewards were attached to worship at certain shrines.

[30] The oath of office and the oath of allegiance.

[31] The story is repeated by Melanchthon in the Apology of the Augsburg Confession, Ch. XIII, Art. xxvii, 38 (Book of Concord, Eng. Trans., p. 288). The "Alexander Coriarius" of text is misleading.

THE FOURTEEN OF CONSOLATION

FOR SUCH AS LABOR AND ARE HEAVY LADEN

(TESSARADECAS CONSOLATORIA)

1520

INTRODUCTION

1. When Luther's Elector, Frederick the Wise (1486-1525), returned to his residence at Torgau, after participating in the election of Emperor Charles V, at Frankfort-on-the-Main, in the summer of 1519, he was stricken with a serious illness, from which there seemed little hope of his recovery Concerned for his noble patron, and urged by Dr. George Spalatin, his friend at court, to prepare a "spiritual consolation" for the Elector, Luther wrote "The Fourteen of Consolation," one of his finest and tenderest devotional writings, and, in conception and execution, one of the most original of all his works.

Its composition falls within the months of August and September of the year 1519. On August 29th, the Day of the Beheading of St. John Baptist, we find him writing in Part I, chapter vi: "Does not the example of St. John Baptist, whom we commemorate on this day as beheaded by Herod, shame and amaze us all?" On September 22d, he sends the completed manuscript (in Latin) to Spalatin, requesting him to make a free translation of it into German and present it to the Elector. By the end of November Spalatin had completed his task (one marvels at the leisureliness of this, in view of the serious condition of the Elector; or was the manuscript translated and administered piecemeal to the noble patient?), and early in December he returned the original, doubtless together with his own translation, to Luther, who had requested its return, "in order to comfort himself therewith."

The work was, therefore, in the strictest sense, a private writing, and not in the least intended for publication.[1] But the importunities of those who had seen it, particularly of Spalatin, prevailed, and on December 18th Luther writes to the latter that "the Tessaradecas, in both Latin and German, is in the hands of the printer." On February 8th, 1520, he sends Spalatin a printed copy of the Latin, and six days later, one of the German edition. The latter contained a dedicatory letter to the Elector, which, however, by an oversight of the printer, and owing to Luther's absence at the time, was omitted in the Latin edition.

In 1535, fifteen years after its first appearance in print, Luther issued his Tessaradecas in a new and final edition, adding a brief prefatory note. He no longer holds many of his former views, and there is much in his little book that he has outgrown and might now correct. But with characteristic unconcern, he lets it all stand, and even restores many passages that had been corrupted or omitted to their original form. It is a revised edition, with the errors, as it were, underscored. It is to be chiefly an historical record, to show the world how far he has progressed since its first writing (1 Tim. 4:15), a mile-post on the road of his inner development.[2] And more than this—and here one fancies he can see the sardonic smile on the battle-scarred face—it is to furnish his enemies with weapons against himself; he desires to show a favor to the hunters of contradictions in his works, "that they may have whereon to exercise their malice."

2. The plan of the work is in the highest degree original and artificial. The title, Tessaradecas consolatoria, which we have rendered "The Fourteen of Consolation," [3] is explained by Luther in the dedicatory epistle to the Elector, pp. 110 ff. The "Fourteen" were the fourteen patron saints of medieval devotion, called the "Defenders from all evils" (defendores, auxiliatores). Whence the cult arose is not altogether certain. It is said to have become popular in Germany since the vision of a Franconian shepherd, in 1446, to whom there appeared, in the fields, the Christ-child surrounded by the fourteen saints. The Vierzehnheiligenkirche at Staffelstein, a famous shrine for pilgrims, marks the spot. The names of the "Fourteen," each of whom was a defender against some particular disease or danger, are as follows: Achatius (Acacius), Aegidius, Barbara (cf. St. Barbara's cress), Blasius (the "defender" of those afflicted with throat diseases), Catharine (cf. St. Catharine's flower), Christopher (cf. St. Christopher's herb), Cyriacus, Dionysius, Erasmus (Italian: San Elmo; cf. St. Elmo's fire), Eustachius, George the Martyr (cf. St. George's herb), Margaret, Pantaleon, and Vitus (cf. St. Vitus's dance). Luther's Sermons on the First Commandment (1516) may be compared lot references to some of these saints and to many others.

As over against these saints, Luther also invents fourteen defenders or comforters, and arranges them in this writing in the form of an altar tablet; but his is not a tablet such as those found in the churches, representing the fourteen defenders, but it is a spiritual tablet or painting, to uplift and strengthen the pious heart of the Elector, and of all others who are weary and heavy laden. The first division, or panel, of this figurative altar-piece contains the images or paintings of seven evils (maia); the second, those of seven blessings (bona). The contemplation of the evils will comfort the weary and heavy laden by showing them how small their evil is in comparison with the evil that they have within themselves, namely, their sin; with the evils they have suffered in the past, and will have to suffer in the future; with the evils which others, their friends and foes, suffer; and, above all, with those which Christ suffered on the cross. Similarly, the contemplation of the blessings will help them to forget their present sufferings; for they are as nothing compared with the blessing within them, namely, their faith; the blessings they enjoyed in the past, and those that await them in the future, as well as those which arc enjoyed by their friends and foes, and, finally, the highest blessing of all, which is Jesus Christ, risen and glorified.

We can only conjecture as to the origin of this unique conception of Luther's. Of course, the evils and blessings came to him from the passage in Ecclesiasticus 11:26.[4] The order and arrangement may follow some contemporary altar-picture of the "Fourteen Saints." There was a famous altar-painting of the "Fourteen," by Lucas Cranach, in St Mary's at Torgau, the residence of the Elector. The fact is suggestive.[5]

3. The Tessaradecas was favorably received by the Elector, was highly praised by Spalatin, who urged its publication, and must have been dear to Luther's own heart, since he desired the return of his manuscript for his own comfort. The little work soon became very popular, and passed through numerous editions, both in Latin and in German. During the first two years five Latin editions were printed, and up to 1525 seven German editions. A translation was published in the Netherlands in 1521, and one in England in 1578. Erasmus commended it to Bishop Christopher of Basle, in 1523; "I am sending your Highness Luther's book of the fourteen pictures, which has won great approbation even from those who oppose his doctrine at every point." Mathesius, Luther's pupil and biographer, judged that there had never before been such words of comfort written in the German language. The Franciscan Lemmens speaks of "the beautiful and Catholic thoughts" in it.

4. Our translation is made from the Latin text, as found in the Weimar edition of Luther's works, volume vi, with continual reference to the German text, as given in the Berlin edition. We regret our inability to obtain a copy of the old English translation (A right comfortable Treatise conteining sundrye pointes of consolation for them that labour and are laden....Englished by W. Gace. T. Vautrollier, London, 1578, sec. ed. 1580), although the form of the title would seem to indicate that it was made from Spalatin's translation, and not from the original.[6]

The many Scripture quotations, all naturally from the Latin Vulgate, and most of them freely quoted from memory, and sometimes "targumed" and woven into the texture of the treatise, are rendered by us, unless the sense should thereby be affected, in the words of the Authorised Version. Important or interesting variations are indicated in the foot-notes.

5. The Tesseradecas deserves to be more widely known and used. Its value is more than merely that of an historical document, representing a transition stage in Luther's reformatory views. It gives us, besides this, a deep insight into the living piety of the man, his great heart so full of the peace of God that passeth all understanding. When we remember that this little work was composed in the midst of a very "tempest" of other writings, chiefly polemical (e.g., the savage onslaughts on Emser), it will appear akin to the little book of Ruth, lying so peacefully between the war-like books of Judges and First Samuel. At the Leipzig Disputation, earlier in the same year, Luther was seen to hold a bouquet of flowers in his hand, and to smell of it when the battle waxed hot. The Tesseradecas is such a bunch of flowers. Its chief glory, however, that of a devotional

classic, has been somewhat dimmed by Luther himself, who with the carelessness of genius refused to revise his outworn views in it; and yet, despite its relics of mediævalism, particularly by reason of its firm evangelical foundation, its scriptural warp and woof, its fervent piety, and its fresh and original treatment, it is not less entitled to a high place in the devotional and ascetic literature of the Church than the much better known Imitatio Christi. In this sense it is herewith offered anew to the English reader, with the hope that "the diligent reading and contemplation of these 'images' may minister some slight comfort."

6. Literature.—(1) The literary and historical introductions to the Tessaradecas in the Weimar, Erlangen, and Berlin editions. (2) Köstlin-Kawerau, Martin Luther, sein Leben und seine Schriften. 5th ed., 1903, vol. I, pp. 280, 281. (3) H. Beck, Die Erbauungslit. der evang. Kirche Deutschlands, 1883. (4) On the fourteen Defenders see articles in Wetzer und Welte and the Catholic Encyclopaedia, and especially the article Nothelfer, by Zöckler, in PRE3, where also see further literature.

A. T. W. Steinhaeuser

Allentown, PA.

FOOTNOTES

[1] Cf. the first sentence of the Prefatory Note, p. 109 of this volume; also the dedicatory epistle of the Treatise on Good Works, p. 184.

[2] We have noted a few of the more glaring relics of mediævalism in the footnotes; the attentive reader will discover and dispose of others for himself.

[3] The title furnishes peculiar difficulties to the translator.

Cole has simply transliterated it, "The Consolatory Terradecad."

Spalatin paraphrased it "Ein trostlichs Buchlein," etc. The

Berlin Edition renders it, "Vierzehn Trostmittel," etc.

[4] See p. 113.

[5] Did the comment of Bernard of Clairvaux, on Romans 8:18, perhaps contribute its quota to the general conception? "The sufferings of this present time are not worthy to be compared with the past guilt, which is forgiven (remittitur); with the present grace of consolation, which is given (immittitur); with the future glory, which is promised (promittitur)."

An English translation, with some omissions that Luther himself did not care to make is found in Henry Cole's Select Works of Martin Luther, vol. II, London, 1824.

THE FOURTEEN OF CONSOLATION

(TESSARADECAS CONSOLATORIA)

1520

PREFATORY NOTE[1]

This book was written, early in my career, for that most excellent prince, Frederick, Duke of Saxony, when he was stricken with a dangerous illness; but many desired that it be printed. After passing through various editions it has now become so sadly corrupted and mutilated that many passages are missing, whose original form I myself have clean forgot. However, I have restored the sense of them, as well as I was able, taking care to set down only such views as I held when the work was first written. I did not care to revise them now, as I might well do. For it is my purpose in this book to put forth a public record of my progress,[2] and also to show a kindness to the "Contradictionists," [3] that they may have whereon to exercise their malice. For me it is enough if I please my Lord Christ and His saints; that I am hated of the devil and his scales, [4] I rejoice with all my heart, and give thanks to God.

DEDICATORY EPISTLE[5]

To the Most Illustrious Prince and Lord, Frederick, Duke of

Saxony, Arch-Marshal and Elector Of the Holy Roman Empire,

Landgrave of THuringia, Margrave of Meissen, his most gracious

Lord.

Our Lord and Saviour Jesus hath left us a commandment, which concerns all Christians alike,—that we should render the duties of humanity, or (as the Scriptures call them) the works of mercy, [Luke 6:36] to such as are afflicted and under calamity; [Matt. 25:34 ff.] that we should visit the sick, endeavor to set free the prisoners, and perform other like acts of kindness to our neighbor, whereby the evils of this present time may in some measure be lightened. And of this command our Lord Jesus Christ hath Himself given us the brightest example, in that, out of infinite love to the race of men. He descended out of the bosom of the Father into our misery and prison-cell, that is, our flesh and life so full of ills, and took upon Him the penalty of our sins, in order that we might be saved; as He saith in Isaiah xliii, "Thou hast made Me to serve with thy sins, and wearied Me with thine iniquities." [Isa. 43:24]

Whoever is not moved by so bright an example, and driven by the authority of the divine command, to show forth such works of mercy, he will deservedly hear, in the last judgment, the voice of the angry Judge saying: "Depart from me, thou cursed, into everlasting fire! For I was sick, and thou didst not visit Me; but, basely ungrateful for the many blessings I bestowed on thee and on all the world, thou wouldest not so much as lift a finger to succor thy brethren, nay Me, Christ, thy God and Saviour, in thy brethren." [Matt. 25:41]

Since, then, most noble Prince, I perceive that your Lordship has been smitten with a dangerous malady, and that Christ has thus fallen sick in you, I have counted it my duty to visit your Lordship with a little writing of mine. For I cannot pretend to be deaf to the voice of Christ crying to me out of your Lordship's flesh and blood, "Behold, here am I sick." For such ills as sickness and the like are endured, not by us Christians, but by Christ Himself, our Lord and Saviour, in Whom we live. Even as He plainly testifies in the Gospel, "Whatsoever ye have done unto one of the least of these My brethren, ye have done it unto Me." [Matt. 25:40] And while we should visit and console all who are afflicted with sickness, yet we owe this duty specially to those who are of the household of faith. For Paul clearly distinguishes between strangers and those of the household, or those who are bound to us by intimate ties, Galatians vi. [Gal. 6:10]

But I have yet other reasons for performing this my duty. For I consider that, as one of your Lordship's subjects, I must needs share in your Lordship's illness, together with the remainder of your many subjects, and suffer with you as a member with the Head, on which all our fortunes, our safety, and our happiness depend. For we recognize in your Lordship another Naaman [2 Kings, 5:1], by whom God is now giving deliverance to Germany, as in times past He gave deliverance to Syria. Wherefore the whole Roman Empire turns its eyes to your Lordship alone, and venerates and receives you as the Father of the Fatherland, and the bright ornament and protector of the whole Empire, but of the German nation in particular.[6]

Nor are we bound only to console your Lordship as much as in us lies, and to make your present sorrow our own, but much more to pray God for your health and safety; which I trust your Lordship's subjects are doing with all diligence and devotion. But as for me, whom your Lordship's many and signal benefactions have made your debtor above all others, I count it my duty to express my gratitude by rendering you some special service. But now, by reason of my poverty both of mind and fortune, it is not possible for me to offer anything of value; therefore I gladly welcomed the suggestion of Doctor George Spalatin, one of your Lordship's court chaplains, that I should prepare a kind of spiritual consolation and present it to your Lordship, to whom, he said, it would be most acceptable. Being unwilling to reject this friendly counsel, I have put together the following fourteen chapters, after the fashion of an altar tablet, and have called them, "The Fourteen." [7] They are to take the place of the fourteen saints whom our superstition has invented and called, "The Defenders against all evil." [8] But this is a tablet not of silver, but of a spiritual sort; nor is it intended to adorn the walls of a church, but to uplift and strengthen a pious heart. I trust it will stand your Lordship in good stead in your present condition. It consists of two divisions; the former containing the images of seven evils, in the contemplation of which your present troubles will grow light; the latter presenting the images of seven blessings, brought together for the same purpose.

May it please your Lordship graciously to accept this little work of mine, and to make such use of it that the diligent reading and contemplation of these "images" may minister some small comfort.

Your Lordship's humble servant,

Martin Luther, Doctor.

PREFACE

The Apostle Paul, treating in Romans xv. of the consolations of Christians, writes, "Whatsoever things were written aforetime were written for our learning, that we through patience and comfort of the scriptures might have hope." [Rom. 15:4] In these words he plainly teaches that our consolations are to be drawn from the Holy Scriptures. Now the Holy Scriptures administer comfort after a twofold fashion, by presenting to our view blessings and evils, most wholesomely intermingled; as the wise Preacher saith, "In the day of evil be mindful of the good, and in the day of good be mindful of the evil." [Ecclus. 11:26] For the Holy Spirit knows that a thing has only such meaning and value for a man as he assigns to it in his thoughts; for what he holds common and of no value will move him but little, either to pleasure when he obtains it, or to grief when he loses it. Therefore He endeavors with all His might to draw us away from thinking about things and from being moved by them; and when He has effected this, then all things whatsoever are alike to us. Now this drawing away is best accomplished by means of the Word, Whereby our thoughts are turned from the thing that moves us at the present moment to that which either is absent or does not at the moment move us. Therefore it is true that we shall attain to this state of mind only through the comfort of the Scriptures, which call us, in the day of evil, to the contemplation of good things, either present or to come, and, in the day of good, to the contemplation of evil things.

But let us, for our better understanding of these two series of pictures or images, divide each of them into seven parts. The first series will treat of the evils, and we shall consider (1) the evil within us, (2) the evil before us, (3) the evil behind us, (4) the evil on our left hand, (5) the evil on our right hand, (6) the evil beneath us, and (7) the evil above us.[9]

CHAPTER I

THE FIRST IMAGE

This is most certain and true—we may believe it or not—that no suffering in a man's experience, be it never so severe, can be the greatest of the evils that are within him. So many more and far greater evils are there within him than any that he feels. And if he were to feel those evils, he would feel the pains of hell; for he holds a hell within himself. Do you ask how this can be? The Prophet says, "All men are liars" [Ps. 116:11] and again, "Every man at his best state is altogether vanity." [Ps. 39:6] But to be a liar and vanity, is to be without truth and reality; and to be without truth and reality, is to be without God and to be nothing; and this is to be in hell and damned. Therefore, when God in His mercy chastens us, He reveals to us and lays upon us only the lighter evils; for if He were to lead us to the full knowledge of our evil, we should straightway perish. Yet even this He has given some to taste, and of them it is written, "He bringeth down to hell, and bringeth up." [1 Sam. 2:6] Therefore they say well who call our bodily sufferings the monitors of the evil within. And the Apostle, in Hebrews xii, calls them God's fatherly chastenings, when he says, "He scourgeth every son whom He receiveth." [Heb. 12:6] And He does this, in order by such scourgings and lesser evils to drive out those great evils, that we may never need to feel them; as it is written, "Foolishness is bound in the heart of a child; but the rod of correction shall drive it far from him." [Prov. 33:15] Do not loving parents grieve more for their sons when they turn out thieves and evil-doers than when they receive a wound? Nay, they themselves beat them until the blood flows, to keep them from becoming evil-doers.[10]

What is it, then, that prevents us from feeling this our true evil? It is, as I have said, so ordered by God, that we may not perish on seeing the evils hidden in the depths of our hearts. For God keeps them hidden, and would have us discern them only by faith, when He points them out to us by means of the evil that we feel. Therefore, "In the day of evil be mindful of the good." [Ecclus. 11:26] Behold, how great a good it is, not to know the whole of our evil! Be mindful of this good, and the evil that you feel will press you less cruelly. Again, "In the day of good be mindful of the evil." That is to say. Whilst you do not feel your true evil, be grateful for this respite; then will the evil that you feel sit lightly upon you. It is clear, then, that in this life a man's freedom from pain is always greater than his pain. Not that his whole evil is not present with him, but he does not think about it and is not moved by it, through the goodness of God, Who keeps it hidden.

How furiously do those men rage against themselves, to whom their true evil has been revealed! How they count as nothing whatever sufferings life may bring, if only they might not feel the hell within! Even so would every one do, who felt or truly believed in the evil within him. Gladly would he call down all external evils on his head, and count them mere child's play; nay, he would never be more sorrowful than when he had no evils to bear, after the manner of certain of the saints, such as David in Psalm vi. [Ps. 6]

Therefore, this is our first image of consolation, that a man should say to himself: "Not yet, O man, dost thou feel thine evil. Rejoice and give thanks that thou dost not need to feel it!" And so the lesser evil grows light by comparison with the greatest evil. That is what others mean when they say, "I have deserved far worse things, yea, hell itself"—a thing easy to say, but horrible to contemplate.

And this evil, though never so deeply hidden, yet puts forth fruits that are plainly enough perceived. These are the dread and uncertainty of a trembling conscience, when faith is assailed, and a man is not sure, or doubts, whether he have a gracious God. And this fruit is bitter in proportion to the weakness of one's faith. Nay, when rightly considered, this weakness alone, being spiritual, far outweighs every weakness of the body, and renders it, in comparison, light as a feather.

Moreover, to the evils within us belong all those tragic experiences described by the Preacher, when he refers again and again to "vanity and vexation of spirit." [Eccl. 1:2, 14] How many of our plans come to naught! How oft our hopes are deceived! How many things that are not to our liking must we see and bear! And the very things that fall out according to our wish fall out also against our wish! So that there is nothing perfect and complete. Finally, all these things are so much greater, the higher one rises in rank and station;[11] for such a one will of necessity be driven about by far more and greater billows, floods, and tempests, than others who labor in a like case. As it is truly said in Psalm ciii,[12] "In the sea of this world there are things creeping innumerable, both small and great beasts," [Ps. 104:25] that is, an infinite number of trials. And Job, for this reason, calls the life of man a "trial." [13]

These evils do not, indeed, cease to be evils because they are less sharply felt by us; but we have grown accustomed to them from having them constantly with us, and through the goodness of God our thoughts and feelings concerning them have become blunted. That is why they move us the more deeply when we do feel them now and then, since we have not learned through familiarity to despise them. So true is it, therefore, that we feel scarce a thousandth part of our evils, and also that we estimate them and feel them or do not feel them, not as they are in themselves, but only as they exist in our thoughts and feelings.[14]

CHAPTER II

THE SECOND IMAGE

THE FUTURE EVIL, OR THE EVIL BEFORE US

It will tend in no small degree to lighten any present evil if a man turn his mind to the evils to come. These are so many, so diverse, and so great, that out of them has arisen one of the strongest emotions of the soul; namely, fear. For fear has been defined by some as the emotion caused by coming evil. Even as the Apostle says in Romans xi, "Be not highminded, but fear." [Rom. 11:30] This evil is all the greater because of our uncertainty in what form and with what force it may come; so that there goes a popular saying, "No age is proof against the itch," although this is but a little children's disease. Even so, no man is safe from the evils that befall any other; for what one has suffered another may suffer also.

Here belong all the tragic histories of the ages, and all the lamentations of the world. Here belong the more than three hundred diseases—which some have observed—with which the human body may be vexed. And if there be so many diseases, how great will be the number of other misfortunes that may befall our possessions, our friends, and even our mind itself, that target of all evils, and trysting-place of sorrow and every ill!

And these evils increase in power and intensity as a man rises to higher rank and dignity;[15] in which estate he must needs dread every moment the coming of poverty, disgrace, and every indignity, which may indeed swiftly overtake him, for they all hang by but a slender thread, not unlike the sword which the tyrant Dionysius suspended above the head of the guest at his table.

And if none of these evils befall us, we should count it our gain, and no small comfort in the evil that does befall us; so that we should feel constrained to say with Jeremiah, "It is of the Lord's mercies that we are not consumed." [Lam. 3:22 f.] For when none of them befall us, it is because they have been kept from us by the right hand of the Most High that compasses us about with such mighty power (as we see in Job) that Satan and all evils can but gnash their teeth in helpless rage. [Job 1:10] From this we see how sweetly we ought to love our Lord, whenever any evil comes upon us. For our most loving Father would by that one evil have us see how many evils threaten us and would fall on us, if He did not Himself stand in the way, as though He said, "Satan and the host of evils have desired to have thee, to sift thee as wheat; [Luke:22:31] but I have marked out bounds for the sea, and have said, Hitherto shaft thou come, and here shall thy proud waves be stayed [Job 38:10]," as He saith in Job xxxviii.

And, granted that perchance, if God please, none of these things will come upon you; nevertheless, that which is known as the greatest of terrors, death, is certain to come, and nothing is less certain than the hour of its coming. Truly, this is so great an evil that there are many who would rather live on amid all the above-named evils than to die once and have them ended. With this one thing the Scriptures, which hold all others in contempt, associate fear, saying, "Remember thy end, and thou shalt never do amiss." [Ecclus. 7:40] Behold, how many meditations, how many books, how many rules and remedies have been brought together, in order, by calling to men's minds this one evil, to keep them from sin, to render the world contemptible, to lighten suffering, to comfort the afflicted,—all by a comparison with this great and terrible, and yet so inevitable, evil of death. This evil even the saints dreaded, and Christ submitted to it with trembling and bloody sweat. [Luke 22:44] So that the divine Mercy hath been nowhere more concerned to comfort our little faith than in the matter of this evil, as we shall see below.[16]

But all these things are common to all men, even as the blessings of salvation under these evils are common to all. For Christians, however, there is another and a particular reason for dreading the evils to come, which easily surpasses all the evils that have been

88

mentioned. It is that which the Apostle portrays in I. Corinthians x, when he says, "He that standeth, let him take heed lest he fall." [1 Cor. 19:12] So unstable is our footing, and so powerful our foe, armed with our own strength (that is, the weapons of our flesh and all our evil lusts), attended by the countless armies of the world, its delights and pleasures on the right hand, its hardships and the plots of wicked men on the left, and, besides all this, master himself of the art of doing us harm, seducing us, and bringing us down to destruction by a thousand different ways. Such is our life that we are not safe for one moment in our good intentions. Cyprian, who in his De Mortalitate[17] touches on many of these matters, teaches that death is to be desired as a swift means of escape from these evils. And truly, wherever there have been high-hearted men, who brought their minds steadily to bear on these infinite perils of hell, we find them, with contempt of life and death (that is, all the aforesaid evils), desiring to die, that so they might be delivered at one and the same time from this evil of the sins in which they now are (of which we spoke in the previous chapter), and of the sins into which they might fall (of which we are treating now). And these are, indeed, two most weighty reasons why we should not only desire death, but also despise all evils, to say nothing of lightly bearing a single evil; if the Lord grant us to be moved thereby. For it is God's gift that we are moved thereby. For what true Christian will not even desire to die, and much more to bear sickness, seeing that, so long as he lives and is in health, he is in sin, and is constantly prone to fall, yea, is falling every day, into more sins; and is thus constantly thwarting the most loving will of his most loving Father! To such a heat of indignation was St. Paul moved, in Romans vii, when after complaining that he did not the good that he would, but the evil that he would not, [Rom. 7:19] he cried out, "O wretched man that I am! who shall deliver me the body of this death? The grace of God," [18] he answers, "through Jesus Christ."

That man loves God his Father but little, who does not prefer the evil of dying to this evil of sinning. For God has appointed death, that this evil might come to an end, and that death might be the minister of life and righteousness, of which more below.[19]

CHAPTER III

THE THIRD IMAGE

THE PAST EVIL, OR THE EVIL BEHIND US

In this image, above all others, the sweet mercy of God our Father shines forth, able to comfort us in every distress. For never does a man feel the hand of God more closely upon him than when he calls to mind the years of his past life. St. Augustine says: "If a man were set before the choice either of dying or of living his past life over, it is certain that he would choose to die, seeing the many perils and evils which he had so hardly escaped." This is a very true saying, if it be rightly pondered.

Here a man may see how often he has done and suffered many things, without any exertion or care of his own, nay, without and against his wish; of which things he took so little thought before they came to pass, or while they were taking place, that, only after all was over, he found himself compelled to exclaim in great surprise: "Whence have all these things come to me, when I never gave them a thought, or when I thought of something very different?" So that the proverb is true, "Man proposeth, but God disposeth"; [Prov. 16:9] that is, God turns things about, and brings to pass something far different from that which man proposes. Therefore, from this consideration alone, it is impossible for us to deny that our life and all our actions are under the direction, not of our own prudence, but of the wonderful power, wisdom, and goodness of God. Here we see how often God was with us when we knew it not, and with what truth Peter has said, "He careth for us all." [1 Peter 5:7]

Therefore, even if there were no books or tracts, yet our very life itself, brought through so many evils and dangers, if we will but consider it, abundantly commends to us the ever present and most tender goodness of God, which, far above all that we purposed or perceived, carried us as it were in its bosom. As Moses says in Deuteronomy xxxii, "The Lord kept him as the apple of His eye, and led him about, and bore him on His shoulders." [Deut. 32:10 ff.][20]

Hence arose those exhortations in the Psalter: "I remember the days of old; I meditate on all Thy works; I muse on the work of Thy hands." [Ps. 143:5] "Surely I will remember Thy wonders of old." [Ps. 77:11] Again, "I remembered Thy judgments of old, O Lord, and have comforted myself," [Ps. 119:52] These exhortations and the like are intended to teach us that, if God was with us when we thought it not, or when He seemed not to be with us, we should not doubt that He is always with us, even when He appears to be far from us. For He Who, in so many necessities, has sustained us without our aid, will not forsake us in our smaller need, even though He seem to be forsaking us. As He saith in Isaiah, "For a small moment have I forsaken thee; but with great mercies will I gather thee." [Isa. 54:7]

Moreover, who had the care of us so many a night, while we slept? Who cared for us when we were at work, or at play, or engaged in all those countless things wherein we had no care for ourselves? Indeed, how much of our time is there in which we have the care of ourselves? Even the miser, careful as he is to gain riches, must perforce put by his care in the midst of all his getting and gaining. And so we see that, whether we will or no, all our care falls back on God alone, and we are scarcely ever left to care for ourselves. Still, God does now and again leave us to care for ourselves, in order to bring home to us His goodness, and to teach us how great the difference between His care and ours. Hence, He suffers us now and then to be assailed by some slight malady or other ill, dissembling His care for us (for He never ceases to care), and yet at the same time preventing the many evils that threaten us on every side from bursting in upon us all together. Hereby He tries us as His well-beloved children, to see whether we will not trust His care, which extends through all our past life, and learn how vain and powerless a thing is any care of ours. How little, indeed, do we or can we do for ourselves, throughout our life, when we are not able to stop a small pain in one of our limbs, even for the shortest space of time?[21]

Why, then, are we so anxious in the matter of a single danger or evil, and do not rather leave our care to Him? For our whole life bears witness to the many evils from which He has delivered us, without our doing. To know this, is indeed to know the works of God, to meditate on His works, [Ps. 143:5, 119:52] and by the remembrance of them to comfort ourselves in our adversities. But they that know this not come under that other word in Psalm xxvii, "Because they regard not the works of the Lord, nor the operations of His hand, He shall destroy them, and not build them up." [Ps. 28:5] For those men are ungrateful toward God for all His care over them during their whole life, who will not, for one small moment, commit their care to Him.

CHAPTER IV

THE FOURTH IMAGE

THE INFERNAL EVIL, OR THE EVIL BENEATH US

Hitherto we have seen, in all the evils that we endure, naught but the goodness of God, which is so great and so near that of all the countless evils with which we are surrounded in this life, and in which we are shut up as in a prison, but a very few are permitted to approach us, and these never for long together. So that, when we are oppressed by any present evil, it is only to remind us of some great gain with which God is honoring us, in that He does not suffer us to be overwhelmed by the multitude of evils with which we are surrounded. For what wonder that a man, at whom an infinite number of blows is aimed, should be touched by one now and then! Nay, it is a mercy not to be struck by all; it is a miracle to be struck by but a few.

The first, then, of the evils beneath us is death, and the other is hell.

If we will but consider the deaths, so diverse and so terrible, with which other sinners are punished, we shall soon see how great a gain is ours in that we suffer far less than we have deserved. How many men are hanged, strangled, drowned or beheaded, who perchance committed less sins than we! And their death and misery are held up to us by Christ as in a mirror, in which we may behold what we have deserved. For it is said in Luke xiii, when they told Him of the Galileans, whose blood Pilate had mingled with their sacrifices, that He replied: "Suppose ye that these Galileans were sinners above all the Galileans, because they suffered these things? I tell you, Nay: but, except ye repent, ye shall all likewise perish. Or those eighteen, upon whom the tower in Siloam fell, and slew them, think ye that they were sinners above all men that dwelt in Jerusalem? I tell you. Nay: but, except ye repent, ye shall all likewise perish." [Luke 13:1 ff.] For we need not expect that we, who have committed the same or even graver sins, shall escape with a lighter punishment. Nor will the justice and truth of God, which hath decreed to render to every man according to his deeds, be turned for our sake into injustice and a lie, unless we hasten to make satisfaction by at least bearing our trifling evil with patience.[22]

And how many thousands are there in hell and everlasting damnation, who have not committed the thousandth part of our sins! How many virgins, youths, and those whom we call innocents, are there! How many monks, priests, and married pairs! These seemed all their life long to be serving God, and, it may be for a single lapse, are now being punished for ever. For, it may not be denied, the justice of God is the same in the case of every sin, whatever it may be, and hates and punishes all sin alike, it matters not in whom it is found. Do we not then see here the inestimable mercy of God, Who hath not condemned us, though we have so many times deserved condemnation? Pray, what are all the sufferings life can bring, compared to eternal punishment, which they indeed justly endure on account of one sin, while we go free and unpunished for our many sins, which God hath covered! [Ps. 32:1] That we take no thought of these benefits of God, or but lightly esteem them, that is ingratitude, and the hardening of our unbelieving heart.

Moreover, we must include here the many infidels, Gentiles, Jews, and infants, who, if to them had been granted the advantages that we enjoy, would not now be in hell, but rather in heaven, and who would have sinned far less than we. For this mirror also does Christ set before us, when He says in Matthew xi: "Woe unto thee, Chorazin! woe unto thee, Bethsaida! for if the mighty works, which were done in you, had been done in Tyre and Sidon, they would have repented long ago in sackcloth and ashes. But I say unto you, It shall be more tolerable for Tyre and Sidon at the day of judgment, than for you. And thou, Capernaum, which art exalted unto heaven, shalt be brought down to hell: for if the mighty works, which have been done in thee, had been done in Sodom, it would have remained to this day. But I say unto you. That it shall be more tolerable for the land of Sodom in the day of judgment, than for thee." [Matt. 11:21 ff.] We see, therefore, what praise and love we owe to our good Lord, in any evil whatsoever of this life; for it is but a tiny drop of the evils which we have deserved, and which Job compares to the sea, and to the sand by the seashore. [Job 6:3]

CHAPTER V

THE FIFTH IMAGE

THE EVIL ON OUR LEFT HAND

Here we must set before our eyes the whole multitude of our adversaries and wicked men, and consider, first, how many evils they would have inflicted on our bodies, our property, our good name, and on our souls, but could not, being prevented by the providence of God. Indeed, the higher one's station and the wider one's sway,[23] the more is he exposed to the intrigues, slanders, plots, and stratagems of his enemies. In all this we may mark and feel the very present hand of God, and need not wonder if we be touched now and then by one of these evils.

Again, let us consider the evils which these men themselves endure; not that we may exult over them, but that we may feel pity for them. For they, too, are exposed to all these same evils, in common with ourselves; as may be seen in the preceding times. Only, they are in a worse plight than we, because they stand outside our fellowship,[24] both as to body and soul. For the evil that we endure is as nothing compared to their evil estate; for they are in sin and unbelief, under the wrath of God, and under the dominion of the devil, wretched slaves to ungodliness and sin, so that, if the whole world were to heap curses on their heads, it could wish them no worse things. If we rightly consider this, we shall see how much more highly favored we are of God, in that we may bear our slight bodily ill in faith, in the kingdom of Christ, and in the service of God; and, indeed, are scarce able to feel it, being so rich in those high blessings. Nay, this wretchedness of theirs must so sorely trouble a pious Christian heart as to make its own troubles seem delights beside them. Thus St. Paul exhorts in Philippians ii, "Look not every man on his own things, but every man also on the things of others. Let this mind be in you, which was also in Christ Jesus: Who, being in the form of God, took upon Him the form of a servant, etc." [Phil. 2:4 ff.] That is to say, Out of fervent love He took our form upon Himself, bearing Himself amidst our evils as though they were His own, and so completely forgetting Himself and all His goods, and humbling Himself, that He was found in all things to be made in the likeness of men, counting nothing human foreign to Himself, and wholly giving Himself over to our evils.

Animated with this love, and moved by this example, the saints are wont to pray for wicked men, even their enemies, [Luke 6:27 f.] and to do all things for them after the example of Christ; and forgetting their own injuries and rights, to take thought only how they may rescue them from their evils, with which they are far more cruelly tormented than with any evils of the body. Even as St. Peter writes of Lot, that he "dwelt among them who from day to day vexed the just soul with unjust works." [2 Peter 2:8]

You see, then, how deep an abyss of evils is here discovered, and how great an opportunity for showing mercy and compassion, as well as for overlooking our own trifling ills, if the love of God dwell in us; since that which God permits us to suffer is as nothing to that which those others endure. But the reason why these things affect us so little is, because the eye of our heart is not clear enough to see how great is the squalor and wretchedness of a man lying in sin; that is, separated from God, and in the possession of the devil. For who is there so hard of heart that he must not sicken at the spectacle of those miserable forms lying at our church doors and in our streets, their faces disputed, and all their members hideously consumed with putrifying sores; so that the mind is horror-struck at the thought and the senses recoil from the sight! And what does God intend, through these lamentable specimens of our flesh and brotherhood, but to open the eyes of our mind, that we may see in how much more dreadful a guise the soul of the sinner shows forth its disease and decay, even though he himself go in purple and gold, and tie among lilies and roses, as a very child of paradise! Yet how many sinners are there to one of those wretched creatures? When these evils on the part of our neighbors, so great both in number and degree, are disregarded by us, it follows that our one evil, be it never so trifling, will appear as the sole evil, and the greatest of all.

But even in respect of bodily evils, the wicked are of necessity in a worse plight than we. For what sweet and pure joy can be theirs, so long as their conscience can find no peace?

Or can there be a more terrible evil than the unrest of a gnawing conscience? Isaiah says, "The wicked are like the troubled sea, when it cannot rest, whose waters cast up mire and dirt. There is no peace, saith my God, to the wicked." [Isaiah 57:20 f.] This also, in Deuteronomy xxviii, applies to them: "The Lord shall give thee a trembling heart, and failing of eyes, and sorrow of mind: and thy life shall hang in doubt before thee; and thou shalt fear day and night, and shalt have none assurance of thy life; in the morning thou shalt say, Would God it were even! and at even thou shalt say, Would God it were morning! for the fear of thine heart wherewith thou shalt fear, and for the sight of thine eyes which thou shalt see." [Deut. 28:65 ff.] In a word, if one regarded all the evils of the wicked in the right spirit, whether they be those of his friends or his foes, he would not only seem to be suffering nothing at all, but he would also, with Moses and the Apostle Paul, [Ex. 32:32, Rom. 9:3] be filled with an hearty desire to die for them, if it might be, and to be blotted out of the book of life, as it is written in Romans ix, that thereby they might be set free. With such zeal and burning was Christ's heart kindled, when He died for us and descended into hell, leaving us an example that we also should be so regardful of the evils of others, and forgetful of our own, nay, rather covetous of evils of our own.

CHAPTER VI

THE SIXTH IMAGE

THE EVIL ON OUR RIGHT HAND

On out right hand are our friends, in the contemplation of whose evils out own will grow light, as St. Peter teaches, I. Peter v, "Resist the devil, steadfast in the faith, knowing that the same afflictions are accomplished in your brethren that are in the world." [1 Pet. 5:9] Thus also does the Church entreat in her prayers, that provoked by the example of the saints, we may imitate the virtue of their sufferings; and thus she sings,

What torments all the Saints endured,

That they might win the martyr's palm!

From such words and hymns of the Church we learn that the feasts of the saints, their memorials, churches, altars, names, and images, are observed and multiplied to the end that we should be moved by their example to bear the same evils which they also bore. And unless this be the manner of our observance, it is impossible that the worship of saints should be free from superstition. Even as there are many who observe all these things in order to escape the evil which the saints teach us should be borne, and thus to become unlike those whose feasts they keep for the sake of becoming like them.

But the finest treatment of this portion of our consolation is given by the Apostle, when he says, in Hebrews xii: "Ye have not yet resisted unto blood, striving against sin. And ye have forgotten the exhortation which speaketh unto you as unto children, My son, demise not thou the chastening of the Lord, nor faint when thou art rebuked of Him; for whom the Lord loveth He chasteneth, and scourgeth every son whom He receiveth. If ye endure chastening, God dealeth with you as with sons; for what son is he whom the father chasteneth not? But if ye be without chastisement, whereof all are partakers, then are ye bastards, and not sons. Furthermore we have had fathers of our flesh which corrected us, and we gave them reverence; shall we not much rather be in subjection unto the Father of spirits, and live? For they verily for a few days chastened us after their good pleasure; but He for our profit, that we might be partakers of His holiness. Now no chastening for the present seemeth to be joyous, but grievous; nevertheless afterward it yieldeth the peaceable fruit of righteousness unto them which are exercised thereby." [Heb. 12:4 ff.] Who must not be terrified at these words of Paul, in which he plainly states that they who are without the chastisement of God are not the sons of God! Again, what greater strengthening and what better comfort can there be than to hear that they who are chastened are beloved of the Lord, that they are sons of God, that they have part in the communion of saints, that they are not alone in their sufferings! So forceful an exhortation must make chastisement a thing to be loved.

Nor is there here any room for the excuse that some have lighter, others heavier, evils to bear. For to every one is given his temptation according to measure, and never beyond his strength. As it is written in Psalm lxxix, "Thou shalt feed us with the bread of tears, and give us for our drink tears in measure";[25] [Ps. 80:5] and as Paul says, "God is faithful, who will not suffer you to be tempted above that ye are able; but will with the temptation also make a way to escape, that ye may be able to bear it." [1 Cor. 10:13] Where there is, therefore, a greater evil, there is also more of divine help, and an easier way to escape; so that the unequal distribution of sufferings appears to be greater than it actually is. Does not the example of St. John Baptist, whom we commemorate on this day[26] as beheaded by Herod, shame and amaze us all!—that so great a man, than whom there was none greater born of woman, [Matt. 11:11] the special friend of the Bridegroom, [John 3:29] the forerunner of Christ, and more than all the prophets, [Matt. 11:9] should have been put to death, not indeed after a public trial, nor on a feigned charge (as it was with Christ), nor yet for the sake of the people; but in a dungeon, and for the sake of a dancing-girl, daughter of an adulteress! [Matt. 14:3-11] This one Saint's ignominious death, and his life so vilely and shamelessly given over into the hands of his sworn and adulterous enemy, must make all our evil light. Where was God then, that He could look on such things? Where was Christ, Who, hearing of it, was altogether silent? He perished as if unknown to God, and men, and every creature. Compared with such a death, what sufferings have we to boast of; nay, what sufferings of which we must not even be ashamed? And where shall we appear, if we are unwilling to endure any suffering, when such a man endured so shameful a death, and so undeserved, and his body, after death, was given up to the insults of his enemies! [1 Pet. 4:18] "Behold," He saith in Jeremiah, "behold, they whose judgment was not to drink of the cup have assuredly drunken: and art thou he that shall altogether go unpunished? thou shalt not go unpunished, but thou shalt surely drink of it." [Jer. 49:12]

Therefore, that hermit, who was used to fall ill every year, did well to weep and lament, when for one whole year he found himself in sound health, because, he said, God had forsaken him and withdrawn His grace from him. So necessary and so salutary is the Lord's chastening for all Christians.

We see, then, that all our sufferings are as nothing, when we consider the nails, dungeons, irons, faggots, wild beasts, and all the endless tortures of the saints; nay, when we ponder the afflictions of men now living, who endure in this life the most grievous persecutions of the devil. For there is no lack of men who are suffering more sharp and bitter pains than we, in soul as well as in body.

But now some will say, "This is my complaint, that my suffering cannot be compared with the sufferings of the saints; because I am a sinner, and not worthy to be compared with them. They, indeed, suffered because of their innocence, but I suffer because of my sins. It is no wonder, then, that they so blithely bore all." That is a very stupid saying. If you suffer because of your sins, then you ought to rejoice that your sins are being purged away. And, besides, were not the saints, too, sinners? But do you fear that you are like Herod, and the thief on Christ's left hand? You are not, if you have patience. For what was it that distinguished the thief on the left hand from him on the right but the patience of the one and the impatience of the other? If you are a sinner, well; the thief, too, was a sinner; but by his patience he merited the glorious reward of righteousness and holiness. Go, and do thou likewise. [Luke 10:37] For you can suffer nothing except it be either on account of your sins or on account of your righteousness; and both kinds of suffering sanctify and save, if you will but love them. And so there is no excuse left. In short, just as soon as you have confessed that you are suffering on account of your sins, you are righteous and holy, even as the thief on the right hand. For the confession of sins, because it is the truth,[27] justifies and sanctifies, and so, in the very moment of this confession, you are suffering no longer on account of your sins, but on account of your innocence. For the righteous man always suffers innocently. But you are made righteous by the confession of your merited sufferings and of your sins. And so your sufferings may truly and worthily be compared with the sufferings of the saints, even as your confession may truly and worthily be compared with the confession of the saints. For one is the truth of all, one the confession of all sins, one the suffering of all evils, and one the true communion of saints in all and through all.[28]

CHAPTER VII

THE SEVENTH IMAGE

THE SUPERNAL EVIL, OR THE EVIL ABOVE US

Finally, let us lift up our hearts, and ascend with the Bride into the mountain of myrrh. [Song of Sol. 4:6] This is Jesus Christ the Crucified, Head of all saints, and Prince of all sufferers; of Whom many have written many things, and all all things, as it is meet.[29] His memory is commended to the Bride, when it is said, "Set Me as a seal upon thine heart, as a seal upon thine arm." [Song of Sol. 8:6] The blood of this Lamb, signed upon the threshold, wards off the destroying angel. [Ex. 12:7, 13] By Him is the Bride praised, because "the hair of her head is as the king's purple"; [Song of Sol. 7:5] that is, her meditation glows red with the remembrance of the Passion of Christ. This is that tree which Moses was commanded to cast into the waters of Marah (that is, the bitterness of suffering), and they were made sweet. [Ex. 15:23 ff.] There is nothing that this Passion cannot sweeten, not even death itself; as the Bride saith, "His lips are lilies, dropping sweet-smelling myrrh." [Song of So. 5:13] What resemblance is there between lips and lilies, since lips are red and lilies white? But she says this in a mystery, signifying that the words of Christ are most fair and pure, and that there is in them naught of blood-red bitterness or guile; nevertheless, in them He drops precious and chosen myrrh, that is, the bitterness of death. These most pure lips and sweet have power to make the bitterest death sweet and fair and bright and dear,—death that, like precious myrrh, removes at once all of sin's corruption.

How does this come to pass? When, forsooth, you hear that Jesus Christ, God's Son, hath, by His most holy touch, consecrated and hallowed all sufferings, even death itself, hath blessed the curse, glorified shame, and enriched poverty, so that death has been made a door to life, curse a fount of blessing, and shame the mother of glory: how can you then be so hard and ungrateful as not to long for and to love all manner of sufferings, now that they have been touched by Christ's most pure and holy flesh and blood, and made unto you holy, harmless, wholesome, blessed, and full of joy?

For if Christ, by the touch of His most innocent flesh, has hallowed all waters unto baptism, yea, and every creature besides; how much more has He, by the same contact of His most innocent flesh and blood, hallowed every form of death, all suffering and loss, every curse and shame, unto the baptism of the Spirit, or the baptism of blood![30] Even as He saith of this same baptism of His Passion, in Luke xii, "I have a baptism to be baptised with; and how am I straitened until it be accomplished!" [Luke 12:50] Behold, how He is straitened, how He pants and thirsts, to sanctify suffering and death, and make them things to be loved! For He sees how we stand in fear of suffering. He marks how we tremble and shrink from death. And so, like a godly pastor or faithful physician, He hastens to set bounds to this our evil, and is impatient to die and by His contact to commend suffering and death unto us. So that the death of a Christian is henceforth to be regarded as the brazen serpent of Moses, [Num. 21:8] which indeed hath in all things the appearance of a serpent, yet is quite without life, without motion, without venom, without sting. Even so the righteous seem, in the sight of the unwise, to die; but they are in peace. We resemble them that die, nor is the outward appearance of our dying unlike that of others; but the thing itself is different, because for us death is dead. In like manner all our sufferings are like the sufferings of other men; but it is only in the appearance. In reality our sufferings are the beginning of our freedom from suffering, as our death is the beginning of our life. This is that which Christ saith in John viii, "If a man keep my saying he shall never see death." [John 8:51] How shall he not see it? Because when he dies, he begins to live, and so he cannot see death for the life that he sees. For here the night shines as the day; [Ps. 139:12] since the life that breaks upon him is brighter far than departing death. These things are assured to all who believe in Christ, to the unbelieving they are not.

Therefore, if you kiss, caress, and embrace, as most sweet relics,[31] consecrated by His touch, the robe of Christ, the vessels, waterpots, and what things soever He touched and used; why will you not the rather caress, embrace, and kiss the pains and evils of this world, disgrace and death, which He not only hallowed by His touch, but sprinkled and blessed with His most holy blood, yea, embraced with willing heart, and great constraining love?[32] The more, since in these there are for you far greater merits, rewards, and blessings than in those relics; for in them there is offered to you the victory over death, and hell, and all sins, but in those relics nothing at all. O could we but see the heart of Christ, when, hanging on the Cross, He was so eager to slay death, and hold it up to our contempt! With what grace and ardor He embraced death and pain for us timid ones, who shrink from them! How willingly He first drinks this cup for us sick ones, that we may not dread to drink it after Him! For we see that naught of evil befell Him, but only good, in His resurrection. Could we see this, then doubtless that precious myrrh, dropping from Christ's lips, and commended by His words, would grow most sweet and pleasant unto us, even as the beauty and fragrance of lilies. Thus saith also St. Peter, I. Peter iv, "Forasmuch as Christ hath suffered for us in the flesh, arm yourselves likewise with the same mind." [1 Pet. 4:1] And St. Paul, Hebrews xii, "Consider Him that endured such contradiction of sinners against Himself, lest ye be wearied and faint in your minds." [Heb. 12:3]

If we have learned, in the foregoing images, beneath us and above us, to bear our evils with patience, surely in this last, lifted above and out of ourselves, caught up unto Christ, and made superior to all evils, we ought not only to bear with them, but to love them, desire them, and seek them out. Whoever is yet far from this state of mind, for him the Passion of Christ has little value; as it is with those who use the sign and arms of Christ[33] to ward off evils and death, that so they may neither suffer pain nor endure death, which is altogether contrary to the cross and death of Christ. Hence, in this image, whatever evils we may have to bear must be swallowed up and consumed, so that they shall not only cause us no pain, but even delight us; if indeed this image find its way into our heart, and fix itself in the inmost affections of our mind.

PART II

The second part also consists of seven images, answering to the first; the first representing the internal blessing, the second the future blessing, the third the past blessing, the fourth the infernal blessing, the fifth the blessing on the left hand, the sixth the blessing on the right hand, and the seventh the supernal blessing.

CHAPTER I

THE FIRST IMAGE

THE BLESSING WITHIN US

Who can recount only those blessings which every one hath in his own person? How great are, first, the gifts and endowments of the body; such as beauty, strength, health, and the lively play of the senses! To these there comes, in the case of the male, a greater nobility of sex, that fits him for the doing of many things both in public and in private life, and for many splendid achievements, to which woman is a stranger. And if, by the grace of God, you enjoy these excellent gifts for ten, twenty, or thirty years, and in all this time endure suffering for a few days now and then, what great matter is that? There is a proverb among knaves, Es ist umb ein bose stund zuthun, and, Ein gutt stund ist eyner posen werdt.[34] What shall be said of us, who have seen so many good hours, yet are not willing to endure evil for a single hour! We see, therefore, how many blessings God showers upon us, and how few evils barely touch us. This is true at least of the most of us.

But not content with these blessings, our gracious God adds to them riches and an abundance of all things; if not in the case of all, certainly in the case of many, and of those especially who are too frail to bear the evil. For as I said before,[35] when He grants fewer bodily gifts and possessions, He gives greater mental gifts; so that all things may be equal, and He the just Judge of all. For a cheerful mind is a greater comfort than much riches. Moreover, to some He grants offspring, and, as men say, the highest pleasure, influence, rank, honor, fame, glory, favor, and the like. And if these be enjoyed for a long or even for a short season, they will soon teach men how they ought to conduct themselves under some small evil.

But more excellent than all these are the blessings of the mind; such as reason, knowledge, judgment, eloquence, prudence. And, here again, God tempers the justice of His dealing, so that when He bestows more of these gifts on some men. He does not therefore prefer them to others, since on these again He confers greater peace and cheerfulness of mind. In all these things we should gratefully mark the bountiful hand of God, and take comfort in our infirmity. For we should feel no surprise if among so many and great blessings there be some intermingling of bitterness; since even for epicures no meat is savory without salt, nor scarce any dish palatable that has not a certain bitter savor, either native or produced by seasoning. So intolerable is a continual and unrelieved sweetness, that it has been truly said, "Every pleasure too long continued begets disgust"; and again, "Pleasure itself turns at length to loathing." That is to say, this life is incapable of enjoying only good things without a tempering of evil, because of the too great abundance of good things, has arisen also this proverb, "It needs sturdy bones to bear good days"; which proverb I have often pondered and much admired for its excellent true sense, namely, that the wishes of men are contrary to one another; they seek none but good days, and, when these arrive, are less able to bear them than evil days.

What, then, would God have us here lay to heart but this, that the cross is held in honor even among the enemies of the cross! For all things must needs be tempered and sanctified with the relics of the cross, lest they decay; even as the meat must be seasoned with salt, that it may not breed worms. And why will we not gladly accept this tempering which God sends, and which, if He did not send it, our own life, weakened with pleasures and blessings, would of itself demand? Hence we see with what truth the Book of Wisdom says of God, "He[36] reacheth from end to end mightily, and ordereth all things sweetly." [Wid. 8:1] And if we examine these blessings, the truth of Moses' words, in Deuteronomy xxxii, will become plain, "He bore him on His shoulders, He led him about, and kept him as the apple of His eye." [Deut. 32:10] With these words we may stop the mouths of those ungrateful praters who hold that there is in this life more of evil than of good. For there is no lack of good things and endless sweet blessings, but they are lacking who ate of the same mind with him who said, "The earth is full of the mercy of the Lord" [Ps. 33:5]; and again, "The earth is full of His praise" [Hab. 3:3]; and in Psalm ciii, "The earth is full of Thy riches" [Ps. 104:24]; "Thou, Lord, hast made me glad through Thy work," [Ps. 92:4] Hence we sing every day in the Mass; [37] "Heaven and earth are full of Thy glory." [Isa. 6:3] Why do we sing this? Because there are many blessings for which God may be praised, but it is done only by those who see the fulness of them. Even as we said concerning the evils of the first image,[38] that a man's evils are only so great as he in his thoughts acknowledges them to be, so it is also with the blessings. Though they crowd upon us from every side, yet they are only so great as we acknowledge them to be. For all things that God made are very good, [Gen. 1:31] but they are not acknowledged as very good by all. Such were they of whom it is said in Psalm lxxvii,[39] "They despised the pleasant land." [Ps. 106:24]

The most beautiful and instructive example of this image is furnished by Job, who when he had lost all said. "Shall we receive good at the hand of God, and shall we not receive evil?" [Job 2:10] Truly, that is a golden saying, and a mighty comfort in temptation. For Job not only suffered, but was tempted to impatience by his wife, who said to him, "Dost thou still retain thine integrity? curse God, and die." [Job 2:9] As who should say, "It is plain that he is not God who is thus forsaking thee. Why, then, dost thou trust in him, and not rather, renouncing him, and thus cursing him, acknowledge thyself a mortal man, for whom naught remains after this life?" These things and the like are suggested to each one of us by his wife (i. e., his carnal mind[40]) in time of temptation; for the carnal mind[40] savoreth not the things that be of God. [Matt. 16:13]

But these are all bodily blessings, and common to all men. A Christian has other and far better blessings within, namely, faith in Christ; of which it is said in Psalm xliv, "The king's daughter is all glorious within; her clothing is of wrought gold." [Ps. 45:14 f.] For, as we said concerning the evil of the first image,[41] that no evil in a man can be so great as to be the worst of the evils within him; so too the greatest of the blessings which are in the Christian, he himself is unable to see. Could he perceive it, he would forthwith be in heaven; since the kingdom of heaven, as Christ says, is within us. [Luke 17:21] For to have faith is to have the Word and truth of God; and to have the Word of God is to have God Himself, the Maker of all. If these blessings, in all their fulness, were discovered to the soul, straightway it would be released from the body, for the exceeding abundance of sweet pleasure. Wherefore, of a truth, all the other blessings which we have mentioned are but as the monitors of those blessings which we have within, and which God would by than commend unto us. For this life of ours could not endure to have than revealed, but God mercifully keeps them hidden, until they have reached their full measure. Even so loving parents give their children foolish little toys, in order thereby to lead them on to look for better things.

Nevertheless, these blessings show themselves at times, and break out of doors, when the happy conscience rejoices in its trust to Godward, is fain to speak of Him, hears His Word with pleasure, and is quick to serve Him, to do good and suffer evil. All these are the evidence of that infinite and incomparable blessing hidden within, which sends forth such little drops and tiny rills. Still, it is sometimes more fully revealed to contemplative souls, who then are rapt away thereby, and know not where they are; as is confessed by St. Augustine and his mother,[42] and by many others.

CHAPTER II

THE SECOND IMAGE

THE FUTURE BLESSING, OR THE BLESSING BEFORE US

Those who are not Christians will find small comfort, amid their evils, in the contemplation of future blessings; since for them all these things are uncertain. Although much ado is made here by that famous emotion called hope, by which we call on each other, in words of human comfort, to look for better times, and continually plan greater things for the uncertain future, yet are always deceived. Even as Christ teaches concerning the man in the Gospel, Luke xii, who said to his soul, "I will pull down my barns, and build greater; and will say to my soul, Soul, thou hast much goods laid up for many years; take thine ease, eat, drink, and be merry. But God said unto him, Thou fool, this night thy soul shall be required of thee; and then whose shall those things be which thou hast provided? So is he that layeth up treasure for himself, and is not rich toward God." [Luke 12:18 ff.]

Nevertheless, God has not so utterly forsaken the sons of men that He will not grant them some measure of comfort in this hope of the passing of evil and the coming of good things. Though they are uncertain of the future, yet they hope with certain hope, and hereby they are meanwhile buoyed up, lest falling into the further evil of despair, they should break down under their present evil, and do some worse thing.[43] Hence, even this sort of hope is the gift of God; not that He would have them lean on it, but that He would turn their attention to that firm hope, which is in Him alone. For He is so long-suffering that He leadeth them to repentance, as it is said in Romans ii, and suffers none to be straightway deceived by this deceitful hope, if haply they may "return to the heart," [44] and come to the true hope.

But Christians have, beside this twofold blessing,[45] the very greatest future blessings certainly awaiting them; yet only through death and suffering. Although they, too, rejoice in that common and uncertain hope that the evil of the present will come to an end, and that its opposite, the blessing, will increase; still, that is not their chief concern, but rather this, that their own particular blessing should increase, which is the truth as it is in Christ, in which they grow from day to day, and for which they both live and hope. But beside this they have, as I have said, the two greatest future blessings in their death. The first, in that through death the whole tragedy of this world's ills is brought to a close; as it is written, "Precious in the sight of the Lord is the death of His saints"; [Ps. 116:15] and again, "I will lay me down in peace and sleep"; [Ps. 4:8] and "Though the righteous be prevented with death, yet shall he be at rest." [Wisd. 4:7] But to the ungodly death is the beginning of evils;

as it is said, "The death of the wicked is very evil," [Ps. 34:21] and, "Evil shall catch the unjust man unto destruction." [46] [Ps. 140:11] Even so Lazarus, who received his evil things in his lifetime, is comforted, while the rich glutton is tormented, because he received his good things here. [Luke 16:25] So that it is always well with the Christian, whether he die or live; so blessed a thing is it to be a Christian and to believe in Christ. Wherefore Paul says, "To me to live is Christ, and to die is gain," [Phil. 1:21] and, in Romans xiv, "Whether we live, we live unto the Lord; and whether we die, we die unto the Lord; whether we live therefore, or die, we are the Lord's." [Rom. 14:8 f.] This security Christ hath won for us by His death and rising again, that He might be Lord of both the living and dead, able to keep us safe in life and in death; as Psalm xxii. saith, "Though I walk through the valley of the shadow of death, I will fear no evil, for Thou art with me." [Ps. 23:4] If this gain of death move us but little, it is proof that our faith in Christ is feeble, and does not prize highly enough the reward and gain of a blessed death, or does not yet believe that death is a blessing; because the old man is still too much alive in us, and the wisdom of the flesh too strong. We should, therefore, endeavor to attain to the knowledge and the love of this blessing of death. It is a great thing that death, which is to others the greatest of evils, is made to us the greatest gain. And unless Christ had obtained this for us, what bad He done that was worthy of the great price He paid, namely, His own self? It is indeed a divine work that He wrought, and none need wonder, therefore, that He made the evil of death to be something that is very good. [Gen. 1:31]

Death, then, to believers is already dead, and hath nothing terrible behind its grinning mask. Like unto a slain serpent, it hath indeed its former terrifying appearance, but it is only the appearance; in truth it is a dead evil, and harmless enough. Nay, as God commanded Moses to lift up a serpent of brass, at sight of which the living serpents perished, [Num. 21:8 f.] even so our death dies in the believing contemplation of the death of Christ, and now hath but the outward appearance of death. With such fine similitudes the mercy of God prefigures to us, in our infirmity, this truth, that though death would not be taken away, He yet has reduced its power to a mere shadow. [Matt. 9:24] For this reason it is called in the Scriptures a "sleep" rather than death. [1 Thess. 4:13 ff.]

The other blessing of death is this, that it not only concludes the pains and evils of this life, but (which is more excellent) makes an end of sins and vices. And this renders death far more desirable to believing souls, as I have said above,[47] than the former blessing; since the evils of the soul, which are its sins, are beyond comparison worse evils than those of the body. This alone, did we but know it, should make death most desirable. But if it does not, it is a sign that we neither feel nor hate our sin as we should. For this our life is so full of perils—sin, like a serpent, besetting us on every side—and it is impossible for us to live without sinning; but fairest death delivers us from these perils, and cuts our sin clean away from us. Therefore, the praise of the just man, in Wisdom iv, concludes on this wise: "He pleased God, and was taken away, and was beloved of Him: so that living among sinners he was translated. Yea, speedily was he taken away, lest that wickedness should alter his understanding, or deceit beguile his soul. For the bewitching of naughtiness doth obscure things that are honest; and the wandering of concupiscence doth undermine the simple mind (O how constantly true is this!). He, being made perfect in a short time, fulfilled a long time; for his soul pleased the Lord: therefore hasted He to take him away from the wicked." [Wisd. 4:10-14]

Thus, by the mercy of God, death, which was to man the punishment for his sin, is made unto the Christian the end of sin, and the beginning of life and righteousness. Wherefore, he that loves life and righteousness must not hate, but love sin, their minister and workshop; else he will never attain to either life or righteousness. But he that is not able to do this, let him pray God to enable him. For to this end are we taught to pray, "Thy will be done," [Matt. 6:10] because we cannot do it of ourselves, since through fear of death we love death and sin rather than life and righteousness. And that God appointed death for the putting to death of sin, may be gathered also from the fact that He imposed death upon Adam immediately after his sin; and that before He drove him out of paradise; in order to show us that death should bring us no evil, but every blessing, since it was imposed in paradise, as a penance and satisfaction.[48] For it is true that, through the envy of the devil, death altered into the world; [Wisd. 2:24] but it is of the Lord's surpassing goodness that, after having thus entered in, it is not permitted to harm us very much, but is taken captive from the very beginning, and set to be the punishment and death of sin.

This He signified when, after having in His commandment foretold the death of Adam, [Gen. 2:17] He did not afterward hold His peace, but imposed death anew, and tempered the severity of His commandment, nay. He did not so much as mention death with a single syllable, but said only, "Dust thou art, and unto dust shalt thou return" [Gen. 3:19]; and, "Until thou return unto the ground, from whence thou wast taken"—as if He then so bitterly hated death that He would not deign to call it by its name, according to the word, "Wrath is in His indignation; and life in His good will." [49] [Ps. 30:5] Thus He seemed to say that, unless death had been necessary to the abolishing of sin, He would not have been willing to know it nor to name it, much less to impose it. And so, against sin, which wrought death, the zeal of God arms none other than this very death again; so that you may here see exemplified the poet's line,[50]

By his own art the artist perisheth.

Even so sin is destroyed by its own fruit, and is slain by the death which it brought forth;[51] as a viper is slain by its own offering. This is a brave spectacle, to see how death is destroyed, not by another's work, but by its own; is stabbed with its own weapon, and, like Goliath, is beheaded with its own sword. [1 Sam. 17:51] For Goliath also was a type of sin, a giant terrible to all save the young lad David—that is Christ,—who single-handed laid him low, and having cut off his head with his own sword, said afterward that there was no better sword than the sword of Goliath (I. Samuel xxi). [1 Sam. 21:9]

Therefore, if we meditate on these joys of the power Christ, and these gifts of His grace, how can any small evil distress us, the while we see such blessings in this great evil that is to come!

CHAPTER III

THE THIRD IMAGE

THE PAST BLESSING, OR THE BLESSING BEHIND US

The consideration of this image is not difficult, in view of its counterpart, of the past evils;[52] we would, however, aid him who undertakes it. Here St. Augustine shows himself an excellent master, in his Confessions, in which he gives a beautiful rehearsal of the benefits of God toward him from his mother's womb.[52] The same is done in that fine Psalm cxxxvii, 'Lord, Thou hast searched me," [Ps. 139:2] where the Psalmist, marveled among other things at the goodness of God toward him, says, "Thou understandest my thoughts afar off, Thou compassest my path and my lying down." Which is as though he said, Whatever I have thought or done, whatever I shall achieve and possess, I see now that it is not the result of my industry, but was ordered long ago by Thy care. "And there is no speech in my tongue."[54] Where is it then? In Thy power.

We learn this from our own experience. For if we reflect on our past life, is it not a wonder that we thought, desired, did and said that which we were not able to foresee? How far different our course would have been, had we been left to our own free will! Now only do we understand it, and see how constantly God's present care and providence were over us, so that we could neither think nor speak nor will anything except as He gave us leave. As it is said in Wisdom vii, "In His hands are both we and our words"; [Wisd. 7:16] and by Paul, "Who worketh all in all." [1 Cor. 12:6] Ought not we, insensate and hard of heart, to bang our heads in shame, when we learn from our own experience how our Lord hath cared for us unto this hour, and given us every blessing? And yet we cannot commit our care to Him in a small present evil, and act as if He had forsaken us, or ever could forsake us! Not so the Psalmist, in Psalm xxxix, "I am poor and needy; yet the Lord thinketh on me." [Ps. 40:17] On which St. Augustine has this comment: "Let Him care for thee, Who made thee. He Who cared for thee before thou wast, how shall He not care for thee now thou art that which He willed thee to be?" [55] But we divide the kingdom with God; to Him we grant (and even that but grudgingly) that He hath made us, but to ourselves we arrogate the care over ourselves; as though He had made us, and then straightway departed, and left the government of ourselves in our own hands.

But if our wisdom and foresight blind us to the care that God hath over us, because perchance many things have fallen out according to our plans, let us turn again, with Psalm cxxxviii, and look in upon ourselves. "My substance was not hid from Thee when I was made in secret"—that is, Thou didst behold and didst fashion my bones in my mother's womb, when as yet I was not, and my mother knew not what was forming in her;—"and my substance was curiously wrought in the lowest parts of the earth"—that is, even the form and fashion of my body in the secret chambers of the womb were not hidden from Thee, for Thou wast fashioning it. What does the Psalmist intend with such words but to show us by this marvelous illustration how God hath always been caring for us without our help! For who can boast that he took any part in his formation in the womb? Who gave to our mother that loving care wherewith she fed and fondled and caressed us, and performed all those duties of motherhood, when we had as yet no consciousness of our life, and when we should neither know nor remember these things, but that, seeing the same things done to others, we believe that they were done to us also? For they were performed on us as though we had been asleep, nay dead, or rather not yet born, so far as our knowledge of them is concerned.

Thus we see how the divine mercies and consolations bear us up, without our doing. And still we doubt, or even despair, that He is caring for us to-day. If this experience does not instruct and move one, I know not what will. For we have it brought home to us again and again, in every little child we meet; so that so many examples proposed to our foolishness and hardness of heart may well fill us with deep shame, if we doubt that the slightest blessing or evil can come to us without the particular care of God. Thus St Peter says, "Casting all your care upon Him, because He careth for you." [1 Pet. 5:7] And Psalm xxxvi, "Cast thy burden upon the Lord, and He will sustain thee." [Ps. 37:5] And St. Augustine, in the Confessions,[56] addresses his soul on this wise: "Why dost thou stand upon thyself, and dost not stand? Cast thyself on Him; for He will not withdraw His hand and let thee fall." Again, we read in I. Peter iv, "Wherefore let them that suffer according to the will of God, commit the keeping of their souls to Him in well doing, as unto a faithful Creator." [1 Pet. 4:10]

O could a man attain unto such a knowledge of his God, how safely, how quietly, how joyfully, would he fare! He would in truth have God on his side, knowing this of a certainty, that all his fortunes, whatever they might be, had come to him, and still were coming, under the guidance of His most sweet will. The word of Peter stands firm, "He careth for you." [1 Pet. 5:7] What sweeter sound than this word can we hear! Therefore, he says, "Cast all your care upon Him." If we do this not, but rather take our care upon ourselves, what is this but to seek to hinder the care of God, and, besides, to make our life a life of sorrow and labor, troubled with many fears and cares and much unrest! And all to no avail; for we accomplish nothing good thereby, but, as the Preacher saith, it is vanity of vanities, and vexation of spirit. [Eccl. 1:2,14] Indeed, that whole book treats of this experience, as written by one who for himself made trial of many things, and found them all only weariness, vanity and vexation of spirit, so that he concludes it is a gift of God that a man may eat and drink and live joyfully with his wife, i. e., when he passes his days without anxiety, and commits his care to God. Therefore, we ought to have no other care for ourselves than this, namely, not to care for ourselves, and rob God of His care for us.

Whatever remains to be said, will easily be gathered from the corresponding image of evils, as I have said,[57] and from the contemplation of one's past life.

CHAPTER IV

THE FOURTH IMAGE

THE INFERNAL BLESSING, OR THE BLESSING BENEATH US

Thus far we have considered the blessings which are ours, and are found within ourselves; let us now turn to those blessings that are without us, and are found in others. The first of these is found in those who are beneath us, that is, the dead and damned. Do you wonder what kind of blessing can be discovered in the dead and damned? But the power of the divine goodness is everywhere so great that it grants us to descry blessings in the very greatest evils. Comparing, then, these poor wretches, first of all, with ourselves, we see how unspeakable is our gain; as may be gathered from the corresponding image of evils.[58] For great as are the evils of death and hell that we see in them, so great certainly are the gains that we behold in ourselves. These things are not to be lightly passed over, for they forcibly commend to us the magnificent mercy of God. And we run the danger, if we lightly esteem them, of being found ungrateful, and of being condemned together with these men, and even more cruelly tormented. Therefore, when we perceive how they suffer and wail aloud, we ought so much the more to rejoice in the goodness of God toward us; according to Isaiah lxv: "Behold, my servants shall eat, but ye shall be hungry; behold, my servants shall drink, but ye shall be thirsty; behold, my servants shall rejoice, but ye shall be ashamed; behold, my servants shall sing for joy of heart, but ye shall cry for sorrow of heart; and shall howl for vexation of spirit. And ye shall leave your name for a curse unto my chosen." [Isa. 65:13 ff.] In short, as I have said,[59] the examples of those who die in their sins and are damned are profitable unto us for admonition and instruction, as St. Gregory also observes in his Dialogues;[60] so that

Happy are they who caution gain

From that that which caused another's pain.

This blessing, indeed, affects us but little, because it is so common and well known; nevertheless, it is to be ranked among the very highest blessings, and is comforted of no slight value by those who have an understanding heart; and many are the passages of Scripture that bear upon it, those, namely, which treat of the wrath, the judgments, and the threatenings of God. These most wholesome teachings are confirmed to us by the examples of those wretched men; and their examples only then have their effect on us, when we enter into the feelings of them that endure such things, and put ourselves as it were in their very place. Then will they move and admonish us to praise the goodness of God, Who has preserved us from those evils.

But let us also compare them with God, that we may see the divine justice in their case. Although this is a difficult task, yet it must be essayed. Now, since God is a just Judge, we must love and laud His justice, and thus rejoice in our God, even when He miserably destroys the wicked, in body and soul; for in all this His high, unspeakable justice shines forth. And so even hell, no less than heaven, is full of God and the highest good. For the justice of God is God Himself; and God is the highest good. Therefore, even as His mercy, so must His justice or judgment be loved, praised, and glorified above all things. In this sense David says, "The righteous shall rejoice when he seeth the vengeance; he shall wash his feet in the blood of the wicked." [Ps. 58:10] It was for this reason that the Lord forbade Samuel to mourn any longer for Saul (I. Samuel xvi), saying, "How long wilt thou mourn for Saul, seeing I have rejected him from reigning over Israel?" [1 Sam. 16:1] As who should say, "Does My will so sorely displease thee, that thou preferrest the will of man to Me?" In short, this is the voice of praise and joy resounding through the whole Psalter,—that the Lord is the judge of the widow, and a father of the fatherless; that He will maintain the cause of the afflicted, and the right of the poor; that His enemies all be confounded, and the ungodly shall perish; [Ps. 68:5, 149:12] and many similar sayings. Should any one be inclined, in foolish pity, to feel compassion for that bloody generation, that killeth the prophets, yea, the Son of God Himself, and for the company of wicked men, he will be found rejoicing in their iniquity, and approving their deeds. Such a one deserves to perish in like manner with them whose sins he would condone, and will hear the word, "Thou lovest thine enemies, and hatest thy friends." [2 Sam. 19:6] For thus Joab said unto David, when he grieved too sorely over his impious and murderous son.

Therefore, in this image, we ought to rejoice in the piety of all the saints, and in the justice of God which justly punishes the persecutors of their piety, that He may deliver His elect out of their hands. And so you may see no small blessings, but the very greatest, shining forth in the dead and damned; even the avenging of the injuries of the saints, and of your own as well, if you be righteous with them. What wonder, then, if God, by means of your present evil, should take vengeance also on your enemy, that is, the sin in your body! You ought the rather to rejoice in this work of the high justice of God, which, even without your prayer, is thus slaying and destroying your fiercest foe, namely, the sin that is within you. But, should you feel pity for it, you will be found a friend of sin, and an enemy to the justice that worketh in you. Of this beware; lest it be said also to you, "Thou lovest thine enemies, and hatest thy friends." Therefore, as you ought joyfully to consent to the justice of God when it rages against your sin, you should do even the same when it rages against sinners, those enemies of all men and of God. You see, then, that in the greatest evils may be found the greatest blessings, and that we are able to rejoice in these evils, not on account of the evils themselves, but on account of the supreme goodness of the justice of God our Avenger.

CHAPTER V

THE FIFTH IMAGE

THE BLESSING ON OUR LEFT HAND

Here are our adversaries who are yet in this life; for in the foregoing image we considered those who are already damned and given over to devils. These we must regard with other feelings, and find in them a twofold blessing. The first is this, that they abound in temporal goods, so that even the prophets were well nigh moved to envy thereby; as we read in

Psalm lxii, "But as for me, my feet were almost gone; my steps had well nigh slipped. For I was envious at the foolish, when I saw the prosperity of the wicked" [Ps. 73:2 f.]; and again, "Behold, these are the ungodly, who prosper in the world; they increase in riches." [Ps. 73:12] And Jeremiah says, "Righteous art Thou, O Lord, when I plead with Thee: yet let me talk with Thee of Thy judgments: wherefore doth the way of the wicked prosper? Wherefore are all they happy that deal very treacherously?" [Jer. 12:1] Why does He lavish and waste so many blessings upon them except to comfort us thereby, and make us to know how good He is to "such as are of a clean heart"? as it is said in that same Psalm lxxii. If He is so good to the wicked, how good will He not be to the good? [Ps. 73:1] Except that He does not vex the wicked with any evil, yet afflicts the good with many evils, in order that they may acknowledge His goodness to them not only in the present blessings, but even in those that are hidden and yet to come, and that they may say, with the same Psalmist, "But it is good for me to draw near to God; I have put my trust in the Lord God." [Ps. 73:28] Which is as though he said. Even though I suffer certain things, from which I see that those men are free, nevertheless I trust that God is far more good to me than He is to them. Thus the blessings which we see the wicked enjoy become to us an incentive to hope for those blessings which are not seen, and to despise the evils which we suffer. Even as Christ, in Matthew vi, bids us behold the foul of the air and the lilies of the field, saying, "Wherefore if God so clothe the grass, which to-day is, and to-morrow is cast into the oven, shall He not much more clothe you, O ye of little faith?" [Matt. 6:26 ff.] Hence, by this comparison of the blessings in which the wicked abound with the evils that we suffer, our faith is exercised, and our consolation is placed in God alone, which is the only holy consolation. So doth He make all things work together for good unto His saints. [Rom. 8:28]

The other blessing, which is more marvelous, is this, that the evils of our adversaries become blessings to us, under the providence of God. For though their sins are a stumbling-block to the weak, to such as are strong they are an exercise of virtue, and an opportunity for conflict and the amassing of greater merit.[61] For, "Blessed is the man that endureth temptation, for when he is tried, he shall receive the crown of life." [Jas. 1:12] What greater temptation can there be than a host of evil examples? For this reason, indeed, the world is called one of the enemies of God's saints, because with its allurements and ungodly works it incites, provokes, and entices us from the way of God to its own way. As we read in Genesis vi, "The sons of God saw the daughters of men, that they were fair, and they were made flesh." [Gen. 6:2,3] And in Numbers xxv, "The people of Israel began to commit whoredom with the daughters of Moab." [Num. 25:1] So it is good for us to be always oppressed with some trouble or other, that we may not, in our weakness, stumble at the offences of the world, and fall into sin. Thus Lot is praised by Peter, in II. Peter ii., because he suffered many things because of the evil example of the people of Sodom, so that he made progress thereby in his righteousness. [2 Pet. 2:8] It must needs be that these offences come, which furnish us an occasion for conflict and for victory; but woe unto the world because of offences! [Matt. 18:7] But if God procures us such great blessings in the sins of others, should we not with our whole heart believe that He will work, us much greater blessings in our own troubles; even though our flesh and blood judge it to be otherwise!

Nor does the world confer a smaller blessing on us from another side of its evils; namely, its adversities. For, when it is unable to swallow us up with its allurements, and through its offences to make us one with itself, it endeavors through sufferings to drive us out, and through pains to cast us forth; always laying snares for us by the example of its sins, or else visiting its fury upon us through the torment of its pains. This is indeed that fabled monster, Chimaera,[62] with the head of a maiden, seductive, the body of a lion, cruel, and the tail of a serpent, deadly. For the end of the world, both of its pleasures and its tyranny, is poison and death everlasting. Hence, even as God grants us to find our blessings in the sins of the world, so also its persecutions, that they may not remain fruitless and in vain, are appointed unto us to increase our blessings; so that the very things that work us harm are turned to our profit. As St. Augustine says, concerning the innocents slain by Herod, "Never could he have done them so much good with his favor as he did with his hatred." And St. Agatha,[63] the blessed martyr, went to prison as to a banquet chamber; "for," said she, "except thou cause my body to be well broken by thy executioners, my soul will not be able to enter paradise, bearing the victor's palm; even as a grain of wheat, except it be stript of its husk, and well beaten on the threshing-floor, is not gathered into the barn."

But why waste words here, when we see the whole of the Scriptures, the writings and sayings of all the Fathers, and the lives and acts of all the saints, agreeing together in this matter; namely, that they who bring the most harm upon believers are their greatest benefactors, if only we bear with them in the right spirit. As St. Peter says, "And who is he that will harm you, if ye be followers of that which is good?" [1 Pet. 3:13] And Psalm lxxxviii, "The enemy shall not exact upon him; nor the son of wickedness afflict him." [Ps. 89:22] How is it that he shall not harm us, seeing that oftentimes he even kills us? Because, forsooth, in harming us he is working us the very greatest gain. [Rom. 8:36] Thus we find ourselves every way dwelling in the midst of blessings, if we are wise, and yet, at the same time, also in the midst of evils. So wondrously are all things tempered together under the rule of the goodness of God.

CHAPTER VI

THE SIXTH IMAGE

THE BLESSING ON OUR RIGHT HAND

This is the Church of the saints, the new creation of God, our brethren and our friends, in whom we see naught but blessing, naught but consolation; not, indeed, always with the eyes of the flesh (to which they would appear to belong rather under the corresponding image of evils),[64] but with the eyes of the spirit Nevertheless, we must not disregard even those blessings of theirs which may be seen, but rather learn from them how God would comfort us. For even the Psalmist did not venture, in Psalm lxxii, to condemn all those who amass riches in this world, but said, "If I say, I will speak thus; behold, I should offend against the generation of Thy children." [Ps. 73:15] That is to say, If I should call all men wicked who possess riches, health, and honor, I should be condemning even Thy saints, of whom there are many such. Paul also instructs Timothy to charge them that are rich in this world, that they be not high minded;[1 Tim. 6:17] but he does not forbid them to be rich. And

Abraham, Isaac, and Jacob were rich men, as the Scriptures record. Daniel, also, and his companions were raised to honor even in Babylon. [Dan. 2:48 f.] Moreover many of the kings of Judah were saintly men. It is with regard to such persons that the Psalmist says, "If I say, I will speak thus; behold, I should offend against the generation of Thy children." [Ps. 73:15] God gives, even to His people, an abundance of these blessings, for their own comfort, and the comfort of others. Still, these things are not their proper blessings, but only shadows and emblems of their true blessings, which consist in faith, hope, love, and other gifts and graces, which love communicates to all.

This is the communion of saints, in which we glory. And whose heart will not be lifted up, even in the midst of great evils, when he believes that which is indeed the very truth; namely, that the blessings of all the saints are his blessings, and that his evil is also theirs! For this is the sweet and pleasant picture which the Apostle Paul depicts, in Galatians vi, "Bear ye one another's burdens, and so fulfil the law of Christ." [Gal. 6:21] Is it not a blessing to be in such a company in which, "whether one member suffer, all the members suffer with it; or one member be honored, all the members rejoice with it"? [1 Cor. 12:26] as it is said in I. Corinthians vi[65]. Therefore, when I suffer, I suffer not alone, but Christ and all Christians suffer with me; as He saith, "He that toucheth you, toucheth the apple of My eye." [Zach. 2:8] Even so others bear my burden, and their strength becomes my own. The Church's faith supports my fearfulness, the chastity of others bears the temptations of my flesh, the fastings of others are my gain, the prayer of another pleads for me. In short, such care have the members one for another, that the comely parts cover, serve, and honor the uncomely; as it is beautifully set forth in I. Corinthians vi.[65] others as though they were my own; and they are truly my own when I find joy and pleasure therein. Let me, then, be base and vile; yet they whom I love and admire are fair and beautiful. And by my love I make not only their blessings, but their very selves my own; so that by their honor my shame is made honorable, by their abundance my poverty is filled, by their merits my sins are healed. Who, then, could despair in his sins? Who would not rejoice in his pains? For it is not he that bears his sins and pains; or if he does bear them, he bears them not alone, but is assisted by so many holy sons of God, yea, even by Christ Himself. So great a thing is the communion of saints, and the Church of Christ.[66]

If any one does not believe this, he is an infidel, and has denied Christ and the Church. For even if it should not be perceived yet it is true; but who could fail to perceive it? For why is it that you do not sink in despair, or grow impatient? Is it your strength? Nay: it is the communion of saints. Otherwise you could not bear even a venial sin,[67] nor endure a word of man against you. So close to you are Christ and the Church. It is this that we confess in the Creed, "I believe in the Holy Ghost; the holy Catholic[68] Church." What is it to believe in the holy Church but to believe in the communion of saints. But what things have the saints in common? Blessings, forsooth, and evils; all things belong to all; as the Sacrament of the Altar signifies, in the bread and wine, where we are all said by the Apostle to be one body, one bread, one cup.[69][1 Cor. 10:17] For who can hurt any part of the body without hurting the whole body? What pain can we feel in the tip of the toe that is not felt in the whole body? Or what honor can be shown to the feet in which the whole body will not rejoice? But we are one body. Whatever another suffers, that I suffer and bear;

whatever good befalls him, befalls me. So Christ says that whatsoever is done unto one of the least of His brethren, is done unto Him. If a man partake of the smallest fragment of the bread of the altar, is he not said to have partaken of the bread? If he despise one crumb of it, is he not said to have despised the bread?

When we, therefore, feel pain, when we suffer, when we die, let us turn hither our eyes,[70] and firmly believe and be sure that it is not we, or we alone, but that Christ and the Church are in pain, are suffering, are dying with us. For Christ would not have us go alone into the valley of death, from which all men shrink in fear; but we set out upon the way of pain and death attended by the whole Church, and the Church bears the brunt of it all. Therefore, we can with truth apply to ourselves the words of Elisha, which he spake to his timid servant, "Fear not: for they that be with us are more than they that be with them. And Elisha prayed, and said, Lord, I pray thee, open his eyes that he may see. And the Lord opened the eyes of the young man; and he saw: and, behold, the mountain was full of horses and chariots of fire round about Elisha." [2 Kings 6:16 f.] This one thing remains for us also; namely, to pray that our eyes may be opened (I mean the eyes of our faith), that we may see the Church round about us. Then there will be nothing for us to fear; as it is said also in Psalm cxxiv, "Mountains are round about it: so the Lord is round about His people from henceforth now and for ever." [Ps. 125:2][71]

CHAPTER VII

THE SEVENTH IMAGE

THE SUPERNAL BLESSING, OR THE BLESSING ABOVE US

I do not now speak of the eternal blessings of Heaven, which the blessed enjoy in the perfect vision of God; or father, I do speak of them in faith, and in so far as they some within our comprehension. For this seventh image is Jesus Christ, the King of glory, rising from the dead; even as, in His Passion and death. He formed the seventh image of evils.[72] Here there is nothing at all of evil; for "Christ, being risen from the dead, dieth no more; death hath no more dominion over him." [Rom. 6:9] Here is that furnace of love and fire of God in Zion; [Isa. 31:9] as Isaiah saith. For Christ is not only born unto us, but He is also given unto us. [Isa. 9:6] Therefore, His resurrection, and all that He wrought by it, are mine, and, as the Apostle exults in exuberant joy, "how hath [73] He not also, with Him, given us all things?" But what is it that He hath wrought by His resurrection? Why, He hath destroyed sin and brought righteousness to light, abolished death and restored life, conquered hell and bestowed on us everlasting glory. These are such inestimably precious blessings that the mind of man dare scarce believe that they have become ours; as it was with Jacob, in Genesis xlv, who, when he heard that his son Joseph was ruler in Egypt, was like one awakened out of deep slumber, and believed them not, until, after telling him all the words of Joseph, they showed him the wagons that Joseph had sent. [Gen 45:26 ff.] So difficult, indeed, would it be for us to believe that in Christ such great blessings have been conferred on us unworthy creatures, did He not teach us to believe it, with many words, and by the evidence of our own experience; even as He manifested Himself to His disciples[74] in divers appearances. [Acts 1:3] Such are our "Joseph's wagons." This is indeed a most godly "wagon," that He is made unto us of God righteousness, and sanctification, and redemption, and wisdom; [1 Cor. 1:30] as the Apostle saith in I. Corinthians i. For, I am a sinner; yet am I drawn in His righteousness, which is given me. I am unclean; but His holiness is my sanctification, in which I pleasurably tide. I am an ignorant fool; but His wisdom carries me forward. I have deserved condemnation; but I am set free by His redemption, a wagon in which I sit secure. So that a Christian, if he but believe it, may boast of the merits of Christ and all His blessings, even as if he had won them all himself. So truly are they his own, that he may even dare to look boldly forward to the judgment of God, unbearable though it be. So great a thing is faith, such blessings does it bring us, such glorious sons of God does it make us. For we cannot be sons without inheriting our Father's goods. Let the Christian say, then, with full confidence: "O death, where is thy victory? O death, where is thy sting? The sting of death is sin; and the strength of sin is the law. But thanks be to God,[75] which giveth us the victory through our Lord Jesus Christ." [1 Cor. 15:55 ff.] That is to say, the law makes us sinners, and sin makes us guilty of death. Who hath conquered these twain? Was it our righteousness, or our life? Nay: it was Jesus Christ, rising from the dead, condemning sin and death, bestowing on us His merits, and holding His hand over us. And now it is well with us, we keep the law, and vanquish sin and death. For all which be honor, praise, and thanksgiving unto our God for ever and ever. Amen.

This, then, is the highest image of all, in which we are lifted up, not only above our evils, but above our blessings as well, and are set down amid strange blessings, brought together by another's labor; whereas we formerly lay among evils, heaped up by another's sin,[76] and added to by our own. We are set down, I say, in Christ's righteousness, with which He Himself is righteous; because we cling to that righteousness by which He is well pleasing to God, intercedes for us as our Mediator, and gives Himself wholly to be our own, as our High-Priest and Protector. Therefore, as it is impossible that Christ, with His righteousness, should not please God, so it is impossible that we should not please Him. Hence it comes that a Christian is almighty, lord of all,[77] having all things, and doing all things, wholly without sin. And even if he have sins, they can in no wise harm him, but are forgiven for the sake of the inexhaustible righteousness of Christ that swalloweth up all sins, on which our faith relies, firmly trusting that He is such a Christ unto us as we have described. But if any one does not believe this, he hears the tale with deaf ears,[78] and does not know Christ, and understands neither what blessings He hath nor how they may be enjoyed.

Therefore, if we considered it aright and with attentive hearts, this image alone would suffice to fill us with so great comfort that we should not only not grieve over our evils, [Rom. 5:3] but even glory in our tribulations, nay, scarcely feel them, for the joy that we have in Christ. In which glorying may Christ Himself instruct us, our Lord and God, blessed for evermore. Amen. [Rom. 9:5]

EPILOGUE

With these prattlings of mine, Most Illustrious Prince, in token of my willingness to serve your Lordship to the best of my poor ability, I commend myself to your Illustrious Lordship, being ready to bring a worthier offering, if ever my mental powers shall equal my desires. For I shall always remain a debtor to every neighbor of mine, but most of all to your Lordship, whom may our Lord Jesus Christ, in His merciful kindness, long preserve to us, and at last by a blessed death take home to Himself. Amen.

Your Most Illustrious Lordship's

Intercessor,

Brother Martin Luther,

Augustinian at Wittenberg.

FOOTNOTES

[1] Written by Luther for the last edition of 1535.

[2] Compare to the Preface to the Complete Works (1545), page 11 of this volume.

[3] Antilogistae; the hunters of contradictions and inconsistencies in Luther's writings, such as John Faber, who published, in 1530, his Antilogiarum Mart. Lutheri Babylonia. Compare also reference in preceding note.

[4] As over against Christ and the saints in His train, the devil and his followers are represented here, as frequently in Luther, under the figure of a dragon with a scaly tail.

[5] Omitted, through on oversight, from the Latin editio princeps. See Introduction, p. 105.

[6] On the political influence of Frederick, as a factor in the

German Reformation, see Hermelink, Reformation und

Gegenreformation (Krüger's Handbuch der Kirchengeschicte, 3.

Teil), p. 67.

[7] Tessaradecas.

[8] See Introduction, pp. 106 f.

[9] In the body of the work Luther places (6) between (3) and (4).

[10] A reminiscence of Luther's childhood?

[11] Luther has particular reference to the Elector's high rank.

[12] Luther follows the Vulgate numbering of the Psalms, which differs from the Hebrew (and the English and German). As far as Ps. 8 both agree; but the Vulgate (following the Greek version) counts Ps. 9 and 10 as one, thus dropping behind one in the numbering. But it divides Ps. 147 into two; vv. 1-11 being counted as Ps. 146, and vv. 12-20 as Ps. 147; and so both versions agree again from Ps. 148 to 150.

[13] Job calls it a "warfare" (militia).

[14] Luther harks back to his discussion of this point in the Preface, p. 113.

[15] Particular reference to the Elector.

[16] See pp. 147 ff.

[17] Cypr. de mortal. c. V.

[18] Vulgate reading.

[19] See pp. 149 f.

[20] From the Vulgate.

[21] Luther is probably thinking of his own experience, when, near Erfurt, he came near bleeding to death from an injury to his ankle. See Köstlin-Kawerau, Martin Luther, I, 44.

[22] Luther no longer held this view of "satisfaction" in 1535. See also pp. 150 and 161.

[23] Luther is thinking here specifically of the Elector.

[24] He means the communion of saints. See next chapter.

[25] According to the Vulgate (Douay Version).

[26] August 29th. See Introduction, p. 105.

[27] Cf. A Discussion of Confession, above, p. 82.

[28] Luther might have considerably revised this whole paragraph.

[29] This seems to refer to the writers of the Holy Scriptures.

[30] A reference to the threefold baptism, commonly accepted, viz., (1) fluminia, (2) flaminis, (3) sanguinis; that is, (1) the Sacrament of baptism, (2) the baptism of the Spirit, or repentance, (3) the baptism of blood, or martyrdom. Cf. PRE3, XIX, 414.

[31] Frederick the Wise was a pious collector of relics, having 5005 of them in the Castle Church at Wittenberg. They had something to do with Luther's choice of October 31st as the date of the posting of the XCV Theses. See Introduction to the Theses, p. 16 of this volume, note 1.

[32] Cf. Letter to George Leiffer, 15 April, 1516. See M. A. Cueriz, The Letters of M. Luther, p. 7.

[33] i. e., The sign of the cross.

[34] As much as, "We are in for a bad hour," and, "A good hour is worth a bad hour."

[35] See p. 134.

[36] In this passage "Wisdom" is the subject.

[37] In the Sanctus.

[38] See p. 118.

[39] Luther quotes a verse from Ps. 106, which sums up the contents of Ps. 78.

[40] Luther uses sensualitas the first time, and sensus the second.

[41] See p.115.

[42] The Confessions of St. Augustine, Book IX, chapter 1.

[43] Luther is probably thinking of the sin of suicide.

[44] From the Vulgate (Douay Version).

[45] Namely, the hope of the passing evil and the coming of good things. See above.

[46] The last two passages read thus in the Vulgate.

[47] See p. 122.

[48] Cf. p. 127, note.

[49] Thus the Vulgate.

[50] Ovid, Ars amat., I, 656.

[51] Cf. Treatise on Baptism, above, p. 66.

[52] See pp. 123 ff.

[53] The Confessions of St. Augustine, Book I, chap. vi.

[54] Thus the Vulgate.

[55] Comm. in Ps. xxxix, No. 27.

[56] Book VIII, chap. xi.

[57] See p. 152.

[58] See pp. 126 ff.

[59] See pp. 126 ff.

[60] Gregor. dialogorum libri iv, containing number of examples of the terrible end of the wicked.

[61] One of the passages Luther did not care to correct. Compare p. 127, note.

[62] Luther here unites the mythological figures of chimaera and alren.

[63] An Italian saint whose festival is observed on February 5th, whose worship flourishes especially in South Italy and Sicily, and whose historical existence is doubtful.

[64] See pp. 133 ff.

[65] Luther has mistaken the chapter.

[66] For the various interpretations of the "communion of the saints" among mediæval theologians, See Reinh. Seeberg, Lehrbuch der Dogmengeschichte, 1st ed., vol. ii, p.127, note. Luther in the Sermon von dem hochwürdigen Sacrament des heiligen wahren Leichnams Christi (1519), still accepts the phrase as meaning the participation in the Sacrament, and through it the participation in "the spiritual possessions of Christ and His saints." In our treatise, it is taken as the definition of "the holy Catholic Church," in the sense of a communion with the saints. In The Papacy at Rome (later in the same year), it becomes the communion or community (consisting of saints, or believers; as a Gemeinde oder Sammlung. Compare the classical passage in the Large Catechism (1529): "nicht Gemenschaft, sondern Gemeine."

[67] See A Discussion of Confession, above, p. 88.

[68] Changed to "Christian" in the Catechisms (1529), although the Latin translations retain catholocism.

[69] The Apostle does not say, "one cup."

[70] The translation here follows the reading of the Jena Ed. (huc feratur intuitus), as against that of the Weimar and Erl. Edd. (huc foratur intutus).

[71] Thus the Vulgate.

[72] See pp. 137 ff.

[73] Vulgate.

[74] Namely, after His resurrection.

[75] Compare the different form of this verse on p. 112.

[76] He means the sin of Adam.

[77] The germ of The Liberty of a Christian Man (1520).

[78] Cf. Terence's surdo narrare fabulam. Heauton., 222.

A TREATISE ON GOOD WORKS,

TOGETHER WITH THE LETTER OF DEDICATION

1520

INTRODUCTION

1. The Occasion of the Work.—Luther did not impose himself as a reformer upon the Church. In the course of a conscientious performance of the duties of his office, to which he had been regularly and divinely called, and without any urging on his part, he attained to this position by inward necessity. In 1515 he received his appointment as the standing substitute for the sickly city pastor, Simon Heinse, from the city council of Wittenberg. Before this time he was obliged to preach only occasionally in the convent, apart from his activity as teacher in the University and convent. Through this appointment he was in duty bound, by divine and human right, to lead and direct the congregation at Wittenberg on the true way to life, and it would have been a denial of the knowledge of salvation which God had led him to acquire, by way of ardent inner struggles, if he had led the congregation on any other way than the one God had revealed to him in His Word. He could not deny before the congregation which had been intrusted to his care, what up to this time he had taught with ever increasing clearness in his lectures at the University—for in the lectures on the Psalms, which he began to deliver in 1513, he declares his conviction that faith alone justifies, as can be seen from the complete manuscript, published since 1885, and with still greater clearness from his Commentary on the Epistle to the Romans (1515-1516), which is accessible since 1908; nor what he had urged as spiritual adviser of his convent brethren when in deep distress—compare the charming letter to Georg Spenlein, dated April 8, 1516,[1]

Luther's first literary works to Appear in print were also occasioned by the work of his calling and of his office in the Wittenberg congregation. He had no other object in view than to edify his congregation and to lead it to Christ when, in 1517, he published his first independent work, the Explanation of the Seven Penitential Psalms. On Oct 31 of the same year he published his 95 Theses against Indulgences. These were indeed intended as controversial theses for theologians, but at the same time it is well known that Luther was moved by his duty toward his congregation to declare his position in this matter and to put in issue the whole question as to the right and wrong of indulgences by means of his theses. His sermon Of Indulgences and Grace, occasioned by Tetzel's attack and delivered in the latter part of March, 1515, as well as his sermon Of Penitence, delivered about the same time, were also intended for his congregation. Before his congregation (Sept., 1516-Feb., 1517) he delivered the Sermons on the Ten Commandments, which were published in 1518, and the Sermons on the Lord's Prayer, which were also published in 1518 by Agricola. Though Luther in the same year published a series of controversial writings, which were occasioned by attacks from outside sources, viz., the Resolutiones disputationis de virtute indulgentiarum, the Asterisci adversus obeliscos Joh. Eccii, and the Ad dialogum Silv. Prieriatis responsio, still he never was diverted by this necessary rebuttal from his paramount duty, the edification of the congregation. The autumn of the year 1518, when he was confronted with Cajetan, as well as the whole year of 1519, when he held his disputations with Eck, etc, were replete with disquietude and pressing labors; still Luther served his congregation with a whole series of writings during this time, and only regretted that he was not entirely at its disposal. Of such writings we mention: Explanation of the Lord's Prayer for the simple Laity (an elaboration of the sermons of 1517); Brief Explanation of the Ten Commandments; Instruction concerning certain Articles, which might be ascribed and imputed to him by his adversaries; Brief Instruction how to Confess; Of Meditation on the Sacred Passion of Christ; Of Twofold Righteousness; Of the Matrimonial Estate; Brief Form to understand and to pray the Lord's Prayer; Explanation of the Lord's Prayer "vor sich und hinter sich"; Of Prayer and Processions in Rogation Week; Of Usury; Of the Sacrament of Penitence; Of Preparation for Death; Of the Sacrament of Baptism; Of the Sacrament of the Sacred Body; Of Excommunication. With but few exceptions these writings all speared in print in the year 1519, and again it was the congregation which Luther sought primarily to serve. If the bounds of his congregation spread ever wider beyond Wittenberg, so that his writings found a surprisingly ready sale, even afar, that was not Luther's fault. Even the Tessaradecas consolatoria,[2] written in 1519 and printed in 1530, a book of consolation, which was originally intended for the sick Elector of Saxony, was written by him only upon solicitation from outside sources.

To this circle of writings the treatise Of Good Works also belongs. Though the incentive for its composition came from George Spalatin, court-preacher to the Elector, who reminded Luther of a promise he had given, still Luther was willing to undertake it only when he recalled that in a previous sermon to his congregation he occasionally had made a similar promise to deliver a sermon on good works;[3] and when Luther actually commenced the composition he had nothing else in view but the preparation of a sermon for his congregation on this important topic.

But while the work was in progress the material so accumulated that it far outgrew the bounds of a sermon for his congregation. On March 25. he wrote to Spatatin that it would become a whole booklet instead of a sermon; on May 5. he again emphasizes the growth of the material; on May 13. he speaks of its completion at an early date, and on June 8. he could send Melanchthon a printed copy. It was entitled: Von den gutenwerckenn: D. M. L. Vuittenherg. On the last page it bore the printer's mark: Getruck zu Wittenberg bey dem iungen Melchior Lotther. Im Tausent funfhundert vnud zweynitzsgen Jar. It filled not less than 58 leaves, quarto. In spite of its volume, however, the intention of the book for the congregation remained, now however, not only for the narrow circle of the Wittenberg congregation, but for the Christian layman in general. In the dedicatory preface Luther lays the greatest stress upon this, for he writes: "Though I know of a great many, and must hear it daily, who think lightly of my poverty and say that I write only small Sexternlein (tracts of small volume) and German sermons for the untaught laity, I will not permit that to move me. Would to God that during my life I had served but one layman for his betterment with all my powers; it would be sufficient for me, I would thank God and suffer all my books to perish thereafter...Most willingly I will leave the honor of greater things to others, and not at all will I be ashamed of preaching and writing German to the untaught laity."

Since Luther had dedicated the afore-mentioned Tessaradecas conolatoria to the reigning Prince,[4] he now, probably on Spalatin's recommendation, dedicated the Treatise on Good Works to his brother John, who afterward, in 1525, succeeded Frederick in the Electorate. There was probably good reason for dedicating the book to a member of the reigning house. Princes have reason to take a special interest in the fact that preaching on good works should occur within their realm, for the safety and sane development of their kingdom depend hugely upon the cultivation of morality on the part of their subjects. Time and again the papal church had commended herself to princes and statesmen by her emphatic teaching of good works. Luther, on the other hand, had been accused—like the Apostle Paul before him (Rom. 3:31)—that the zealous performance of good works had abated, that the bonds of discipline had slackened and that, as a necessary consequence, lawlessness and shameless immorality were being promoted by his doctrine of justification by faith alone. Before 1517 the rumor had already spread that Luther intended to do away with good works. Duke George of Saxony had received no good impression from a sermon Luther had delivered at Dresden, because he feared the consequences which Luther's doctrine of justification by faith alone might have upon the morals of the masses. Under these circumstances it would not have been surprising if a member of the Electoral house should harbor like scruples, especially since the full comprehension of Luther's preaching on good works depended on an evangelical understanding of faith, as deep as was Luther's own. The Middle Ages had differentiated between fides informis, a formless faith, and fides formata or informata, a formed or ornate faith. The former was held to be a knowledge without any life or effect, the latter to be identical with love, for, as they said, love which proves itself and is effective in good works must be added to the formless faith, as its complement and its content, well pleasing to God. In Luther's time every one who was seriously interested in religious questions was reared under the influence of these ideas.[5]

Now, since Luther had opposed the doctrine of justification by love and its good works, he was in danger of being misunderstood by strangers, as though he held the bare knowledge and assent to be sufficient for justification, and such preaching would indeed have led to frivolity and disorderly conduct. But even apart from the question whether or not the brother of the Elector was disturbed by such scruples, Luther must have welcomed the opportunity, when the summons came to him, to dedicate his book Of Good Works to a member of the Electoral house. At any rate the book could serve to acquaint him with the thoughts of his much-abused pastor and professor at Wittenberg, for never before had Luther expressed himself on the important question of good works in such a fundamental, thorough and profound way.

2. Contents of the Work.—A perusal of the contents shows that the book, in the course of its production, attained a greater length than was originally intended. To this fact it must be attributed that a new numeration of sections begins with the argument on the Third Commandment, and is repeated at every Commandment thereafter, while before this the sections were consecutively numbered. But in spite of this, the plan of the whole is clear and lucid. Evidently the whole treatise is divided into two parts: the first comprising sections 1-17, while the second comprises all the following sections. The first, being fundamental, is the more important part. Luther well knew of the charges made against him that "faith is so highly elevated" and "works are rejected" by him; but he knew, too, that "neither silver, gold and precious stone, nor any other precious thing had experienced so much augmentation and diminution" as had good works "which should all have but one simple goodness, or they are nothing but color, glitter and deception." But especially was he aware of the fact that the Church was urging nothing but the so-called self-elected works, such as "running to the convent, singing, reading, playing the organ, saying the mass, praying matins, vespers, and other hours, founding and ornamenting churches, altars, convents, gathering chimes, jewels, vestments, gems and treasures, going to Rome and to the saints, curtsying and bowing the knees, praying the rosary and the psalter," etc., and that she designated these alone as truly good works, while she represented the faithful performance of the duties of one's calling as a morality of a lower order. For these reasons it is Luther's highest object in this treatise to make it perfectly clear what is the essence of good works. Whenever the essence of good works has been understood, then the accusations against him will quickly collapse.

In the fundamental part he therefore argues; Truly good works are not self-elected works of monastic or any other holiness, but such only as God has commanded and as are comprehended within the bounds one's particular calling, and all works, let the name be what it may, become good only when they flow from faith, the "first, greatest, and noble of good works." (John 6:19.) In this connection the essence of faith, that only source of all truly good works, must of course be rightly understood. It is the sure confidence in God, that all my doing is well-pleasing to him; it is trust in His mercy even though He appear angry and puts sufferings and adversities upon us; it is the assurance of the divine good will even though "God should reprove the conscience with sin, death and hell, and deny it all grace and mercy, as though He would condemn and show His wrath eternally." Where such faith lives in the heart, there the works are good "even though they were as insignificant as the picking up of a straw"; but where it is wanting, there are only such works as "heathen, Jew and Turk" may have and do. Where such faith possesses the man, he needs no teacher in good works, as little as does the husband or the wife, who only look for love and favor from one another, nor need any instruction therein "how they are to stand toward each other, what they are to do, to leave undone, to say, to leave unsaid, to think."

This faith, Luther continues, is "the true fulfilment of the First Commandment, apart from which there is no work that could do justice to this Commandment." With this sentence he combines, on the one hand, the whole argument of faith, as the best and noblest of good works, with his opening proposition (there are no good works besides those commanded of God), and, on the other hand, he prepares the way for the following argument, wherein he proposes to exhibit the good works according to the Ten Commandments. For the First Commandment does not forbid this and that, nor does it require this and that; it forbids but one thing, unbelief; it requires but one thing, faith, "that confidence in God's good will at all times." Without this faith the best works are as nothing, and if man would think that by them he could be well-pleasing to God, he would be lowering God to the level of a "broker or a laborer who will not dispense his grace and kindness gratis."

This understanding of faith and good works, so Luther now addresses his opponents, should in fairness be kept in view by those who accuse him of declaiming against good works, and they should learn from it, that though he has preached against "good works," it was against such as are falsely so called and as contribute toward the confusion of consciences, because they are self-elected, do not flow from faith, and are done with the pretension of doing works well-pleasing to God.

This brings us to the end of the fundamental part of the treatise. It was not Luther's intention, however, to speak only on the essence of good works and their fundamental relation to faith; he would show, too, how the "best work," faith, must prove itself in every way a living faith, according to the other commandments. Luther does not proceed to this part, however, until in the fundamental part he has said with emphasis, that the believer, the spiritual man, needs no such instruction (1. Timothy 1:9), but that he of his own accord and at all times does good works "as his faith, his confidence, teaches him." Only "because we do not all have such faith, or are unmindful of it," does such instruction become necessary.

Nor does he proceed until he has repeated his oft repeated words concerning the relation of faith to good works to the relation of the First to the other Commandments. From the fact, that according to the First Commandment, we acquire a pure heart and confidence toward God, he derives the good work of the Second Commandment, namely, "to praise God, to acknowledge His grace, to render all honor to Him alone." From the same source he derives the good work of the Third Commandment, namely, "to observe divine services with prayer and the hearing of preaching, to incline the imagination of our hearts toward

God's benefits, and, to that end, to mortify and overcome the flesh." From the same source he derives the works of the Second Table.

The argument on the Third and Fourth Commandments claims nearly one-half of the entire treatise. Among the good works which, according to the Third Commandment, should be an exercise and proof of faith, Luther especially mentions the proper hearing of mass and of preaching, common prayer, bodily discipline and the mortification of the flesh, and he joins the former and the latter by an important fundamental discussion of the New Testament conception of Sabbath rest.

Luther discusses the Fourth Commandment as fully as the Third. The exercise of faith, according to this Commandment, consists in the faithful performance of the duties of children toward their parents, of parents toward their children, and of subordinates toward their superiors in the ecclesiastical as well as in the common civil sphere. The various duties issue from the various callings, for faithful performance of the duties of one's calling, with the help of God and for God's sake, is the true "good work."

As he now proceeds to speak of the spiritual powers, the government of the Church, he frankly reveals their faults and demands a reform of the present rulers. Honor and obedience in all things should be rendered unto the Church, the spiritual mother, as it is due to natural parents, unless it be contrary to the first Three Commandments. But as matters stand now the spiritual magistrates neglect their peculiar work, namely, the fostering of godliness and discipline, like a mother who runs away from her children and follows a lover, and instead they undertake strange and evil works, like parents whose commands are contrary to God. In this case members of the Church must do as godly children do whose parents have become mad and insane. Kings, princes, the nobility, municipalities and communities must begin of their own accord and put a check to these conditions, so that the bishops and the clergy, who are now too timid, may be induced to follow. But even the civil magistrates must also suffer reforms to be enacted in their particular spheres; especially are they called on to do away with the rude "gluttony and drunkenness," luxury in clothing, the usurious sale of rents and the common brothels. This, by divine and human right, is a part of their enjoined works according to the Fourth Commandment.

Luther, at last, briefly treats of the Second Table of the Commandments, but in speaking of the works of these Commandments he never forgets to point out their relation to faith, thus holding fast this fundamental thought of the book to the end. Faith which does not doubt that God is gracious, he says, will find it an easy matter to be graciously and favorably minded toward one's neighbor and to overcome all angry and wrathful desires. In this faith in God the Spirit will teach us to avoid unchaste thoughts and thus to keep the Sixth Commandment. When the heart trusts in the divine favor, it cannot seek after the temporal goods of others, nor cleave to money, but according to the Seventh Commandment, will use it with cheerful liberality for the benefit of the neighbor. Where such confidence is present there is also a courageous, strong and intrepid heart, which will at all times defend the truth, as the Eighth Commandment demands, whether neck or coat be at stake, whether it be against pope or kings. Where such faith is present there is also strife against the evil lust, as forbidden in the Ninth and Tenth Commandments, and that even unto death.

3. The Importance of the Work.—Inquiring now into the importance of the book, we note that Luther's impression evidently was perfectly correct, when he wrote to Spalatin, long before its completion—as early as March 15.—that he believed it to be better than anything he had heretofore written. His book, indeed, surpasses all his previous German writings in volume, as well as all his Latin and German ones in clearness, richness and the fundamental importance of its content. In comparison with the prevalent urging of self-elected works of monkish holiness, which had arisen from a complete misunderstanding of the so-called evangelical counsels (comp. esp. Matthew 19:16-22) and which were at that time accepted as self-evident and zealously urged by the whole church, Luther's argument must have appeared to all thoughtful and earnest souls as a revelation, when he so clearly amplified the proposition that only those works are to be regarded as good works which God has commanded, and that therefore, not the abandoning of one's earthly calling, but the faithful keeping of the Ten Commandments in the course of one's calling, is the work which God requires of us. Over against the wide-spread opinion, as though the will of God as declared in the Ten Commandments referred only to the outward work always especially mentioned, Luther's argument must have called to mind the explanation of the Law, which the Lord had given in the Sermon on the Mount, when he taught men to recognize only the extreme point and manifestation of a whole trend of thought in the work prohibited by the text, and when he directed Christians not to rest in the keeping of the literal requirement of each Commandment, but from this point of vantage to inquire into the whole depth and breadth of God's will—positively and negatively—and to do His will in its full extent as the heart has perceived it. Though this thought may have been occasionally expressed in the expositions of the Ten Commandments which appeared at the dawn of the Reformation, still it had never before been so clearly recognized as the only correct principle, much less had it been so energetically carried out from beginning to end, as is done in this treatise. Over against the deep-rooted view that the works of love must bestow upon faith its form, its content and its worth before God, it must have appeared as the dawn of a new era (Galatians 3:13-35) when Luther in this treatise declared, and with victorious certainty carried out the thought, that it is true faith which invests the works, even the best and greatest of works, with their content and worth before God.

This preposition, which Luther here amplifies more clearly than ever before, demanded nothing less than a breach with the whole of prevalent religious views, and at that time must have been perceived as the discovery of a new world, though it was no more than a return to the dear teaching of the New Testament Scriptures concerning the way of salvation. This, too, accounts for the fact that in this writing the accusation is more impressively repelled than before, that the doctrine of justification by faith lone resulted in moral laxity, and that, on the other hand, the fundamental and radical importance of righteousness by faith for the whole moral life is revealed in such a heart-refreshing manner. Luther's appeal in this treatise to kings, princes, the nobility, municipalities and communities, to declare against the misuse of spiritual powers and to abolish various abuses in civil life, marks this treatise as a forerunner of the great Reformation writings, which appeared in the same year (1520), while, on the other hand, his espousal of the rights of the "poor man"—to be met with here for the first time—shows that the Monk of Wittenberg, coming from the narrow limits of the convent, had an intimate and sympathetic knowledge of the social needs of his time. Thus he proved by his own example that to take a stand in the center of the Gospel does not narrow the vision nor harden the heart, but rather produces courage in the truth and sympathy for all manner of misery.

Luther's contemporaries at once recognized the great importance of the treatise, for within the period of seven months it passed through eight editions; these were followed by six more editions between the years of 1521 and 1525; in 1521 it was translation into Latin, and in this form passed through three editions up to the year 1525; and all this in spite of the fact that in those years the so-called three great Reformation writings of 1520 were casting all else into the shadow. Melanchthon, in a contemporaneous letter to John Hess, called it Luther's best book. John Mathesius, the well-known pastor at Joachimsthal and Luther's biographer, acknowledged that he had learned the "rudiments of Christianity" from it.

Even to-day this book has its peculiar mission to the Church. The seeking after self-elected works, the indifference regarding the works commanded of God, the foolish opinion, that the path of works leads to God's grace end good-will, are even to-day widely prevalent within the kingdom of God. To all this Luther's treatise answers: Be diligent in the works of your earthly calling as commanded of God, but only after having first strengthened, by the consideration of God's mercy, the faith within you, which is the only source of all truly good works and well-pleasing to God.

M. Reu.

Wartburg Seminary, Dubuque, Iowa.

FOOTNOTES

[1] (Enders, Luther's Briefwechsel, I, p. 29.) Luther here writers: Learn Christ, dear Brother, learn Christ crucified; learn to sing unto him and, despairing of self, to say: "Thou, Lord Jesus art my righteousness, I, however, am Thy sin. Thou has taken unto Thyself what was mine, and has given me what is Thine." In this faith, receive the erring brethren, make their sins your own, and if you have anything good, let it be theirs.

[2] Above, pp. 103-171.

[3] On Feb. 24, Luther answered Spalatin: Die sermone bonorum operum nibil memini; sed et tot jam edidi, ut periculum sit, ne emtores tandem fatigam; but on Feb. 26, he wrote again: Memoria mihi rediit de operibus bonis sermone tractandis, in concione scilicet id promisi; dabo operam, ut fiat. (De Weite, Luther's Briefe, I, p. 419, 421, 430 ff.)

[4] See Dedicatory Letter, above, p. 107.

[5] We mention but one of many testimonies. John Dietenberger in his book, Der leye. Obe der gelaub allein selig mache, printed in Strassburg 1523, says on leaf B26: "Faith is a gift of God, which may appear bare or ornate; still it remains but one faith, which, however, has another effect when ornate than when bare. Ornate faith makes man a child of grace, an heir of the kingdom of heaven and justified. Bare faith, however, does not separate man from devils, helps not to the kingdom of heaven, and leads to no justification."

A TREATISE ON GOOD WORKS

1520

DEDICATION

JESUS[1]

To the Illustrious, High-born Prince and Lord, John, Duke of

Saxony, Landgrave of Thuringia, Margrave of Meissen, my gracious

Lord and Patron.

Illustrious, High-born Prince, gracious Lord! My humble duty and my feeble prayer for your Grace always remembered!

For a long time, gracious Prince and Lord, I have wished to show my humble respect and duty toward your princely Grace, by the exhibition of some such spiritual wares as are at my disposal; but I have always considered my powers too feeble to undertake anything worthy of being offered to your princely Grace.

Since, however, my most gracious Lord Frederick, Duke of Saxony, Elector and Vicar of the Holy Roman Empire, your Grace's brother, has not despised, but graciously accepted my slight book,[2] dedicated to his electoral Grace, and now published—though such was not my intention—I have taken courage from his gracious example and ventured to think that the princely spirit, like the princely blood, may be the same in both of you, especially in gracious kindness and good will. I have hoped that your princely Grace likewise would not despise this my humble offering which I have felt more need of publishing than any other of my sermons or tracts. For the greatest of all questions has been raised, the question of Good Works, in which is practised immeasurably more trickery and deception than in anything else, and in which the simple-minded man is so easily misled that our Lord Christ has commanded us to watch carefully for the sheep's clothing under which the wolves hide themselves. [Matt. 7:15]

Neither silver, gold, precious stones, nor any rare thing has such manifold alloys and flaws as have good works, which ought to have a single simple goodness, and without it are mere color, show and deceit.

And although I know and daily hear many people, who think slightingly of my poverty, and say that I write only little pamphlets[3] and German sermons for the unlearned laity, this shall not disturb me. Would to God I had in all my life, with all the ability I have, helped one layman to be better! I would be satisfied, thank God, and be quite willing then to let all my little books perish.

Whether the making of many great books is an art and a benefit to the Church, I leave others to judge. But I believe that if I were minded to make great books according to their art, I could, with God's help, do it more readily perhaps than they could prepare a little discourse after my fashion. If accomplishment were as easy as persecution, Christ would long since have been cast out of heaven again, and God's throne itself overturned. Although we cannot all be writers, we all want to be critics.

I will most gladly leave to any one else the honor of greater things, and not be at all ashamed to preach and to write in German for the unlearned laymen. Although I too have little skill in it, I believe that if we had hitherto done, and should henceforth do more of it, Christendom would have reaped no small advantage, and have been more benefited by this than by the great, deep books and quaestiones[4], which are used only in the schools, among the learned.

Then, too, I have never forced or begged any one to hear me, or to read my sermons. I have freely ministered in the Church of that which God has given me and which I owe the Church. Whoever likes it not, may hear and read what others have to say. And if they are not willing to be my debtors, it matters little. For me it is enough, and even more than too much, that some laymen condescend to read what I say. Even though there were nothing else to urge me, it should be more than sufficient that I have learned that your princely Grace is pleased with such German books and is eager to receive instruction in Good Works and the Faith, with which instruction it was my duty, humbly and with all diligence to serve you.

Therefore, in dutiful humility I pray that your princely Grace may accept this offering of mine with a gracious mind, until, if God grant me time, I prepare a German exposition of the Faith in its entirety. For at this time I have wished to show how in all good works we should practice and make use of faith, and let faith be the chief work. If God permit, I will treat at another time of the Faith[5] itself—how we are daily to pray or recite it.

I humbly commend myself herewith to your princely Grace,

Your Princely Grace's

Humble Chaplain,

Dr. Martin Luther.

From Wittenberg, March 39th, A.D. 1520.

THE TREATISE

[Sidenote: Faith and the Commandments]

I. We ought first to know that there are no good works except those which God has commanded, even as there is no sin except that which God has forbidden. Therefore whoever wishes to know and to do good works needs nothing else than to know God's commandments. Thus Christ says, Matthew xix, "If thou wilt enter into life, keep the commandments." [Matt. 19:17] And when the young man asks Him, Matthew xix, what he shall do that he may inherit eternal life, Christ sets before him naught else but the Ten Commandments. [Matt. 19:18 f.] Accordingly, we must learn how to distinguish among good works from the Commandments of God, and not from the appearance, the magnitude, or the number of the works themselves, nor from the judgment of men or of human law or custom, as we see has been done and still is done, because we are blind and despise the divine Commandments.

[Sidenote: Faith the Best Work]

II. The first and highest, the most precious of all good works is faith in Christ, as He says, John vi. When the Jews asked Him: "What shall we do that we may work the works of God?" He answered: "This is the work of God, that ye believe on Him Whom He hath sent." [John 6:28 f.] When we hear or preach this word, we hasten over it and deem it a very little thing and easy to do, whereas we ought here to pause a long time and to ponder it well. For in this work[6] all good works must be done and receive from it the inflow of their goodness, like a loan. This we must put bluntly, that men may understand it.

We find many who pray, fast, establish endowments, do this or that, lead a good life before men, and yet if you should ask them whether they are sure that what they do pleases God, they say, "No"; they do not know, or they doubt. And there are some very learned men, who mislead them, and say that it is not necessary to be sure of this; and yet on the other hand, these same men do nothing else but teach good works. Now all these works are done outside of faith, therefore they are nothing and altogether dead. For as their conscience stands toward God and as it believes, so also are the works which grow out of it. Now they have no faith, no good conscience toward God, therefore the works lack their head, and all their life and goodness is nothing. Hence it comes that when I exalt faith and reject such works done without faith, they accuse me of forbidding good works, when in truth I am trying hard to teach real good works of faith.

[Sidenote: All Works done in Faith are Good]

III. If you ask further, whether they count it also a good work when they work at their trade, walk, stand, eat, drink, sleep, and do all kinds of works for the nourishment of the body or for the common welfare, and whether they believe that God takes pleasure in them because of such works, you will find that they say, "No"; and they define good works so narrowly that they are made to consist only of praying in church, fasting, and almsgiving. Other works they consider to be in vain, and think that God cares nothing for them. So through their damnable unbelief they curtail and lessen the service of God, Who is served by all things whatsoever that are done, spoken or thought in faith.

So teaches Ecclesiastes ix: "Go thy way with joy, eat and drink, and know that God accepteth thy works. Let thy garments be always white; and let thy head lack no ointment. Live joyfully with the wife whom thou lovest all the days of the life of thy vanity." [Eccles. 9:7] "Let thy garments be always white," that is, let all our works be good, whatever they may be, without any distinction. And they are white when I am certain and believe that they please God. Then shall the head of my soul never lack the ointment of a joyful conscience.

So Christ says, John viii: "I do always those things that please Him." [John 8:29] And St. John says, I. John iii: "Hereby we know that we are of the truth, if we can comfort our hearts before Him and have a good confidence. And if our heart condemns or frets us, God is greater than our heart, and we have confidence, that whatsoever we ask, we shall receive of Him, because we keep His Commandments, and do those things that are pleasing in His sight." [1 John 3, 19 ff.] Again: "Whosoever is born of God, that is, whoever believes and trusts God, doth not commit sin, and cannot sin." [1 John 3, 9] Again, Psalm xxxiv: "None of them that trust in Him shall do sin." [Ps. 34:22] And in Psalm ii: "Blessed are all they that put their trust in Him." [Ps. 2:12] If this be true, then all that they do must be good, or the evil that they do must be quickly forgiven. Behold, then, why I exalt faith so greatly, draw all works into it, and reject all works which do not flow from it.

IV. Now every one can note and tell for himself when he does what is good or what is not good; for if he finds his heart confident that it pleases God, the work is good, even if it were so small a thing as picking up a straw. If confidence is absent, or if he doubts, the work is not good, although it should raise all the dead and the man should give himself to be burned. [1 Cor. 13:3] This is the teaching of St. Paul, Romans xiv: "Whatsoever is not done of or in faith is sin." [Rom. 14:23] Faith, as the chief work, and no other work, has given us the name of "believers on Christ." For all other works a heathen, a Jew, a Turk, a sinner, may also do; but to trust firmly that he pleases God, is possible only for a Christian who is enlightened and strengthened by grace.

That these words seem strange, and that some call me a heretic because of them, is due to the fact that men have followed blind reason and heathen ways, have set faith not above, but beside other virtues, and have given it a work of its own, apart from all works of the other virtues; although faith alone makes all other works good, acceptable and worthy, in that it trusts God and does not doubt that for it all things that a man does are well done. Indeed, they have not let faith remain a work, but have made a habitus[7] of it, [John 6:29] as they say, although Scripture gives the name of a good, divine work to no work except to faith alone. Therefore it is no wonder that they have become blind and leaders of the blind. [Matt. 15:14] And this faith brings with it at once love, peace, joy and hope. For God gives His Spirit at once to him who trusts Him, as St. Paul says to the Galatians: "You received the Spirit not became of your good works, but when you believed the Word of God." [Gal. 3:2]

V. In this faith all works become equal, and one is like the other; all distinctions between works fall away, whether they be great, small, short, long, few or many. For the works are acceptable not for their own sake, but because of the faith which alone is, works and lives in each and every work without distinction, however numerous and various they are, just as all the members of the body live, work and have their name from the head, and without the head no member can live, work and have a name.

From which it further follows that a Christian who lives in this faith has no need of a teacher of good works, but whatever he finds to do he does, and all is well done; as Samuel said to Saul: "The Spirit of the Lord will come upon thee, and thou shalt be turned into another man; then do thou as occasion serves thee; for God is with thee." [1 Sam. 10:6] So also we read of St. Anna, Samuel's mother: "When she believed the priest Eli who promised her God's grace, she went home in joy and peace, and from that time no more turned hither and thither," [1 Sam. 1:17 f.] that is, whatever occurred, it was all one to her. St. Paul also says: "Where the Spirit of Christ is, there all is free." [Rom. 8:2] For faith does not permit itself to be bound to any work [1 Cor. 3:17], nor does it allow any work to be taken from it, but, as the First Psalm says "He bringeth forth his fruit in his season," [Ps. 1:3] that is, as as a matter of course.

[Sidenote: An Analogy]

VI. This we may see in a common human example. When a man and a woman love and are pleased with each other, and thoroughly believe in their love, who teaches them how they are to behave, what they are to do, leave undone, say, not say, think? Confidence alone teaches them all this, and more. They make no difference in works: they do the great, the long, the much, as gladly as the small, the short, the little, and vice versa; and that too with joyful, peaceful, confident hearts, and each is a free companion of the other. But where there is a doubt, search is made for what is best; then a distinction of works is imagined whereby a man may win favor; and yet he goes about it with a heavy heart, and great disrelish; he is, as it were, taken captive, more than half in despair, and often makes a fool of himself.

[Sidenote: The First Stage of Faith: Works]

So a Christian who lives in this confidence toward God, knows all things, can do all things, undertakes all things that are to be done, and does everything cheerfully and freely; not that he may gather many merits and good works, but because it is a pleasure for him to please God thereby, and he serves God purely for nothing, content that his service pleases God. On the other hand, he who is not at one with God, or doubts, hunts and worries in what way he may do enough and with many works move God. He runs to St. James of Compostella,[8] to Rome, to Jerusalem, hither and yon, prays St. Bridget's prayer[9] and the rest, fasts on this day and on that, makes confession here, and makes confession there, questions this man and that, and yet finds no peace. He does all this with great effort, despair and disrelish of heart, so that the Scriptures rightly call such works in Hebrew Aven amal [Ps. 90:10], that is, labor and travail. And even then they are not good works, and are all lost. Many have been crazed thereby; their fear has brought them into all manner of misery. Of these it is written, Wisdom of Solomon v: "We have wearied ourselves in the wrong way; and have gone through deserts, where there lay no way; but as for the way of the Lord, we have not known it, and the sun of righteousness rose not upon us." [Wisd. 5:6 f.]

[Sidenote: The Second Stage of Faith: Sufferings]

132

VII. In these works faith is still slight and weak; let us ask further, whether they believe that they are well-pleasing to God when they suffer in body, property, honor, friends, or whatever they have, and believe that God of His mercy appoints their sufferings and difficulties for them, whether they be small or great. This is real strength, to trust in God when to all our senses and reason He appears to be angry; and to have greater confidence in Him than we feel. Here He is hidden, as the bride says in the Song of Songs: "Behold he standeth behind our wall, he looketh forth at the windows" [Song 2:9]; that is, He stands hidden among the sufferings, which would separate us from Him like a wall, yea, like a wall of stone, and yet He looks upon me and does not leave me, for He is standing and is ready graciously to help, and through the window of dim faith He permits Himself to be seen. And Jeremiah says in Lamentations, "He casts casts off men, but He does it not willingly." [Lam. 3:32]

This faith they do not know at all, and give up, thinking that God has forsaken them and is become their enemy; they even lay the blame of their ills on men and devils, and have no confidence at all in God. For this reason, too, their suffering is always an offence and harmful to them, and yet they go and do some good works, as they think, and are not aware of their unbelief. But they who in such suffering trust God and retain a good, firm confidence in Him, and believe that He is pleased with them, these see in their sufferings and afflictions nothing but precious merits and the rarest possessions, the value of which no one can estimate. For faith and confidence make precious before God all that which others think most shameful, so that it is written even of death in Psalm cxvi, "Precious in the sight of the Lord is the death of His saints." [Ps. 116:13] And just as the confident and faith are better, higher and stronger at this stage than in the first stage, so and to the same degree do the sufferings which are borne in this faith excel all works of faith. Therefore between such works and sufferings there is an immeasurable difference and the sufferings are infinitely better.

[Sidenote: The Highest Stage of Faith: Torments of Conscience]

VIII. Beyond all this is the highest stage of faith, when God punishes the conscience not only with temporal sufferings, but with death, hell, and sin, and refuses grace and mercy, as though it were His will to condemn and to be angry eternally. This few men experience, but David cries out in Psalm vi, "O Lord, rebuke me not in Thine anger." [Ps. 6:1] To believe at such times that God, in His mercy, is pleased with us, is the highest work that can be done by and in the creature;[10] but of this the work-righteous and doers of good works know nothing at all. For how could they here look for good things and grace from God, as long as they are not certain in their works, and doubt even on the lowest step of faith.

[Sidenote: The Works Rejected]

In this way I have, as I said, always praised faith, and rejected all works which are done without such faith, in order thereby to lead men from the false, pretentious, Pharisaic, unbelieving good works, with which all monastic houses, churches, homes, low and higher classes are overfilled, and lead them to the true, genuine, thoroughly good, believing works. In this no one opposes me except the unclean beasts, which do not divide the hoof, [Lev. 11:4] as the Law of Moses decrees; who will suffer no distinction among good works, but go lumbering along: if only they pray, fast, establish endowments, go to confession, and do enough, everything shall be good, although in all this they have had no faith in God's grace and approval. Indeed, they consider the works best of all, when they have done many, great and long works without any such confidence, and they look for good only after the works are done; and so they build their confidence not on divine favor, but on the works they have done, that is, on sand and water, from which they must at last take a cruel fall, as Christ says, Matthew vii. [Matt. 7:16] This good-will and favor, on which our confidence rests, was proclaimed by the angels from heaven, when they sang on Christmas night: "Gloria in excel sis Deo, Glory to God in the highest, peace to earth, gracious favor to man." [Luke 2:14][11]

[Sidenote: The First Commandment]

[Sidenote: Its Work is Faith]

IX. Now this is the work of the First Commandment, which commands: "Thou shalt have no other gods," went which means: "Since I alone am God, thou shalt place all thy confidence, trust and faith on Me alone, and on no one have a god, if you call him God only with your lips, or worship him with the knees or bodily gestures; but if you trust Him with the heart, and look to Him for all good, grace and favor, whether in works or sufferings, in life or death, in joy or sorrow; as the Lord Christ says to the heathen woman, John iv: "I say unto thee, they that worship God must worship Him in spirit and in truth." [John 4:24] And this faith, faithfulness, confidence deep in the heart, is the true fulfilling of the First Commandment; without this there is no other work that is able to satisfy this Commandment. And as this Commandment is the very first, highest and best, from which all the others proceed, in which they exist, and by which they are directed and measured, so also its work, that is, the faith or confidence in God's favor at all times, is the very first, highest and best, from which all others must proceed, exist, remain, be directed and measured. Compared with this, other works are just as if the other Commandments were without the First, and there were no God. Therefore St. Augustine well says that the works of the First Commandment are faith, hope and love. As I said above,[12] such faith and confidence bring love and hope with them. Nay, if we see it aright, love is the first, or comes at the same instant with faith. For I could not trust God, if I did not think that He wished to be favorable and to love me, which leads me, in turn, to love Him and to trust Him heartily and to look to Him for all good things.

134

X. Now you see for yourself that all those who do not at at all times trust God and do not in all their works or sufferings, life and death, trust in His favor, grace and good-will, but seek His favor in other things or in themselves, do not keep this Commandment, and practise real idolatry, even if they were to do the works of all the other Commandments, and in addition had all the prayers, fasting, obedience, patience, chastity, and innocence of all the saints combined. For the chief work is not present, without which all the others are nothing but mere sham, show and pretence, with nothing back of them; against which Christ warns us, Matthew vii: "Beware of false prophets, which come to you in sheep's clothing." [Matt. 7:15] Such are all who wish with their many good works, as they say, to make God favorable to themselves, and to buy God's grace from Him, as if He were a huckster or a day-laborer, unwilling to give His grace and favor for nothing. These are the most perverse people on earth, who will hardly or never be converted to the right way. Such too are all who in adversity run hither and thither, and look for counsel and help everywhere except from God, from Whom they are most urgently commanded to seek it; whom the Prophet Isaiah reproves thus, Isaiah ix: "The mad people turneth not to Him that smiteth them" [Isa. 9:13]; that is, God smote them and sent them sufferings and all kinds of adversity, that they should run to Him and trust Him. But they run away from Him to men, now to Egypt, now to Assyria, perchance also to the devil; and of such idolatry much is written in the same Prophet and in the Books of the Kings. This is also the way of all holy hypocrites when they are in trouble: they do not run to God, but flee from Him, and only think of how they may get rid of their trouble through their own efforts or through human help, and yet they consider themselves and let others consider them pious people.

[Sidenote: Faith Must Do all Works]

XI. This is what St. Paul means in many places, where he ascribes so much to faith, that he says: Justus ex fide sua vivit, "the righteous man draws his life out of his faith," [Rom. 1:17] and faith is that because of which he is counted righteous before God. If righteousness consists of faith, it is clear that faith fulfils all commandments and makes all works righteous, since no one is justified except he keep all the commands of God. Again, the works can justify no one before God without faith. So utterly and roundly does the Apostle reject works and praise faith, that some have taken offence at his words and say: "Well, then, we will do no more good works," [Rom. 3:8] although he condemns such men as erring and foolish.

So men still do. When we reject the great, pretentious works of our time, which are done entirely without faith, they say: Men are only to believe and not to do anything good. For nowadays they say that the works of the First Commandment are singing, reading, organ-playing, reading the mass, saying matins and vespers and the other hours, the founding and

135

decorating of churches, altars, and monastic houses, the gathering of bells, jewels, garments, trinkets and treasures, running to Rome and to the saints. Further, when we are dressed up and bow, kneel, pray the rosary and the Psalter, and all this not before an idol, but before the holy cross of God or the pictures of His saints: this we call honoring and worshiping God, and, according to the First Commandment, "having no other gods"; although these things usurers, adulterers and all manner of sinners can do too, and do them daily.

Of course, if these things are done with such faith that we believe that they please God, then they are praiseworthy, not because of their virtue, but because of such faith, for which all works are of equal value, as has been said.[13] But if we doubt or do not believe that God is gracious to us and is pleased with us, or if we presumptuously expect to please Him only through and after our works, then it is all pure deception, outwardly honoring God, but inwardly setting up self as a false god. This is the reason why I have so often spoken against the display, magnificence and multitude of such works and have rejected them, because it is as clear as day that they are not only done in doubt or without faith, but there is not one in a thousand who does not set his confidence upon the works, expecting by them to win God's favor and anticipate His grace; and so they make a fair[14] of them, a thing which God cannot endure, since He has promised His grace freely, and wills that we begin by trusting that grace, and in it perform all works, whatever they may be.

[Sidenote: Works and Faith Contrasted]

XII. Note for yourself, then, how far apart these two are: keeping the First Commandment with outward works only, and keeping it with inward trust. For this last makes true, living children of God, the other only makes worse idolatry and the most mischievous hypocrites on earth, who with their apparent righteousness lead unnumbered people into their way, and yet allow them to be without faith, so that they are miserably misled, and are caught in the pitiable babbling and mummery. Of such Christ says, Matthew xxiv: "Beware, if any man shall say unto you, Lo, here is Christ, or there" [Matt. 24:23]; and John iv: "I say unto thee, the hour Cometh, when ye shall neither in this mountain nor yet at Jerusalem worship God, for the Father seeketh spiritual worshipers." [John 4:21 f.]

These and similar passages have moved me and ought to move everyone to reject the great display of bulls, seals, flags, indulgences, by which the poor folk are led to build churches, to give, to endow, to pray, and yet faith is not mentioned, and is even suppressed. For since faith knows no distinction among works, such exaltation and urging of one work above another cannot exist beside faith. For faith desires to be the only service of God, and will grant this name and honor to no other work, except in so far as faith imparts it, as it does when the work is done in faith and by faith. This perversion is indicated in the Old Testament, when the Jews left the Temple and sacrificed at other places, in the green parks and on the mountains. [Isa. 65:3, 66:17] This is what these men also do: they are zealous to do all works, but this chief work of faith they regard not at all.

XIII. Where now are they who ask, what works are good; what they shall do; how they shall be religious? Yes, and where are they who say that when we preach of faith, we shall neither teach nor do works? Does not this First Commandment give us more work to do than any man can do? If a man were a thousand men, or all men, or all creatures, this Commandment would yet ask enough of him, and more than enough, since he is commanded to live and walk at all times in faith and confidence toward God, to place such faith in no one else, and so to have only one, the true God, and none other.

Now, since the being and nature of man cannot for an instant be without doing or not doing something, enduring or running away from something (for, as we see, life never rests), let him who will be pious and filled with good works, begin and in all his life and works at all times exercise himself in this faith; let him learn to do and to leave undone all things in such continual faith; then will he find how much work he has to do, and how completely all things are included in faith; how he dare never grow idle, because his very idling must be the exercise and work of faith. In brief, nothing can be in or about us and nothing can happen to us but that it must be good and meritorious, if we believe (as we ought) that all things please God. So says St. Paul: "Dear brethren, all that ye do, whether ye eat or drink, do all in the Name of Jesus Christ, our Lord." [1 Cor. 10:31] Now it cannot be done in this Name except it be done in this faith. Likewise, Romans viii: "We know that all things work together for good to the saints of God." [Rom. 8:26]

Therefore, when some say that good works are forbidden when we preach faith alone, it is as if I said to a sick man: "If you had health, you would have the use of all your limbs; but without health, the works of all your limbs are nothing"; and he wanted to infer that I had forbidden the works of all his limbs; whereas, on the contrary, I meant that he must first have health, which will work all the works of all the members. So faith also must be in all works the master-workman and captain, or they are nothing at all.

[Sidenote: Why Laws are Given]

XIV. You might say: "Why then do we have so many laws of the Church and of the State, and many ceremonies of churches, monastic houses, holy places, which urge and tempt men to good works, if faith does all things through the First Commandment?" I answer; Simply because we do not all have faith or do not heed it. If every man had faith, we would need no more laws, but every one would of himself at all times do good works, as his confidence in God teaches him.

But now there are four kinds of men: the first, just mentioned, who need no law, of whom St. Paul says, I. Timothy "The law is not made for a righteous man," [1 Tim. 1:9] that is, for the believer, but believers of themselves do what they know and can do, only because they finally trust that God's favor and grace rests upon them in all things. The second class want to abuse this freedom, put a false confidence in it, and grow lazy; of whom St. Peter says, I. Peter ii, "Ye shall live as free men, but not using your liberty for a cloak of maliciousness," [1 Pet. 2:16] as if he said: The freedom of faith does not permit sins, nor will it cover them, but it sets us free to do all manner of good works and to endure all things as they happen to us, so that a man is not bound only to one work or to a few. So also St. Paul, Galatians v: "Use not your liberty for an occasion to the flesh." [Gal. 5:13] Such men must be urged by laws and hemmed in by teaching and exhortation. The third class are wicked men, always ready for sins; these must be constrained by spiritual and temporal laws, like wild horses and dogs, and where this does not help, they must be put to death by the worldly sword, as St. Paul says, Romans xiii: "The worldly ruler bears the sword, and serves God with it, not as a terror to the good, but to the evil." [Rom. 13:3 f.] The fourth class, who are still lusty, and childish in their understanding of faith and of the spiritual life, must be coaxed like young children and tempted with external, definite and prescribed decorations, with reading, praying, fasting, singing, adorning of churches, organ-playing, and such other things as are commanded and observed in monastic houses and churches, until they also learn to know the faith. Although there is great danger here, when the rulers, as is now, alas! the case, busy themselves with and insist upon such ceremonies and external works as if they were the true works, and neglect faith, which they ought always to teach along with these works, just as a mother gives her child other food along with the milk, until the child can eat the strong food by itself.

[Sidenote: Charity Endures Unnecessary Works]

XV. Since, then, we are not all alike, we must tolerate such people, share their observances and burdens, and not despise them, but teach them the true way of faith. So St. Paul teaches, Romans xiv: "Him that is weak in the faith receive ye, to teach him." [Rom. 14:1] And so he did himself, I. Corinthians ix: "To them that are under the law, I became as under the law, although I was not under the law." [1 Cor. 9:20] And Christ, Matthew xvii, when He was asked to pay tribute, which He was not obligated to pay, argues with St. Peter, whether the children of kings must give tribute, or only other people. St. Peter answers; "Only other people." Christ said: "Then are the children of kings free; notwithstanding, lest we should offend them, go thou to the sea, and cast an hook, and take up the fish that first Cometh up; and in his mouth thou shalt find apiece of money; take that and give it for me and thee." [Matt. 17:25]

Here we see that all works and things are free to a Christian through his faith; and yet, because the others do not yet believe, he observes and bears with them what he is not obligated to do. But this he does freely, for he is certain that this is pleasing to God, and he does it willingly, accepts it as any other free work which comes to his hand without his choice, because he desires and seeks no more than that he may in his faith do works to please God.[15]

But since in this discourse we have undertaken to teach what righteous and good works are, and are now speaking of the highest work, it is clear that we do not speak of the second, third and fourth classes of men, but of the first, into whose likeness all the others are to grow, and until they do so the first class must endure and instruct them. Therefore we must not despise, as if they were hopeless, these men of weak faith, who would gladly do right and learn, and yet cannot understand because of the ceremonies to which they cling; we must rather blame their ignorant, blind teachers, who have never taught them the faith, and have led them so deeply into works. They must be gently and gradually led back again to faith, as a sick man is treated, and must be allowed for a time, for their conscience sake, to cling to some works and do them as necessary to salvation, so long as they rightly grasp the faith; lest if we try to tear them out so suddenly, their weak consciences be quite shattered and confused, and retain neither faith nor works. But the hardheaded, who, hardened in their works, have no heed to what is said of faith, and fight against it, these we must, as Christ did and taught, let go their way, that the blind may lead the blind.

[Sidenote: The Contradiction of Faith and Daily Sins]

XVI. But you say: How can I trust surely that all my works are pleasing to God, when at times I fall, and talk, eat, drink and sleep too much, or otherwise transgress, as I cannot help doing? Answer: This question shows that you still regard faith as a work among other works, and do not set it above all works. For it is the highest work for this very reason, because it remains and blots out these daily sins by not doubting that God is so kind to you as to wink at such daily transgression and weakness. Aye, even if a deadly sin should occur (which, however, never or rarely happens to those who live in faith and trust toward God), yet faith rises again and does not doubt that Sin is already gone; as it is written I. John ii: "My little children, these things I write unto you, that ye sin not. And if any man sin, we have an Advocate with God the Father, Jesus Christ, Who is the propitiation of all our sins." [1 John 2:1] And Wisdom xv: "For if we sin, we are Thine, knowing Thy power." [Wis. 15:2] And Proverbs xxiv: "For a just man falleth seven times, and riseth up again." [Prov. 24:16] Yes, this confidence and faith must be so high and strong that the man knows that all his life and works are nothing but damnable sins before God's judgment, as it is written, Psalm cxliii: "In thy sight no man living be justified" [Ps. 143:2]; and he must entirely despair of his works, believing that they cannot be good except through this faith, which looks for no judgment, but only for pure grace, favor, kindness and mercy, like David, Psalm xxvi: "Thy loving kindness is ever before mine eyes, and I have trusted in Thy truth" [Ps. 26:3]; Psalm iv: "The light of Thy countenance is lift up upon us (that is, the knowledge of Thy grace through faith), and thereby hast Thou put gladness in my heart" [Ps. 4:7]; for as faith trusts, so it receives.

See, thus are works forgiven, are without guilt and are good, not by their own nature, but by the mercy and grace of God because of the faith which trusts on the mercy of God. Therefore we must fear because of the works, but comfort ourselves because of the grace of God, as it is written, Psalm cxlvii: "The Lord taketh pleasure in them that fear Him, in those that hope in His mercy." [Ps. 147:11] So we pray with perfect confidence: "Our Father," and yet petition: "Forgive us our trespasses"; we are children and yet sinners; are acceptable and yet do not do enough; and all this is the work of faith, firmly grounded in God's grace.

[Sidenote: The Source of Faith]

XVII. But if you ask, where the faith and the confidence can be found and whence they come, this it is certainly most necessary to know. First: Without doubt faith does not come from your works or merit, but alone from Jesus Christ, and is freely promised and given; as St. Paid writes, Romans v: "God commendeth His love to us as exceeding sweet and kindly, in that, while we were yet sinners, Christ died for us" [Rom. 5:8]; as if he said: "Ought not this give us a strong unconquerable confidence, that before we prayed or cared for it, yes, while we still continually walked in sins, Christ dies for our sin?" St. Paul concludes; "If while we were yet sinners Christ died for us, how much more then, being justified by His blood, shall we be saved from wrath through Him; and if, when we were enemies, we were reconciled to God by the death of His Son, much more, being reconciled, shall we be saved by His life."

Lo! thus must thou form Christ within thyself and see how in Him God holds before thee and offers thee His mercy without any previous merits of thine own, and from such a view of His grace must thou draw faith and confidence of the forgiveness of all thy sins. Faith, therefore, does not begin with works, neither do they create it, but it must spring up and flow from the blood, wounds and death of Christ, if thou see in these that God is so kindly affectioned toward thee that He gives even His Son for thee, then thy heart also must in its turn grow sweet and kindly affectioned toward God, and so thy confidence must grow out of pure good-will and love—God's love toward thee and thine toward God. We never read that the Holy Spirit was given to any one when he did works, but always what men have heard the Gospel of Christ and the mercy of God. From this same Word and from no other source must faith still come, even in our day and always. For Christ is the rock out of which men suck oil and honey, as Moses says, Deuteronomy xxxii. [Deut. 32:13]

[Sidenote: The Second Commandment]

140

XVII. So far we have treated of the first work and of the First Commandment, but very briefly, plainly and hastily, for very much might be said of it. We will now trace the works farther through the following Commandments.

[Sidenote: The Second Commandment]

The second work, next to faith, is the work of the Second Commandment, that we shall honor God's Name and not take it in vain. This, like all the other works, cannot be done without faith; and if it is done without faith, it is all sham and show. After faith we can do no greater work than to praise, preach, sing and in every way exalt and magnify God's glory, honor and Name.

And although I have said above,[16] and it is true, that there is no difference in works where faith is and does the work, yet this is true only when they are compared with faith and its works. Measured by one another there is a difference, and one is higher than the other. Just as in the body the members do not differ when compared with health, and health works in the one as much as in the other; yet the works of the members are different, and one is higher, nobler, more useful than the other [Rom. 12:4, 1 Cor. 12]; so, here also, to praise God's glory and Name is better than the works of the other Commandments which follow; and yet it must be done in the same faith as all the others.

But I know well that this work is lightly esteemed, and has indeed become unknown. Therefore we must examine it further, and will say no more about the necessity of doing it in the faith and confidence that it pleases God. Indeed there is no work in which confidence and faith are so much experienced and felt as in honoring God's Name; and it greatly helps to strengthen and increase faith, although all works also help to do this, as St. Peter says, II. Peter i: "Wherefore the rather, brethren, give diligence through good works to make your calling and election sure."

[Sidenote: Its Positive Works]

XIX. The First Commandment forbids us to have other gods, and thereby commands that we have a God, the true God, by a firm faith, trust, confidence, hope and love, which are the only works whereby a man can have, honor and keep a God; for by no other work can one find or lose God except by faith or unbelief, by trusting or doubting; of the other works none reaches quite to God. So also in the Second Commandment we are forbidden to use His Name in vain. Yet this is not to be enough, but we are thereby also commanded to honor, call upon, glorify, preach and praise His Name. And indeed it is impossible that God's Name should not be dishonored where it is not rightly honored. For although it be honored with the lips, bending of the knees, kissing and other postures, if this is not done in the heart by faith, in confident trust in God's grace, it is nothing else than an evidence and badge of hypocrisy.

See now, how many kinds of good works a man can do under this Commandment at all times and never be without the good works of this Commandment, if he will; so that he truly need not make a long pilgrimage or seek holy places. For, tell me, what moment can pass in which we do not without ceasing receive God's blessings, or, on the other hand, suffer adversity? But what else are God's blessings and adversities than a constant urging and stirring up to praise, honor, and bless God, and to call upon His Name? Now if you had nothing else at all to do, would you not have enough to do with this Commandment alone, that you without ceasing bless, sing, praise and honor God's Name? And for what other purpose have tongue, voice, language and mouth been created? As Psalm li. says: "Lord, open Thou my lips, and my mouth shall show forth Thy praise." [Ps. 51:15] Again: "My tongue shall sing aloud of Thy mercy." [Ps. 51:14]

What work is there in heaven except that of this Second Commandment? As it is written in Psalm lxxxiv: "Blessed are they that dwell in Thy house: they will be for ever praising Thee." [Ps. 84:4] So also David says in Psalm xxxiv: "God's praise shall be continually in my mouth." [Ps. 34:1] And St. Paul, I. Corinthians x: "Whether therefore ye eat or drink, or whatsoever ye do, do all to the glory of God." [1 Cor. 10:31] Also Colossians iii: "Whatsoever ye do in word or deed, do all in the Name of the Lord Jesus, giving thanks to God and the Father." [Col. 3:17] If we were to observe this work, we would have a heaven here on earth and always have enough to do, as have the saints in heaven.

[Sidenote: The Praise of God]

XX. On this is based the wonderful and righteous judgment of God, that at times a poor man, in whom no one can see many great works, in the privacy of his home joyfully praises God when he fares well, or with entire confidence calls upon Him when he fares ill, and thereby does a greater and more acceptable work than another, who fasts much, prays much, endows churches, makes pilgrimages, and burdens himself with great deeds in this place and in that. Such a fool opens wide his mouth, looks for great works to do, and is so blinded that he does not at all notice this greatest work, and praising God is in his eyes a very small matter compared with the great idea he has formed of the works of his own devising, in which he perhaps praises himself more than God, or takes more pleasure in them than he does in God; and thus with his good works he storms against the Second Commandment and its works. Of all this we have an illustration in the case of the Pharisee and the Publican in the Gospel. [Luke 18:10 f.] For the sinner calls upon God in his sins, and praises Him, and so has hit upon the two highest Commandments, faith and God's honor. The hypocrite misses both and struts about with other good works by which he praises himself and not God, and puts his trust in himself more than in God. Therefore he is justly rejected and the other chosen.

The reason of all this is that the higher and better the works are, the less show they make; and that every one thinks they are easy, because it is evident that no one pretends to praise God's Name and honor so much as the very men who never do it and with their show of doing it, while the heart is without faith, cause the precious work to be despised. So that the Apostle St. Paul dare say boldly, Romans ii, that they blaspheme God's Name who make their boast of God's Law. [Rom. 2:23] For to name the Name of God and to write His honor on paper and on the walls is an easy matter; but genuinely to praise and bless Him in His good deeds and confidently to call upon Him in all adversities, these are truly the most rare, highest works, next to faith, so that if we were to see how few of them there are in Christendom, we might despair for very sorrow. And yet there is a constant increase of high, pretty, shining works of men's devising, or of works which look like these true works, but at bottom are all without faith and without faithfulness; in short, there is nothing good back of them. Thus also Isaiah xlviii. rebukes the people of Israel: "Hear ye this, ye which are called by the name of Israel, which swear by the Name of the Lord, and make mention of the God of Israel neither in truth, nor in righteousness" [Is. 48:1]; that is, they did it not in the true faith and confidence, which is the real truth and righteousness, but trusted in themselves, their works and powers, and yet called upon God's Name and praised Him, two things which do not fit together.

XXI. The first work of this Commandment then is, to praise God in all His benefits, which are innumerable, so that such praise and thanksgiving ought also of right never to cease or end. For who can praise Him perfectly for the gift of natural life, not to mention all other temporal and eternal blessings? And so through this one part of the Commandment man is overwhelmed with good and precious works; if he do these in true faith, he has indeed not lived in vain. And in this matter none sin so much as the most resplendent saints, who are pleased with themselves and like to praise themselves or to hear themselves praised, honored and glorified before men.

[Sidenote: Avoiding the Praise of Self]

Therefore the second work of this Commandment is, to be on one's guard, to flee from and to avoid all temporal honor and praise, and never to seek a name for oneself, or fame and a great reputation, that every one sing of him and tell of him; which is an exceedingly dangerous sin, and yet the most common of all, and, alas! little regarded. Every one wants to be of importance and not to be the least, however small he may be; so deeply is nature sunk in the evil of its own conceit and in its self-confidence contrary to these two first Commandments.

Now the world regards this terrible vice as the highest virtue, and this makes it exceedingly dangerous for those who do not understand and have not had experience of God's Commandments and the histories of the Holy Scriptures, to read or hear the heathen books and histories. For all heathen books are poisoned through and through with this striving after praise and honor; in them men are taught by blind reason that they were not nor could be men of power and worth, who are not moved by praise and honor; but those are counted the best, who disregard body and life, friend and property and everything in the effort to win praise and honor. All the holy Fathers have complained of this vice and with one mind conclude that it is the very last vice to be overcome, St, Augustine says: "All other vices are practised in evil works; only honor and self-satisfaction are practised in and by means of good works."

Therefore if a man had nothing else to do except this second work of this Commandment, he would yet have to work all his life-time in order to fight this vice and drive it out, so common, so subtle, so quick and insidious is it. Now we all pass by this good work and exercise ourselves in many other lesser good works, nay, through other good works we overthrow this and forget it entirely. So the holy Name of God, which alone should be honored, is taken in vain and dishonored through our own cursed name, self-approval and honor-seeking. And this sin is more grievous before God than murder and adultery; but its wickedness is not so clearly seen as that of murder, because of its subtilty, for it is not accomplished in the coarse flesh, but in the spirit.

[Sidenote: The Seeking of Honor as a Motive for Good]

XXII. Some think it is good for young people that they be enticed by reputation and honor, and again by shame and dishonor, and so be induced to do good. For there are many who do the good and leave the evil undone out of fear of shame and love of honor, and so do what they would otherwise by no means do or leave undone. These I leave to their opinion. But at present we are seeking how true good works are to be done, and they who are inclined to do them surely do not need to be driven by the fear of shame and the love of honor; they have, and are to have a higher and far nobler incentive, namely, God's commandment, God's fear, God's approval, and their faith and love toward God. They who have not, or regard not this motive, and let shame and honor drive them, these also have their reward, [Matt. 6:2] as the Lord says, Matthew vi; and as the motive, so is also the work and the reward: none of them is good, except only in the eyes of the world.

Now I hold that a young person could be more easily trained and incited by God's fear and commandments than by any other means. Yet where these do not help, we must ensure that they do the good and leave the evil for the sake of shame and of honor, just as we must also endure wicked men or the imperfect, of whom we spoke above; nor can we do more than tell them that their works are not satisfactory and right before God, and so leave them until they learn to do right for the sake of God's commandments also. Just as young children are induced to pray, fast, learn, etc., by gifts and promises of the parents, even though it would not be good to treat them so all their lives, so that they never learn to do good in the fear of God: far worse, if they become accustomed to do good for the sake of praise and honor.

[Sidenote: The Need and the Danger of a Good Name]

XXIII. But this is true, that we must none the less have a good name and honor, and every one ought so to live that nothing evil can be said of him, and that he give offence to no one, as St. Paul says, Romans xii: "We are to be zealous to do good, not only before God, but also before all men." [Rom. 12:17] And II. Corinthians iv: "We walk so honestly that no man knows anything against us." [2 Cor. 4:2] But there must be great diligence and care, lest such honor and good name puff up the heart, and the heart find pleasure in them. Here the saying of Solomon holds: "As the fire in the furnace proveth the gold, so man is proved by the mouth of him that praises him." [Prov. 27:21] Few and most spiritual men must they be, who, when honored and praised, remain indifferent and unchanged, so that they do not care for it, nor feel pride and pleasure in it, but remain entirely free, ascribe all their honor and fame to God, offering it to Him alone, and using it only to the glory of God, to the edification of their neighbors, and in no way to their own benefit or advantage; so that a man trust not in his own honor, nor exalt himself above the most incapable, demised man on earth, but acknowledge himself a servant of God, Who has given him the honor in order that with it he may serve God and his neighbor, just as if He had commanded him to distribute some gulden[17] to the poor for His sake. So He says, Matthew v: "Your light shall shine before men, so that they may see your good works and glorify your Father Who is in heaven." [Matt. 5:16] He does not say, "they shall praise you," but "your works shall only serve them to edification, that through them they may praise God in you and in themselves." This is the correct use of God's Name and honor, when God is thereby praised through the edification of others. And if men want to praise us and not God in us, we are not to endure it, but with all our powers forbid it and flee from it as from the most grievous sin and robbery of divine honor.

[Sidenote: The Profitableness of Dishonor]

XXIV. Hence it comes that God frequently permits a man to fall into or remain in grievous sin, in order that he may be put to shame in his own eyes and in the eyes of all men, who otherwise could not have kept himself from this great vice of vain honor and fame, if he had remained constant in his great gifts and virtues; so God must ward off this sin by means of other grievous sins, that His Name alone may be honored; and thus one sin becomes the other's medicine, because of our perverse wickedness, which not only does the evil, but also misuses all that is good.

Now see how much a man has to do, if he would do good works, which always are at hand in great number, and with which he is surrounded on all sides; but, alas! because of his

145

blindness, he passes them by and seeks and runs after others of his own devising and pleasure, against which no man can sufficiently speak and no man can sufficiently guard. With this all the prophets had to contend, and for this reason they were all slain, only because they rejected such self-devised works and preached only God's commandments, as one of them says, Jeremiah vii: "Thus saith the God of Israel unto you: Take your burnt-offerings unto all your sacrifices and eat your burnt-offerings and you yourselves; for concerning these things I have commanded nothing, but this thing commanded I you: Obey My voice (that is, not what seems right and good to you, but what I bid you), and walk in the way that I have commanded you." [Jer. 7:21] And Deuteronomy xii: "Thou shalt not do whatsoever is right in thine own eyes, but what thy God has commanded thee." [Deut 12:8, 32]

These and numberless like passages of Scripture are spoken to tear man not only from sins, but also from the works which seem to men to be good and right, and to turn men, with a single mind, to the simple meaning of God's commandment only, that they shall diligently observe this only and always, as it is written, Exodus xiii: "These commandments shall be for a sign unto thee upon thine hand, and for a memorial between thine eyes." [Ex. 13:9] And Psalm i: "A godly man meditates in God's Law day and night." [Ps. 1:2] For we have more than enough and too much to do, if we are to satisfy only God's commandments. He has given us such commandments that if we understand them aright, we dare not for a moment be idle, and might easily forget all other works. But the evil spirit, who never rests, when he cannot lead us to the left into evil works, fights on our right through self-devised works that seem good, but against which God has commanded, Deuteronomy xxviii, and Joshua xxiii, "Ye shall not go aside from My commandments to the right hand or to the left." [Deut 28:14, Josh. 23:6]

[Sidenote: Calling on God's Name]

XXV. The third work of this Commandment is to call upon God's Name in every need. For this God regards as keeping His Name holy and greatly honoring it, if we name and call upon it in adversity and need. And this is really why He sends us so much trouble, suffering, adversity and even death, and lets us live in many wicked, sinful affections, that He may thereby urge man and give him much reason to run to Him, to cry aloud to Him, to call upon His holy Name, and thus to fulfil this work of the Second Commandment, as He says in Psalm l: "Call upon Me in the day of trouble; I will deliver you and thou shalt glorify Me; for I desire the sacrifice of praise." [Ps. 50:15] And this is the way whereby thou canst come unto salvation; for through such works man perceives and learns what God's Name is, how powerful it is to help all who call upon it; and Thereby confidence and faith grow mightily, and these are the fulfilling of the first and highest Commandment. This is the experience of David, Psalm liv: "Thou hast delivered me out of all trouble, therefore will I praise Thy Name and confess that it is lovely and sweet." [Ps. 54:7] And Psalm xci says, "Because he hath set his hope upon Me, therefore will I deliver him: I will help him, because he hath known My Name." [Ps. 91:14]

Lo! what man is there on earth, who would not all his life long have enough to do with this work? For who lives an hour without trials? I will not mention the trials of adversity, which are innumerable. For this is the most in dangerous trial of all, when there is no trial and everything is and goes well; for then a man is tempted to forget God, to become too bold and to misuse the times of prosperity. Yea, here he has ten times more need to call upon God's Name than when in adversity. Since it is written, Psalm xci, "A thousand shall fail on the left hand and ten thousand on the right hand." [Ps. 91:7]

So too we see in broad day, in all men's daily experience, that more heinous sins and vice occur when there is peace, when all things are cheap and there are good times, than when war, pestilence, sicknesses and all manner of misfortune burden us; so that Moses also fears for his people, lest they forsake God's commandment for no other reason than because they are too full, too well provided for and have too much peace, as he says, Deuteronomy xxxii: "My people is waxed rich, full and fat; therefore has it forsaken its God." [Deut. 32:15] Wherefore also God let many of its enemies remain and would not drive them out, in order that they should not have peace and must exercise themselves in the keeping of God's commandments, as it is written, Judges iii [Judges 3:1 ff.]. So He deals with us also, when sends us all kinds of misfortune: so exceedingly careful is He of us, that He may teach us and drive us to honor and call upon His Name, to gain confidence and faith toward Him, and so to fulfil the first two Commandments.

[Sidenote: The Error of Calling on Other Names]

XXVI. Here foolish men run into danger, and especially the work-righteous saints, and those who want to be more than others; they teach men to make the sign of the cross; one arms himself with letters, another runs to the fortune-tellers; one seeks this, another that, if only they may thereby escape misfortune and be secure. It is beyond telling what a devilish allurement attaches to this trifling with sorcery, conjuring and superstition, all of which is done only that men may not need God's Name and put no trust in it. Here great dishonor is done the Name of God and the first two Commandments, in that men look to the devil, men or creatures for that which should be sought and found in God alone, through naught but a pure faith and confidence, and a cheerful meditation of and calling upon His holy Name.

Now examine this closely for yourself and see whether this is not a gross, mad perversion: the devil, men and creatures they must believe, and trust to them for the best; without such faith and confidence nothing holds or helps. How shall the good and faithful God reward us for not believing and trusting Him as much or more than man and the devil, although

147

He not only promises help and sure assistance, but also commands us confidently to look for it, and gives and urges all manner of reasons why we should place such faith and confidence in Him? Is it not lamentable and pitiable that the devil or man, who commands nothing and does not urge, but only promises, is set above God, Who promises, urges and commands; and that more is thought of them than of God Himself? We ought truly to be ashamed of ourselves and learn from the example of those who trust the devil or men. For if the devil, who is a wicked, lying spirit, keeps faith with all those who ally themselves with him, how much more will not the most gracious, all-truthful God keep faith, if a man trusts Him? Nay, is it not rather He alone Who will keep faith? A rich man trusts and relies upon his money and possessions, and they help him; and we are not willing to trust and rely upon the living God, that He is willing and able to help us? We say: Gold makes bold; and it is true, as Baruch iii. says, "Gold is a thing wherein men trust." [Bar. 3:17] But far greater is the courage which the highest eternal Good gives, wherein trust, not men, but only God's children.

[Sidenote: Motives for Calling on God's Name]

XXVII. Even if none of these adversities constrain us to call upon God's Name and to trust Him, yet were an alone more than sufficient to train and to urge us on in this work. For sin has hemmed us in with three strong, mighty armies. The first is our own flesh, the second the world, the third the evil spirit, by which three we are without ceasing oppressed and troubled; whereby God gives us occasion to do good works without ceasing, namely, to fight with these enemies and sins. The flesh seeks pleasure and peace, the world seeks riches, favor, power and honor, the evil spirit seeks pride, glory, that a man be well thought of, and other men be despised.

And these three are all so powerful that each one of them is alone sufficient to fight a man, and yet there is no way we can overcome them, except only by calling upon the holy Name of God in a firm faith, as Solomon says, Proverbs xviii: "The Name of the Lord is a strong tower; the righteous runneth into it, and is set aloft." [Prov. 18:10] And David, Psalm cxvi: "I will drink the cup of salvation, and call upon the Name of the Lord." [Ps. 116:13] Again, Psalm xviii: "I will call upon the Lord with praise: so shall I be saved from all mine enemies." [Ps. 18:3] These works and the power of God's Name have become unknown to us, because we are not accustomed to it, and have never seriously fought with sins, and have not needed His Name, because we are trained only in our self-devised works, which we were able to do with our own powers.

[Sidenote: Other Works of the Second Commandment]

XXVIII. Further works of this Commandment are: that we shall not swear, curse, lie, deceive and conjure with the holy Name of God, and otherwise misuse it; which are very simple matters and well known to every one, being the sins which have been almost exclusively preached and proclaimed under this Commandment. These also include, that we shall prevent others from making sinful use of God's Name by lying, swearing, deceiving, cursing, conjuring, and otherwise. Herein again much occasion is given for doing good and warding off evil.

[Sidenote: The Greatest Work of the Second Commandment:

Preaching]

But the greatest and most difficult work of this Commandment is to protect the holy Name of God against all who misuse it in a spiritual manner, and to proclaim it to all men. For it is not enough that I, for myself and in myself, praise and call upon God's Name in prosperity and adversity. I must step forth and for the sake of God's honor and Name bring upon myself the enmity of all men, as Christ said to His disciples: "Ye shall be hated of all men for My Name's sake." Here we must provoke to anger father, mother, and the best of friends. Here we most strive against spiritual and temporal powers, and be accused of disobedience. Here we must stir up against us the rich, learned, holy, and all that is of repute in the world. And although this is especially the duty of those who are commanded to preach God's Word, yet every Christian is also obligated to do so when time and place demand. For we must for the holy Name of God risk and give up all that we have and can do, and show by our deeds that we love God and His Name, His honor and His praise above all things, and trust Him above all things, and expect good from Him; thereby confessing that we regard Him as the highest good, for the sake of which we let go and give up all other goods.

[Sidenote: Against Wrong]

XXIX. Here we must first of all resist all wrong, where truth or righteousness suffers violence or need, and dare make no distinction of persons, as some do, who fight most actively and busily against the wrong which is done to the rich, the powerful, and their own friends; but when it is done to the poor, or the demised or their own enemy, they are quiet and patient. These see the Name and the honor of God not as it is, but through a painted glass, and measure truth or righteousness according to the persons, and do not consider their deceiving eye, which looks more on the person than on the thing. These are hypocrites within and have only the appearance of defending the truth. For they well know that there is no danger when one helps the rich, the powerful, the learned and one's own friends, and can in turn enjoy their protection and be honored by them.

Thus it is very easy to fight against the wrong which is done to popes, kings, princes, bishops and other big-wigs.[18] Here each wants to be the most pious, where there is no great need. O how sly is here the deceitful Adam with his demand; how finely does he cover his greed of profit with the name of truth and righteousness and God's honor! But when something happens to a poor and insignificant man, there the deceitful eye does not find much profit, but cannot help seeing the disfavor of the powerful; therefore he lets the poor man remain unhelped. And who could tell the extent of this vice in Christendom? God says in the lxxxii. Psalm, "How long will ye judge unjustly, and accept the persons of the wicked? Judge the matter of the poor and fatherless, demand justice for the poor and needy; deliver the poor and rid the forsaken out of the hand of the wicked." [Ps. 82:2 ff.] But it is not done, and therefore the text continues: "They know not, neither will they understand; they walk on in darkness"; [Ps. 82:5] that is, the truth they do not see, but they stop at the reputation of the great, however unrighteous they are; and do not consider the poor, however righteous they are.

[Sidenote: The Sin of Silence]

XXX. See, here would be many good works. For the greater portion of the powerful, rich and friends do injustice and oppress the poor, the lowly, and their own opponents; and the greater the men, the worse the deeds; and where we cannot by force prevent it and help the truth, we should at least confess it, and do what we can with words, not take the part of the unrighteous, not approve them, but speak the truth boldly.

What would it help a man if he did all manner of good, made pilgrimages to Rome and to all holy places, acquired all indulgences, built all churches and endowed houses, if he were found guilty of sin against the Name and honor of God, not speaking of them and neglecting them, and regarding his possessions, honor, favor and friends more than the truth (which is God's Name and honor)? Or who is he, before whose door and into whose house such good works do not daily come, so that he would have no need to travel far or to ask after good works? And if we consider the life of men, how in every place men act so very rashly and lightly in this respect, we must cry out with the prophet, Omnis homo mendax, "All men are liars, lie and deceive" [Ps. 116:11]; for the real good works they neglect, and adorn and paint themselves with the most insignificant, and want to be pious, to mount to heaven in peaceful security.

But if you should say: "Why does not God do it alone and Himself, since He can and knows how to help each one?" Yes, He can do it; but He does not want to do it alone; He wants us to work with Him, and does us the honor to want to work His work with us and through us. And if we are not willing to accept such honor, He will, after all, perform the work alone, and help the poor; and those who were unwilling to help Him and have despised the great honor of doing His work, He will condemn with the unrighteous, because they have made common cause with the unrighteous. Just as He alone is blessed, but He wants to do us the honor and not be alone in His blessedness, but have us to be blessed with Him. And if He were to do it alone, His Commandments would be given us in vain, because no one would have occasion to exercise himself in the great works of these

Commandments, and no one would test himself to see whether he regards God and His Name as the highest good, and for His sake risks everything.

[Sidenote: Against Spiritual Wickedness]

XXXI. It also belongs to this work to resist all false, seductive, erroneous, heretical doctrines, every misuse of spiritual power. Now this is much higher, for these use the holy Name of God itself to fight against the Name of God. For this reason it seems a great thing and a dangerous to resist them, because they assert that he who resists them resists God and all His saints, in whose place they sit and whose power they use, saying that Christ said of them, "He that heareth you, heareth Me, and he that despiseth you, despiseth Me." [Luke 10:6] On which words they lean heavily, become insolent and bold to say, to do, and to leave undone what they please; put to the ban, accurse, rob, murder, and practise all their wickedness, in whatever way they please and can invent, without any hindrance.

Now Christ did not mean that we should listen to them in everything they might say and do, but only then when they present to us His Word, the Gospel, not their word, His work, and not their work. How else could we know whether their lies and sins were to be avoided? There must be some rule, to what extent we are to hear and to follow them, and this rule cannot be given by them, but must be established by God over them, that it may serve us as a guide, as we shall hear in the Fourth Commandment.

It must be, indeed, that even in the spiritual estate the greater part preach false doctrine and misuse spiritual power, so that thus occasion may be given us to do the works of this Commandment, and that we be tried, to see what we are willing to do and to leave undone against such blasphemers for the sake of God's honor.

Oh, if we were God-fearing in this matter, how often would the knaves of officiales[19] have to decree their papal and episcopal ban in vain! How weak the Roman thunderbolts would become! How often would many a one have to hold his tongue, to whom the world must now give ear! How few preachers would be found in Christendom! But it has gotten the upper hand: whatever they assert and in whatever way, that must be right. Here no one fights for God's Name and honor, and I hold that no greater or more frequent sin is done in external works than under this head. It is a matter so high that few understand it, and, besides, adorned with God's Name and power, dangerous to touch. But the prophets of old were masters in this; also the apostles, especially St. Paul, who did not allow it to trouble them whether the highest or the lowest priest had said it, or had done it in God's Name or in his own. They looked on the works and words, and held them up to God's Commandment, no matter whether big John or little Nick said it, or whether they had done it in God's Name or in man's. And for this they had to die, and of such dying there would be much more to say in our time, for things are much worse now. But Christ and St. Peter and Paul must cover all this with their holy names, so that no more infamous cover for infamy has been found on earth than the most holy and most blessed Name of Jesus Christ!

One might shudder to be alive, simply because of the misuse and blasphemy of the holy Name of God; through which, if it shall last much longer, we will, as I fear, openly worship the devil as a god; so completely do the spiritual authorities and the learned lack all understanding in these things. It is high time that we pray God earnestly that He hallow His Name. But it will cost blood, and they who enjoy the inheritance of the holy martyrs and are won with their blood, must again make martyrs. Of this more another time.[20]

[Sidenote: The Third Commandment]

I.[21] We have now seen how many good works there are in the Second Commandment, which however are not good in themselves, unless they are done in faith and in the assurance of divine favor; and how much we must do, if we take heed to this Commandment alone, and how we, alas! busy ourselves much with other works, which have no agreement at all with it. Now follows the Third Commandment: "Thou shalt hallow the day of rest." [22] In the First Commandment is prescribed our heart's attitude toward God in thoughts, in the Second, that of our mouth in words, in this Third is prescribed our attitude toward God in works; and it is the first and right table of Moses, on which these three Commandments are written, and they govern man on the right side, namely, in the things which concern God, and in which God has to do with man and man with God, without the mediation of any creature.

[Sidenote: Worship]

The first works of this Commandment are plain and outward, which we commonly call worship,[23] such as going to mass, praying, and hearing a sermon on holy days. So understood there are very few works in this Commandment; and these, if they are not done in assurance of and with faith in God's favor, are nothing, as was said above. Hence it would also be a good thing if there were fewer saint's days, since in our times the works done on them are for the greater part worse than those of the work days, what with loafing, gluttony, and drunkenness, gambling and other evil deeds; and then, the mass and the sermon are listened to without edification, the prayer is spoken without faith. It almost happens that men think it is sufficient that we look on at the mass with our eyes, hear the preaching with our ears, and say the prayers with our mouths. It is all so formal and superficial! We do not think that we might receive something out of the mass into our hearts, learn and remember something out of the preaching, seek, desire and expect something in our prayer. Although in this matter the bishops and priests, or they to whom the work of preaching is entrusted, are most at fault, because they do not preach the

152

Gospel, and do not teach the people how they ought to look on at mass, hear preaching and pray. Therefore, we will briefly explain these three works.

[Sidenote: The Mass]

II. In the mass it is necessary that we attend with our hearts also; and we do attend, when we exercise faith in our hearts. Here we must repeat the words of Christ, when He institutes the mass and says, "Take and eat, this is My Body, which is given for you" [Matt. 26:26 ff., Luke 22:19 ff.]; in like manner over the cup, "Take and drink ye all of it: this is a new, everlasting Testament in My Blood, which is shed for you and for many for the remission of sins. This shall ye do, as oft as ye do it, in remembrance of Me." [1 Cor. 11:23 ff.] In these words Christ has made for Himself a memorial or anniversary,[24] to be daily observed in all Christendom, and has added to it a glorious, rich, great testament, in which no interest, money or temporal possessions are bequeathed and distributed, but the forgiveness of all sins, grace and mercy into eternal life, that all who come to this memorial shall have the same testament; and then He died, whereby this testament has become permanent and irrevocable. In proof and evidence of which, instead of letter and seal, He has left with us His own Body and Blood under the bread and wine.[25]

Here there is need that a man practise the first works of this Commandment right well, that he doubt not that what Christ has said is true, and consider the testament sure, so that he make not Christ a liar. For if you are present at mass and do not consider nor believe that here Christ through His testament has bequeathed and given you forgiveness of all your sins, what else is it, than as if you said: "I do not know or do not believe that it is true that forgiveness of my sins is here bequeathed and given me"? Oh, how many masses there are in the world at present! but how few who hear them with such faith and benefit! Most grievously is God provoked to anger thereby. For this reason also no one shall or can reap any benefit form the mass except he be in trouble of soul and long for divine mercy, and desire to be rid of his sins; or, if he have an evil intention, he must be changed during the mass, and come to have a desire for this testament. For this reason in olden times no open sinner was allowed to be present at the mass.

When this faith is rightly present, the heart must be made joyful by the testament, and grow warm and melt in God's love. Then will follow praise and thanksgiving with a pure heart, from which the mass is called in Greek Eucharista, that is, "thanksgiving," because we praise and thank God for this comforting, rich, blessed testament, just as he gives thanks, praises and is joyful, to whom a good friend has presented a thousand and more gulden. Although Christ often fares like those who make several persons rich by their testament, and these persons never think of them, nor praise or thank them. So our masses at present are merely celebrated, without our knowing why or wherefore, and consequently we neither give thanks nor love nor praise, remain parched and hard, and have enough with our little prayer. Of this more another time.

III. The sermon ought to be nothing else than the proclamation of this testament. But who can hear it if no one preaches it? [Rom. 10:14] Now, they who ought to preach it, themselves do not know it. This is why the sermons ramble off into other unprofitable stories,[26] and thus Christ is forgotten, while we fare like the man in II. Kings vii: we see our riches but do not enjoy them. [2 Kings 7:19] Of which the Preacher also says, "This is a great evil, when God giveth a man riches, and giveth him not power to enjoy them." [Eccles. 6:2] So we look on at unnumbered masses and do not know whether the mass be a testament, or what it be, just as if it were any other common good work by itself. O God, how exceeding blind we are! But where this is rightly preached, it is necessary that it be diligently heard, grasped, retained, often thought of, and that the faith be thus strengthened against all the temptation of sin, whether past, or present, or to come.

Lo! this is the only ceremony or practice which Christ has instituted, in which His Christians shall assemble, exercise themselves and keep it with one accord; and this He did not make to be a mere work like other ceremonies, but placed into it a rich, exceeding great treasure, to be offered and bestowed upon all who believe on it.

This preaching should induce sinners to grieve over their sins, and should kindle in them a longing for the treasure. It must, therefore, be a grievous sin not to hear the Gospel, and to despise such a treasure and so rich a feast to which we are bidden; but a much greater sin to preach the Gospel, and to let so many people who would gladly hear it perish, since Christ has so strictly commanded that the Gospel and this testament be preached, that He does not wish even the mass to be celebrated, unless the Gospel be preached, as He says: "As oft as ye do this, remember me"; that is, as St. Paul says, "Ye shall preach of His death." [1 Cor. 11:26] For this reason it is dreadful and horrible in our times to be a bishop, pastor and preacher; for no one any longer knows this testament, to say nothing of their preaching it, although this is their highest and only duty and obligation. How heavily must they give account for so many souls who must perish because of this lack in preaching.

IV. We should pray, not as the custom is, counting many pages or beads, but fixing our mind upon some pressing need, desire it with all earnestness, and exercise faith and confidence toward God in the matter, in such wise that we do not doubt that we shall be heard. So St Bernard[27] instructs his brethren and says: "Dear brethren, you shall by no means despise your prayer, as if it were in vain, for I tell you of a truth that, before you have uttered the words, the prayer is already recorded in heaven; and you shall confidently expect from God one of two things: either that your prayer will be granted, or that, if it will not be granted, the granting of it would not be good for you."

Prayer is, therefore, a special exercise of faith, and faith makes the prayer so acceptable that either it will surely be granted, or something better than we ask will be given in its stead. So also says St. James: "Let him who asketh of God not waver in faith; for if he wavers, let not that man think that he shall receive any thing of the Lord." [Jas. 1:6 f.] This is a clear statement, which says directly: he who does not trust, receives nothing, neither that which he asks, nor anything better.

And to call forth such faith, Christ Himself has said, Mark xi: "Therefore I say unto you. What things soever ye desire, when ye pray, believe that ye receive them, and ye shall surely have them." [Mark 11:24] And Luke xi: "Ask, and it shall be given you; seek, and ye shall find; knock, and it shall be opened unto you; for every one that asketh receiveth; and he that seeketh findeth; and to him that knocketh it shall be opened. Or what father is there of you, who, if his son shall ask bread, will he give him a stone? or if he ask a fish, will he give him a serpent? or if he ask an egg, will he give him a scorpion? But if you know how to give good gifts to your children, and you yourselves are not naturally good, how much more shall your Father which is in heaven give a good spirit to all them that ask Him!" [Luke 11:9 ff.]

[Sidenote: Mistaken Prayer]

V. Who is so hard and stone-like, that such mighty words ought not to move him to pray with all confidence joyfully and gladly? But how many prayers must be reformed, if we are to pray aright according to these words! Now, indeed, all churches and monastic houses are full of praying and singing, but how does it happen that so little improvement and benefit result from it, and things daily grow worse? The reason is none other than that which St. James indicates when he says: "You ask much and receive not, because ye ask amiss." [Jas. 4:3] For where this faith and confidence is not in the prayer, the prayer is dead, and nothing more than a grievous labor and work. If anything is given for it, it is none the less only temporal benefit without any blessing and help for the soul; nay, to the great injury and blinding of souls, so that they go their way, babbling much with their mouths, regardless of whether they receive, or desire, or trust; and in this unbelief, the state of mind most opposed to the exercise of faith and to the nature of prayer, they remain hardened.

From this it follows that one who prays aright never doubts that his prayer is surely acceptable and heard, although the very thing for which he prays be not given him. For we are to lay our need "before God in prayer, but not prescribe to Him a measure, number, time or place; but if He wills to give it to us better or in another way than we think, we are to leave it to Him; for frequently we do not know what we pray, as St. Paul says, Romans viii [Rom. 8:26]; and God works and gives above all that we understand, as he says, Ephesians iii [Eph. 3:20], so that there be no doubt that the prayer is acceptable and heard, and we yet leave to God the time, place, measure and limit; He will surely do what is right. They are the true worshipers, who worship God in spirit and in truth. [John 4:24] For they who believe not that they will be heard, sin upon the left hand against this Commandment, and go far astray with their unbelief. But they who set a limit for Him, sin upon the other side, and come too close with their tempting of God. So He has forbidden both, that we should err from His Commandment neither to the left nor to the right [Deut 6:16, 28:14], that is, neither with unbelief nor with tempting, but with simple faith remain on the straight road, trusting Him, and yet setting Him no bounds.

[Sidenote: Weak Faith no Reason for not Praying]

VI. Thus we see that this Commandment, like the Second, is to be nothing else than a doing and keeping of the First Commandment, that is, of faith, trust, confidence, hope and love to God, so that in all the Commandments the First may be the captain, and faith the chief work and the life of all other works, without which, as was said, they cannot be good.

But if you say: "What if I cannot believe that my prayer is heard and accepted?" I answer: For this very reason faith, prayer and all other good works are commanded, that you shall know what you can and what you cannot do. And when you find that you cannot so believe and do, then you are humbly to confess it to God, and so begin with a weak spark of faith and daily strengthen it more and more by exercising it in all your living and doing. For as touching infirmity of faith (that is, of the First and highest Commandment), there is no one on earth who does not have his good share of it. For even the holy Apostles in the Gospel, and especially St. Peter, were weak in faith, so that they also prayed Christ and said: "Lord, increase our faith" [Luke 17:5]; and He very frequently rebukes them because they have so little faith [Matt. 14:30].

Therefore you shall not despair, nor give up, even if you find that you do not believe as firmly as you ought and wish, in your prayer or in other works. Nay, you shall thank God with all your heart that He thus reveals to you your weakness, through which He daily teaches and admonishes you how much you need to exercise yourself and daily strengthen yourself in faith. For how many do you see who habitually pray, sing, read, work and seem to be great saints, and yet never get so far as to know where they stand in respect of the chief work, faith; and so in their blindness they lead astray themselves and others; think they are very well off, and so unknowingly build on the sand of their works without any faith, not on God's mercy and promise through a firm, pure faith.

Therefore, however long we live, we shall always have our hands full to remain, with all our works and sufferings, pupils of the First Commandment and of faith, and not to cease to learn. No one knows what a great thing it is to trust God alone, except he who attempts it with his works.

[Sidenote: Prayer Without Ceasing]

VII. Again: if no other work were commanded, would not prayer alone suffice to exercise the whole life of man in faith? For this work the spiritual estate has been specially established, as indeed in olden times some Fathers prayed day and night. Nay, there is no Christian who does not have time to pray without ceasing. But I mean the spiritual praying, that is: no one is so heavily burdened with his labor, but that if he will he can, while working, speak with God in his heart, lay before Him his need and that of other men, ask for help, make petition, and in all this exercise and strengthen his faith.

This is what the Lord means, Luke xviii, when He says, "Men ought always to pray, and never cease," [Luke 18:1] although in Matthew vi. He forbids the use of much speaking and long prayers, because of which He rebukes the hypocrites; not because the lengthy prayer of the lips is evil, but because it is not that true prayer which can be made at all times, and without the inner prayer of faith is nothing. For we must also practise the outward prayer in its proper time, especially in the mass, as this Commandment requires, and wherever it is helpful to the inner prayer and faith, whether in the house or in the field, in this work or in that; of which we have no time now to speak more. For this belongs to the Lord's Prayer, in which all petitions and spoken prayer are summed up in brief words.

[Sidenote: Prayer is Work]

VIII. Where now are they who desire to know and to do good works? Let them undertake prayer alone, and lightly exercise themselves in faith, and they will find that it is true, as the holy Fathers have said, that there is no work like prayer. Mumbling with the mouth is easy, or at least considered easy, but with earnestness of heart to follow the words in deep devotion, that is, with desire and faith, so that one earnestly desires what the words say, and not to doubt that it will be heard: that is a great deed in God's eyes.

Here the evil spirit hinders men with all his powers. Oh, how often will he here prevent the desire to pray, not allow us to find time and place, nay, often also raise doubts, whether a man is worthy to ask anything of such a Majesty as God is, and so confuse us that a man himself does not know whether it is really true that he prays or not; whether it is possible that his prayer is acceptable, and other such strange thoughts. For the evil spirit knows well how powerful one man's truly believing prayer is, and how it hurts him, and how it benefits all men. Therefore he does not willingly let it happen.

When so tempted, a man must indeed be wise, and not doubt that he and his prayer are, indeed, unworthy before such infinite Majesty; in no wise dare he trust his worthiness, or because of his unworthiness grow faint; but he must heed God's command and cast this up to Him, and hold it before the devil, and say: "Because of my worthiness I do nothing, because of my unworthiness I cease from nothing. I pray and work only because God of His pure mercy has promised to hear and to be gracious to all unworthy men, and not only promised it, but He has also most sternly, on pain of His everlasting displeasure and wrath, commanded us to pray, to trust and to receive. If it has not been too much for that high Majesty so solemnly and highly to obligate His unworthy worms to pray, to trust, and to receive from Him, how shall it be too much for me to take such command upon myself with all joy; however worthy or unworthy I may be?" Thus we must drive out the devil's suggestion with God's command. Thus will he cease, and in no other way whatever.

[Sidenote: What Men Shall Pray For]

IX. But what are the things which we must bring before Almighty God in prayer and lamentation, to exercise faith thereby? Answer: First, every man's own besetting need and trouble, of which David says, Psalm xxxii: "Thou art my refuge in all trouble which compasseth me about; Thou art my comfort, to preserve me from all evil which surrounds me." [Ps. 32:7] likewise, Psalm cxlii: "I cried unto the Lord with my voice; with my voice unto the Lord did I make my supplication. I poured out my complaint before Him; I showed before Him my trouble." [Ps. 142:2] In the mass a Christian shall keep in mind the short-comings or excesses he feels, and pour out all these freely before God with weeping and groaning, as woefully as he can, as to his faithful Father, who is ready to help him. And if you do not know or recognise your need, or have no trouble, then you shall know that you are in the worst possible plight. For this is the greatest trouble, that you find yourself so hardened, hard-hearted and insensible that no trouble moves you.

There is no better mirror in which to see your need than simply the Ten Commandments, in which you will find what you lack and what you should seek. If, therefore, you find in yourself a weak faith, small hope and little love toward God; and that you do not praise and honor God, but love your own honor and fame, think much of the favor of men, do not gladly hear mass and sermon, are indolent in prayer, in which things every one has faults, then you shall think more of these faults than of all bodily harm to goods, honor and life, and believe that they are worse than death and all mortal sickness. These you shall earnestly before God, lament and ask for help, and with all confidence expect help, and believe that you are heard and shall obtain help and mercy.

Then go forward into the Second Table of the Commandments, and see how disobedient you have been and still are toward father and mother and all in authority; how you sin against your neighbor with anger, hatred and evil words; how you are tempted to unchastity, covetousness and injustice in word and deed against your neighbor; and you will doubtless find that you are full of all need and misery, and have reason enough to weep even drops of blood, if you could.[28]

X. But I know well that many are so foolish as not to want to ask for such things, unless they first be conscious that they are pure, and believe that God hears no one who is a sinner. All this is the work, of those false preachers, who teach men to begin, not with faith and trust in God's favor, but with their own works.

Look you, wretched man! if you have broken a leg, or the peril of death overtakes you, you call upon God, this Saint and that, and do not wait until your leg is healed, or the danger is past: you are not so foolish as to think that God hears no one whose leg is broken, or who is in bodily danger. Nay, you believe that God shall hear most of all when you are in the greatest need and fear. Why, then, are you so foolish here, where there is immeasurably greater need and eternal hurt, and do not want to ask for faith, hope, love, humility, obedience, chastity, gentleness, peace, righteousness, unless you are already free of all your unbelief, doubt, pride, disobedience, unchastity, anger, covetousness and unrighteousness. Although the more you find yourself lacking in these things, the more and more diligently you ought to pray or cry.

So blind are we: with our bodily sickness and need we run to God; with the soul's sickness we run from Him, and are unwilling to come back before we are well, exactly as if there could be one God who could help the body, and another God who could help the soul; or as if we would help ourselves in spiritual need, although it really is greater than the bodily need. Such plan and counsel is of the devil.

Not so, my good man! If you wish to be cured of sin, you must not withdraw from God, but run to Him, and pray with much more confidence than if a bodily need had overtaken you. God is not hostile to sinners, but only to unbelievers, that is, to such as do not recognize and lament their sin, nor seek help against it from God, but in their own presumption wish first to purify themselves, are unwilling to be in need of His grace, and will not suffer Him to be a God Who gives to everyone and takes nothing in return.

XI. All this has been said of prayer for personal needs, and of prayer in general. But the prayer which really belongs to this Commandment and is called a work of the Holy Day, is far better and greater, and is to be made for all Christendom, for all the need of all men, of foe and friend, especially for those who belong to the parish or bishopric.

Thus St. Paul commanded his disciple Timothy: "I exhort thee, that thou see to it, that prayers and intercessions be made for all men, for kings, and for all that are in authority, that we may lead a quiet and peaceable life in all godliness and honesty. For this is good and acceptable in the sight of God our Saviour." [1 Tim. 2:1 ff.] For this reason Jeremiah, chapter xxix, commanded the people of Israel to pray for the city and land of Babylon, because in the peace thereof they should have peace. [Jer. 29:7] And Baruch i: "Pray for the life of the king of Babylon and for the life of his son, that we may live in peace under their rule." [Bar. 1:21 f.]

This common prayer is precious and the most powerful, [Isa. 56:7] and it is for its sake that we come together. For this reason also the Church is called a House of Prayer [Matt. 21:13], because in it we are as a congregation with one accord to consider our need and the needs of all men, present than before God, and call upon Him for mercy. But this must be done with heart-felt emotion and sincerity, so that we feel in our hearts the need of all men, and that we pray with true empathy for them, in true faith and confidence. Where such prayers are not made in the mass, it were better to omit the mass. For what sense is there in our coming together into a House of Prayer, which coming together shows that we should make common prayer and petition for the entire congregation, if we scatter these prayers, and so distribute them that everyone prays only for himself, and no one has regard for the other, nor concerns himself for another's need? How can that prayer be of help, good, acceptable and a common prayer, or a work of the Holy Day and of the assembled congregation, which they make who make their own petty prayers, one for this, the other for that, and have nothing but self-seeking, selfish prayers, which God hates?

XII. A suggestion of this common prayer has been retained from ancient practice, when at the end of the sermon the Confession of Sins is said and prayer is made on the pulpit for all Christendom. But this should not be the end of the matter, as is now the custom and fashion; it should be an exhortation to pray throughout the entire mass for such need as the preacher makes us feel; and in order that we may pray worthily, he first exhorts us because of our sin, and thereby makes us humble. This should be done as briefly as possible, that then the entire congregation may confess their own sin and pray for every one with earnestness and faith.

[Sidenote: The Power of Common Prayer]

Oh, if God granted that any congregation at all heard mass and prayed in this way, so that a common earnest heart-cry of the entire people would rise up to God, what immeasurable virtue and help would result from such a prayer! What more terrible thing could happen to all the evil spirits? What greater work could be done on earth, whereby so many pious souls would be preserved, so many sinners converted?

For, indeed, the Christian Church on earth has no greater power or work than such common prayer against everything that may oppose it. This the evil spirit knows well, and therefore he does all that he can to prevent such prayer. Gleefully he lets us go on building churches, endowing many monastic houses, making music, reading, singing, observing many masses, and multiplying ceremonies beyond all measure. This does not grieve him, nay, he helps us do it, that we may consider such things the very best, and think that thereby we have done our whole duty. But in that meanwhile this common, effectual and fruitful prayer perishes and its omission is unnoticed because of such display, in this he has what he seeks. For when prayer languishes, no one will take anything from him, and no one will withstand him. But if he noticed that wished to practise this prayer, even if it were under a straw roof or in a pig-sty, he would indeed not endure it, but would fear such a pig-sty far more than all the high, big and beautiful churches, towers and bells in existence, if such prayer be not in them. It is indeed not a question of the places and buildings in which we assemble, but only of this unconquerable prayer, that we pray it and bring it before God as a truly common prayer.

[Sidenote: Proof From the Scriptures]

XIII. The power of this prayer we see in the fact that in olden times Abraham prayed for the five cities, Sodom, Gomorrah, etc., Genesis xviii [Gen. 18:32], and accomplished so much, that if there had been ten righteous people in them, two in each city, God would not have destroyed them. What then could many men do, if they united in calling upon God earnestly and with sincere confidence?

St. James also says: "Dear brethren, pray for one another, that ye may be saved. For the prayer of a righteous man availeth much, a prayer that perseveres and does not cease" [Jas. 5:16 ff.] (that is, which does not cease asking ever more and more, although what it asks is not immediately granted, as some timid men do). And as an example in this matter he sets before us Elijah, the Prophet, "who was a man," he says, "as we are, and prayed, that it might not rain; and it rained not by the space of three years and months. And he prayed again, and it rained, and everything became fruitful." There are many texts and examples in the Scriptures which urge us to pray, only that it be done with earnestness and faith. As David says, "The eyes of the Lord are upon the righteous, and His ears are open unto their cry." [Ps. 33:18] Again, "The Lord is nigh unto all them that call upon Him, to all that call upon Him in truth." [Ps. 145:18] Why does he add, "call upon Him in truth"? Because that is not prayer nor calling upon God when the mouth alone mumbles.

[Sidenote: Thoughtless Prayer]

161

What should God do, if you come along with your mouth, book or Paternoster,[29] and think of nothing except that you may finish the words and complete the number? So that if some one were to ask you what it all was about, or what it was that you prayed for, you yourself would not know; for you had not thought of laying this or that matter before God or desiring it. Your only reason for praying is that you are commanded to pray this and so much, and this you intend to do in full. What wonder that thunder and lightning frequently set churches on fire, because we thus make of the House of Prayer a house of mockery, and call that prayer in which we bring nothing before God and desire nothing from Him.

But we should do as they do who wish to ask a favor of great princes. These do not plan merely to babble a certain number of words, for the prince would think they mocked him, or were insane; but they put their request very plainly, and present their need earnestly, and then leave it to his mercy, in good confidence that he will grant it. So we must deal with God of definite things, namely, mention some present need, commend it to His mercy and good-will, and not doubt that it is heard; for He has promised to hear such prayer, which no earthly lord has done.

[Sidenote: Earnest Prayer]

XIV. We are masters in this form of prayer when suffer bodily need; when we are sick we call here upon St. Christopher, there upon St. Barbara[30]; we vow a pilgrimage to St. James[31], to this place and to that; then we make earnest prayer, have a good confidence and every good kind of prayer. But when we are in our churches during mass, we stand like images of saints;[32] know nothing to speak of or to lament; the beads rattle, the pages rustle and the mouth babbles; and that is all there is to it.

But if you ask what you shall speak of and lament in your prayer, you can easily learn from the Ten Commandments and the Lord's Prayer. Open your eyes and look into your life and the life of all Christians, especially of the Spiritual estate, and you will find how faith, hope, love, obedience, chastity and every virtue languish, and all manner of heinous vices reign; what a lack there is of good preachers and prelates; how only knaves, children, fools and women rule. Then you will see that there were need every hour without ceasing to pray everywhere with tears of blood to God, Who is so terribly angry with men. And it is true that it has never been more necessary to pray than at this time, and it will be more so from now on to the end of the world. If such terrible crimes do not move you to lament and complain, do not permit yourself to be led astray by your rank, station, good works at prayer: there is no Christian vein or trait in you, however righteous you may be. But it has all been foretold, that when God's anger is greatest and Christendom suffers the greatest need, then petitioners and supplicants before God shall not be found, as Isaiah says with tears, chapter lxiv: "Thou art angry with us, and there is none that calleth upon Thy Name, that stirreth up himself to take hold of Thee." [Isa. 64:7] Likewise, Ezekiel xxii: "I sought for a man among them, that should make up the hedge, and stand in the gap before me for the land, that I should not destroy it; but I found none. Therefore have I poured out Mine indignation upon them; I have consumed them with the fire of My wrath." [Ezek. 22:30] With these words God indicates how He wants us to withstand Him and turn away His anger from one another [Ex. 32:11 ff.], as it is frequently written of the Prophet Moses, that he restrained God, [Num. 14:13 ff., 21:7] lest His anger should overwhelm the people of Israel. [Ps. 106:23]

[Sidenote: The Indifference of Man]

XV. But what will they do, who not only do not regard such misfortune of Christendom, and do not pray against Men it, but laugh at it, take pleasure in it, condemn, malign, sing and talk of their neighbor's sin, and yet dare, unafraid and unashamed, go to church, hear mass, say prayers, and regard themselves and are regarded as pious Christians? These truly are in need that we pray twice for them, if we pray once for those whom they condemn, talk about and laugh at. That there would be such is also prophesied by Luke the thief on Christ's left band, who blasphemed Him in His suffering, weakness and need; [Luke 23:39, 35] also by all those who reviled Christ on the Cross, when they should most of all have helped Him.

O God, how blind, nay, how insane have we Christians become! When will there be an end of wrath, O heavenly Father? That we mock at the misfortune of Christendom, to pray for which we gather together in Church and at the mass, that we blaspheme and condemn men, this is the fruit of our mad materialism.[33] If the Turk destroys cities, country and people, and ruins churches, we think a great injury has been done Christendom. Then we complain, and urge kings and princes to war. But when faith perishes, love grows cold, God's Word is neglected, and all manner of sin flourishes, then no one thinks of fighting, nay, pope, bishops, priests and clergy, who ought to be generals, captains and standard-bearers in this spiritual warfare against these spiritual and many times worse Turks, these are themselves the very princes and leaders of such Turks and of the devil host, just as Judas was the leader of the Jews when they took Christ [Luke 24:47]. It had to be an apostle, a bishop, a priest, one of the number of the best, who began the work of slaying Christ. So also must Christendom be laid waste by no others than those who ought to protect it, and yet are so insane that they are ready to eat up the Turk, and at home themselves set house and sheep-cote on fire and let them burn up with the sheep and all other contents, and none the less worry about the wolf in the woods. Such are our times, and this is the reward we have earned by our ingratitude toward the endless grace which Christ has won for us freely with His precious blood, grievous labor and bitter death.

[Sidenote: Prayer Better than Good Works]

XVI. Lo! where are the idle ones, who do not know how to do good works? Where are they who run to Rome, to St. James, hither and thither? Take up this one single work of the mass, look on your neighbor's sin and ruin, and have pity on him; let it grieve you, tell it to God, and pray over it. Do the same for every other need of Christendom, especially of the rulers, whom God, for the intolerable punishment and torment of us all, allows to fall and be misled so terribly. If you do this diligently, be assured you are one of the best fighters and captains, not only against the Turks, but also against the devils and the powers of hell. But if you do it not, what would it help you though you performed all the miracles of the saints, and murdered all the Turks, and yet were found guilty of having disregarded your neighbor's need and of having thereby sinned against love? For Christ at the last day will not ask how much you have prayed, fasted, pilgrimaged, done this or that yourself, but how much good you have done to others, even the very least. [Matt. 25:40, 45]

Now without doubt among the "least" are also those who are in sin and spiritual poverty, captivity and need, of whom there are at present far more than of those who suffer bodily need. Therefore take heed: our own self-assumed good works lead us to and into ourselves, that we seek only our own benefit and salvation; but God's commandments drive us to our neighbor, that we may thereby benefit others to their salvation. Just as Christ on the Cross prayed not for Himself alone, but rather for us, when He said, "Father, forgive them, for they know not what they do," [Luke 23:14] so we also must pray for one another. From which every man may know that the slanderers, frivolous judges and despisers of other people are a perverted, evil race, who do nothing else than heap abuse on those for whom they ought to pray; in which vice no one is sunk so deep as those very men who do many good works of their own, and seem to men to be something extraordinary, and are honored because of their beautiful, splendid life in manifold good works.

[Sidenote: The Lord's Day]

XVII. Spiritually understood, this Commandment has a yet far higher work, which embraces the whole nature of man. Here it must be known that in Hebrew "Sabbath" means "rest," because on the seventh day God rested and ceased from all His works, which He had made. Genesis ii [Gen. 2:3]. Therefore He commanded also that the seventh day should be kept holy and that we cease from our works which we do the other six days. This Sabbath has now for us been changed into the Sunday, and the other days are called work-days; the Sunday is called rest-day or holiday or holy day. And would to God that in Christendom there were no holiday except the Sunday; that the festivals of Our Lady and of the Saints were all transferred to Sunday; then would many evil vices be done away with through the labor of the work-days, and lands would not be so drained and impoverished. But now we are plagued with many holidays, to the destruction of souls, bodies and goods; of which matter much might be said.

164

This rest or ceasing from labors is of two kinds, bodily and spiritual. For this reason this Commandment is also to be understood in two ways.

[Sidenote: The Rest of the Body]

The bodily rest is that of which we have spoken above, namely, that we omit our business and work, in order that we may gather in the church, see mass, hear God's Word and make common prayer. This rest is indeed bodily and in Christendom no longer commanded by God, as the Apostle says, Colossians ii, "Let no man obligate you to any holiday whatever" [Col. 2:16]—for they were of old a figure, but now the truth has been fulfilled, so that all days are holy days, as Isaiah says, chapter lxvi, "One holy day shall it follow the other" [Is. 66:23]; on the other hand, all days are workdays. Yet it is a necessity and ordained by the Church for the sake of the imperfect laity and working people, that they also may be able to come to hear God's Word. For, as we see, the priests and clergy celebrate mass every day, pray at all hours and train themselves in God's Word by study, reading and hearing. For this reason also they are freed from work before others, supported by tithes and have holy-day every day, and every day do the works of the holy-day, and have no work-day, but for them one day is as the other. And if we were all perfect, and knew the Gospel, we might work every day if we wished, or rest if we could. For a day of rest is at present not necessary nor commanded except only for the teaching of God's Word and prayer.

[Sidenote: The Rest of the Soul]

The spiritual rest, which God particularly intends in this Commandment, is this: that we not only cease from our labor and trade, but much more, that we let God alone work in us and that we do nothing of our own with all our powers. But how is this done? In this way: Man, corrupted by sin, has much wicked love and inclination toward all sins, as the Scriptures say, Genesis viii, "Man's heart and senses incline always to the evil," [Gen. 8:21] that is, to pride, disobedience, anger, hatred, covetousness, unchastity, etc., and summa summarum, in all that he does and leaves undone, he seeks his own profit, will and honor rather than God's and his neighbor's. Therefore all his works, all his words, all his thoughts, all his life are evil and not godly.

Now if God is to work and to live in him, all this vice and wickedness must be choked and up-rooted, so that there may be rest and a cessation of all our works, thoughts and life, and that henceforth (as St. Paul says, Galatians ii. [Gal. 2:20]) it may be no longer we who live, but Christ Who lives, works and speaks in us. This is not accomplished with comfortable, pleasant days, but here, we must hurt our nature and let it be hurt. [Gal. 5:17] Here begins the strife between the spirit and the flesh; here the spirit resists anger, lust, pride, while the flesh wants to be in pleasure, honor and comfort. Of this St. Paul says, Galatians v, "They that are our Lord Christ's have crucified the flesh with its affections and lusts." [Gal. 5:24]

165

Then follow the good works,—fasting, watching, labor, of which some say and write so much, although they know neither the source nor the purpose of these good works. Therefore we will now also speak of them.

[Sidenote: The Two Means to the Rest of the Soul]

XVIII. This rest, namely, that our work cease and God alone work in us, is accomplished in two ways. First, through our own effort, secondly, through the effort or urging of others.

Our own effort is to be so made and ordered that, in the first place, when we see our flesh, senses, will and thoughts tempting us, we resist them and do not heed them, as the Wise Man says: "Follow not thine own desires." [Sir. 18:30] And Moses, Deuteronomy xii: "Thou shalt not do what is right in thine own eyes." [Deut. 12:8]

Here a man must make daily use of those prayers which David prays: "Lord, lead me in Thy path, and let me not walk in my own ways," [Ps. 110:35, 37] and many like prayers, which are all summed up in the prayer, "Thy kingdom come." For the desires are so many, so various, and besides at times so nimble, so subtle and specious, through the suggestions of the evil one, that it is not possible for a man to control himself in his own ways. He must let hands and feet go, commend himself to God's governance, and entrust nothing to his reason, as Jeremiah says, "O Lord, I know that the way of man is not in his own power." [Jer. 10:26] We see proof of this, when the children of Israel went out of Egypt through the Wilderness, where there was no way, no food, no drink, no help. Therefore God went before them, by day in a bright cloud, by night in a fiery pillar [Ex. 13:21; 16:4 f.], fed them with manna from heaven, and kept their garments and shoes that they waxed not old [Deut. 29:5 f.], as we read in the Books of Moses. For this reason we pray: "Thy kingdom come, that Thou rule us, and not we ourselves," for there is nothing more perilous in us than our reason and will—And this is the first and highest work of God in us and the best training, that we cease from our works, that we let our reason and will be idle, that we rest and commend ourselves to God in all things, especially when they seem to be spiritual and good.

[Sidenote: Fasting]

XIX. After this comes the discipline of the flesh, to kill its gross, evil lust, to give it rest and relief. This we must kill and quiet with fasting, watching and labor, and from this we learn how much and why we shall fast, watch and labor.

There are, alas! many blind men, who practise their castigation, whether it be fasting, watching or labor, only because they think these are good works, intending by them to gain much merit. Far blinder still are they who measure their fasting not only by the quantity or duration, as these do, but also by the nature of the food, thinking that it is of far greater worth if they do not eat meat, eggs or butter. Beyond these are those who fast according to the saints, and according to the days; one fasting on Wednesday, another on Saturday, another on St. Barbara's day, another on St. Sebastian's day,[34] and so on. These all seek in their fasting nothing beyond the work itself: when they have performed that, they think they have done a good work. I will here say nothing of the fact that some fast in such a way that they none the less drink themselves full; some fast by eating fish and other foods so lavishly that they would come much nearer to fasting if they ate meat, eggs and butter, and by so doing would obtain far better results from their fasting. For such fasting is not fasting, but a mockery of fasting and of God.

Therefore I allow everyone to choose his day, food and quantity for fasting, as he will, on condition that he do not stop with that, but have regard to his flesh; let him put upon it fasting, watching and labor according to its lust and wantonness, and no more, although pope, Church, bishop, father-confessor or any one else whosoever have commanded it. For no one should measure and regulate fasting, watching and labor according to the character or quantity of the food, or according to the days, but according to the withdrawal or approach of the lust and wantonness of the flesh, for the sake of which alone the fasting, watching and labor is ordained, that is, to kill and to subdue them. If it were not for this lust, eating were as meritorious as fasting, sleeping as watching, idleness as labor, and each were as good as the other without all distinction.

[Sidenote: The Limitation of Fasting]

XX. Now, if some one should find that more wantonness arose in his flesh from eating fish than from eating eggs and meat, let him eat meat and not fish. Again, if he find that his head becomes confused and crazed or his body and stomach injured through fasting, or that it is not needful to kill the wantonness of his flesh, he shall let fasting alone entirely, and eat, sleep, be idle as is necessary for his health, regardless whether it be against the command of the Church, or the rules of monastic orders: for no commandment of the Church, no law of an order can make fasting, watching and labor of more value than it has in serving to repress or to kill the flesh and its lusts. Where men go beyond this, and the fasting, eating, sleeping, watching are practised beyond the strength of the body, and more than is necessary to the killing of the lust, so that through it the natural strength is ruined and the head is racked; then let no one imagine that he has done good works, or excuse himself by citing the commandment of the Church or the law of his order. He will be regarded as a man who takes no care of himself, and, as far as in him lies, has become his own murderer.

167

For the body is not given us that we should kill its natural life or work, but only that we kill its wantonness; unless its wantonness were so strong and great that we could not sufficiently resist it without ruin and harm to the natural life. For, as has been said, in the practice of fasting, watching and labor, we are not to look upon the works in themselves, not on the days, not on the number, not on the food, but only on the wanton and lustful Adam, that through them he may be cured of his evil appetite.

[Sidenote: Foolish Fasting and Foolish Neglect of Fasting]

XXI. From this we can judge how wisely or foolishly some women act when they are with child, and how the sick are to be treated. For the foolish women cling so firmly to their fasting that they run the risk of great danger to the fruit of their womb and to themselves, rather than not to fast when the others fast. They make a matter of conscience where there is none, and where there is matter of conscience they make none. This is all the fault of the preachers, because they continually prate of fasting, and never point out its true use, limit, fruit, cause and purpose. So also the sick should be allowed to eat and to drink every day whatever they wish. In brief, where the wantonness of the flesh ceases, there every reason for fasting, watching, laboring, eating this or that, has already ceased, and there no longer is any binding commandment at all.

But then care must be taken, lest out of this freedom there grow a lazy indifference about killing the wantonness of the flesh; for the roguish Adam is exceedingly tricky in looking for permission for himself, and in pleading the ruin of the body or of the mind; so some men jump right in and say it is neither necessary nor commanded to fast or to mortify the flesh, and are ready to eat this and that without fear, just as if they had for a long time had much experience of fasting, although they have never tried it.

No less are we to guard against offending those who, not sufficiently informed, regard it a great sin if we do not fast or eat as they do. These we must kindly instruct, and not haughtily despise, nor eat this or that in despite of them, but we must tell them the reason why it is right to do so, and thus gradually lead them to a correct understanding. But if they are stubborn and will not listen, we must let them alone, and do as we know it is right to do.

[Sidenote: Suffering]

XXII. The second form of discipline which we receive at the hands of others, is when men or devils cause us suffering, as when our property is taken, our body sick, and our honor taken away; and everything that may move us to anger, impatience and unrest. For God's work rules in us according to His wisdom, not according to our wisdom, according to His purity and chastity, not according to the wantonness of our flesh; for God's work is wisdom and purity, our work is foolishness and impurity, and these shall rest: so in like manner it should rule in us according to His peace, not our anger, impatience and lack of peace. For peace too is God's work, impatience is the work of our flesh; this shall rest and be dead, that we thus in every way keep a spiritual holiday, let our works stand idle, and let God work in us.

Therefore in order to kill our works and the Adam in us, God heaps many temptations upon us, which move us to anger, many sufferings, which rouse us to impatience, and last of all death and the world's abuse; whereby He seeks nothing else than that He may drive out anger, impatience and lack of peace, and attain to His work, that is, to peace, in us. Thus says Isaiah xxviii, "He does the work of another that He may come to His own work." [Is. 28:21] What does this mean? He sends us suffering and trouble that He may teach us to have patience and peace; He bids us die that He may make us live, until a man, thoroughly trained, becomes so peaceful and quiet that he is not disturbed, whether it go well or ill with him, whether he die or live, be honored or dishonored. There God Himself dwells alone, and there are no works of men. This is rightly keeping and hallowing the day of rest; then a man does not guide himself, then he desires nothing for himself, then nothing troubles him; but God Himself leads him, there is naught but godly pleasure, joy and peace with all other works and virtues.

[Sidenote: The Holiness of Adversity]

XXIII. These works He considers so great that He commands us not only to keep the day of rest, but also to hallow it or regard it as holy, whereby He declares that there are no more precious things than suffering, dying, and all manner of misfortune.[35] For they are holy and sanctify a man from his works to God's works, just as a church is consecrated from natural works to the worship of God. Therefore a man shall also recognise them as holy things, be glad and thank God when they come upon him. For when they come they make him holy, so that he fulfils this Commandment and is saved, redeemed from all his sinful works. Thus says David: "Precious in the sight of the Lord is the death of His saints." [Ps. 116:15]

In order to strengthen us thereto He has not only commanded us to keep such a rest (for nature is very unwilling to die and to suffer, and it is a bitter day of rest for it to cease from its works and be dead); but He has also comforted us in the Scriptures with many words and told us, Psalm xci, "I will be with him in all his trouble, and will deliver him." [Ps. 91:15] Likewise Psalm xxxiv: "The Lord is nigh unto all them that suffer, and will help them." [Ps. 34:18]

As if this were not enough, He has given us a powerful, strong example of it, His only, dear Son, Jesus Christ, our Lord, who on the Sabbath lay in the tomb the entire day of rest, free from all His works, and was the first to fulfil this Commandment, although He needed it not for Himself, but only for our comfort, that we also in all suffering and death should be quiet and have peace. Since, as Christ was raised up after His rest and henceforth lives only in God and God in Him, so also shall we by the death of our Adam, which is perfectly accomplished only through natural death and burial, be lifted up into God, that God may live and work in us forever. Lo! these are the three parts of man: reason, desire, aversion; in which all his works are done. These, therefore, must be slain by these three exercises, God's governance, our self-mortification, the hurt done to us by others; and so they must spiritually rest before God, and give Him room for His works.

[Sidenote: The Circle of the Three Commandments]

XXIV. But such works are to be done and such sufferings to be endured in faith and in sure confidence of God's favor, in order that, as has been said,[36] all works remain in the First Commandment and in faith, and that faith, for the sake of which all other commandments and works are ordained, exercise and strengthen itself in them. See, therefore, what a pretty, golden ring these three Commandments and their works naturally form, and how from the First Commandment and faith the Second flows on to the Third, and the Third in turn drives through the Second up into the First. For the first work is to believe, to have a good heart and confidence toward God. From this Sows the second good work, to praise God's Name, to confess His grace, to give all honor to Him alone. Then follows the third, to worship by praying, hearing God's Word, thinking of and considering God's benefits, and in addition chastising one's self, and keeping the body under.

But when the evil spirit perceives such faith, such honoring of God and such worship, he rages and stirs up persecution, attacks body, goods, honor and life, brings upon us sickness, poverty, shame and death, which God so permits and ordains. See, here begins the second work, or the second rest of the Third Commandment; by this faith is very greatly tried, even as gold in the fire. [Ecclus. 2:5] For it is a great thing to retain a sure confidence in God, although He sends us death, shame, sickness, poverty; [1 Pet. 4:12] and in this cruel form of wrath to regard Him as our all-gracious Father, as must be done in this work of the Third Commandment. Here suffering contains faith, that it must call upon God's Name and praise it in such suffering, and so it comes through the Third Commandment into the Second again; and through that very calling on the Name of God and praise, faith grows, and becomes conscious of itself, and so strengthens itself, through the two works of the Third and of the Second Commandment. Thus faith goes out into the works and through the works comes to itself again; just as the sun goes forth into its setting and comes again unto its rising. [Ps. 19:6] For this reason the Scriptures associate the day with peaceful living in works, the night with passive living in adversity, and faith lives and works, goes out and comes in, in both, as Christ says, John ix. [John 9:4]

[Sidenote: The Parallel with the Lord's Prayer]

XXV. This order of good works we pray in the Lord's Prayer. The first is this, that we say: "Our Father, Who art in heaven"; these are the words of the first work of faith, which, according to the First Commandment, does not doubt that it has a gracious Father in heaven. The second: "Hallowed be Thy Name," in which faith asks that God's Name, praise and honor be glorified, and calls upon it in every need, as the Second Commandment says. The third: "Thy kingdom come," in which we pray for the true Sabbath and rest, peaceful cessation of our works, that God's work alone be done in us, and so God rule in us as in His own kingdom, as He says, Luke xvii, "Behold, God's kingdom is nowhere else except within you." [Luke 17:21] The fourth petition is "Thy will be done"; in which we pray that we may keep and have the Seven Commandments of the Second Table, in which faith is exercised toward our neighbor; just as in the first three it is exercised in works toward God alone. And these are the petitions in which stands the word "Thou, Thy, Thy, Thy," because they seek only what belongs to God; all the others say "our, us, our," etc.; for in them we pray for our goods and blessedness.

Let this, then, suffice as a plain, hasty explanation of the First Table of Moses, pointing out to simple folk what are the highest of good works.

[Sidenote: Second Table]

The Second Table follows.

[Sidenote: The Fourth Commandment]

"Thou shalt honor thy father and thy mother."

From this Commandment we learn that after the excellent works of the first three Commandments there are no better works than to obey and serve all those who are set over us as superiors. For this reason also disobedience is a greater sin than murder, unchastity, theft and dishonesty, and all that these may include. For we can in no better way learn how to distinguish between greater and lesser sins than by noting the order of the Commandments of God, although there are distinctions also within the works of each Commandment. For who does not know that to curse is a greater sin than to be angry, to strike than to curse, to strike father and mother more than to strike any one else? Thus these seven Commandments teach us how we are to exercise ourselves in good works toward men, and first of all toward our superiors.

The first work is that we honor our own father and mother. And this honor consists not only in respectful demeanor, but in this: that we obey them, look up to, esteem and heed their words and example, accept what they say, keep silent and endure their treatment of us, so long as it is not contrary to the first three Commandments; in addition, when they need it, that we provide them with food, clothing and shelter. For not for nothing has He said: "Thou shalt honor them"; He does not say: "Thou shalt love them," although this also must be done. But honor is higher than mere love and includes a certain fear, which unites with love, and causes a man to fear offending them more than he fears the punishment. Just as there is fear in the honor we pay a sanctuary, and yet we do not flee from it as from a punishment, but draw near to it all the more. Such a fear mingled with love is the true honor; the other fear without any love is that which we have toward things which we despise or flee from, as we fear the hangman or punishment. There is no honor in that, for it is a fear without all love, nay, fear that has with it hatred and enmity. Of this we have a proverb of St. Jerome: What we fear, that we also hate. With such a fear God does not wish to be feared or honored, nor to have us honor our parents; but with the first, which is mingled with love and confidence.

II. This work appears easy, but few regard it aright. For where the parents are truly pious and love their children not according to the flesh, but (as they ought) instruct and direct them by words and works to serve God according to the first three Commandments, there the child's own will is constantly broken, and it must do, leave undone, and suffer what its nature would most gladly do otherwise; and thereby it finds occasion to despise its parents, to murmur against them, or to do worse things. There love and fear depart, unless they have God's grace. In like manner, when they punish and chastise, as they ought (at times even unjustly, which, however, does not harm the soul's salvation), our evil nature resents the correction. Beside all this, there are some so wicked that they are ashamed of their parents because of poverty, lowly birth, deformity or dishonor, and allow these things to influence them more than the high Commandment of God, Who is above all things, and has with benevolent intent given them such parents, to exercise and try them in His Commandment. But the matter becomes still worse when the child has children of its own; then love descends to them, and detracts very much from the love and honor toward the parents.

But what is said and commanded of parents must also be understood of those who, when the parents are dead or absent, take their place, such as relatives, god-parents, sponsors, temporal lords and spiritual fathers. For every one must be ruled and be subject to other men. Wherefore we here see again how many good works are taught in this

Commandment, since in it all our life is made subject to other men. Hence it comes that obedience is so highly praised and all virtue and good works are included in it.

[Sidenote: Love without Fear]

III. There is another dishonoring of parents, much more dangerous and subtle than this first, which adorns itself and passes for a real honor; that is, when a child has its own way, and the parents through natural love allow it. Here there is indeed mutual honor, here there is mutual love, and on all sides it is a precious thing, parents and child take mutual pleasure in one another.

This plague is so common that instances of the first form of dishonoring[37] are very seldom seen. This is due to the fact that the parents are blinded, and neither know nor honor God according to the first three Commandments; hence also they cannot see what the children lack, and how they ought to teach and train them. For this reason they train them for worldly honors, pleasure and possessions, that they may by all means please men and reach high positions: this the children like, and they obey very gladly without gainsaying.

Thus God's Commandment secretly comes to naught while all seems good, and that is fulfilled which is written in the Prophets Isaiah and Jeremiah, that the children are destroyed by their own parents [Is. 57:5, Jer. 7:31; 32:35], and they do like the king Manasseh, who sacrificed his own son to the idol Moloch and burned him, II. Kings xxi [2 Kings 21:6]. What else is it but to sacrifice one's own child to the idol and to burn it, when parents train their children more in the way of the world than in the way of God? let them go their way, and be burned up in worldly pleasure, love, enjoyment, possessions and honor, but let God's love and honor and the desire of eternal blessings be quenched in them?

O how perilous it is to be a father or a mother, where flesh and blood are supreme! For, truly, the knowledge and fulfilment of the first three and the last six Commandments depends altogether upon this Commandment; since parents are commanded to teach them to their children, as Psalm lxxviii. says, "How strictly has He commanded our fathers, that they should make known God's Commandments to their children, that the generation to come might know them and declare them to their children's children." [Ps. 78:5] This also is the reason why God bids us honor our parents, that is, to love them with fear; for that other love is without fear, therefore it is more dishonor than honor.

Now see whether every one does not have good works enough to do, whether he be father or child. But we blind men leave this untouched, and seek all sorts of other works which are not commanded.

[Sidenote: The Folly of Parents]

IV. Now where parents are foolish and train their children after the fashion of the world, the children are in no way to obey them; for God, according to the first three Commandments, is to be more highly regarded than the parents [Acts 5:29]. But training after the fashion of the world I call it, when they teach them to seek no more than pleasure, honor and possessions of this world or its power.

To wear decent clothes and to seek an honest living is a necessity, and not sin. Yet the heart of a child must be taught to be sorry that this miserable earthly life cannot well be lived, or even begun, without the striving after more adornment and more possessions than are necessary for the protection of the body against cold and for nourishment. Thus the child must be taught to grieve that, without its own will, it must do the world's will and play the fool with the rest of men, and endure such evil for the sake of something better and to avoid something worse. So Queen Esther wore her royal crown, and yet said to God, Esther xiv, "Thou knowest, that the sign of my high estate, which is upon my head, has never yet delighted me, and I abhor it as a menstruous rag, and never wear it when I am by myself, but when I must do it and go before the people." [Beth. 14:16 Vulgate] The heart that is so minded wears adornment without peril; for it wears and does not wear, dances and does not dance, lives well and does not live well. And these are the secret souls, hidden brides of Christ, but they are rare; for it is hard not to delight in great adornment and parade. Thus St. Cecilia[38] wore golden clothes at the command of her parents, but within against her body she wore a garment of hair.

Here some men say: "How then could I bring my children into society, and marry them honorably? I must make some display." Tell me, are not these the words of a heart which despairs of God, and trusts more on its own providing than on God's care? Whereas St. Peter teaches and says, I. Peter v, "Cast all your care upon Him, and be certain that He cares for you." [1 Pet. 5:7] It is a sign that they have never yet thanked God for their children, have never yet rightly prayed for them, have never yet commended them to Him; otherwise they would know and have experienced that they ought to ask God also for the marriage dower of their children, and await it from Him. Therefore also He permits them to go their way, with cares and worries, and yet succeed poorly.

[Sidenote: Training Children a Good Work]

V. Thus it is true, as men say, that parents, although they had nothing else to do, could attain salvation by training their own children; if they rightly train them to God's service, they will indeed have both hands full of good works to do. For what else are here the hungry, thirsty, naked, imprisoned, sick, strangers, [Matt 25:35] than the souls of your own children? with whom God makes of your house a hospital, and sets you over them as chief nurse, to wait on them, to give them good words and works as meat and drink, that they may learn to trust, believe and fear God, and to place their hope on Him, to honor His Name, not to swear nor curse, to mortify themselves by praying, fasting, watching, working, to attend worship and to hear God's Word, and to keep the Sabbath, that they may learn to despise temporal things, to bear misfortune calmly, and not to fear death nor to love this life.

See, what great lessons are these, how many good works you have before you in your home, with your child, that needs all these things like a hungry, thirsty, naked, poor, imprisoned, sick soul. O what a blessed marriage and home were that where such parents were to be found! Truly it would be a real Church, a chosen cloister, yea, a paradise. Of such says Psalm cxxviii: "Blessed are they that fear God, and walk in His Commandments; thou shalt eat of the labor of thine hands; therefore thou shalt be happy, and it shall be well with thee. Thy wife shall be as a fruitful vine in thine house, and thy children shall be as the young scions of laden olive trees about thy table. Behold, thus shall the man be blessed, that feareth the Lord," [Ps. 128:1-4] etc. Where are such parents? Where are they that ask after good works? Here none wishes to come. Why? God has commanded it; the devil, flesh and blood pull away from it; it makes no show, therefore it counts for nothing. Here this husband runs to St. James, that wife vows a pilgrimage to Our Lady; no one vows that he will properly govern and teach himself and his child to the honor of God; he leaves behind those whom God has commanded him to keep in body and soul, and would serve God in some other place, which has not been commanded him. Such perversity no bishop forbids, no preacher corrects; nay, for covetousness' sake they confirm it and daily only invent more pilgrimages, elevations of saints,[39] indulgence-fairs. God have pity on such blindness.

[Sidenote: Neglect of Children a Cause for Condemnation]

VI. On the other hand, parents cannot earn eternal punishment in any way more easily than by neglecting their own children in their own home, and not teaching them the things which have been spoken of above. Of what help is it, that they kill themselves with fasting, praying, making pilgrimages, and do all manner of good works? God will, after all, not ask them about these things at their death and in the day of judgment, but will require of them the children whom He entrusted to them. This is shown by that word of Christ, Luke xxiii, "Ye daughters of Jerusalem, weep not for me, but for yourselves and for your children. The days are coming, in which they shall say; Blessed are the wombs that never bare, and the paps which never gave suck." [Luke 23:28 f.] Why shall they lament, except because all their condemnation comes from their own children? If they had not had children, perhaps they might have been saved. Truly, these words ought to open the eyes of parents, that they may have regard to the souls of their children, so that the poor children be not deceived by their

175

false, fleshly love, as if they had rightly honored their parents when they are not angry with them, or are obedient in worldly matters, by which their self-will is strengthened; although the Commandment places the parents in honor for the very purpose that the self-will of the children may be broken, and that the children may become humble and meek.

Just as it has been said of the other Commandments, that they are to be fulfilled in the chief work,[40] so here too let no one suppose that the training and teaching of his children is sufficient of itself, except it be done in confidence of divine favor, so that a man doubt not that he is well-pleasing to God in his works, and that he let such works be nothing else than an exhortation and exercise of his faith, that he trust God and look to Him for blessings and a gracious will; without which faith no work lives, or is good and acceptable; for many heathen have trained their children beautifully, but it is all lost, because of their unbelief.

[Sidenote: Obedience to the Church]

VII. The second work of this Commandment is to honor and obey the spiritual mother, the holy Christian Church, the spiritual power, so that we conform to what she commands, forbids, appoints, orders, binds and looses, and honor, fear and love the spiritual authority as we honor, love and fear our natural parents, and yield to it in all things which are not contrary to the first three Commandments.

[Sidenote: The Neglected Duty of the Church]

Now with regard to this work, things are almost worse than with regard to the first. The spiritual authority should punish sin with the ban and with laws, and constrain its spiritual children to be good, in order that they might have reason to do this work and to exercise themselves in obeying and honoring it. Such zeal one does not see now; they act toward their subjects like the mothers who forsake their children and run after their lovers, as Hosea ii. [Hos. 2:5] says; they do not preach, they do not teach, they do not hinder, they do not punish, and there is no spiritual government at all left in Christendom.

What can I say of this work? A few fast-days and feast-days are left, and these had better be done away with. But no one gives this a thought, and there is nothing left except the ban for debt, and this should not be. But spiritual authority should look to it, that adultery, unchastity, usury, gluttony, worldly show, excessive adornment, and such like open sin and shame might be most severely punished and corrected; and they should properly manage the endowments, monastic houses, parishes and schools, and earnestly maintain worship in them, provide for the young people, boys and girls, in schools and cloisters, with learned, pious men as teachers, that they might all be well trained, and so the older people give a good example and Christendom be filled and adorned with fine young people. So St. Paul teaches his disciple Titus, that he should rightly instruct and govern all classes, young and old, men and women. [Tit. 2:1-10] But now he goes to school who wishes; he is taught who governs and teaches himself; nay, it has, alas! come to such a pass that the places where good should be taught have become schools of knavery, and no one at all takes thought for the wild youth.

[Sidenote: The Worldliness of the Church]

VIII. If the above order prevailed, one could say how honor and obedience should be given to the spiritual authority. But now the case is like that of the natural parents who let their children do as they please; at present the spiritual authority threatens, dispenses, takes money, and pardons more than it has power to pardon. I will here refrain from saying more; we see more of it than is good; greed holds the reins, and just what should be forbidden is taught; and it is clearly seen that the spiritual estate is in all things more worldly than the worldly estate itself. Meanwhile Christendom must be ruined, and this Commandment perish.

If there were a bishop who would zealously provide for all these classes, supervise, make vitiations and be faithful as he ought, truly, one city would be too much for him. For in the time of the Apostles, when Christendom was at its best estate, each city had a bishop, although the smallest part of the inhabitants were Christians. How may things go when one bishop wants to have so much, another so much, this one the whole world, that one the fourth of it.

It is time that we pray God for mercy. Of spiritual power we have much; but of spiritual government nothing or little. Meanwhile may he help who can, that endowments, monastic houses, parishes and schools be well established and managed; and it would also be one of the works of the spiritual authority that it lessen the number of endowments, monastic houses and schools, where they cannot be cared for. It is much better that there be no monastic house or endowment than that there be evil government in them, whereby God is the more provoked to anger.[41]

[Sidenote: Abuses in the Church]

IX. Since, then, the authorities so entirely neglect their work, and are perverted, it must assuredly follow that they misuse their power, and undertake other and evil works, just as parents do when they give some command contrary to God. Here we must be wise; for the Apostle has said, that those times shall be perilous in which such authorities shall rule. [1 Tim. 4:1 ff.] For it seems as if we resisted their power if we do not do and leave undone all that they prescribe. [2 Tim. 3:1 ff.] Therefore we must take hold of the first three

177

Commandments and the First Table, and be certain that no man, neither bishop, nor pope, nor angel, may command or determine anything that is contrary to or hinders these three Commandments, or does not help them; and if they attempt such things, it is not valid and amounts to nothing; and we also sin if we follow and obey, or even tolerate such acts.

From this it is easy to understand that the commands of fasting do not include the sick, the pregnant women, or those who for other reasons cannot fast without injury. And, to rise higher, in our time nothing comes from Rome but a fair of spiritual wares, which are openly and shamelessly bought and sold, indulgences, parishes, monastic houses, bishoprics, provostships, benefices, and every thing that has ever been founded to God's service far and wide; whereby not only is all money and wealth of the world drawn and driven to Rome (for this would be the smallest harm), but the parishes, bishoprics and prelacies are torn to pieces, deserted, laid waste, and so the people are neglected, God's Word and God's Name and honor come to naught, and faith is destroyed, so that at last such institutions and offices fall into the hands not only of unlearned and unfit men, but the greater part into the hands of the Romans, the greatest villains in the world. Thus what has been founded for God's service, for the instruction, government and improvement of the people, must now serve the stable-boys, mule-drivers, yea, not to use plainer language, Roman whores and knaves; yet we have no more thanks than that they mock us for it as fools.

[Sidenote: The Duty of Resisting Abuses in the Church]

X. If then such unbearable abuses are all carried on in the Name of God and St. Peter, just as if God's Name and the spiritual power were instituted to blaspheme God's honor, to destroy Christendom, body and soul: we are indeed in duty bound to resist in a proper way as much as we can. And here we must do like pious children whose parents have become insane, and first see by what right that which has been founded for God's service in our lands, or has been ordained to provide for our children, must be allowed to do its work in Rome, and to lapse here, where it ought to serve. How can we be so foolish?

Since then bishops and spiritual prelates stand idle in this matter, offer no opposition or are afraid, and thus allow Christendom to perish, it is our duty first of all humbly to call upon God for help to prevent this thing, then to put our hand to work to the same end, send the courtesans[42] and those who bear letters from Rome about their business, in a reasonable, gentle way inform them that, if they wish to care for their parishes properly, they shall live in them and improve the people by preaching or by good example; or if not, and they do live in Rome or elsewhere, lay waste and debauch the churches, then let the pope feed them, whom they serve. It is not fitting that we support the pope's servants, his people, yes, his knaves and whores, to the destruction and injury of our souls.

Lo! these are the true Turks, whom the kings, princes and the nobility ought to attack first: not seeking thereby their own benefit, but only the improvement of Christendom, and the prevention of the blasphemy and disgracing of the divine Name; and so to deal with the clergy as with a father who has lost his sense and wits; who, if one did not restrain him and resist him (although with all humility and honor), might destroy child, heir and everybody. Thus we are to honor Roman authority as our highest father; and yet, since they have gone mad and lost their senses, not allow them to do what they attempt, lest Christendom be destroyed thereby.

[Sidenote: The Hopelessness of General Councils]

XI. Some think, this should be referred to a General Council. To this I say: No! For we have had many councils in which this has been proposed, namely, at Constance, Basel and the last Roman Council;[43] but nothing has been accomplished, and things have grown ever worse. Moreover, such councils are entirely useless, since Roman wisdom has contrived the device that the kings and princes must beforehand take an oath to let the Romans remain what they are and keep what they have, and so has put up a bar to ward off all reformation, to retain protection and liberty for all their knavery, although this oath is demanded, forced and taken contrary to God and the law, and by it the doors are locked against the Holy Spirit, Who should rule the councils.[44] But this would be the best, and also the only remedy remaining, if kings, princes, nobility, cities and communities themselves began and opened a way for reformation, so that the bishops and clergy, who now are afraid, would have reason to follow. For here nothing else shall and must be considered except God's first three Commandments, against which neither Rome, nor heaven nor earth can command or forbid anything. And the ban or threatening with which they think they can prevent this, amounts to nothing; just as it amounts to nothing if an insane father severely threatens the son who restrains him or locks him up.[45]

[Sidenote: Obedience to the Temporal Authorities]

XII. The third work of this Commandment is to obey the temporal authority, as Paul teaches, Romans xiii [Rom. 13:1], and Titus iii [Tit. 3:1], and St. Peter, I. Peter ii [1 Pet. 2:14 f.]: "Submit yourselves to the king as supreme, and to the princes as his ambassadors, and to all the ordinances of the worldly power." But it is the work of the temporal power to protect its subjects, and to punish thievery, robbery, and adultery, as St. Paul says, Romans xiii: "It beareth not the sword in vain; it serves God with it, to the terror of evil doers, and to the protection of the good." [Rom. 13:4]

Here men sin in two ways. First, if they lie to the government, deceive it, and are disloyal, neither obey nor do as it has ordered and commanded, whether with their bodies or their possessions. For even if the government does injustice, as the King of Babylon did to the

179

people of Israel, yet God would have it obeyed, without treachery and deception. Secondly, when men speak evil of the government and curse it, and when a man cannot revenge himself and abuses the government with grumbling and evil words, publicly or secretly.

In all this we are to regard that which St. Peter bids us regard, namely, that its power, whether it do right or wrong, cannot harm the soul, but only the body and property; unless indeed it should try openly to compel us to do wrong against God or men; [1 Pet. 2:19 ff.] as in former days when the magistrates were not yet Christians, and as the Turk is now said to do. For to suffer wrong destroys no one's soul, nay, it improves the soul, although it inflicts loss upon the body and property; but to do wrong, that destroys the soul, although it should gain all the world's wealth.

XIII. This also is the reason why there is not such great danger in the temporal power as la the spiritual, when it does wrong. For the temporal power can do no harm, since it has nothing to do with preaching and faith and the first three Commandments. But the spiritual power does harm not only when it does wrong, but also when it neglects its duty and busies itself with other things, even if they were better than the very best works of the temporal power. Therefore, we must resist it when it does not do right, and not resist the temporal power although it does wrong. For the poor people believe and do as they see the spiritual power believing and doing; if they are not set an example and are not taught, then they also believe nothing and do nothing; since this power is instituted for no other reason than to lead the people in faith to God. All this is not found in the temporal power; for it may do and leave undone what it will, my faith to God still goes its way and works its works, because I need not believe what it believes.

Therefore, also, the temporal power is a very small thing in God's sight, and far too slightly regarded by Him, that for its sake, whether it do right or wrong, we should resist, become disobedient and quarrel. On the other hand, the spiritual power is an exceeding great blessing, and far too precious in His eyes, that the very least of Christians should endure and keep silent, if it departs a hair's breadth from its own duty, not to say when it does the very opposite of its duty, as we now see it do every day.

XIV. In this power also there is much abuse. First, when it follows the flatterers, which is a common and especially harmful plague of this power, against which no one can sufficiently guard and protect himself. Here it is led by the nose, and oppresses the common people, becomes a government of the like of which a heathen says: "The spider-webs catch the small flies, but the mill-stones roll through." So the laws, ordinances and government of one and the same authority hold the small men, and the great are free; and where the prince is not himself so wise that he needs nobody's advice, or has such a standing that they fear him, there will and must be (unless God should do a special wonder) a childish government.

For this reason God has considered evil, unfit rulers the greatest of plagues, as He threatens, Isaiah iii, "I will take away from them every man of valor, and will give children to be their princes and babes to rule over them." [Is. 3:2] Four plagues God has named in Scripture, Ezekiel xiv. [Ezek. 14:13 ff.] the first and slightest, which also David chose [2 Sam. 24:13 f.], is pestilence, the second is famine, the third is war, the fourth is all manner of evil beasts, such as lions, wolves, serpents, dragons; these are the wicked rulers. For where these are, the land is destroyed, not only in body and property, as in the others, but also in honor, discipline, virtue and the soul's salvation. For pestilence and famine make people good and rich; but war and wicked rulers bring to naught everything that has to do with temporal and eternal.

[Sidenote: Wisdom Needed in the Exercise of Authority]

XV. A prince must also be very wise and not at all times undertake to enforce his own will, although he may have the authority and the very best cause. For it is a far nobler virtue to endure wrong to one's authority than to risk property and person, if it is advantageous to the subjects; since worldly rights attach only to temporal goods.

Hence, it is a very foolish saying: I have a right to it, therefore I will take it by storm and keep it, although all sorts of misfortune may come to others thereby. So we read of the Emperor Octavianus,[46] that he did not wish to make war, however just his cause might be, unless there were sure indications of greater benefit than harm, or at least that the harm would not be intolerable, and said: "War is like fishing with a golden net; the loss risked is always greater than the catch can be." For he who guides a wagon must walk far otherwise than if he were walking alone; when alone he may walk, jump, and do as he will; but when he drives, he must so guide and adapt himself that the wagon and horses can follow him, and regard that more than his own will. So also a prince leads a multitude with him and must not walk and act as he wills, but as the multitude can, considering their need and advantage more than his will and pleasure. For when a prince rules after his own mad will and follows his own opinion, he is like a mad driver, who rushes straight ahead with horse and wagon, through bushes, thorns, ditches, water, up hill and down dale, regardless of roads and bridges; he will not drive long, all will go to smash.

Therefore it would be most profitable for rulers, that they read, or have read to them, from youth on, the histories, both in sacred and in profane books, in which they would find more examples and skill in ruling than in all the books of law; as we read that the kings of Persia did, Esther vi. [Esth. 6:1 ff.] For examples and histories benefit and teach more than the laws and statutes: there actual experience teaches, here untried and uncertain words.

[Sidenote: Good Works for Rulers]

[Sidenote: Economic Reforms: Gluttony]

XVI. Three special, distinct works all rulers might do in our times, particularly in our lands. First, to make an end of the horrible gluttony and drunkenness, not only because of the excess, but also because of its expense. For through seasonings and spices and the like, without which men could well live, no little loss of temporal wealth has come and daily is coming upon our lands. To prevent these two great evils would truly give the temporal power enough to do, for the inroads they have made are wide and deep. And how could those in power serve God better and thereby also improve their own land?

[Sidenote: Luxury]

[Sidenote: Rent-charges]

Secondly, to forbid the excessive cost of clothing, whereby so much wealth is wasted, and yet only the world and the flesh are served; it is fearful to think that such abuse is to be found among the people who have been pledged, baptised and consecrated to Christ, the Crucified, and who should bear the Cross after Him and prepare for the life to come by dying daily. If some men erred through ignorance, it might be borne; but that it is practised so freely, without punishment, without shame, without hindrance, nay, that praise and fame are sought thereby, this is indeed an unchristian thing. Thirdly, to drive out the usurious buying of rent-charges,[47] which in the whole world ruins, consumes and troubles all lands, peoples and cities through its cunning form, by which it appears not to be usury, while in truth it is worse than usury, because men are not on their guard against it as against open usury. See, these are the three Jews, as men say, who suck the whole world dry. Here princes ought not to sleep, nor be lazy, if they would give a good account of their office to God.

[Sidenote: Exections of the Church]

XVII. Here too ought to be mentioned the knavery which is practised by officiales[48] and other episcopal and spiritual officers, who ban, load, hunt and drive the poor people with great burdens, as long as a penny remains. This ought to be prevented by the temporal sword, since there is no other help or remedy.

[Sidenote: Vice]

O, would God in heaven, that some time a government might be established that would do away with the public bawdy-houses, as was done among the people of Israel! It is indeed an unchristian sight, that public houses of are maintained among Christians, a thing formerly altogether unheard of. It should be a rule that boys and girls should be married early and such vice be prevented. Such a rule and custom ought to be sought for by both the spiritual and the temporal power. If it was possible among the Jews, why should it not also be possible among Christians? Nay, if it is possible in villages, towns and some cities, as we all see, why should it not be possible everywhere?

But the trouble is, there is no real government in the world. No one wants to work, therefore the mechanics must give their workmen holiday: then they are free and no one can tame them. But if there were a rule that they must do as they are bid, and no one would give them work in other places, this evil would to a large extent be mended. God help us! I fear that here the wish is far greater than the hope; but this does not excuse us.

Now see, here only a few works of magistrates are indicated, but they are so good and so many, that they have superabundant good works to do every hour and could constantly serve God. But these works, like the others, should also be done in faith, yea, be an exercise of faith, so that no one expect to please God by the works, but by confident trust in His favor do such works only to the honor and praise of his gracious God, thereby to serve and benefit his neighbor.

[Sidenote: Obedience to Masters]

XVIII. The fourth work of this Commandment is obedience of servants and workmen toward their lords and ladies, masters and mistresses. Of this St. Paul says, Titus ii: "Thou shalt exhort servants that they highly honor their masters, be obedient, do what pleases them, not cheating them nor opposing them" [Tit. 2:9 f. 8]; for this reason also: because they thereby bring the doctrine of Christ and our faith into good repute, that the heathen cannot complain of us and be offended [1 Tim. 6:1]. St. Peter also says: "Servants, be subject to your masters, for the fear of God, not only to the good and gentle, but also to the froward and harsh. For this is acceptable with God, if a man suffers harshness, being innocent." [1 Pet. 2:18 f.]

Now there is the greatest complaint in the world about servants and working men, that they are disobedient, unfaithful, unmannerly, and over-reaching; this is a plague sent of God. And truly, this is the one work of servants whereby they may be saved; truly they need not make pilgrimages or do this thing or the other; they have enough to do if their heart is only set on this, that they gladly do and leave undone what they know pleases their masters and mistresses, and all this in a simple faith [Eph. 6:5]; not that they would by their works gain much merit, but that they do it all in the confidence of divine favor [Col. 3:22] (in which all merits are to be found), purely for nothing, out of the love and good-will toward God which grows out of such confidence. And all such works they should think of as an exercise and exhortation ever to strengthen their faith and confidence more and more. For, as has now been frequently said, this faith makes all works good, yea, it must do them and be the master-workman.

[Sidenote: Duties of Masters]

XIX. On the other hand, the masters and mistresses should not rule their servants, maids and workingmen roughly, not look to all things too closely, occasionally overlook something, and for peace' sake make allowances. For it is not possible that everything be done perfectly at all times among any class of men, as long as we live on earth in imperfection. Of this St. Paul says, Colossians iv, "Masters, do unto your servants that which is just and equal, knowing that ye also have a Master in heaven." [Col. 4:1] Therefore as the masters do not wish God to deal too sharply with them, but that many things be overlooked through grace, they also should be so much the more gentle toward their servants, and overlook some things, and yet have a care that the servants do right and learn to fear God.

But see now, what good works a householder and a mistress can do, how finely God offers us all good works so near at hand, so manifold, so continuously, that we have no need of asking after good works, and might well forget the other showy, far-off, invented works of men, such as making pilgrimages, building churches, seeking indulgence, and the like.

[Sidenote: Husband and Wife]

Here I ought naturally also to say how a wife ought to be obedient, subject to her husband as to her superior, give way to him, keep silent and give up to him, where it is a matter not contrary to God's commands. On the other hand, the husband should love his wife, overlook a little, and not deal strictly with her, of which matter St. Peter [1 Pet. 3:6 ff.] and St. Paul [Eph. 5:22 ff., Col. 3:18 ff.] have said much. But this has its place in the further explanation of the Ten Commandments, and is easily inferred from these passages.

XX. But all that has been said of these works is included in these two, obedience and considerateness.[49] Obedience is the duty of subjects, considerateness that of masters, that they take care to rule their subjects well, deal kindly with them, and do everything whereby they may benefit and help them. That is their way to heaven, and these are the best works they can do on earth; with these they are more acceptable to God than if without these they did nothing but miracles. So says St. Paul, Romans ii: "He that ruleth, let him do it with diligence"; [Rom. 12:8] as who should say: "Let him not allow himself to be led astray by what other people or classes of people do; let him not look to this work or to that, whether it be splendid or obscure; but let him look to his own position, and think only how he may benefit those who are subject to him; by this let him stand, nor let himself be torn from it, although heaven stood open before him, nor be driven from it, although hell were chasing him. This is the right road that leads him to heaven."

Oh, if a man were so to regard himself and his position, and attended to its duties alone, how rich in good works would he be in a short time, so quietly and secretly that no one would notice it except God alone! But now we let all this go, and one runs to the Carthusians,[50] another to this place, a third to that, just as if good works and God's Commandments had been thrown into corners and hidden; although it is written in Proverbs i, that divine wisdom crieth out her commandments publicly in the streets, in the midst of the people and in the gates of the cities; [Prov. 1:20 f.] which means that they are present in profusion in all places, in all stations of life and at all times, and we do not see hem, but in our blindness look for them elsewhere. This Christ declared, Matthew xxiv: "If they shall say unto you: Lo, here is Christ, or there, believe it not. If they shall say: Behold, He is in the desert, go not forth; behold, He is in the secret chambers, believe it not; they are false prophets and false Christs." [Matt. 24:23-26]

XXI. Again, obedience is the duty of subjects, that they direct all their diligence and effort to do and to leave undone what their over-lords desire of them, that they do not allow themselves to be torn or driven from this, whatever another do. Let no man think that he lives well or does good works, whether it be prayer or fasting, or by whatever name it may be called, if he does not earnestly and diligently exercise himself in this.

But if it should happen, as it often does, that the temporal power and authorities, as they are called, should urge a subject to do contrary to the Commandments of God, or hinder him from doing them, there obedience ends, and that duty is annulled. Here a man must say as St. Peter says to the rulers of the Jews: "We ought to obey God rather than men." [Acts 5:29] He did not say: "We must not obey men"; for that would be wrong; but he said: "God rather than men." Thus, if a prince desired to go to war, and his cause was manifestly unrighteous, we should not follow nor help him at all; since God has commanded that we shall not kill our neighbor, nor do him injustice. Likewise, if he bade us bear false witness, steal, lie or deceive and the like. Here we ought rather give up goods, honor, body, and life, that God's Commandments may stand.

[Sidenote: The Fifth Commandment]

The four preceding Commandments have their works in the understanding, that is, they take a man captive, rule him and make him subject, so that he rule not himself, approve not himself, think not highly of himself; but in humility know himself and allow himself to be led, that pride be prevented. The following Commandments deal with the passions and lust of men, that these also be killed.

[Sidenote: The Duty of Meekness]

[Sidenote: False Meekness]

I. The passions of anger and revenge, of which the Fifth Commandment says, "Thou shalt not kill." This Commandment has one work, which however includes many and dispels many vices, and is called meekness.[51] Now this is of two kinds. The one has a beautiful splendor, and there is nothing back of it. This we practice toward our friends and those who do us good and give us pleasure with goods, honor and favor, or who do not offend us with words nor with deeds. Such meekness irrational animals have, lions and snakes, Jews, Turks, knaves, murderers, bad women. These are all content and gentle when men do what they want, or let them alone; and yet there are not a few who, deceived by such worthless meekness, cover over their anger and excuse it, saying: "I would indeed not be angry, if I were left alone." Certainly, my good man, so the evil spirit also would be meek if he had his own way. Dissatisfaction and resentment overwhelm you in order that they may show you how full of anger and wickedness you are, that you may be admonished to strive after meekness and to drive out anger.

[Sidenote: True Meekness]

The second form of meekness is good through and through, that which is shown toward opponents and enemies, does them no harm, does not revenge itself, does not curse nor revile, does not speak evil of them, does not meditate evil against them, although they had taken away goods, honor, life, friends and everything. Nay, where it is possible, it returns good for evil, speaks well of them, thinks well of them, prays for them. Of this Christ says, in Matthew v: "Do good to them that despitefully use you. Pray for them that persecute you and revile you." [Matt. 5:44] And Paul, Romans xii: "Bless them which curse you, and by no means curse them, but do good to them." [Rom. 12:14 f.]

II. Behold how this precious, excellent work has been lost among Christians, so that nothing now everywhere prevails except strife, war, quarreling, anger, hatred, envy, back-biting, cursing, slandering, injuring, vengeance, and all manner of angry works and words; and yet, with all this, we have our many holidays, hear masses, say our prayers, establish churches, and more such spiritual finery, which God has not commanded. We shine resplendently and excessively, as if we were the most holy Christians there ever were. And so because of these mirrors and masks we allow God's Commandment to go to complete ruin, and no one considers or examines himself, how near or how far he be from meekness and the fulfilment of this Commandment; although God has said, that not he who does such works, but he who keeps his Commandments, shall enter into eternal life. [John 14:15, 21; 15:10]

[Sidenote: Enemies an Occasion for Good Works]

How, since no one lives on earth upon whom God does not bestow an enemy and opponent as a proof of his own anger and wickedness, that is, one who afflicts him in goods, honor, body or friends, and thereby tries whether anger is still present, whether he can be well-disposed toward his enemy, speak well of him, do good to him, and not intend any evil against him; let him come forward who asks what he shall do that he may do good works, please God and be saved. Let him set his enemy before him, keep him constantly before the eyes of his heart, as an exercise whereby he may curb his spirit and train his heart to think kindly of his enemy, wish him well, care for him and pray for him; and then, when opportunity offers, speak well of him and do good to him. Let him who will, try this and if he find not enough to do all his life long, he may convict me of lying, and say that my contention was wrong. But if this is what God desires, and if He will be paid in no other coin, of what avail is it, that we busy ourselves with other great works which are not commanded, and neglect this? Therefore God says, Matthew v, "I say unto you, that whosoever is angry with his neighbor, is in danger of the judgment; but whosoever shall say to his brother, Thou fool (that is, all manner of invective, cursing, reviling, slandering), he shall be in danger of everlasting fire." [Matt. 5:22] What remains then for the outward act, striking, wounding, killing, injuring, etc., if the thoughts and words of anger are so severely condemned?

III. But where there is true meekness, there the heart is pained at every evil which happens to one's enemy. And these are the true children and heirs of God and brethren of Christ, Whose heart was so pained for us all when He died on the holy Cross. Even so we see a pious judge passing sentence upon the criminal with sorrow, and regretting the death which the law imposes. Here the act seems to be one of anger and harshness. So thoroughly good is meekness that even in such works of anger it remains, nay, it torments the heart most sorely when it must be angry and severe.

[Sidenote: The Limits of Meekness]

But here we must watch, that we be not meek contrary to God's honor and Commandment. For it is written of Moses that he was the very meekest man on earth, and yet, when the Jews had worshiped the golden calf and provoked God to anger [Sir. 45:4], he put many of them to death, and thereby made atonement before God. [Ex. 32:28] Likewise it is not fitting that the magistrates should be idle and allow sin to have sway, and that we say nothing. My own possessions, my honor, my injury, I must not regard, nor grow angry because of them; but God's honor and Commandment we must protect, and injury or injustice to our neighbor we must prevent, the magistrates with the sword, the rest of us with reproof and rebuke, yet always with pity for those who have merited the punishment.

This high, noble, sweet work can easily be learned, if we perform it in faith, and as an exercise of faith. For if faith does not doubt the favor of God nor question that God is gracious, it will become quite easy for a man to be gracious and favorable to his neighbor, however much he may have sinned; for we have sinned much more against God. Behold, a short Commandment this, but it presents a long, mighty exercise of good works and of faith.

Thou shalt not commit adultery.

[Sidenote: The Sixth Commandment: The Duty of Purity]

In this Commandment, too a good work is commanded, which includes much and drives away much vice; it is called purity, or chastity, of which much is written and preached, and it is well known to every one, only that it is not as carefully observed and practised as other works which are not commanded. So ready are we to do what is not commanded and to leave undone what is commanded. We see that the world is full of shameful works of unchastity, indecent words, tales and ditties, temptation to which is daily increased through gluttony and drunkenness, idleness and frippery. Yet we go our way as if we were Christians; when we have been to church, have said our little prayer, have observed the fasts and feasts, then we think our whole duty is done.

Now, if no other work were commanded but chastity alone, we would all have enough to do with this one; so perilous and raging a vice is unchastity. It rages in all our members: in the thoughts of our hearts, in the seeing of our eyes, in the hearing of our ears, in the words of our mouth, in the works of our hands and feet and all our body. To control all these requires labor and effort; and thus the Commandments of God teach us how great truly good works are, nay, that it is impossible for us of our own strength to conceive a good work, to say nothing of attempting or doing it. St Augustine says, that among all the conflicts of the Christian the conflict of chastity is the hardest, for the one reason alone, that it continues daily without ceasing, and chastity seldom prevails. This all the saints have wept over and lamented, as St. Paul does, Romans vii: "I find in me, that is in my flesh, no good thing." [Rom. 7:18]

[Sidenote: Helps Against Unchastity]

II. If this work of chastity is to be permanent, it will drive to many other good works, to fasting and temperance over against gluttony and drunkenness, to watching and early rising over against laziness and excessive sleep, to work and labor over against idleness. For gluttony, drunkenness, lying late abed, loafing and being without work are weapons of unchastity, with which chastity is quickly overcome. [Rom. 13:12 f.] On the other hand, the holy Apostle Paul calls fasting, watching and labor godly weapons, with which unchastity is mastered; but, as has been said above, these exercises must do no more than overcome unchastity, and not pervert nature.

Above all this, the strongest defence is prayer and the Word of God; namely, that when evil lust stirs, a man flee to prayer, call upon God's mercy and help, read and meditate on the Gospel, and in it consider Christ's sufferings. Thus says Psalm cxxxvii: "Happy shall he be, that taketh and dasheth the little ones of Babylon against the rock," [Ps. 137:9] that is, if the heart runs to the Lord Christ with its evil thoughts while they are yet young and just beginning; for Christ is a Rock, on which they are ground to powder and come to naught.

See, here each one will find enough to do with himself, and more than enough, and will be given many good works to do within himself. But now no one uses prayer, fasting, watching, labor for this purpose, but men stop in these works as if they were in themselves the whole purpose, although they should be arranged so as to fulfil the work of this Commandment and purify us daily more and more. Some have also indicated more things which should be avoided, such as soft beds and clothes, that we should avoid excessive adornment, and neither associate nor talk with members of the opposite sex, nor even look upon them, and whatsoever else may be conducive to chastity. In all these things no one can fix a definite rule and measure. Each one must watch himself and see what things are needful to him for chastity, in what quantity and how long they help him to be chaste, that he may thus choose and observe them for himself; if he cannot do this, let him for a time give himself up to be controlled by another, who may hold him to such observance until he can learn to rule himself. This was the purpose for which the monastic houses were established of old, to teach young people discipline and purity.

III. In this work a good strong faith is a great help, more noticeably so than in almost any other; so that for this reason also Isaiah xi. says that "faith is a girdle of the reins," [Is. 11:5] that is, a guard of chastity. For he who so lives that he looks to God for all grace, takes pleasure in spiritual purity; therefore he can so much more easily resist fleshly impurity: and in such faith the spirit tells him of a certainty how he shall avoid evil thoughts and everything that is repugnant to chastity. For as the faith in divine favor lives without ceasing and works in all works, so it also does not cease its admonitions in all things that are pleasing to God or displease Him; as St. John says in his Epistle: "Ye need not that any man teach you: for the divine anointing, that is, the Spirit of God, teacheth you of all things." [1 John 2:27]

Yet we must not despair if we are not soon rid of the temptation, nor by any means immune that we are free from it as long as we live, and we must regard it only as an incentive and admonition to prayer, fasting, watching, laboring, and to other exercises for the quenching of the flesh, especially to the practice and exercise of faith in God. For that chastity is not precious which is at ease, but that which is at war with unchastity, and fights, and without ceasing drives out all the poison with which the flesh and the evil spirit attack it. Thus St. Peter says, "I beseech you, abstain from fleshly desires and lusts, which war always against the soul." [1 Pet. 2:11] And St Paul, Romans vi, "Ye shall not obey the body in its lusts." [Rom. 6:12] In these and like passages it is shown that no one is without evil lust; but that everyone shall and must daily fight against it. But although this brings uneasiness and pain, it is none the less a work that gives pleasure, in which we shall have our comfort and satisfaction. For they who think they make an end of temptation by yielding to it, only set themselves on fire the more; and although for a time it is quiet, it comes again with more strength another time, and finds the nature weaker than before.

Thou shalt not steal.

This Commandment also has a work, which embraces very many good works, and is opposed to many vices, and is called in German Mildigkeit, "benevolence;" which is a work ready to help and serve every one with one's goods. And it fights not only against theft and robbery, but against all stinting in temporal goods which men may practise toward one another: such as greed, usury, overcharging and plating wares that sell as solid, counterfeit wares, short measures and weights, and who could tell all the ready, novel, clever tricks,[52] which multiply daily in every trade, by which every one seeks his own gain through the other's loss, and forgets the rule which says; "What ye wish that others do to you, that do ye also to them." [Matt. 7:12] If every one kept this rule before his eyes in his trade, business, and dealings with his neighbor, he would readily find how he ought to buy and sell, take and give, lend and give for nothing, promise and keep his promise, and the like. And when we consider the world in its doings, how greed controls all business, we would not only find enough to do, if we would make an honorable living before God, but also be overcome with dread and fear for this perilous, miserable life, which is so exceedingly overburdened, entangled and taken captive with cares of this temporal life and dishonest seeking of gain.

[Sidenote: Greed]

II. Therefore the Wise Man says not in vain: "Happy is the rich man, who is found without blemish, who does not run after gold, and has not set his confidence in the treasures of money. Who is he? We will praise him, that he has done wondrous things in his life." [Sir. 31:8 f.] As if he would say; "None such is found, or very few indeed." Yea, they are very few who notice and recognise such lust for gold in themselves. For greed has here a very beautiful, fine cover for its shame, which is called provision for the body and natural need, under cover of which it accumulates wealth beyond all limits and is never satisfied; so that he who would in this matter keep himself clean, must truly, as he says, do miracles or wondrous things in his life.

Now see, if a man wish not only to do good works, but even miracles, which God may praise and be pleased with, what need has he to look elsewhere? Let him take heed to himself, and see to it that he run not after gold, nor set his trust on money, but let the gold run after him, and money wait on his favor, and let him love none of these things nor set his heart on them; then he is the true, generous, wonder-working, happy man, as Job xxxi says: "I have never yet relied upon gold, and never yet made gold my hope and confidence." [Job 31:24] And Psalm lxii: "If riches increase, set not your heart upon them." [Ps. 62:10] So Christ also teaches, Matthew vi, that we shall take no thought, what we shall eat and drink and wherewithal we shall be clothed, since God cares for this, and knows that we have need of all these things. [Matt. 6:31 f.]

But some say: "Yes, rely upon that, take no thought, and see whether a roasted chicken will fly into your mouth!" I do not say that a man shall not labor and seek a living; but he shall not worry, not be greedy, not despair, thinking that he will not have enough; for in Adam we are all condemned to labor, when God says to him, Genesis iii, "In the sweat of thy face shalt thou eat bread." [Gen. 3:19] And Job v, "As the birds to flying, so is man born into labor." [Job 5:7 Vulgate] Now the birds fly without worry and greed, and so we also should labor without worry and greed; but if you do worry and are greedy, wishing that the roasted chicken fly into your mouth: worry and be greedy, and see whether you will thereby fulfil God's Commandment and be saved!

[Sidenote: Faith the Source of Benevolence]

191

III. This work faith teaches of itself. For if the heart looks for divine favor and relies upon it, how is it possible that a man should be greedy and worry? He must be sure beyond a doubt that God cares for him; therefore he does not cling to money; he uses it also with cheerful liberality for the benefit of his neighbor, and knows well that he will have enough, however much he may give away. For his God, Whom he trusts, will not lie to him nor forsake, him, as it is written, Psalm xxxvii: "I have been young, and now am old; never have I seen a believing man, who trusts God, that is a righteous man, forsaken, or his child begging bread." [Ps. 37:25] Therefore the Apostle calls no other sin idolatry except covetousness [Col. 3:5], because this sin shows most plainly that it does not trust God for anything, expects more good from its money than from God; and, as has been said, it is by such confidence that God is truly honored or dishonored.

And, indeed, in this Commandment it can be clearly seen how all good works must be done in faith; for here every one most surely feels that the cause of covetousness is distrust and the cause of liberality is faith. For because a man trusts God, he is generous and does not doubt that he will always have enough; on the other hand, a man is covetous and worries because he does not trust God. Now, as in this Commandment faith is the master-workman and the doer of the good work of liberality, so it is also in all the other Commandments, and without such faith liberality is of no worth, but rather a careless squandering of money.

[Sidenote: The Test of Liberality]

IV. By this we are also to know that this liberality shall extend even to enemies and opponents. For what manner of good deed is that, if we are liberal only to our friends? As Christ teaches, Luke vi, even a wicked man does that to another who is his friend. [Luke 6:32 f.] Besides, the brute beasts also do good and are generous to their kind. Therefore a Christian must rise higher, let his liberality serve also the undeserving, evil-doers, enemies, and the ungrateful, even as his heavenly Father makes His sun to rise on good and evil, and the rain to fall on the grateful and ungrateful. [Matt. 5:45]

But here it will be found how hard it is to do good works according to God's Commandment, how nature squirms, twists and writhes in its exposition to it, although it does the good works of its own choice easily and gladly. Therefore take your enemies, the ungrateful, and do good to them; then you will find how near you are to this Commandment or how far from it, and how all your life you will always have to do with the practice of this work. For if your enemy needs you and you do not help him when you can, it is just the same as if you had stolen what belonged to him, for you owed it to him to help him. So says St. Ambrose, "Feed the hungry; if you do not feed him, you have, as far as you are concerned, slain him." And in this Commandment are included the works of mercy, which Christ will require at men's hands at the last day. [Matt. 25:35 f.]

But the magistrates and cities ought to see to it that the vagabonds, pilgrims and mendicants from foreign lands be debarred, or at least allowed only under restrictions and rules, so that knaves be not permitted to run at large under the guise of mendicants, and their knavery, of which there now is much, be prohibited; I have spoken at greater length of this Commandment in the Treatise on Usury.[53]

Thou shall not bear false witness against thy neighbor.

[Sidenote: The Eight Commandment: The Duty of Truthfulness]

[Sidenote: In Worldly Matters]

This Commandment seems small, and yet is so great, that he who would rightly keep it must risk and imperil life and limb, goods and honor, friends and all that he has; and yet it includes no more than the work of that small member, the tongue, and is called in German Wahrheit sagen, "telling the truth" and, where there is need, gainsaying lies; so that it forbids many evil works of the tongue. First: those which are committed by speaking, and those which are committed by keeping silent. By speaking, when a man has an unjust lawsuit, and wants to prove and maintain his case by a false argument, catch his neighbor with subtilty, produce everything that strengthens and furthers his own cause, and withhold and discount everything that further his neighbor's good cause; in doing which he does not do to his neighbor as he would have his neighbor do to him. [Matt. 7:12] This some men do for the sake of gain, some to avoid loss or shame, thereby seeking their own advantage more than God's Commandment, and excuse themselves by saying: Vigilanti jura subveniunt, "the law helps him who watches"; just as if it were not as much their duty to watch for their neighbor's cause as for their own. Thus they intentionally allow their neighbor's cause to be lost, although they know that it is just. This evil is at present so common that I fear no court is held and no suit tried but that one side sins against this Commandment. And even when they cannot accomplish it, they yet have the unrighteous spirit and will, so that they would wish the neighbor's just cause to be lost and their unjust cause to prosper. This sin is most frequent when the opponent is a prominent man or an enemy. For a man wants to revenge himself on his enemy: but the ill will of a man of prominence he does not wish to bring upon himself; and then begins the flattering and fawning, or, on the other hand, the withholding of the truth. Here no one is willing to run the risk of disfavor and displeasure, loss and danger for the truth's sake; and so God's Commandment must perish. And this is almost universally the way of the world. He who would keep this Commandment, would have both hands full doing only those good works which concern the tongue. And then, how many are there who allow themselves to be fenced and swerved aside from the truth by presents and gifts! so that in all places it is truly a high, great, rare work, not to be a false witness against one's neighbor.

II. There is a second bearing of witness to the truth, which is still greater, with which we must fight against the evil spirits; and this concerns not temporal matters, but the Gospel and the truth of faith, which the evil spirit has at no time been able to endure, and always so manages that the great among men, whom it is hard to resist, must oppose and persecute it. Of which it is written in Psalm lxxxii, "Rid the poor out of the hand of the wicked, and help the forsaken to maintain his just cause." [Ps. 82:3 f.]

Such persecution, it is true, has now become infrequent; but that is the fault of the spiritual prelates, who do not stir up the Gospel, but let it perish, and so have abandoned the very thing because of which such witnessing and persecution should arise; and in its place they teach us their own law and what pleases them. For this reason the devil also does not stir, since by vanquishing the Gospel he has also vanquished faith in Christ, and everything goes as he wishes. But if the Gospel should be stirred up and be heard again, without doubt the whole world would be aroused and moved, and the greater portion of the kings, princes, bishops, doctors and clergy, and all that is great, would oppose it and rage against it, as has always happened when the Word of God has come to light; for the world cannot endure what comes from God. This is proved in Christ, Who was and is the very greatest and most precious and best of all that God has; yet the world not only did not receive Him, but persecuted Him more cruelly than all others who had ever come forth from God.

Therefore, as at that time, so at all times there are few who stand by the divine truth, and imperil and risk life and limb, goods and honor, and all that they have, as Christ has foretold: "Ye shall be hated of all men for My Name's sake." [Matt. 14:9 f.] And: "Many of them shall be offended in Me." Yea, if this truth were attacked by peasants, herdsmen, stable-boys and men of no standing, who would not be willing and able to confess it and to bear witness to it? But when the pope, and the bishops, together with princes and kings attack it, all men flee, keep silent, dissemble, in order that they may not lose goods, honor, favor and life.

III. Why do they do this? Because they have no faith in God, and expect nothing good from Him. For where such faith and confidence are, there is also a bold, defiant, fearless heart, that ventures and stands by the truth, though it cost life or cloak, though it be against pope or kings; as we see that the martyrs did. For such a heart is satisfied and rests easy because it has a gracious, loving God. Therefore it despises all the favor, grace, goods and honor of men, lets them come and go as they please; as is written in Psalm xv: "He contemneth them that contemn God, and honoreth them that fear the Lord" [Ps. 15:4]; that is, the tyrants, the mighty, who persecute the truth and despise God, he does not fear, he does not regard them, he despiseth them; on the other band, those who are persecuted for the truth's sake, and fear God more than men, to these he clings, these he defends, these he honors, let it vex whom it may; as it is written of Moses, Hebrews xi, that he stood by his brethren, regardless of the mighty king of Egypt. [Heb. 11:24 ff.]

Lo, in this Commandment again you see briefly that faith must be the master-workman in this work also, so that without it no one has courage to do this work: so, entirely are all works comprised in faith, has has now been often said. Therefore, apart from faith all works, are dead, however good the form and name they bear. For as no one does the work of this Commandment except he be firm and fearless in the confidence of divine favor: so also he does no work of any other Commandment without the same faith: thus every one may easily by this Commandment test and weigh himself whether he be a Christian and truly believe in Christ, and thus whether he is doing good works or no. Now we see how the Almighty God has not only set our Lord Jesus Christ before us that we should believe in Him with such confidence, but also holds before us in Him an example of this same confidence and of such good works, to the end that we should believe in Him, follow Him and abide in Him forever; as He says, John xiv: "I am the Way, the Truth and the life," [John 14:6]—the Way, in which we follow Him; the Truth, that we believe in Him; the life, that we live in Him forever.

From all this it is now manifest that all other works, which are not commanded, are perilous and easily known: such as building churches, beautifying them, making pilgrimages, and all that is written at so great length in the Canon Law and has misled and burdened the world and ruined it, made uneasy consciences, silenced and weakened faith, and has not said how a man, although he neglect all else, has enough to do with all his powers to keep the Commandments of God, and can never do all the good works which he is commanded to do; why then does he seek others, which are neither necessary not commanded, and neglect those that are necessary and commanded?

[Sidenote: The Ninth and Tenth Commandments]

The last two Commandments, which forbid evil desires of the body for pleasure and for temporal goods, are clear in themselves; these evil desires do no harm to our neighbor, and yet they continue unto the grave, and the strife in us against them endures unto death; therefore these two Commandments are drawn together by St. Paul into one, Romans vii, and are set as a goal unto which we do not attain, and only in our thoughts reach after until death. For no one has ever been so holy that he felt in himself no evil inclination, especially when occasion and temptation were offered. [Rom. 7:7] For original sin is born in us by nature and may be checked, but not entirely uprooted, except through the death of the body; which for this reason is profitable and a thing to be desired.[54] To this may God help us. Amen.

FOOTNOTES

[1] Col. 3:17. See above p. 25, note 1.

[2] The Tessaradecas consolatoria, printed in the present volume, pp. 109-171.

[3] Sexternlein.

[4] Questions debated in the schools.

[5] Here "the Faith" means the Creed, as a statement of faith.

[6] I.e., In faith.

[7] A quality, state or condition, independent of works.

[8] St. Jacob di Compostella, a place in Spain, where the Apostle James, the son of Zebedee, who was killed in Jerusalem (Acts 12:2), is in Spanish tradition said to have died a martyr's death; since the Ninth Century a noted and much frequented goal of pilgrimages. The name Compostella is a corruption of Giacomo Postolo, that is "James the Apostle."

[9] St. Bridget of Ireland, who died in 523, was considered a second Virgin Mary, the "Mary of the Irish." Perhaps here confused with another Bridget, or Brigita, who died 1373, a Scottish saint, who wrote several prayers, printed for the first time in 1492 and translated into almost all European languages.

[10] I.e., by us men.

[11] This translation indicates the imperfection of the German form of Bible quotation throughout this treatise.

[12] Page 190.

[13] Page 190.

[14] A Jarmarkt; the reference here being to the bargaining common at such fairs.

[15] The theme developed in the treatise De Libertate, 1520.

[16] Page 190.

[17] A gold coin, the value of which is very uncertain. It was an adaptation of the florin, which was first coined in Florence in the year 1252, and was worth about $2.50. Of the value of the gold gulden of Luther's time various estimates are given. Schaff, Church History, 3 vi., p. 470, calls it a guilder and says it was equal to about $4.00 of the present day. Preserved Smith, Life of Luther, p. 367, fixes its intrinsic value at about fifty cents, but believes its purchasing power was almost twenty times as great. To us a gold piece worth fifty cents seems almost impossible; but the New English Dictionary quotes, under the year 1611: "Florin or Franc: an ancient coin of gold in France, worth ij s. sterling." As the gold coins of those times were not made of pure gold, rarely 17 carats fine, the possibility may be granted. But in 1617, the Dictionary quotes "The Gold Rehnish Guldens of Germany are almost of the same standard as the Crowne Gold of England," and the Crown was worth at the time 6s. 3 1/2 d.—somewhat more than $1.50.

The later silver gulden, worth about forty cents was current in Europe until modern times, and a gulden, worth 48 1/2 cents, was, until recently, a standard coin in Austro-Hungary.

[18] Grosse Hansen.

[19] Men who exercised a delegated authority and acted as the representatives of pope and bishop in matters of church law.

[20] See especially the Address to the Christian Nobility and the Babylonian Captivity.

[21] On the number of the sections see the Introduction, p. 178.

[22] Here, as also in his Catechism, Luther departs from the Old Testament form of the Third Commandment. His restatement of it is extremely difficult to put into English, because of the various meanings of the word Feiertag. It may mean "day of rest," or "holiday," or "holy day." By the use of this word Luther avoids the difficulty of first retaining the Jewish Sabbath in the Commandment and then rejecting it in favor of the Christian Sunday in the explanation.

[23] Gottesdienst.

[24] A reference to the Requiem Mass, sung both at the burial of the dead, and on the anniversary of the day of death. The word translated "memorial," Begängniss, is literally, "a burial service."

[25] See also the Treatise on the New Testament, elsewhere in this volume.

[26] The sermons were frequently either scholastic arguments or popular, often comic tirades against current immorality; the materials were taken from the stories of the saints as much as from the Bible.

[27] Lived 1091-1153. Founder of the Cistercian monastery at Clairvaux, of whom Luther says: "If there ever lived on earth a God-fearing and holy monk, it was Saint Bernard, of Clairvaux." Erl. Ed., 36, 8.

[28] Cf. Discussion of Confession, above, p. 81 f.

[29] The prayer-book and the rosary. The Breviary, a collection of prayers, was used by the clergy; the Rosary, the beads of which represent prayers, the smaller and more numerous Ave Marias, the larger of the Lord's Prayer, Paternoster, was the layman's prayer book.

[30] Cf. Introduction to The Fourteen of Consolation, p. 106.

[31] See note, p. 191.

[32] The German, Oelgötzen, means the wooden images of saints, which were painted with oil paints. It was transferred to any dull person, block-head, sometimes also to priests, who were anointed with oil at their consecration.

[33] Sinnlichkeit.

[34] St. Barbara, a legendary saint, whose day falls on December 4, was thought to protect against storm and fire. See above, p. 237. St. Sebastian, a martyr of the third century, whose day falls on January 20, was supposed to ward off the plague.

[35] Cf. The Fourteen of Consolation, above, p. 162.

[36] Page 194 f.

[37] I. e., by fear without love.

[38] The patron saint of music, of whose life and martyrdom little that is definite is known.

[39] Canonisations, giving a dead man the rank of a saint, who may be or shall be worshiped.

[40] I.e., faith.

[41] Cf. the similar statements in the Sermon vom Wucher (Weimar Ed., VI, 59) and in the Address to the Christian Nobility (ibid., 438).

[42] A name for the dependents of the papal court at Rome.

[43] At Constance, 1414-1443; at Rome, the Lateran council, 1512-1517.

[44] Or, "Who is said to rule the councils."

[45] This program of reform is further elaborated in the Address to the Christian Nobility.

[46] Augustus Caesar, first Roman Emperor (B.C. 63-A.D. 14), the Caesar Augustus of Luke 2:1.

[47] "The purchase of a rent-charge (rent, census, Zins) was one of the methods of investing money frequently resorted to during the later middle ages. From the transfer from one person to another of the right to receive a rent already due the step was but a short one to the creation of an altogether new rent-charge, for the express purpose of raising money by the sale of it...The practice seems to have arisen spontaneously, and to have been by no means a mere evasion of the prohibition of usury." Dictionary of Political Economy, ed. by R. H. Inglish Palgrave, vol. ii. Cf. Ashley, Economic History, vol. i, p.t. ii, §§ 66, 74, 75. For a fuller discussion of the subject by Luther, see the Sermon vom Wucher (Weimar Ed., VI, 51-60).

[48] See note above, p. 220.

[49] Sorgfäitigkeit, Luther's translation of the Vulgate solicitndo in Rom. 12:8, where our English Version reads "diligence." The word as Luther uses it includes the two kinds of carefulness and considerateness.

[50] A most strict monastic order; the phrase here is equivalent to "becomes a monk."

[51] Sanftmüthlgkeit.

[52] Luther discusses these tricks in detail in his Sermon von Kaufhandlung und Wucher (1524) Weimar Ed., XV, pp. 279 ff.

[53] Sermon von dem Wucher, Weimar Ed., VI, 36 ff. Cf. also Address to the German Nobility.

[54] Cf. The Fourteen of Consolation above, p. 149.

A TREATISE ON THE NEW TESTAMENT

THAT IS THE HOLY MASS

1520

INTRODUCTION

The Treatise on the New Testament, that is, on the Holy Mass, was published in the year 1520[1] In the beginning of August of that year, Luther's Address to the Christian Nobility of the German Nation had appeared, in which he had touched upon the subject of the mass,[2] but refused to express himself fully at that time, promising to take up this question later, a promise which he had already made in his Treatise on Good Works, of May, 1520.[3] He must have begun the preparation of this Treatise on the New Testament while the Address to the Christian Nobility was still in press, because on Aug. 3 it was already finished and ready for publication.[4] The treatise, therefore, takes its place between Luther's two famous writings, the Address to the Christian Nobility and the Babylonian Captivity of the Church, which appeared in Oct, 1520. Its tone is remarkably quiet, and its aim predominantly constructive. It is one of those devotional tracts which Luther issued from time to time between his larger publications, and which appear like roses among the thorns of his polemical writings.

The doctrine of the Lord's Supper was one of the most corrupt doctrines of the Roman Church, and it was, therefore, but natural that Luther should have written extensively on this subject, even at the beginning of the work of reformation. From this period, when the opposition of the Sacramentarians[5] to the doctrine of the Real Presence had not yet arisen we have four writings of Luther in which he makes this sacrament a subject of special discussion. These are (1) his mild-toned Sermon von dem hochwürdigen Sacrament, etc., of 1519; (2) the present Sermon von dem neuen Testament, etc., of Aug., 1520; (3) the Babylonian Captivity of the Church, of Oct., 1520; (4) the strongly polemical tract On the Abuse of the Mass, 1522.[6] We shall have occasion to refer to some interesting points of comparison among these works.

This treatise is divided into sections, ending with number 40, but section 32 is omitted, so that there are only 39 in all. Section 1 contains the introduction, section 40 the conclusion. Sections 2-15 are the positive, constructive part of the treatise, dealing with the question. What is the Lord's Supper? In sections 16-34 the sacrificial theory of the Roman Church is rejected; sections 35-31 discuss (1) in how far we may speak of making an offering in the sacrament, and (2) what follows for the conception of a true priesthood in the Church, viz., the priesthood of all believers. Sections 33-39 deal, among other things, with the abuses to which an unscriptural conception of the Lord's Supper has led. Of special interest is section 12, in which Luther gives a summary of all that enters into the Sacrament of the Altar.

Knowing, as we do, that Luther developed his doctrine of the Lord's Supper gradually[7] and under stress of much opposition from all sides, it is interesting for us to note the stage of that development which this treatise represents. We may, therefore, inquire how he stood at this time on the question of the Real Presence. This question is answered under the fourth point of section 12. The true presence of the body and blood cannot be more clearly admitted than is done in sections 11 and 12 of this treatise. We can safely say that there never was a time when Luther was uncertain on this point. The point of view from which he discusses the significance of the sacrament in the Sermon von dem hochwürdigen Sacrament (1519) has sometimes been cited to the contrary, but even in this Sermon, with its emphasis upon the spiritual body of Christ, of which even those may be partakers whom the pope might exclude from the external communion, he speaks of the bread and wine as being changed into the Lord's "true, natural flesh" and into His "natural, true blood," [8] which shows that Luther at that time, nine months before the appearance of this Treatise on the New Testament, still held even to the conception of transubstantiation. He cannot, therefore, have had doubts about the Real Presence.

In view, however, of the rapid development of Luther's doctrinal conceptions, we might further ask: Did Luther still retain his belief in transubstantiation at the time when he wrote the Treatise on the New Testament? At the beginning of October in this same year, in his Babylonian Captivity, Luther comes out for the first time with an attack on this Roman doctrine. He regards it as a mere human opinion, which one may accept or not accept, and clearly inclines to the belief that after consecration not only the form (Gestalt; species), but also the substance of bread and wine is still present.[9] In the Sermon von dem hochwürdigen Sacrament he spoke of the "shape and form of the bread"; in the present treatise he chooses the expression: "His own true flesh and blood under the bread and wine" (sec. 12). This would soon to indicate that in this writing he already holds the opinion which he soon afterward expressed in the Babylonian Captivity. But while he believed in the real presence of Christ's "own true flesh and blood," this body of Christ he regards—at this time, when he has not yet had to meet the spiritualistic interpretation of the Sacramentarians—as a sign only, a thing signifying the blessing of the sacrament, which is forgiveness of sins and life eternal (sec 10). Exactly the same view is expressed in the Sermon of 1519[10]. "Luther does not yet speak of 'any value which this body, sacramentally imparted, is supposed to have in and of itself.'" [11]

The question next arises: How does the recipient of the sign (body and blood under bread and wine) become partaker of that which is thereby signified? It is through faith, as the receiving organ (sec. 13). So, too, in the Sermon of 1519, where it is called the "third part of the sacrament," "in which the power lies" (wo die Macht anliegt). At a later time Luther found it necessary to emphasize the fact that it is not through the faith of the recipient that the sacrament gains its power and efficacy, since this attaches to it simply by virtue of the Word[12]; but that faith is the receiving organ for the blessing of the sacrament is a conviction which he never gave up.

The object of faith is the Gospel, i. e., the promise of the forgiveness of sins contained in the Words of Institution, which are a "testament," a "new and eternal testament" (secs. 5-10). Hence the title of the work, Treatise on the New Testament. While the Sermon of 1519 speaks of the Gospel only in general, we have here a special emphasis on the words of institution as embracing "in a short summary" the whole Gospel (sec. 33). The words of institution are still further emphasized and interpreted in the work On Abuse of the Mass, of 1522. Because of the importance of the Word in the sacrament, Luther declares that the words of institution should be spoken aloud, not whispered, as was and is done in the Roman churches, and in a language which is understood by the people (sec. 16).

An especially striking feature of this treatise is the repeated assertion that faith, which leans on the Word, and is the "principal part of the mass," does not absolutely need the sacrament. "I can daily enjoy the sacrament in the mass if only I keep before my eyes the testament, that is, the words and covenant of Christ, and feed and strengthen my faith thereby" (sec. 17) [13]. He quotes Augustine: "Only believe, so hast thou already partaken of the sacrament." In interpreting this passage we must remember that Luther was writing at a time when he was daily expecting to hear that the pope had excommunicated him from the Church. His comfort was that he and his followers could not be excluded by papal dictum from the communion of true believers and saints, nor deprived of the spiritual feeding upon the true spiritual body of Christ.

In this treatise Luther also attacks for the first time the Roman doctrine of the mass as a bloodless repetition of the sacrifice once made on Calvary—a theory which forgets that the mass is a testament and a sacrament, in which God promises and gives something to us, not we to Him (sec. 19). In much stronger language, and quoting Scripture more extensively, Luther exposes and rejects this error, so fundamental to the Roman system, in his work of 1522, On the Abuse of the Mass. In the Babylonian Captivity he remarks, "When I published my Sermon of the Supper,[14] I was still caught in the prevailing conception, and was indifferent whether the pope was right or not." [15] In this treatise, then, we have the first clear statement of the reformer on this subject.

It shows, however, the beautifully conservative character of Luther that even here, where he is compelled to reject the Roman sacrificial theory, we see him laboring to detect at least an element of scriptural truth in the refuted doctrine. He says (secs. 26, 27) that in the Supper we use Christ as our Sacrifice and Mediator, by bringing our prayer and thanksgiving to the Father through Him. And this furnishes the basis on which he builds the evangelical doctrine of the priesthood of all believers (sec. 28); alle Christenmänner Pfaffen, alle Weiber Pfaffinnen, es sei jung oder alt, etc. This is still more strongly emphasized in the Abuse of the Mass of 1522.

Two more points need to be mentioned,—the withholding of the cup from the laity and the number of the sacraments. In the Sermon of 1519 Luther attaches little importance to the communion in both kinds, though he thinks it would be well for the Church in a General Council to restore the two elements to all Christians. But in this treatise of 1520 he is already beginning to use stronger language. He would like to know who gave the power to withhold the cup (sec. 34). In the Babylonian Captivity and in the Abuse of the Mass he unsparingly condemns the Roman practice. On the number of the sacraments, Luther seems not yet to have been entirely in the clear when he wrote this work. In Section 24 he mentions, besides baptism and the Lord's Supper, "confirmation, penance, extreme unction, etc." In the Babylonian Captivity he definitely reduces the seven sacraments of the Roman Church to baptism, the Lord's Supper and penance, but he had his doubts on this point before he wrote this present work, as we may conclude from a remark in the Sermon of 1519, in which he distinguishes "baptism and the bread" as the two "principal sacraments," and also from a letter to Spalatin,[16] in which he writes that no one need expect from him a publication on the other sacraments until he shall first have been taught by what passage of Scripture he may justify them.[17] In conclusion, it may be said that this whole Treatise on the New Testament is a beautiful illustration of the constructive power of Luther's work. In the work of tearing down he proceeds with the greatest care, ever mindful of his duty to replace the old with something new which can stand the test of Scripture.

J. L. NEVE.

Wittenberg Theological Seminary,

Springfield, O.

FOOTNOTES

[1] As the earliest prints, the following may be mentioned: (1) By Joh. Gruenenberg in Wittenberg, 11520 (the basis of the Weimar text); (2) by the same publisher, 1520; (3) by Melchior Lotther in Wittenberg, 1520; (4) by Silanus Ottmar in Wittenberg, Aug. 21st, 1520 (this is the text of the Erlangen Edition); (5) a Wittenberg print with no mention of the publisher, but otherwise identical in appearance with No. 4; (6) by Fridrichen Peypus at Nürnberg, 1520; (7) a Wittenberg print, 1520, with no mention of the publisher; (8) by Adam Petri in Basel, 1520; (9) a Wittenberg edition of 1520, revised by Luther (anderweit gecorigiert durch D. Mart. Luther); this edition in octavo, all the preceding in quarto. The text of this treatise in the following collections of Luther's works, Wittenberg, VII, 25 ff.; Jena, I, 329 ff.; Altenburg, I, 514 ff.; Leipzig, XVII 490 ff.; Walch XIX, 1256 ff.; Erlangen XXVII, 141 ff.; Weimar VI. 353 ff.

[2] By the word "mass" Luther means the celebration of the Lord's Supper. Even after this sacrament was understood in an evangelical sense, the Lutherans for a long time kept the name mass. Thus Melanchthon writes in the Augs. Conf., Art. xxiv, "Our churches are falsely accused of abolishing the mass; for the mass is retained on our part, and celebrated with the greatest reverence."

[3] Page 224.

[4] De Weite, Luther's Briefe, I, 475.

[5] The name given by the Lutheran theologians to those who denied the real presence of the body and blood of Christ in the Lord's Supper.

[6] Two more might have been mentioned: (1) a discourse on the proper preparation of the Lord's Supper (Erl. Ed., XVII, 55 ff.) and (2) the Discourse on Excommunication (Ibid., XXVII, 29 ff.)

[7] In the Introduction to The Babylonian Captivity of the Church he writes: "I am compelled, whether I will or not, to become daily more learned, having so many notable teachers diligently pushing me on and keeping me at work." (Weimar Ed., VI, 497.

[8] Cf. Koëstlin-Kawäeau, Martin Luther, 4th ed., I, 284; Koëstlin-Hay, Theology of Luther, I, 399 f; Luther's Werke, Berlin Ed., III, 261-264, 374.

[9] Weimar Ed., VI, 511 f.

[10] Cf. Koëstlin-Hay, op. cit., I, 340.

[11] Ibid., p. 350.

[12] Erl. Ed., XVI, 33, 92 ff.

[13] So also with much emphasis in the Sermon v. d. hochw. Sac., 1519.

[14] He means the Serm. v. d. hochw. Sac., 1519.

[15] Weimar Ed., VI, 502.

[16] De Weite, Briefe, I, 378

[17] Koëstlin-Hay, op. cit., I, 355.

A TREATISE ON THE NEW TESTAMENT,

THAT IS THE HOLY MASS

1519

JESUS[1]

[Sidenote: The Multiplying of Laws]

1. Experience, all chronicles, and the Holy Scriptures besides, teach us this truth: the less law, the more justice; the fewer commandments, the more good works. No well-regulated community ever existed long, if at all, where there were many laws. Therefore, before the ancient law of Moses, the Patriarchs of old had no prescribed law and order for the service of God other than the sacrifices; as we read of Adam, Abel, Noah and others. Afterward, circumcision was enjoined upon Abraham and his household, until the time of Moses, through whom God gave the people of Israel divers laws, forms, and practices, for the sole purpose of teaching human nature how utterly useless many laws are to make people pious. For although the law leads and drives away from evil to good works, it is still impossible for man to do them willingly and gladly; but he has at all times an aversion for the law and would rather be free. Now where there is unwillingness, there can never be a good work. For what is not done willingly is not good, and only seems to be good. Consequently, all the laws cannot make one really pious without the grace of God, for they can produce only dissemblers, hypocrites, pretenders, and proud saints, such as have their reward here [Matt. 6:2], and never please God. Thus He says to the Jews, Malachi i: "I have no pleasure in you; for who is there among you that would even as much as shut a door for me, willingly and out of love?" [Mal. 1:10]

[Sidenote: Sects and Divisions]

2. Another result of many laws is this, that many sects and divisions in the congregations [Gemeinden] arise from them. One adopts this way, another that, and there grows up in each man a false, secret love for his own sect, and a hatred, or at least a contempt for, and a disregard of the other sects, whereby brotherly, free, common love perishes, and selfish

love prevails. So Jeremiah and Hosea speak, [Jer. 2:28, Hos. 8:11,12] yea, all the profits lament that the people of Israel divided themselves into as many sects as there were cities in the land; each desiring to outdo the others. Thence also arose the Sadducees and Pharisees in the Gospel.

So we observe to-day, that through the Spiritual Law[2] but little justice and piety have arisen in Christendom; the world has been filled with dissemblers and hypocrites and with so many sects, orders, and divisions of the one people of Christ, that almost every city is divided into ten parties or more. And they daily devise new ways and manners (as they think) of serving God, until it has come to this, that priests, monks, and laity have become more hostile toward each other than Turks and Christians. Yea, the priests and the monks are deadly enemies, wrangling about their self-conceived ways and methods like fools and madmen, not only to the hindrance, but to the very destruction of Christian love and unity. Each one clings to his sect and despises the others; and they regard the laymen as though they were no Christians. This lamentable condition is only a result of the laws.

[Sidenote: The Mass Christ's Law]

3. Christ, in order that He might prepare for Himself an acceptable and beloved people, which should be bound together in unity through love, abolished the whole law of Moses. And that He might not give further occasion for divisions, He did not again appoint more than one law or order for His entire people, and that the holy mass. For, although baptism is also an external ordinance, yet it takes place but once, and is not a practice of the entire life, like the mass. Therefore, after baptism there is to be no other external order for the service of God except the mass. And where the mass is used, there is a true service, even though there be no other form, with singing, playing, bell-ringing, vestments, ornaments and postures; for everything of this sort is an addition invented by men. When Christ Himself first instituted this sacrament and held the first mass, there were do patens, no chasuble, no singing, no pageantry, but only thanksgiving to God, and the use of the sacrament. After this same simplicity the Apostles and all Christians long time held mass, until the divers forms and additions arose, by which the Romans held mass one way, the Greeks another; and now it has finally come to this, that the chief thing in the mass has become unknown, and nothing is remembered except the additions of men.

[Sidenote: Christ's Institution and Man's Ordinances]

4. The nearer, now, our masses are to the first mass of Christ, the better, without doubt, they are; and the farther from Christ's mass, the more perilous. For that reason we may not boast of ourselves, against the Russians or Greeks, that we alone have a right to hold mass; as little as a priest who wears a red chasuble may boast against him who wears one of white or black. For such external additions and differences may by their dissimilarity make sects

207

and dissensions, but they can never make the mass better. Although I neither wish nor am able to displace or discard all such additions, still, because such pompous forms are perilous, we must never permit ourselves to be led away by them from the simple institution by Christ and from the right use of the mass. And, indeed, the greatest and most useful art is to know what really and properly belongs to the mass, and what is added and foreign. For where there is no clear distinction, the eyes and the heart are easily misled by such shamming into a false impression and delusion; so that what men have invented is reckoned the mass, and what the mass is, is never experienced, to say nothing of deriving benefit from it. Thus, alas! it happens in our times; for, I fear, every day more than a thousand masses are said, of which perhaps not one is a real mass. O dear Christian, to have many masses is not to have the mass. There is more to it than that.

[Sidneote: The Chief Thing in the Mass]

5. If we desire to say mass rightly and understand it, then we must give up everything that the eyes and all the senses behold and suggest in this act, such as vestments, in bells, songs, ornaments, prayers, processions, elevations, prostrations, or whatever happens in the mass, until we first lay hold of and consider well the words of Christ, by which He completed and instituted the mass and commanded us to observe it. For therein lies the whole mass, its nature, work, profit and benefit, and without them (i. e., the words) no benefit is derived from the mass. But these are the words: Take and eat, this is My body, which is given for you. [Matt. 26:26] Take and drink ye all of it, this is the cup of the new and eternal testament in My blood, [Mark 14:22, 23, 24] which is shed for you and for many for the forgiveness of sins [Luke 22:19, 20]. These words every Christian must have before him in the mass and hold fast to them as the chief part of the mass, in which also the really good preparation for the mass and sacrament is taught; this we shall see.

[Sidenote: Faith and God's Promises]

6. If man is to deal with God and receive anything from Him, it must happen in this wise, not that man begin lay the first stone, but that God alone, without any entreaty or desire of man, must first come and give him a promise.[3] This word of God is the beginning, the foundation, the rock, upon which afterward all works, words and thoughts of man must build. This word man must gratefully accept, and faithfully believe the divine promise, and by no means doubt that it is and comes to pass just as He promises. This trust and faith is the beginning, middle, and end of all works and righteousness. For, because man does God the honor of regarding and confessing Him as true. He becomes to him a gracious God, Who in turn honors him and regards and confesses him as true. Thus it is not possible that man, of his own reason and strength, should by works ascend to heaven and anticipate God, moving Him to be gracious; but God must anticipate all works and thoughts, and make a promise clearly expressed in words, which man then takes and keeps with a good, firm faith. Then follows the Holy Spirit, Who is given him because of this same faith.

7. Such a promise was given to Adam after his fall, when God spake to the serpent: "I will put enmity between thee and the woman, between her seed and thy seed: she shall crush thy head; and thou shalt lie in wait for her foot." [Gen. 3:15] [4] In these words, however obscurely, God promises help to human nature, namely, that by a woman the devil shall again be overcome. This promise of God sustained Adam and Eve and all their children until the time of Noah; in this they believed, and by this faith they were saved; else they had despaired. [Gen. 9:9 f.] In like manner, after the flood, He made a covenant with Noah and his children, until the time of Abraham (Genesis xii), whom He summoned out of his fatherland [Gen. 12:1, 3], and promised that in his seed all nations should be blessed [Gen. 18:18]. This promise Abraham believed and obeyed, and thereby was justified and became the friend of God. [Gen. 22:18; 15:6] In the same book this promise to Abraham is many times repeated, enlarged and made more definite, until Isaac is promised him, who was to be the seed from which Christ and every blessing should come. In this faith upon the promise Abraham's children were kept until the time of Christ, although in the mean time it was continually renewed and made more definite by David and many prophets This promise the Lord in the Gospel calls "Abraham's bosom," [Luke 16:22, 23] because in it were kept all who with a right faith clung thereto, and, with Abraham, waited for Christ Then came Moses, who declared the same promise under many forms in the Law. [Ex. 3:6, 7, 8] Through him God promised the people of Israel the land of Canaan, while they were still in Egypt; which promise they believed, and by it they were sustained and led into that land.

[Sidenote: God's Promise in the Mass—the Testament]

8. In the New Testament, likewise, Christ has made a promise or solemn vow, which we are to believe and thereto come to godliness and salvation. This promise is the word in which Christ says: "This is the cup of the New Testament." [Luke 22:20] This we shall now examine.

Not every vow is called a testament, but only a last irrevocable will of one who is about to die, whereby he bequeaths his goods, allotted and assigned to be distributed to whom he will. Just as St. Paul says to the Hebrews that a testament must be made operative by death, and avails nothing while he still lives who made the testament. [Heb. 9:16, 17] For other vows, made for this life, may be hindered or recalled, and hence are not called testaments. Therefore, wherever in Scripture God's testament is referred to by the prophets, in that very word the prophets are taught that God would become man and die and rise again, to the end that His Word, in which He promised such a testament, might be fulfilled and confirmed. For if He is to make a testament as He promised, then He must die; if He is to die, He must be a man. And so that little word "testament" is a short summary of all God's wonders and grace, fulfilled in Christ.

9. He also distinguishes this testament from others and says, "It is a new and everlasting testament, in His own blood, for the forgiveness of sins"; whereby He disannuls the old testament. For the little word "new" makes the testament of Moses old and ineffective, one that avails no more. The old testament was a promise made through Moses to the people of Israel, to whom was promised the land of Canaan. For this testament God did not die, but the paschal lamb had to die instead of Christ and as a type of Christ; and so it was a temporal testament in the blood of the paschal lamb, which was shed for the obtaining and possessing of that land of Canaan. And as the paschal lamb, which died in the old testament for the land of Canaan, was a temporal and transitory thing, so too the old testament, together with that possession or land of Canaan allotted and promised therein, was temporal and transitory.

But Christ, the true Paschal Lamb, is an eternal divine Person, Who dies to establish the new testament; therefore the testament and the possessions therein bequeathed are eternal and abiding. And that is what He means when He contrasts this testament with that other, and says: A new testament—so that the other may become old and of none effect. An eternal testament, [Heb. 8:13] He says, not temporal like that other; not to dispose of temporal lands or possessions, but of eternal. In My blood, He says, not in the blood of a lamb. All this is to the end that the old should be altogether annulled and give place to the new alone.

10. What then is this testament, and what is bequeathed us therein by Christ? Forsooth, a great, eternal and unspeakable treasure, namely, the forgiveness of all sins, as the words plainly state, "This is the cup of a new eternal testament in My blood, that is shed for you and for many for the remission of sin." [Matt. 26:8, Luke 22:30] As though He said: Behold, man, in these words I promise and bequeath thee forgiveness of all thy sin and eternal life. And in order that thou mayest be certain and know that such promise remains irrevocably thine, I will die for it, and will give My body and blood for it, and will leave them both to thee as sign and seal, that by them thou mayest remember Me." [1 Cor. 11:25] So He says: "As oft as ye do this, remember Me." [Luke 22:19] Even as a man who bequeathes something includes therein what shall be done for him afterward [1 Cor. 11:25], as is the custom at present in the requiems and masses for the dead, so also Christ has ordained a requiem for Himself in this testament; not that He needs it, but because it is necessary and profitable for us to remember Him; whereby we are strengthened in faith, confirmed in hope and made ardent in love. For as long as we live on earth our lot is such that the evil spirit and all the world assail us with joy and sorrow, to extinguish our love for Christ, to blot out our faith, and to weaken our hope. Wherefore we sorely need this sacrament, in

which we may gain new strength when we have grown weak, and may daily exercise ourselves into the strengthening and uplifting of the spirit.

[Sidenote: Promises and Signs]

11. Furthermore, in all His promises God has usually given a sign in addition to the word, for the greater assurance and strengthening of our faith. Thus He gave Noah the sign of the rainbow. [Gen. 9:9, 13] To Abraham He gave circumcision as a sign. [Gen. 17:11] To Gideon He gave the rain on the ground and on the fleece [Judg. 6:37 ff.]; and we constantly find in the Scriptures many of these signs, given along with the promises. For so also worldly testaments are made; not only are the words written down, but seals and notaries' marks are affixed thereto, that they may always be binding and authentic. Thus Christ has done in this testament and has affixed to the words a powerful and most precious seal and sign; this is His own true body and blood under the bread and wine. For we poor men, since we live in our five senses, must always have, along with the words, at least one outward sign, on which we may lay hold, and around which we may gather; but in such wise that this sign may be a sacrament, that is, that it may be external and yet contain and express something spiritual, so that through the external we may be drawn into the spiritual, comprehending the external with the eyes of the body, the spiritual and inward with the eyes of the heart.

[Sidenote: The Parts of the Testament]

12. Now we see how many parts there are in this testament, or the mass. There is, first, the testator who makes the testament, Christ. Second, the heirs to whom the testament is bequeathed, we Christians. Third, the testament in itself, the words of Christ when He says: "This is My body which is given for you. This is My blood which is shed for you, a new eternal testament, etc." Fourth, the seal or token, the sacrament, bread and wine, and under them His true body and blood. For everything that is in this sacrament must live; therefore He did not put it in dead writ and seal, but in living words and signs which we use from day to day.

And this is what is meant when the priest elevates the host,[5] by which act he addresses us rather than God, as though he said to us: Behold, this is the seal and sign of the testament in which Christ has bequeathed us remission of all an and eternal life. With this agrees also that which is sung by the choir: "Blessed be He that cometh to us in the name of God" [Matt. 21:9]?[6] so that we testify how we receive therein blessings from God, and do not sacrifice nor give to Him. Fifth, the bequeathed blessing which the words signify, namely, remission of sin and eternal life. Sixth, the obligation, remembrance or requiem which we should observe for Christ, to wit, that we preach this His love and grace, hear and meditate upon it, by it be incited and preserved unto love and hope in Him, as St. Paul explains it:

"As oft as ye eat this bread and drink of this cup ye show the death of Christ." [1 Cor. 11:26] And this is what an earthly testator does, who bequeaths something to his heirs, that he may leave behind him a good name, the good will of men and a blessed memory, that he be not forgotten.

[Sidenote: How the Mass Should be Regarded]

13. From all this it is now easily seen what the mass is, how one should prepare himself for it, how observe and how use it, and how many are the abuses of it. For just as one would act if ten thousand gulden were bequeathed him by a good friend: so, and with far more reason, we ought to conduct ourselves toward the mass, which is nothing else than an exceeding rich and everlasting and good testament bequeathed us by Christ Himself, and bequeathed in such wise that He would have had no other reason to die except that He wished to make such a testament; so fervently desirous was He to pour out His eternal treasures, as He says: "With desire I have desired to eat this passover with you before I die." [Luke 22:15] Hence, too, it comes that in spite of many masses we remain so blind and cold, for we do not know what the mass is, what we do in it, nor what we get from it.

[Sidenote: Faith in the word the True Preparation for the Mass]

Since then it is nothing else than a testament, the first and by far the best preparation for the mass is a hungry soul and a firm joyful faith of the heart accepting such a testament Who would not go with great and joyful desire, hope and comfort, and demand a thousand gulden, if he knew that at a certain place they had been bequeathed him; especially if there were no other condition than that he remember, honor, and praise the testator? So, in this matter, you must above all else take heed to your heart, that you believe the words of Christ, and admit their truth, when He says to you and to all: "This is My blood, a new testament, by which I bequeath you forgiveness of all sins and eternal life." How could you do Him greater dishonor and show greater disrespect to the holy mass than by not believing or by doubting? For He desired this to be so certain that He Himself even died for it. Surely such doubt would be naught else than denying and blaspheming Christ's sufferings and death, and every blessing which He has thereby obtained.

14. For this reason, I have said, everything depends upon the words of this sacrament, which are the words of Christ, and which we verily should set in pure gold and precious stones, and keep nothing more diligently before the eyes of the heart, that faith be exercised thereby. Let another pray, fast, go to confession, prepare himself for mass and the sacrament as he will. Do thou the same, but know that all that is pure fool's-work and self-deception, if you do not set before you the words of the testament and arouse yourself to believe and desire them. A long time would you have to polish your shoes, pick the lint[7] off your clothes, and deck yourself out to get an inheritance, if you had no letter and seal

with which you could prove your right to it. But if you have letter and seal, and believe, desire, and seek it, it must be given you, even though you were scaly, scabby, stinking and most unclean. So if you would receive this sacrament and testament worthily, see to it that you bring forward these living words of Christ, rely thereon with a strong faith, and desire what Christ has therein promised you: then it will be given you, then are you worthy and well prepared. This faith and confidence must and will make you joyful, and awaken a bold love for Christ, by means of which you will begin with joy to lead a really good life and with all your heart to flee from sin. For he who loves Christ will surely do what pleases Him, and leave undone what does not please Him. But who will love Him except he taste the riches of this testament which Christ, out of pure mercy, has freely bequeathed to poor sinners? This taste comes by the faith which believes and trusts the testament and promise. If Abraham had not believed the promise of God he would never have amounted to anything. Just as certainly, then, as Abraham, Noah, and David accepted and believed their promises: so certainly must we also accept and believe this testament and promise.

[Sidenote: Who is Worthy]

15. Now there are two temptations which never cease to assail you; the first, that you are entirely unworthy of so rich a testament, the second, that even were you worthy, the blessing is so great that human nature is terrified by the greatness of it; for what do not forgiveness of all sin and eternal life bring with them? If either of these temptations comes to you, you must, as I have said, esteem the words of Christ more than such thoughts. It will not be He that lies to you; your thoughts will be deceiving you.

Just as though a poor beggar, yea, a very knave, were bequeathed a thousand gulden: he would not demand them because of his merit or worthiness, nor fail to claim them because of the greatness of the sum; and if any one should cast up to him his unworthiness and the greatness of the sum, he would certainly not allow anything of that sort to frighten him, but would say: "What is that to you? I know full well that I am unworthy of the inheritance; I do not demand it on my merits, as though it had been due me, but on the favor and grace of the testator. If he did not think it too much to bequeath to me, why should I so despise myself and not claim and take it?" So also must a timid, dejected conscience insist, against its own thoughts, upon the testament of Christ, and be stubborn in firm faith, despite its own unworthiness and the greatness of the blessing. For this very reason that which brings to such unworthy ones so great a blessing is a divine testament, by which God desires above all things to awaken love to Him. So Christ comforted those dejected ones who thought the blessing too great and said: "Faint-hearted little flock, fear not; it hath pleased your Father to give you the eternal Kingdom." [Luke 12:32]

[Sidenote: Abuses of the Mass: 1. The Suppression of the Words]

16. But see now what they have made of the mass! In the first place, they have hidden these words of the testament, and have taught that they are not to be spoken to the laity, that they are secret words to be spoken in the mass only by the priest. Has not the devil here in a masterly way stolen from us the chief thing in the mass and put it to silence? For who has ever heard it preached that one should give heed in the mass to these words of the testament and insist upon them with a firm faith? And yet this should have been the chief thing. Thus they have been afraid, and have taught us to be afraid, where there is no cause for fear, nay, where all our comfort and safety lie.

How many miserable consciences, which perished from fear and sorrow, could have been comforted and rescued by these words! What devil has told them that the words which should be the most familiar, the most openly spoken among all Christians, priests and laity, men and women, young and old, are to be hidden in greatest secrecy? How should it be possible for us to know what the mass is, or how to use and observe it, if we are not to know the words in which the very mass consists?[8]

But would to God that we Germans could say mass in German, and sing these "most secret" words loudest of all! Why should not we Germans say mass in our own language, when the Latins, Greeks and many others observe mass in their language? Why should we not also keep secret the words of baptism: "I baptise thee in the name of the Father and of the Son and of the Holy Ghost, Amen"? [Matt. 28:19] If every one may speak in German, and aloud, these words, which are no less the holy Word and promise of God, why should not every one also be permitted to hear and speak those words of the mass aloud and in German?

[Sidenote: Word and Sign in the Sacraments]

17. Let us learn, then, that in every covenant[9] of God there are two things which one must consider; these are Word and Sign. In baptism these are the words of the baptiser and the dipping in water.[10] In the mass they are the words and the bread and wine. The words are the divine covenant, promise and testament. The signs are sacraments, that is sacred signs. Now since the testament is far more important than the sacrament, so the words are much more important than the signs. For the signs might be lacking, if only one have the words, and thus one might be saved without sacrament, yet not without testament. For I can daily enjoy the sacrament in the mass, if I only keep before my eyes the testament, that is, the words and covenant of Christ, and feed and strengthen my faith thereby.

We see, then, that the best and greatest part of all sacraments and of the mass is the words and covenant of God, without which the sacraments are dead and are nothing at all; like a body without a soul, a cask without wine, a purse without gold, a type without fulfilment, a letter without spirit, a sheath without a knife, and the like; whence it is true that when we

214

use, hear, or see the mass without the words or testament, and look only to the sacrament and sign, we do not even half keep the mass. For sacrament without testament is keeping the case without the jewel, quite an unequal separation and division.

[Sidenote: The Testament ignored]

18. I fear, therefore, that there is at present more idolatry in Christendom through the masses than ever occurred among the Jews. For we hear nowhere that the mass is directed toward the feeding and strengthening of faith, for which alone it was ordained by Christ, but is only used as a sacrament without the testament.

Many have written of the fruits of the mass, and indeed have greatly exalted them; nor do I question the value of these fruits. But take heed that you regard them all, compared to this one thing, as the body compared to the soul. God has here prepared for our faith a pasture, table and feast; [Ps. 23] but faith is fed with nothing except the Word of God alone. Therefore you must take heed above all things to the words, exalt them, highly esteem them, and hold them fast; then you will have not simply the little drops of blessing[11] that drip from the mass, but the very head-waters of faith, from which springs and flows all that is good, as the Lord says in John vii, "Whosoever believeth in Me, out of his belly shall flow streams of living water" [John 4:14, 15]; again: "Whosoever shall drink of the water which I give, he shall never thirst, and there shall be in him a spring of living water unto everlasting life." We see, then, the first abuse of the mass is this—that we have lost the chief blessing, to wit, the testament and the faith. What consequences this has had we now shall see.

19. It follows of necessity, where faith and the Word or promise of God decline or are neglected, that there arise in their place works and a false, presumptuous trust in them. For where there is no promise of God there is no faith. Where there is no faith, there everyone presumptuously undertakes to better himself by means of works, and to make himself well-pleasing to God. When this happens, false security and presumption arise therefrom, as though man were well-pleasing to God because of his own works. When this does not happen, the conscience has no rest, and knows not what to do, that it may become well-pleasing to God.

[Sidenote: Abuses of the Mass: 2. The Mass a Good Work]

So too I fear that many have made out of the mass a good work, whereby they thought to do a great service to Almighty God. Now, if we have rightly understood what has been said above, namely, that the mass is nothing else than a testament and sacrament, in which God pledges Himself to us and gives us grace and mercy, I think it is not fitting that we should make a good work or merit out of it. For a testament is not beneficium acceptum, sed

215

datum;[12] it does not derive benefit from us, but brings us benefit. Who has ever heard that he who receives an inheritance does a good work? He does derive benefit. Likewise in the mass we give Christ nothing, but only take from Him; unless they are willing to call this a good work, that a man be quiet and permit himself to be benefited, to be given food and drink, to be clothed and healed, helped and redeemed. Just as in baptism, in which there is also a divine testament and sacrament, no one gives God anything or does Him a service, but instead takes something; so too in all the other sacraments, and in the sermon. For if one sacrament cannot be a meritorious good work, then no other can be a work; because they are all of one kind, and it is the nature of a sacrament or testament that it is not a work, but only an exercise of faith.

[Sidenote: Good Works Connected with the Mass]

20. It is true, indeed, that when we come together to the mass to receive the testament and sacrament, and to nourish and strengthen faith, we there offer our prayer with one accord, and this prayer, which arises out of faith, and is for the increase of faith, is truly a good work; and we also distribute alms among the poor; as was done aforetime when the Christians gathered food and other needful things, which after the mass were distributed among the needy, as we learn from St. Paul. But this work and prayer are quite another thing than the testament and sacrament, [1 Cor. 11:21, 22] which no one can offer or give to God or to men, but every one takes and receives of it for himself only, in proportion as he believes and trusts. Now just as I cannot receive or give the sacrament of baptism, of penance, or of extreme unction in any one's stead or for his benefit, but I take for myself alone the blessing therein offered by God, and there is here not officium, but beneficium, i. e., not work or service, but reception and benefit alone; so also, no one can say or hear mass for another, but each one for himself alone, for it is purely a taking and receiving.

This is all easily understood, if one only considers what the mass really is, namely, a testament and sacrament; that is, God's Word and promise, together with a sacred sign, the bread and the wine, under which Christ's body and blood are truly present. For by what process of reasoning could a man be said to do a good work for another when, like the others, he comes as one in need, and takes to himself the words and sign of God in which God promises and grants him grace and help? Surely, to receive God's Word, sign, and grace is not the imparting of good, or the doing of a good work, but is simply a "taking to oneself."

[Sidenote: Abuses of the Mass: 3. The Mass as a Sacrifice]

21. Now, since the whole world has made a sacrifice of the mass, wherein they bring an offering to God, which without doubt is the third and very worst abuse, we must clearly distinguish between what we offer and what we do not offer in the mass.

Beyond all doubt the word "offering" in the mass has arisen and has remained until now, because in the times of the Apostles, when some of the practices of the Old Testament were still observed, the Christians brought food, money and necessities, which were distributed in connection with mass among the needy, as I have said before.[13] For so we still read in Acts iv, that the Christians sold all that they had, and brought it to the feet of the Apostles, who then had it distributed and gave of the common possessions to every one as he needed. [Acts 4:34, 35] Even so the Apostle Paul teaches, that all food and whatsoever we use shall be blessed with prayer and the Word of God, and thanks be given to God therefor [Rom. 14:6, 7; 1 Cor. 10:30,31]; hence we say the Benedicite and Gratias[14] at table. Thus it was the custom of the Old Testament, when men thanked God for gifts received, that they lifted them up in their hands to God; as is written in the law of Moses. [Exod. 34:26; Num.15:19, 20] Therefore, the apostles also lifted up the offerings in this way, thanked God, and blessed, with the Word of God, food and whatever the Christians gathered. And Christ Himself, as St. Luke writes, lifted up the cup, gave thanks to God, drank of it, and gave to the others, before He instituted the sacrament and testament. [Luke 22:17]

[Sidenote: The Collect and Offeratory]

22. Traces of this usage have survived in three customs. The first, that the first and last prayer of the mass are called "collects," that is, "collections"; which indicates that these prayers were spoken as a blessing and thanksgiving over the food which had been collected, to bless it and give thanks to God, according to the teaching of St. Paul [1 Cor. 10:30, 31]. The second, when the people after the Gospel proceed to the offering; from which the chant which is sung at that time is called "Offertory," that is, an offering. The third, that the priest elevates in the paten and offers to God the still unblessed host, at the same time that the offertory is being sung and the people are making their offering; by which is shown that the sacrament is not offered to God by us, but only these "collects" and offerings of food and gifts that have been gathered, in order that God may be thanked for them, and they may be blessed, to be distributed to the needy.

For afterward, when the priest, in the "low mass," [15] elevates the blessed host and cup, there is not a word said about the sacrifice, where he should most of all make mention of the sacrifice, if the mass were a sacrifice: but, as I have said above,[16] he elevates it not toward God, but toward us, to remind us of the testament, and to incite us to faith in the same. In like manner, when he receives or administers the sacrament, he does not mention the sacrifice by a single word; which must and should be done were the sacrament a sacrifice. Therefore, the mass dare not and cannot be called or be a sacrifice because of the sacrament, but only because of the food which is gathered and the prayer with which God is thanked and with which it is blessed.

23. Now the custom of gathering food and money at the mass has fallen into disuse, and not more than a trace of it remains in the offering of the pfennig on the high festivals, and especially on Easter Day, when they still bring cakes, meat, eggs, etc., to church to be blessed. Now in place of such offerings and collections, endowed churches, monastic houses and hospitals have been erected, and should be maintained for the sole purpose that the needy in every city may be given all they need, that there be no beggar or needy one among the Christians, but that each and all may have from the mass enough for body and soul.

But all this is reversed. Just as the mass is not rightly explained to men, but is understood as a sacrifice, not as a testament, so, on the other hand, that which is and ought to be the offering, namely, the possessions of the churches and monastic houses, is no longer offered and is not given, with the thanksgiving and blessing of God, to the needy to whom it ought to be given. Therefore God is provoked to anger, and now permits the possessions of the churches and monastic houses to become the occasion of war, of worldly pomp, and of such abuse that no other blessing is so shamefully and blasphemously managed and wasted. And since it does not serve the poor, for whom it was appointed, it is indeed meet and right that it should remain unworthy to serve for anything but sin and shame.

[Sidenote: The Mass Not a Sacrifice]

24. Now if you ask what is left in the mass to give it the name of a sacrifice, since so much is said in the Office about the sacrifice, I answer: Nothing is left. For, to be brief and to the point, we must let the mass be a sacrament and testament, and this is not and cannot be a sacrifice any more than the other sacraments—baptism, confirmation, penance, extreme unction, etc.—are sacrifices.[17] Otherwise we should lose the Gospel, Christ, the comfort of the sacrament and every grace of God. Therefore we must separate the mass clearly and distinctly from the prayers and ceremonies which have been added by the holy fathers, and keep the two as far apart as heaven and earth, that the mass may remain nothing else than the testament and sacrament comprehended in the words of Christ. What there is over and beyond these words we are to regard, in comparison with the words of Christ, as we regard the monstrance[18] and corporal[19] in comparison with the host and the sacrament itself; and these we regard as nothing but additions for the reverent and seemly administration of the sacrament. Now just as we regard the monstrance, corporal and altar-cloths compared with the sacrament, so we are to look upon all added words, works and ceremonies of the mass compared with the words of Christ Himself, in which He gives and ordains this testament. For if the mass or sacrament were a sacrifice, we would have to say that it is a mass and sacrifice when the sacrament is brought to the sick in their home, or when those in health receive it in the church, and that there are as many masses and sacrifices as the number of those who approach the sacrament. If in this case it is not a sacrifice, how is it a

218

sacrifice in the hand of the priest, since it is still one and the same sacrament, one and the same use, one and the same benefit, and in all respects the same sacrament and testament with all of us?

[Sidenote: The Spiritual Sacrifice in the Mass]

25. We should, therefore, give careful heed to this word "sacrifice," that we do not presume to give God something in the sacrament, when it is He who therein gives us all things. We should bring spiritual sacrifices, since the external sacrifices have ceased and have been changed into the gifts to churches, monastic houses and charitable institutions. What sacrifices then are we to offer? Ourselves, and all that we have, with constant prayer, as we say: "Thy will be done on earth as in heaven." [Matt. 6:10] Whereby we are to yield ourselves to the will of God, that He may do with us what He will, according to His own pleasure; in addition, we are to offer Him praise and thanksgiving with our whole heart, for His unspeakable, sweet grace and mercy, which He has promised and given us in this sacrament. And although such a sacrifice occurs apart from the mass, and should so occur, for it does not necessarily and essentially belong to the mass, as has been said,[20] yet it is more precious, more seemly, more mighty and also more acceptable when it takes place with the multitude and in the assembly where men provoke, move and inflame one another to press close to God, and thereby attain without all doubt what they desire.

For so has Christ promised; where two are gathered together in His name there He is in the midst of them, and where two agree on earth as touching anything that they shall ask, all shall be done that they ask. [Matt. 18:19, 20] How much more shall they obtain what they ask, when a whole city comes together to praise God and to pray with one accord! We would not need many indulgence-letters if we proceeded aright in this matter. Souls also would easily be redeemed from purgatory and innumerable blessings would follow. But, alas! that is not the way it goes. Everything is reversed; what the mass is intended to do, we take upon us and want to do ourselves; what we ought to do we give over to the mass. All this is the work of unlearned, false preachers.

26. To be sure, this sacrifice of prayer, praise and thanksgiving, and of ourselves, we are not to present before God in our own person, but we are to lay it on Christ and let Him present it, as St. Paul teaches in Hebrews xiii: "Let us offer the sacrifice of praise to God continually, that is, the fruit of the lips which confess Him and praise Him," [Heb. 13:15] and all this through Christ. For He is also a priest, as Psalm cx says: "Thou art a priest forever after the order of Melchizedek" [Ps. 110:4]; because He intercedes for us in heaven, receives our prayer and sacrifice, and through Himself, as a godly priest, makes them pleasing to God [Heb. 5:6, 10, etc.], as St. Paul says again in Hebrews ix: "He is ascended into Heaven to be a mediator in the presence of God for us" [Heb. 9:24]; and: "It is Christ Jesus that died, yea, rather, that is risen again, Who is even at the right hand of God, Who also maketh intercession for us." [Rom. 8:34]

From these words we learn that we do not offer Christ as a sacrifice, but that Christ offers us. And in this way it is permissible, yea, profitable, to call the mass a sacrifice, not on its own account, but because we offer ourselves as a sacrifice along with Christ; that is, we lay ourselves on Christ by a firm faith in His testament, and appear before God with our prayer, praise and sacrifice only through Him and through His mediation; and we do not doubt that He is our priest and minister in heaven before God. Such faith, forsooth, brings it to pass that Christ takes up our cause, presents us, our prayer and praise, and also offers Himself for us in heaven. If the mass were so understood and therefore called a sacrifice, it would be well. Not that we offer the sacrament, but that by our praise, prayer and sacrifice we move Him and give Him occasion to offer Himself for us in heaven, and ourselves with Him. As though I were to say, I had brought a king's son to his father as an offering, when, indeed, I had done no more than induce that son to present my need and petition to the king, and made the son my mediator.

27. Few, however, understand the mass in this way. For they suppose that only the priest offers the mass as a sacrifice before God, although this is done and should be done by everyone who receives the sacrament, yea, also by those who are present at the mass and do not receive the sacrament. Furthermore, such offering of sacrifice every Christian may make, wherever he is and at all times, as St. Paul says: "Let us offer the sacrifice of praise continually through Him," [Heb. 13:15] and Psalm cx: "Thou art a priest forever." [Ps. 110:4] If He is a priest forever, then He is at all times a priest and is offering sacrifices without ceasing before God. But we cannot be continually the same, and therefore the mass has been instituted that we may there come together and offer such sacrifice in common.

But let him who understands the mass otherwise or uses it otherwise than as a testament and sacrifice of this kind take heed how he understands it. I understand it, as has been said, to be really nothing else than this, that we receive the testament and at the same time admonish ourselves and be minded to strengthen our faith and not doubt that Christ is our priest in heaven, who offers Himself for us without ceasing and presents us and our prayer and praise, and makes them acceptable; just as though I were to offer the human priest as a sacrifice in the mass and appoint him to present my need and my praise of God, and he were to give me a token that he would do it. In this case I would be offering the priest as a sacrifice; and it is in this wise that I offer Christ, in that I desire and believe that He accepts me and my prayer and praise, and presents it to God in His own person, and to strengthen this faith, gives me a token that He will do it. This token is the sacrament of bread and wine. Thus it becomes clear that it is not the priest alone who offers the sacrifice of the mass, but every one's faith, which is the true priestly office, through which Christ is offered as a sacrifice to God. This office the priest, with the outward ceremonies of the mass, simply represents. Each and all are, therefore equally spiritual priests before God. [Rev. 1:6; 5:10, 1 Pet. 2:9]

[Sidenote: Faith the True Priestly Office]

28. From this you can see for yourself that there are many who rightly observe mass and make this sacrifice, who themselves know nothing about it, nay, who do not realize that they are priests and can observe mass. Again, there are many who take great pains and apply themselves with all diligence, thinking that they are keeping the mass properly and offering a right sacrifice, and yet there is nothing right about it. For all those who have the faith that Christ is a priest for them in heaven before God, and who lay on Him their prayers and praise, their need and their whole selves, and present them through Him, not doubting that He does this very thing, and offers Himself for them, these take the sacrament and testament, outwardly or spiritually, as a sign of all this, and do not doubt that all sin is thereby forgiven, that God has become their gracious Father and that everlasting life is prepared for them.

All such, then, wherever they may be, are true priests, observe the mass aright and also obtain by it what they desire. For faith must do everything. It alone is the true priestly office and permits no one else to take its place. Therefore all Christians are priests; the men, priests, the women, priestesses, be they young or old, masters or servants, mistresses or maids, learned or unlearned. Here there is no difference, unless faith be unequal. Again, all who do not have such faith, but presume to make much of the mass as a sacrifice, and perform this office before God, are figure-heads. They observe mass outwardly and do not themselves know what they are doing, and cannot be well pleasing to God. For without true faith it is impossible to please Him, as St. Paul says in Hebrews xi. [Heb. 11:6] Now there are many who, hidden in their hearts, have such true faith, and themselves know not of it; many there are who do not have it, and of this, too, they are unaware.

[Sidenote: Masses for the Dead]

39. It has become a wide-spread custom to found masses for the dead, and many books have been written about it. If we ask now, Of what benefit are the masses celebrated for the souls which are kept in purgatory? the answer is: What is custom! God's Word must prevail and remain true, to wit, that the mass is nothing else than a testament and sacrament of God, and cannot be a good work or a sacrifice, although it may be taken to include sacrifice and good works, as was said above.[21]

221

There is no doubt, therefore, that whoever observes mass without the faith aforementioned benefits neither himself nor any one else. For the sacrament in itself, without faith, does nothing; nay, God Himself, Who indeed doeth all things, does and can do good to no one unless he firmly believes Him; how much less can the sacrament. It is easy to say, a mass is effective whether it be performed by a pious or a wicked priest, that it is acceptable opere operati, not opere operantis.[22] But to produce no other argument except that many say this, and it has become a custom, is poor proof that it is right. Many have praised pleasures and riches and have grown accustomed to them; that does not make them right; we should produce Scripture or reason for it. Therefore let us take heed lest we be made fools. I cannot conclude that the institution of so many masses and requiems can be without abuse, especially since all this is done as a good work and sacrifice by which to pay God, whereas in the mass there is nothing else than the reception and enjoyment of divine grace, promised and given us in His testament and sacrament.

30. I will gladly agree that the faith which I have called[23] the true priestly office, which makes of us all priests and priestesses, through which in connection with the sacrament we offer ourselves, our need, prayer, praise and thanksgiving in Christ and through Christ, and thereby offer Christ before God, that is, give Him cause and move Him to offer Himself for us and us with Himself—this faith, I say, is truly able to do all things in heaven, earth, hell and purgatory, and to this faith no one can ascribe too much. And as I have said above,[24] if Christ promises to two persons the answers to all their prayers [Matt. 18:19], how much more may so many obtain from Him what they desire!

I know full well that some will be very ready to call me a heretic in this. But, dear fellow, you should also consider whether you can prove as easily as you slander. I have read all that, and I know the books on which you rely, so you need not think I do not know your art. But I say that your art has no foundation, and that you cannot defend it, and that out of a sacrament or testament of God you will never make a sacrifice or a work of satisfaction, and, indeed, satisfaction itself is more of a human than a divine law.[25]

Therefore my advice is, let us hold fast to that which is sure[26] and let the uncertain go; that is, if we would help these poor souls in purgatory or any one else, let us not take the risk of relying upon the mass as a sufficient work, but rather come together to mass, and with priestly faith[27] present every besetting need, in Christ and with Christ, praying for the souls [of the departed], and not doubting that we will be heard. Thus we may be sure that the soul is redeemed. For the faith which rests on the promise of Christ never deceives nor fails.

[Sidenote: The Need for the Sacrament]

31. So we read that St. Monica, St Augustine's mother, on her death-bed, desired to be remembered in the mass.[28] If the mass were sufficient of itself to help everyone, what need would there be for faith and prayer? But you might say, if this is true, anyone might observe mass and offer such a sacrifice, even in the open fields. For every one may indeed have such a faith in Christ in the open fields, and offer and commit to Him his prayer, praise, need and cause, to bring it before God in heaven, and besides he may also think of the sacrament and testament, heartily desire it, and in this way spiritually receive it. For he who desires it and believes, receives it spiritually, as St. Augustine teaches.[29]

What need is there then to observe mass in the churches? I answer: It is true, such faith is enough, and truly accomplishes everything, but how could you think of this faith, sacrifice, sacrament and testament if it were not visibly administered in certain designated places and churches? The same is true in the case of baptism and absolution, although faith is sufficient without them, where no more can be done; still if there were no place for their administration, who could think of them and believe in them, or who could know or say anything of them? Moreover, since God has so ordered this sacrament, we must not despise it, but receive it with great reverence, praise and gratitude. For if there were no other reason why we should observe mass outwardly and not be satisfied with inward faith alone, yet were this sufficient, that God so orders and wills it. And His will ought to please us above all things and be sufficient reason to do or omit anything.

There is also this advantage: since we are still living in the flesh and are not all perfect enough to rule ourselves in spirit, we need to come together to enkindle such a faith in one another by example, prayer, praise, and thanksgiving, as I have said above,[30] and through the outward seeing and receiving of the sacrament and testament to move each other to the increase of this faith. There are many saints, who like St. Paul the Hermit,[31] remained for years in the desert without mass, and yet were never without mass. But such a high spiritual example cannot be imitated by everyone or by the whole Church.

[Sidenote: The Mass a Proclamation of the Gospel]

33. But the chief reason for outwardly holding mass is the Word of God, which no one can do without, and which must daily be used and studied. Not only because every day Christians are born, baptised and trained, but because we live in the midst of the world, the flesh and the devil, who do not cease to tempt us and drive us into sin, against which the most powerful weapon is the holy Word of God, as St. Paul also calls it, "a spiritual sword," [Eph. 6:17] which is powerful against all sin. This the Lord indicated when He instituted the mass and said: "This do in remembrance of Me" [Luke 22:19]; as though He said, "As often as you use this sacrament and testament you shall preach of Me," As also St. Paul says in I. Corinthians xi, "As oft as ye eat this bread and drink this cup ye shall preach and proclaim the death of the Lord until He come" [1 Cor. 11:26]; and Psalm cii, "They shall declare the glory of the Lord in Zion and His praise in Jerusalem, as often as the kings (that is, the

bishops and rulers) and the people come together to serve the lord" [Ps. 102:21, 22]; and Psalm cxi, "He hath instituted a memorial of His wonders in that He has given meat to all who fear Him." [Ps. 111:4, 5]

In these passages you see how the mass was instituted to preach and praise Christ, to glorify His sufferings and all His grace and goodness, that we may be moved to love Him, hope and believe in Him, and thus, in addition to this Word or sermon, receive an outward sign, that is, the sacrament, to the end that our faith, provided with and confirmed by divine words and signs, may become strong against all sin, suffering, death and hell and everything that is against us. And but for the preaching of the Word He would nevermore have instituted the mass. He is more concerned about the Word than about the sign. For the preaching ought to be nothing but an explanation of the words of Christ when He institutes the mass and says: "This is My body. This is My blood, etc." What is the whole Gospel but an explanation of this testament? Christ has comprehended the whole Gospel in a short summary with the words of this testament or sacrament. For the whole Gospel is nothing but a proclamation of God's grace and of the forgiveness of all sins, granted us through the sufferings of Christ, as St. Paul proves in Romans x [Rom. 10:9, 11, 13]; and Christ in Luke xxiv [Luke 24:46, 47]. This same thing the words of this testament contain, as we have seen.

34. From this we may see what a pity and perversion it is that so many masses are said, and yet the Gospel is kept altogether silent. They stand and preach, and give to poor souls chaff for wheat, yea, death for life, intending afterward to make up for it with many masses. What sort of baptism would that be, if the water were poured upon the child and not a word were said? I fear that the holy words of the testament are read so secretly, and kept hidden from the laity, because God in His wrath is testifying thereby that the whole Gospel is no longer publicly preached to the people, that even as the summary of the Gospel is hidden, so also its public explanation has ceased.

[Sidenote: The Withdrawal of the Cup]

Next, they took entirely from us the one element, the wine, although that does not matter much, for the Word is more important than the sign. Still, I should like to know who gave them the power to do such a thing. In the same way they might take from us the other element and give us the empty monstrance to kiss as a relic, and at last abolish everything that Christ has instituted. I fear it is a figure and type that augurs nothing good in these perilous, perverted latter days. It is said that the pope has the power to do it; I say that is all fiction, he does not have a hair's breadth of power to change what Christ has made; and whatever of these things he changes, that he does as a tyrant and Antichrist. I should like to hear how they will prove it.

Not that I wish to cause a turmoil about it, for I regard the Word as mightier than the sign, but I cannot permit the outrage when they not only do us wrong, but wish to have a right thereto, and force us not only to permit such a wrong, but also to praise it as right and good. Let them do what they will, so long as we are not obliged to acknowledge wrong as right. It is enough that we permit ourselves, with Christ, to be smitten on the cheek [John 18:22], but it is not for us to praise it, as though they had done well therein and earned God's reward.

[Sidenote: Superstitious Use of Mass]

35. But what of those poor priests and laymen who have departed so far from the true meaning of the mass and of faith that they have even made of it a sort of magic? Some men have masses said that they may become rich and prosper in their business, others because they think if they hear mass in the morning they will be safe during the day from all danger and want; some, again, on account of sickness; others for still more foolish, yea, even sinful reasons, and yet they find priests perverted enough to take their money and do their bidding.

[Sidenote: Distinction of Masses]

Furthermore, they have now made one mass better than another; one is valued as useful for this, another for that. Thus they have made seven "Golden Masses." [33] The "Mass of the Holy Cross" has come to have a different virtue from the "Mass of Our Lady." In this matter every one is silent and permits the people to go on for the sake of the cursed, filthy pfennigs, which through these various titles and virtues of the mass come piling in. So must faith, like Christ, be sold by its Judas, that is, by covetousness and the thirst for money. [Matt. 26:15, 16]

Some are to be found also who have mass said privately, for this and for that; in short, the mass must do all kinds of things, except its own peculiar work—faith, which no one regards. They now are the best men on earth who have many masses said, as though they thought thereby to lay up many good works. All of this is the work of ignorance, which does not separate the hymns and prayers, which have been added, from the true, original mass. For one mass is like another and there is no difference, except in the faith. For the mass is best to him who believes most, and it serves only to increase faith, and for nothing else. True, indeed, the added prayers do serve, one this purpose, another that, according to the meaning of their words, but they are not the mass or the sacrament.

[Sidenote: Reduction in the Number of Masses]

36. I would advise then, that where the masses are not directed toward such faith, they be abolished, and that there be fewer masses endowed for the souls of the dead. Truly we provoke God to anger with them more than we conciliate Him. To what purpose are the priests in the chapter houses and cloisters so strictly bound to observe the yearly[34] masses, since they are not only without such faith, but also are often of necessity unfit. Christ Himself did not desire to bind anyone thereto and left us wholly free when He said: "This do ye, as oft as ye do it, in remembrance of Me." [1 Cor. 11:25] And we men bind ourselves so fast and drive ourselves on against our own conscience. I see too that such an institution often has no good reason, but a secret greed is at the bottom of the obligation and that we burden ourselves with many masses in order that we may have sufficient income in temporal things; afterward we say that we do it for God's sake. I fear few would be found who gratuitously and for God's sake would thus burden themselves. But if all these masses are observed in the faith above mentioned, which I scarcely expect, they are to be tolerated. But if not, then it would be best that there be only one mass a day in a city, and that it be held in a proper manner in the presence of the assembled people. If at any time, however, we desire to have more, the people should be divided into as many parts as there are masses, and each part should be made to attend its own mass, there to exercise their faith and to offer their prayer, praise and need in Christ, as was said above.[35]

[Sidenote: Proper Preparation for the Mass]

37. If, then, the mass is a testament and sacrament in which the forgiveness of sins and every grace of God are promised and sealed with a sign, it follows of itself, what is the best preparation for it. Without doubt, it is given to them that need it and desire it. But who needs forgiveness of sins and God's grace more than just these poor miserable consciences that are driven and tormented by their sins, are afraid of God's anger and judgment, of death and of hell, that would be glad to have a gracious God and desire nothing more greatly? These are truly they who are well-prepared for mass. For them these words have force and meaning, when Christ says: "Take and drink, this is My blood, which is shed for you for the remission of sins." [Matt. 26:27] Where such a soul believes these words, as it ought, it receives from the mass all the fruits of the mass, that is, peace and joy, and is thus well and richly fed by it in spirit. But where there is no faith, there no prayer helps, nor the hearing of many masses; things can only become worse. As Psalm xxiii says: "Thou preparest a table before me against all my enemies." [Ps. 23:5] Is this not a clear passage? What greater enemies are there than sin and an evil conscience which at all times fears God's anger and never has rest? Again, Psalm cxi says: "He hath made His wonderful works to be remembered and hath given meat to them that fear Him." [Ps. 111:4, 5] It is certain then that for bold, confident spirits, whose sin does not prick them, the mass is of no value, for they have as yet no hunger for this food, but are still too full. The mass demands and must have a hungry soul, which longs for forgiveness of sins and divine favor.

[Sidenote: The Mass a Remedy against Despair and Doubt]

38. But because this despair and unrest of conscience are nothing but an infirmity of faith, the severest malady which man can have in body and soul, and which cannot at once or speedily be cured, it is useful and necessary that the more restless a man's conscience, the more should he approach the sacrament or hear mass, provided that he picture to himself therein the Word of God, and feed and strengthen his faith by it, and ever see to it that he do not make a work or sacrifice of it, but let it remain a testament and sacrament, out of which he shall take and enjoy a benefit freely and of grace, by which his heart may become sweet toward God and obtain a comforting confidence toward Him. For so sings the Psalter, Psalm civ, "The bread strengtheneth man's heart, and the wine maketh glad the heart of man." [Ps. 104:15]

[Sidenote: A Sacrament for the Deaf and Dumb]

39. Some have asked whether the sacrament is to be offered also to the deaf and dumb. Some think it a kindness to practice a pious fraud upon them, and think they should be given unblessed wafers. This mockery is not right, and will not please God, Who has made them Christians as well as us; and the same things are due to them as to us. Therefore, if they have sound understanding and can show by indubitable signs that they desire it in true Christian devotion, as I have often seen, we should leave to the Holy Spirit what is His work and not refuse Him what He demands. It may be that inwardly they have a better understanding and faith than we, and this no one should presumptuously oppose. Do we not read of St. Cyprian,[36] the holy martyr, that in Carthage, where he was bishop, he gave both elements to the children, although that has now ceased, for good reasons? Christ permitted the children to come to Him, and would not suffer any one to forbid them [Mark 10:13 ff.]. And in like manner He has withheld His blessings neither from dumb or blind, nor from the lame; why should not His sacrament also be for those who heartily and in a Christian spirit desire it?

[Sidenote: Conclusion]

40. Thus we see with how very few laws and works Christ has weighed down His holy Church, and with how many promises He has lifted it up to faith; although now, alas! all is turned about, and we are driven by many long and burdensome laws and works to become pious; and nothing comes of it. But Christ's burden is light [Matt. 11:30] and soon produces an abundant piety, which consists in faith and trust, and fulfils what Isaiah says: "A little perfection shall bring a flood full of all piety." [Isa. 10:32 (Vulgate)] That burden is faith, which is a little thing, to which belong neither laws nor works, nay it cuts off all laws and works and fulfils all laws and works. Therefore there flows from it nothing but righteousness. For so perfect is faith, that without any other labor and law, it makes everything that man does acceptable and well-pleasing to God. As I have further said of it in my little book "Of Good Works." [37]

Therefore, let us beware of sins, but much more of laws and good works, and only give heed to the divine promise and to faith; then good works will come of themselves. To this may God help us. Amen.

FOOTNOTES

[1] See above, p. 25, note 1.

[2] Luther's customary term for the law of the Church, or "Canon Law."

[3] For the application of this principle to the sacrament of penance, see the Discussion of Confession above, p. 82 f.

[4] Luther quotes from the Vulgate, St. Jerome's Latin version of the Bible.

[5] The bread of the Lord's Supper.

[6] The Sanctus in the mass.

[7] Luther says "feathers."

[8] Darinnen die Messe steht und geht.

[9] Gelübde, literally "vow."

[10] On the mode of baptism see the Treatise on Baptism in this volume. Cf. Small Catechism, Part IV, 4, and Large Catechism, Part IV.

[11] Tropffrüchtlein.

[12] "Not a benefit received, but a benefit conferred."

[13] See p. 309.

[14] i. e., Blessing and Thanksgiving at Table; cf. Appendix II. of the Small Catechism.

[15] Called the "still" mass because said without music.

[16] See p. 302.

[17] Luther at this period still acknowledges seven sacraments. But see the Babylonian Captivity, written in October 1520.

[18] The receptacle in which the consecrated host is shown to the people.

[19] The corporal-cloth spread over the altar during the communion service.

[20] See p. 306.

[21] See pp. 308 f., 311 ff.

[22] It is the teaching of the Roman Church that a sacrament is effective ex opere operato, i. e., simply as a sacrament ordained of God. Intended to guard against the idea that the validity of the sacrament depended on the character of the priest or of the recipient, it gave rise to the notion that the sacrament worked a sort of sacred magic.

[23] See p. 316.

[24] See p. 313.

[25] Cf. XCV Theses, pp. 19, 41.

[26] Lasst uns des gewissen spielen.

[27] See p. 316.

[28] Confessions of St. Augustine, Book IX, Chapter XI.

[29] This is the votum sacramenti, which, according to Roman teaching, suffices for salvation if participation in the sacrament is impossible.

[30] See p. 313.

[31] Paul of Thebes, an Egyptian hermit of the III. Century, whose life was written by St. Jerome.

[32] The translators have followed the numbering of the text in the Weimar and Erlangen Editions, which omit No. 32 in numbering the paragraphs.

[33] The mass held for the Blessed Virgin in Hildsheim on the second Sunday after St. Michael's Day is, on account of its magnificence, called "golden." Du Cange.

[34] The masses which are observed every day throughout the year.

[35] See p. 313 f.

[36] Bishop of Carthage, died 258.

[37] See above, pp. 187 ff.

THE PAPACY AT ROME

AN ANSWER TO THE CELEBRATED ROMANIST AT LEIPZIG

1520

INTRODUCTION

Luther's declaration of emancipation from the spiritual pre-eminence of the Church of Rome, which, said he, "is proven solely by the by the empty papal decretals of the last four hundred years, and against which there stands the testimony of the authentic history of eleven hundred years, the text of Holy Scripture, and the decree of the Nicene Council," appeared in print in spring 1519.[1] It was in the form of a counter-thesis[2] to Eck's specious and celebrated "Thirteenth Thesis." It culminated in the Leipzig Disputation in July.

Before another summer had passed, this Disputation bore marvelous and unlooked-for fruits. In a series of epochal pamphlets, written in part for the clergy, and in part for the newly awakened laity, Luther with remarkable rapidity developed his new and scriptural teaching on the nature of the Church, on the duties of the state, on the essence of the sacraments, and on the inner life of the individual Christian.

The tractates of 1520, to which that on "The Papacy at Rome" belongs, like most of Luther's writings, were drawn forth from him in large part defensively, under provocation from the other side, or by the exigencies of the occasion. His correspondence[3] during the first half of 1520 reveals them as a result (with fresh causes arising) of the stir at Leipzig.

Said Luther (February, 1520), "You cannot make a pen out of a sword: the Word of God is a sword. I was unwilling to be forced to come forward in public; and the more unwilling I am, the more I am drawn into the contest." Widely and eagerly read, these piquant publications made Luther the awakener, the developer, and as Harnack declares, the spiritual center of the reformatory thought that was now rising to a crisis.

Fortunate it was, that the infancy of modern and the birth of Luther were contemporary, and that Luther turned to the printing press to such an extent in that critical period, that in the single year under discussion the number of printed German works was doubled.

Our little book of June 26, 1520, is the earliest of his writings to present a full outline of his teaching on the nature of the Christian Church. Driven by an antagonist, to whom his work is a reply, to write[4] in German for the laity, Luther gives them a clear and fundamental insight into this burning subject. His teachings "which he had just one year before maintained at the Leipzig Disputation are here unfolded, following to their logical conclusions and clearly presented."[5] This flying counter-attack against the "famous Romanist at Leipzig" thus becomes, in the judgment of Köstlin,[6] "one of the most important of his general doctrinal treatise of that period."

Luther's reply was written in short order during the last two weeks in May.[7] It came about in this wise: Eck at the Disputation had driven Luther to declare that belief in the divine supremacy of Rome was not necessary to salvation. Following this, in fall, a Franciscan friar, Augustine von Avleld, had risen to attack Luther and glorify the papacy, having received an appointment from Adolph, the Bishop of Merseburg (who had posted the inhibition on the Leipzig churches against the Disputation,[8] to write against the Reformer. Alveld's work, justifying the divine right of the Apostolic Chair, to all learned men, appeared early in May,[9] in the Latin language, in a first edition full of errors, followed quickly by a second edition.[10] Alveld attempted to cut Luther to pieces with "seven swords," of which the first was recta ratio; the second, canonica scriptura; the third, vera scientia (gained through the Church teachers and scholastics); the fourth, pietas sacra; the fifth, sanus intellectus; the sixth, simplex et pudica sapientia; the seventh, pura et integra scientia.

On Alved's miserable jumble, in which the Reformer is alluded to as a "heretic," "lunatic," "wolf," Luther was not willing to waste any time (despite a threatening letter from Alveld); but jotted down some points for John Lonicer,[11] who on June 1st, published a sharp exposé[12] of the Leipzig Romanist's weaknesses[13]. Although the monastic authorities at Leipzig, fearing Luther, now attempted to suppress Alveld, that worthy at once came out[14] with a new work[15] on the same theme and this time in the German language[16]. It stirred Luther's blood. "If the jackanapes had not issued his little book in German to poison the defenceless laity," he said, "I would have looked on it as too small a matter to take up." As it was, with great rapidity he wrote his "The Papacy at Rome against the Celebrated Romanist at Leipzig." Going to press in May, the book was completed on the 26th of June. The twelve known editions are all quartos and range in size from twenty-two to thirty-two leaves. The first[17] two editions were printed by Melchior Lotther in Wittenberg; one by Peypus in Nuremberg; two by Silvan Otmar in Augsburg; one by George Nadler in Augsburg; one by Adam Petri in Basel and one by Andrew Exatander.[18]

Incidentally Luther handles the "Alveld Ass" [19] and the Roman cause without gloves, but in substance he explains to the layman what Christianity really is,[20] i. e., unfolds to them the essence of the Christian Church.[21] In doing so he takes advanced ground for civil and religious liberty. The traditional mediæval idea of universal monarchy is dealt a heavy blow. Neither in Civil Government nor in the Church is the need of a single monarchical head. "The Roman Empire governed itself for a long time, and very well, without the one head, and many other countries in the world did the same. How does the Swiss Confederacy govern itself at present?"

Against the modern demand that the Church shall socialize itself, that it shall organize as a public center in a community of the people's civic life, that it shall enter the nation's political activities for moral uplift, and that ministers should become what Luther would call "preachers of dreams in material communities," our book places itself on record[22].

Against the widespread demand that Christianity should get together into one world-wide visible ecclesiastical order, Luther's words are peremptory. He declares that the one true Church is already a spiritual community composed of all the believers in Christ upon the earth, that it is not a bodily assembly, but "an assembly of the hearts in one faith," that the true Church is "a spiritual thing, and not anything external or outward," that "external unity is not the fulfilment of a divine commandment," and that those who emphasize the externalization of the Church into one visible or national order "are in reality Jews."[23]

Luther refers to those without the unity of the Roman Church as still within the true Church. "For the Muscovites, Russians, Greeks, Bohemians, and many other great peoples in the world, all these believe as we do, baptise as we do, preach as we do, live as we do."

But if Luther attacks the supremacy of the outer organization in the Church, he no less forcibly disputes the supremacy of man's own inner thinking, his reasoning, in theology. He defines human reason as "our ability which is drawn from experience in temporal things" and declares it ridiculous to place this ability on a level with divine law[24]. He compares the man who uses his reason to defend God's law with the man who in the thick of battle would use his bare hand and head to protect his helmet and sword. He insists that Scripture is the supreme and only rule of faith[25], and ridicules the Romanists who inject their reason into the Scriptures, "making out of them what they wish, as though they were a nose of wax to be pulled around at will."

As might be supposed, Luther's book, thus set against the external unity of human ecclesiastical organization, and against the inner rule of human thinking, is equally strong against the human visualization of divine worship. He argues against those who "turn spiritual edification into an outward show", and those who chiefly apply the name Church to an assembly in which "the external rites are in use, such as chanting, reading, vestments; and the name 'spiritual estate' is given to the members of the holy orders, not on account of their faith (which perhaps they do not have), but because they have been consecrated with an external anointing, wear distinctive dress, make special prayers and do special works, have their places in the choir, and seem to attend to all such external matters of worship."[26]

The fallacy of the argument that because the Old Testament was a type of the New, therefore the material types of the Old Testament must be reproduced in the New, is exposed by him. [27] The open and fearless opposition to the popedom at Rome, which already appeared in the Diet at Augsburg in 1518, and more circumspectly, in the Leipzig Disputation in 1519, is very free[28] in this booklet to the laity of 1520, and is preliminary to the more intense antagonism which will appear in "The Babylonian Captivity." At Leipzig, Eck had laid emphasis on the Scripture passage, "Feed my sheep," and both this passage[29] and the one of Matthew 16:18 ("Thou art Peter, and upon this rock I will build my Church") are explained by Luther for the laity. He charges the popes with having forsaken the faith, with living under the power of Satan, and with being themselves heretical.[30]

This tractate applies doctrine to existing institutions, and makes the truth clear to the laity. We see in it the power of Luther in stirring the popular mind. We do not regard the coarse invectives of Luther (which many cultured men of to-day seem to cite with outward horror—and inner enjoyment) as a remark of low peasant birth, or of crudeness of breeding, but as the language of a great leader who, in desperate struggle with the powers that be, knew how to attach himself to the mind of his age in such way as to influence it. How noble and great is his own remark at the close of his booklet on others' allusion to himself in print! "Whoever will, let him freely slander and condemn my person and my life. It is already forgiven him. God has given me a glad and fearless spirit, which they shall not embitter for me, I trust, not in all eternity."

Luther in this pamphlet, insists that none are to be regarded as heretics simply because they are not under the Pope; and that the Pope's decrees, to stand, must endure the test of Scripture. Luther wrote in May. In June he told Spalatin that if the Pope did not reform, he would appeal to the Emperor and German nobility. Within another month that appeal appeared.

The men of Leipzig feared the work of Luther, and the rector of the University had pled for mercy. Luther replied that Leipzig deserved to be placed in the pillory[31], that he had no desire to make sport of the city and its university, but was pressed into it by the bombast of the Romanist, who boasted that he was a "public teacher of the Holy Scripture at Leipzig"; and by the fact that Alveld had dedicated his work to the city and its Council. Alveld answered Lonicer and Luther bitterly, but Luther replied no more.

Theodore E. Smauk.

Lebanon, Pennsylvania.

FOOTNOTES

[1] Still earlier, in his Resolutions to the 95 Theses (Resolut. Disputat., etc. Erl. Fr. Ed. II, 122 sqq., 137 sqq.) Luther had in an historical and objective way spoken of a time when the

Roman Church had not been exalted over the other churches, at least not above those of Greece; that it was thus yet in the time of Pope Gregory I.

[2] Luther's Thirteen Theses against Eck's Thirteen Theses. Frater Mar. Luth. Dsupt. etc., Erl.-Fr. Ed. III, 4 sqq., 11 sqq. "Bruder Martin Luther's Disputation und Entschuldigung wider die Anschuldigungen des D. Johann Eck." St. Louis Ed. XVIII, 718. The oldest print is doubtless one in possession of the University at Halle.

[3] January 10, 1520, to Spalatin; January 26, to John Lang; February 5, to Spalatin; February 18, to Spalatin; April, Alved to Luther; Ma 5, May 17, May 31, June 8, and June 20, to Spalatin, with a letter of July or August to Peter Mosellanus, rector of the University at Leipzig.

[4] He alluded to the subject in his Sermon on the Ban.

[5] Köstlin, Theology of Luther, translated by Hay, I, 363.

[6] Martin Luther, I, 299.

[7] Alved's second book, the Confutatio Inepti, was dedicated to the Council and honorable citizens of the city of Leipzig on the 23d of April, and appeared in print in the middle of May. Its smooth and popular form roused Luther to this reply, which was put in press before the end of May, and published before the end of June.

[8] See Luther to Spalatin, July 20, 1519.

[9] See Luther to Spalatin, May 5, 1520. "Exiit tandem frater Augustinus Afveidenais cum sus offs," etc. He characterises Alved in this letter, and refers to the approval it found in Meissen in his letter to Spalatin of May 17th.

[10] The title is as follows: "Super apostolica ne-de, An Videlicet diuino sit iure nec ne, anque potifex qui Papa dici caeptus est, iure diuino in ea ipea president, no paru laudanda ex sacro Biblior. canone declaratio. sedita p. F. Augustinu Ahldesem Franciscanu, regularis (vt dicit) observuatíae sacredote, Prouin ciae Saxoniae, Sancte crucia, Sa-criq Biblioru canonis publi-cu lectore i couetu Lipsico, ad Reurendu in Chro patre & dom, dom Adolphu pricipe Illust. i Anhaldt ic Episcope Mersen-burge sem." See Super apostolica sed declario

edita per Augustinum Alveldensem Bl.; E. S. Cyprian, Nütsliche Urkunden, Leipzig, 1718, II S. 160 f.

[11] Luther's famulus. "Ich werde meinem Bruder Famulus anstellen."—To Spalatin already on May 5th.

[12] "Contra Romanistam fratrem Augustinu, Alulden. Fran-ciscanu Leipaica Canonis Biblici publicu lictore eiusdem. F. Joanes Lonicerus. Augustinianus. VVITTENBERGAE, APVD, COLLEGIVM NOVVM. ANNO. M.D.XX."

[13] Lonicer's reply had been preceded by one more detailed and less impetuous by Bernardi Feldkirch, teacher in the Wittenberg High School. This work is wrongly regarded as Melanchton's. Its title is: "CONFUTATIO INEP-ti & impli Libelli F. August. AL-VELD. Franciscani Lipsici, pro D. M. Luthero. Vmittenbergae, apud Melciorem Lottherum iuniorem, Anno M. D. XX."

[14] He requested the Nuncio Milits to secure authority for him to write.

[15] Cf. Luther in the Tractate: "They cling to me like mud to a wheel."

[16] "Eyn gar fruchtbar vu nutsbarlich buchbleyn vo dë Babstliche stul: vmud von sant Peter: vund vo den, die warhafftige schef-lein Christi sein, die Christus vner herr Petro befolen hat in sein hute vnd reglrung, gemacht durch bruder Augustinu Alueldt sant Francisci ordens tzu Leiptsk."

See Cyprian, Urkunden, II, 161 f.

On May 31, Luther puts the whole situation graphically in a letter to Spalatin as follows: "Lonicers Schrift wird morgen fergig sein. Die Leipziger sind besorgt, ihre Schülter zu behalten; sie rühmen, dases Erasmus zu ihnen kommen werde. Wie geschäftig und doch wie unglüchlich ist der Neid. Vor einem Jahre, da sie ührer uns, als währen wir besiegt, spotteten, saben sie nicht voraus, dass ihnen dies Kreut bevorstebe. Der Herr regiert…Ochsenfart soll sich wider das Büchlein Feldkirchens rüston, in welchem er durch gehechbelt wird. Ich habe ein deutsches Buch wider den Esel von Alveld fertiggestellt, welches jetzt unter der Presse ist."

[17] "Von dem Bapstum zu Rome: wid der den hochberupton Romanisten zu Leipzck D. Martinus Lu-ther ther Agust. Vuittenberg." 50 leaves, quarto, last page blank.

[18] For titles of these editions see Weimar Ed., vi, 281.

[19] Luther in this tractate aims beyond the "undersized scribe of the barefoot friars at Leipzig," at the "brave and great flag-bearers who remain in hiding, and would win a notable victory in another's name," namely Prierias, Cajetan, Eck, Emser and the Universities of Cologne and Louvaine. Luther uses the epithet quoted above in one of his letters to Spalatin.

[20] "I welcome the opportunity to explain something of the nature of Christianity for the laity."

[21] "I must first of all explain what these things mean, the Church, and the One Head of the Church."

[22] "On this point we must hear the word of Christ, Who, when Pilate asked Him concerning His Kingdom answered, My Kingdom is not of this world. This is indeed a clear passage in which the Church is made separate from all temporal communities. Is not this a cruel error, when one places the Christian Church, separated by Christ Himself from temporal cities and places, and transferred to spiritual realms, is made a part of material communities?"

"No hope is left on earth except in the temporal."

[23] Among many things that Luther says on this point are the following: "According to the Scriptures the Church is called the assembly of all the believers in Christ upon the earth. This community consists of all those who live in true faith, hope and love, so that the essence, life and nature of the Church is not a bodily assembly, but an assembly of the hearts in one faith. Thus, though they be a thousand miles apart in body, they are yet called an assembly in spirit, because each one preaches, believes, hopes, loves, and lives like the other. So we sing of the Holy Ghost: 'Thou, Who through diverse tongues gatherest together the nations in the unity of the faith.' That means spiritual unity. And this unity is of itself sufficient to make a Church, and without it no unity, be it of place, of time, of person, of work, or of whatever else, makes a Church."

"A man is not reckoned a member of the Church according to his body, but according to his soul, nay, according to his faith...It is plain that the Church can be classed with a temporal community as little as spirits with bodies. Whosoever would not go astray should therefore hold fast to this, that the Church is a spiritual assembly of souls in one faith, that no one is reckoned a Christian for his body's sake; that the true, real, essential, Church is a spiritual thing, and not anything external or outward."

"All those who make the Christian communion a material and outward thing, like other communities, are in reality Jews, who wait for their Messiah to establish an external kingdom at a certain definite place, namely Jerusalem; and so sacrifice the faith, which alone makes the kingdom of Christ a thing spiritual or of the heart."

In this and the following notes, for brevity's sake, various quotations are summarized and connected.

[24] "For the teachings of human experience and (Deut. xii:8) reason are far below the divine law. The Scriptures expressly forbid us to follow our own reason, Deut. xii: 'Ye shall not do...every man whatsoever is right in his own eyes'; for human reason ever strives against the law (Gen. vi:5) of God. Therefore the attempt to establish or defend divine order with human reason, unless that reason has previously been established and enlightened by faith, is just as futile, as if I would throw a light upon the sun with a lightless lantern, or rest a rock upon a reed. For Isaiah vii makes reason subject to faith, when he says (vii:9): 'Except ye believe, ye shall not have understanding or reason.' He does not say, Except ye have reason, ye shall not believe. Therefore this scribe would better not have put forth a claim to establish the faith and the divine law by mere reason."

[25] "That the serpent lifted up by Moses, signifies Christ, is taught by John iii. If it were not for that passage, my reasoning might evolve many strange and weird fancies out of that type. That Adam was a type of Christ, I learn not from myself, but from St. Paul. That the rock in the wilderness represents Christ is not taught by my reason, but by St. Paul. None other explains the type but the Holy Spirit Himself. He has given the type and wrought the fulfillment, that both type and fulfillment and the interpretation may be God's own and not man's, and our faith he founded not on human, but on divine words. What leads the Jews astray but that they interpret the types as they please, without the Scriptures? What has led so many heretics astray but the interpretation of the types without reference to the Scriptures?"

[26] "The word Church, when it is used for such external affairs, whereas it concerns the faith alone, is done violence to; yet this manner of using it has spread everywhere, to the great injury of many souls, who think that such outward show is the spiritual and only true estate in Christendom. Of such a purely external Church, there is not one letter in the Holy

Scriptures. The building and increase of the Church, which is the body of Christ, cometh alone from Christ, Who is its head. Christendom is ruled with outward show; but that does not make us Christians. The Church is a spiritual and not a bodily thing, for that which one believes is not bodily or visible. The external marks whereby one can perceive this Church is on earth, are Baptism, the Sacrament and the Gospel. For where Baptism and the Gospel are no one may doubt that there are saints, even if it were only the babes in their cradles."

[27] "It is evident that a type is material and external, and fulfilment of the type is spiritual and internal; what the type reveals to the bodily eye, its fulfilment must reveal to the eye of faith alone. The bodily assembly of the people signifies the spiritual and internal assembly of the Christian people in faith. Moses set a serpent on a pole and whosoever looked upon it was made whole. That signifies Christ on the cross. Whosoever believeth in Him is saved. And so throughout the entire Old Testament, all the bodily visible things in it signify in the New Testament spiritual and inward things, which one cannot see, but only possess in faith. St. Augustine says on John iii: 'This is the difference between the type and its fulfilment: the type gave temporal goods and life, but the fulfilment gives spiritual and eternal life.'"

"Aaron was a type of Christ and not of the Pope. Paul says the high priest typifies Christ; you say St. Peter. Paul says Christ entered not into a temporal building. You make the fulfilment to be earthly and external. If Aaron was a type in external authority, vestments and state, why was he not a type in all other external and bodily matters? The Old Testament high priest was not permitted to have his head shorn. But why does the Pope have a tonsure? The Old Testament high priest was a subject. Why then does the Pope have men kiss his feet and aspire to be king, which Christ Himself did not? Wherein is the type fulfilled?"

[28] Luther to Spalatin, June 8th: "Gegen den Esel von Alveld werde ich menen Angriff so enrichten dass ich des römischen Pabstes nich uneingedenk bin, und werde keinem von beiden etwas schenken. Denn solches erfordert der Stoff mit Nothwendigkeith. Endlicheinmal müssen die Geheimnisse des Antichrist offenbart werden. Denn so drangen sie sich selbst hervor, und wollen nicht weiter vorborgen sein."

To this Luther adds the significant statement: "Ich habe vor, einen öffentlichen Zettel auszulassen an den Kaiser und den Adel im ganzen Deutschland, wider die Tyrannei und die Nichstwürdigkeit des römischen Hofes."

[29] "'Feeding' in the Roman sense means to burden Christendom with many and hurtful laws. In 'feeding' it means to sit in the highest place and to have an office, it follows that whoever is doing this work of feeding is a saint, whether he be a knave, or a rogue, or what not. Where there is no love, there is no feeding. The papacy either must be a love, or it cannot be a feeding of the sheep."

[30] "The greater part of the Roman communion, and even some of the popes themselves, have forsaken the faith wantonly and without struggle, and live under the power of Satan. The majority of those who hold so strongly to the authority of the Pope, and lean upon it, are themselves possessed by the powers of hell. Some of the popes were heretics themselves and gave heretical laws. These Roman knaves come along, place the Pope above Christ and make him a judge over the Scriptures. They say that he cannot err."

[31] "Das Bemulhen der Leipziger Gehässigkeit." To Spalatin, Jan. 10. "Die Nichstwürdigkeitem der Leipziger." To Joh. Lang, Jan. 26. "Die Kunstangriffder Leipziger Partei." To Spalatin, Feb. 5.

TO THE PAPACY AT ROME

AN ANSWER TO THE CELEBRATED ROMANIST AT LEIPZIG[1]

1520

[Sidenote: A New Adversary]

After all these years of fruitful rain and abundant growth something new has appeared on the scene. Many have essayed to attack me heretofore with vile abuse and glorious lies, yet without much success. But the latest to distinguish themselves are the brave heroes at Leipzig on the market-place, who desire not only to be seen and admired, but to break a lance with every one. Their armor is so wonderful that I have never seen the like before. They have put the helmet on the feet, the sword on the head, shield and breastplate on the back, they hold the spear by the point, and the whole armor becomes them so well as to mark them as horsemen of a new sort.[2] They would prove thereby not only that they have not frittered away their time with dream-books without learning anything, as I accused them, but would also achieve a great name as people who were conceived, born, nursed, cradled, fondled, brought up, and grown up in the Holy Scriptures. It would be no more than fair that whoever could, should be afraid of them, so that their labor and their good intentions might not be entirely in vain. Leipzig, to produce such giants, must indeed be rich soil.

That you may understand what I mean, observe: Sylvester, Cajetan, Eck, Emser,[3] and now Cologne and Louvaine have shown their knightly prowess against me in most strenuous endeavor, and received the honor and glory they deserved; they have defended the cause of the pope and of indulgences against me in such a manner that they might well wish to have had better luck, finally, some of them thought the best thing to do was to attack me in the same manner as the pharisees attacked Christ [Matt. 22:35]. They put forward a champion,

240

and thought: If he wins, we all win with him; if he is defeated, he suffers defeat alone. And the super-learned, circumspect Malvolio[4] thinks I will not notice it. Very well, in order that all their plans may not miscarry, I will pretend not to understand their game. And I beg them in return, not to take notice, that when I strike the pack, I am aiming at the mule. And if they will not grant this request, I stipulate that, whenever I say anything against the newest Roman heretics and blasphemers of the Scriptures, not merely the poor, immature scribe of the bare-foot friars at Leipzig shall take it to himself, but rather the great-hearted flag-bearers, who remain in hiding, and yet would win a notable victory in another's name.

I pray every honest Christian to receive my words—though sometimes barbed with scorn or satire—as coming from a heart that is made to break with sorrow and to turn seriousness into jesting at the sight now beheld at Leipzig, where there are also pious people who would venture body and soul for God's Word and the Scriptures, but where a blasphemer can thus openly speak and write, who esteems and treats God's holy words no better than if they were the fabled pratings of some fool or jester at the carnival. Because my Lord Christ and His holy Word, even He who gave His own blood as the purchase-price, is held to be but mockery and fools' wit, I must likewise drop all seriousness, and see whether I, too, have learned how to play the fool and clown. Thou knowest, my Lord Jesus Christ, how my heart stands toward these arch-blasphemers. That is my reliance, and I will let matters take their course in Thy name. Amen. They must ever abide Thee as the Lord. Amen.

I notice that these poor people are seeking naught else than to gain renown at my expense. They cling to me like mud to a wheel. They would rather have questionable honor shamefully acquired than remain quiet, and the evil spirit uses the designs of such people only to hinder me from doing more useful things. But I welcome the opportunity to give the laity[6] some explanation of the nature of the Church,[7] and to contradict the words of these seductive masters. Therefore I intend to treat of the subject-matter directly, rather than to answer their senseless prattle. I will not mention their names, lest they achieve their true purpose and boastfully regard themselves capable of arguing with me in the Scriptures.

THE STATEMENT OF THE CASE

We are discussing a matter which, taken by itself, is unnecessary, for any one could be a Christian without knowing anything about it. But these idlers who tread under foot all the great essentials of the Christian faith, must needs pursue such things and worry other people, in order to have some object in life.

[Sidenote: The Foundation of Papal Power]

This then is the question: Whether the papacy at Rome, possessing the actual power over all Christendom (as they say), is of divine or of human origin,[8] and this being decided, whether it is possible for Christians to say that all other Christians in that world are heretics and apostates, even if they agree with us in holding to the same baptism, Sacrament, Gospel, and all the articles of faith, but merely do not have their priests and bishops confirmed by Rome, or, as it is now, buy such confirmation with money and let themselves be mocked and made fools of like the Germans. Such are the Muscovites, Russians, Greeks, Bohemians, and many other great peoples in the world. For all these believe as we do, baptise as we do, preach as we do, live as we do, and also give due honor to the pope, only they will not pay for the confirmation of their bishops and priests. They will not, like the drunken, stupid Germans, submit to extortion and abuse with indulgences, bulls, seals, parchments, and other Roman stock in trade. They are ready, too, to hear the Gospel from the pope, or the pope's ambassadors, and yet they are not sent to them.

Now the question is, whether all these may properly be called heretics by us Christians (for of such alone, and of no others, do I speak and write), or whether we are not rather the heretics and apostates, because we brand such Christians as heretics and apostates solely for the sake of money. For when the pope does not send the Gospel to them, and his messengers to proclaim it, although they are eager to receive them, it is clear as day that he is grasping for power and money through this confirmation of bishops and priests. But to this they will not agree, and therefore they are branded as heretics and apostates.

Now I have held, and still hold, that they are not heretics and apostates, but perhaps better Christians than we are, although not all, even as we are not all good Christians. This is challenged, after all its predecessors, by the fine little bare-foot book[9] of Leipzig, which comes along on clogs—nay, on stilts. It imagines that it alone (among all the others) does not step into the mud; perhaps it would gladly dance if some one would buy it a flute. I must have a try at it.

[Sidenote: The Insincerity of the Roman Claims]

I say, first of all: No one should be so foolish as to believe that it is the serious opinion of the pope and of all his Romanists and flatterers, that his great power is of divine right. Pray observe, of all that is by divine right not the smallest jot or tittle is observed in Rome, nay, if they think of it at all, it is scorned as foolishness; all of which is as clear as day. They even suffer the Gospel and Christian faith everywhere to go to rack and ruin, and do not intend to lose a hair for it. Yea, all the evil examples of spiritual and temporal infamy flow from Rome, as out of a great sea of universal wickedness, into all the world. All these things cause laughter in Rome, and if any one grieves over them, he is called a Bon Christian, i. e., a fool. If they really took the commands of God seriously, they would find many thousand things more necessary to be done, especially those at which they now laugh and mock. For St. James says, "He that keepeth not one commandment of God, breaketh all." [Jas. 2:10] Who would be so stupid as to believe that they seek God's command in one thing, and yet make a mockery of all the others? It is impossible that any one should take one command of God to heart, and not at least be moved by all the others. Now there are ever so many

242

who zealously guard the power of the pope, yet none of them ever ventures a word in favor of even one of the other much greater and more necessary commandments, which are so blasphemously mocked and scornfully rejected at Rome.

Furthermore, if all Germany were to fall on its knees, and to pray that the pope and the Romans should keep this power, and confirm our bishops and priests without payment, for nothing—even as the Gospel says, "Freely ye have received, freely give" [Matt. 10:8]—and provide all our churches with good preachers, because they have a sufficient abundance of riches to give money instead of taking it; and if it were urged and pressed, that this is their duty according to divine command: believe it surely, we should find all of them arguing with more insistence than any one ever did before, that it is not a divine command to go to so much trouble without pay. They would soon find a little gloss[10] with which to wind themselves out of it, just as they now find what they desire, to weave themselves into it. All our beseechings would not drive them to it. But since it means money, everything they dare to put forth must be divine command.

[Sidenote: Roman Greed and Extortion]

The bishopric of Mainz alone, within the memory of men now living, has bought eight pallia[11] in Rome, every one costing about 30,000 gulden—not to mention the innumerable other bishoprics, prelacies and benefices. Thus are we German fools to be led by the nose and then they say: It is a divine command to have no bishop without Roman confirmation. I am surprised that Germany, which is by one-half or more in the possession of the Church,[12] still has so much as one pfennig left by reason of the unspeakable, innumerable, insufferable Roman thieves, knaves and robbers. It is said that Antichrist shall find the treasures of the earth; I trow the Romanists have found them to such an extent as to make our very life a burden. If the German princes and the nobility will not interfere very shortly, and with decisive courage, Germany will yet become a wilderness and be compelled to devour itself. That would furnish the greatest pleasure for the Romanists, who do not think of us otherwise than as brutes, and have made a proverb concerning us at Rome: "Squeeze the gold from German fools, in any way you can."

The pope does not prevent this scandalous villainy. They all wink at it, yea, they think far more highly of these supreme arch-villains than they do of the holy Gospel of God. They pretend that we are hopeless fools, and that it is a divine command that the pope should have his finger in every pie and do as he pleases with every one, just as if he were a god on earth, and should not rather be the servant of all,[13] without any pay, if he wished to be— or were—the very highest. But before consenting to this, they would much rather surrender this power and not call this a divine command any more than any other.

But I hear you say, why do they fight so hard against you in this matter? Answer: I have attacked some higher things, which concern faith and God's Word. And when they were not able to contradict me, and saw that Rome does not trouble itself about such good things, they dropped them too, and attacked me on indulgences and the authority of the pope, in the hope of thus attaining the prize. For they knew very well that where money was concerned, the chief school of knaves in Rome would support them and not remain quiet. But Dr. Luther is just a little proud, and pays very little attention to the grunting and squealing of the Romanists; and this is well-nigh heartbreaking to them. But that does not bother my Lord Jesus, nor Dr. Luther, for we believe that the Gospel will and must continue. Let a layman ask such Romanists, and let them give answer, why they despoil and mock all of God's commandments, and rant so violently about this power, whereas they cannot show at all why it is necessary, or what it is good for. For ever since it has arisen, it has accomplished nothing but the devastation of Christendom, and no one is able to show anything good or useful that has resulted from it. Of this I will speak more fully if this Romanist comes again, and then, please God, I will throw light upon the Holy Chair at Rome and expose it as it deserves to be exposed.

I have said this, not as a sufficient argument for disputing papal power, but in order to show the perverted opinions of those who strain the gnats, but let elephants go through [Matt. 23:24], who behold the mote in the brother's eye and permit the beams in their own to remain [Matt. 7:3], only to the end that others may be stifled by superfluous and unnecessary things, or at least branded as heretics or by any other epithet that occurs to them. One of than is this delicate, pious Romanist at Leipzig. Let us now have a look at him.

I find three strong arguments by which this fruitful and noble little book[14] of the Romanist at Leipzig attacks me.

[Sidenote: The Arguments of the Romanists—1. Luther a Heretic and a Fool]

The first, and by far the strongest, is, that he calls me names—a heretic, a blind, senseless fool, one possessed by the devil, a serpent, a poisonous reptile, and many other names of similar import; not simply once, but throughout the book, almost on every page.[15] Such reproaches, slanders and calumnies are of no account in other books. But when a book is made at Leipzig, and issued from the cloister of the bare-foot friars, by a Romanist of the high and holy observance[16] of St. Frauds, such names are not merely fine examples of mediation, but likewise strong arguments with which to defend papal power, indulgences, Scripture, faith and the Church.[17] It is not necessary that any one of these should be proved by Scripture or by reason; it is quite enough that they have been put down in his book by a Romanist and holy observant of the order of St. Francis.

And inasmuch as this Romanist himself writes that the Jews had overcome Christ on the cross with such arguments, I, too, must surrender, and acknowledge that as far as cursing and scolding, abuse and slander are concerned, the Romanist has surely beaten Dr. Luther. On this point he doubtless wins.

[Sidenote: The Argument from Reason]

The second argument, to express it tersely, is that of natural reason.

This is the argument: A. Every community[18] on earth, if it is not to fall to pieces, must have a bodily head, under the true head, which is Christ.

B. Inasmuch as all Christendom is one community on earth, it must have a head, which is the pope.

[Sidenote: The Futility of the Argument]

This argument I have designated with the letters A and B for the sake of clearness, and also to show that this Romanist has learned his A-B-C all the way down to B. However, to answer this argument: Since the question is whether the pope's power is by divine right, is it not a bit ridiculous that human reason (that ability which is drawn from experience in temporal things) is brought in and placed on a level with the divine law, especially since it is the intention of this poor presumptuous mortal to bring the divine law against me. For the teachings of human experience and reason are far below the divine law. The Scriptures expressly forbid us to follow our own reason, Deuteronomy xii, "Ye shall not do...every man whatsoever is right in his own eyes" [Deut. 12:8]; for human reason ever strives against the law of God, as Genesis vi. says: "Every thought and imagination of man's heart is only evil continually." [Gen. 6:5] Therefore the attempt to establish or defend divine order with human reason, unless that reason has previously been established and enlightened by faith, is just as futile as if I would throw light upon the sun with a lightless lantern, or rest a rock upon a reed. For Isaiah vii. makes reason subject to faith, when it says: "Except ye believe, ye shall not have understanding or reason." [Isa. 7:9] It does not say, "Except ye have reason, ye shall not believe." Therefore this scribe would better have left his perverted reason at home, or first have well established it with texts of Scripture, so as not to put forth so ridiculous and preposterous a claim and establish the faith and the divine law by mere reason. For if this reason of ours draws the conclusion that a visible community must have a visible overlord or cease to exist, it also must draw the further conclusion, that as a visible community does not exist without wives, therefore the whole Church[19] must have a visible, common wife, in order not to perish. What a valiant woman that would needs be! Again, a visible community does not exist without a common visible city, house and

245

country; therefore the Church[19] must have a common city, house and country. But where will you find that? Verily, in Rome they are seeking just this with impatient eagerness, for they have made nearly the whole world their very own. Again, the Church[19] would likewise need to have in common its visible property, servants, maids, cattle, food, etc., for no community exists without them. See how gracefully human reason stalks along on its stilts.

A professor of theology ought to have considered in advance the clumsiness of such an argument, and proved the divine laws and works by the Scriptures, and not by temporal analogies and worldly reason. For it is written that the divine commandments are justified in and by themselves, and not by any external help.[20] [Ps. 19:9]

Again, the wise man says of the wisdom of God: "Wisdom hath overcome the proud with her power." [Prov. 11:3] It is most deplorable that we should attempt with our reason to defend God's Word, whereas the Word of God is rather our defence against all our enemies, as St. Paul teaches us. [Eph. 6:17] Would he not be a great fool who in the thick of battle sought to protect his helmet and sword with bare hand and unshielded head? It is no different when we essay, with our reason, to defend God's law, which should rather be our weapon.

From this, I hope, it is clear that the flimsy argument of this prattler fails utterly, and, together with everything he constructs upon it, is found to be without any basis whatever. But that he may the better understand his own mummery, even in case I should grant that a process of reasoning might be entirely valid without the Scriptures, I will show that neither of his arguments is valid, neither the first, A, nor the second, B.

[Sidenote: The Argument Answered]

The first, A, is that every community on earth must have one visible head under Christ. This is simply not true. How many principalities, castles, cities, and houses we find where two brothers or lords reign—and with equal authority. The Roman empire governed itself for a long time, and very well, without the one head, and many other countries in the world did the same. How does the Swiss confederacy govern itself at present? Thus in the government of the world there is not one single overlord, yet we are all one human race, descended from the one father, Adam. The kingdom of France has its own king, Hungary its own, Poland, Denmark, and every other kingdom its own, and yet they are one people, the temporal estate in Christendom, without one common head; and still this does not cause these kingdoms to perish. And if there were no government constituted in just this manner, who could or would prevent a community from choosing not one, but many overlords, all clothed with equal power? Therefore it is a very poor procedure to measure the things which are of God's appointing by such vacillating analogies of worldly things, when they do not hold even in the appointments of men. But suppose I should grant this dreamer that his dream is true, and that no community can exist without one visible head; how does it follow that it must likewise be so in the Church?[21] I know very well that the poor dreamer has a certain conception, according to which a Christian community is the same as any other temporal community.[22] He thus reveals plainly that he has never learned to know what Christendom, or the Christian community, really is. I had not believed it possible to meet such dense, massive, stubborn error and ignorance in any man, much less in a saint of Leipzig.

For the benefit, therefore, of this numskull, and of those led astray by him, I must first of all explain what is meant by these things—the Church,[23] and the One Head of the Church.[23] I must talk bluntly, however, and use the same words which they have so barbarously perverted.

[Sidenote: What is the Church?]

[Sidenote: The Communion of Saints]

[Sidenote: The Unity of the Church Not External]

The Scriptures speak of the Church[23] quite simply, and use the term in only one sense; these men have added and brought into general use two more. The first use, according to the Scriptures, is this, that the Church[23] is called the assembly of all the believers in Christ upon earth, just as we pray in the Creed: "I believe in the Holy Ghost, a communion of saints." This community or assembly consists of all those who live in true faith, hope and love; so that the essence, life and nature of the Church[23] is not a bodily assembly, but an assembly of hearts in one faith, as St. Paul says, Ephesians iv, "One baptism, one faith, one Lord." [Eph. 4:5] Thus, though they be a thousand miles apart in body, yet they are called an assembly in spirit because each one preaches, believes, hopes, loves, and lives like the other. So we sing of the Holy Ghost: "Thou, who through divers tongues gatherest together the nations in the unity of the faith."[24] That means in reality a spiritual unity, because of which men are called a communion of saints. And this unity is of itself sufficient to make a Church,[23] and without it no unity, be it of place, of time, of person, of work, or of whatever else, makes a Church.[23] On this point we must hear the word of Christ, Who, when Pilate asked Him concerning His kingdom, answered: "My kingdom is not of this world." [John 18:36] This is indeed a dear passage, in which the Church[23] is made separate from all temporal communities, as not being anything external. And this blind Romanist makes of it an external community, like any other. Christ says even more clearly, Luke xvii, "The kingdom of God cometh not with observation: neither shall they say, Lo, here, or lo, there! for behold, the kingdom of God is within you." [Luke 17:20, 21]

I am astounded, that such strong, clear words of Christ are treated as a farce by these Romanists. For by these words it is clear to every one that the kingdom of God (for so He calls His Church[25]) is not at Rome, nor is it bound to Rome or any other place, but it is where there is faith in the heart, be a man at Rome, or here, or elsewhere. It is a nauseating lie,[26] and Christ is made a liar when it is said that the Church[25], is in Rome, or is bound to Rome—or even that the head and the authority are there by divine right.

Moreover, in Matthew xxiv. He foretold the gross deception which now rules under the name of the Roman Church, when He says: "Many false prophets and false Christs shall come in My name, saying: I am Christ; and shall deceive many, and show great signs, that if possible they shall deceive the very elect. Wherefore, if they shall say unto you: Behold, in the secret chambers is Christ, believe it not; behold, He is in the desert, go not forth. Behold, I have told you before." [Matt. 24:24-26] Is this not a cruel error, when the unity of the Christian Church[25], separated by Christ Himself from all material and temporal cities and places, and transferred to spiritual realms, is included by these preachers of dreams in material communities,[27] which must of necessity be bound to localities and places. How is it possible, or whose reason can grasp it, that spiritual unity and material unity should be one and the same? There are those among Christians who are in the external assembly and unity, who yet by their sins exclude themselves from the inner, spiritual unity.

Therefore, whosoever maintains that an external assembly or an outward unity makes a Church,[25] sets forth arbitrarily what is merely his own opinion, and whoever endeavors to prove it by the Scriptures, brings divine truth to the support of his lies, and makes God a false witness, just as does this miserable Romanist, who explains everything that is written concerning the Church[28] as meaning the outward show of Roman power; and yet he cannot deny that the large majority of these people, particularly in Rome itself, because of unbelief and evil lives, is not in the spiritual unity, i. e., the true Church.[28] For if to be in the external Roman unity made men true Christians, there would be no sinners among them, neither would they need faith nor the grace of God to make them Christians; this external unity would be enough.

[Sidenote: What Makes a Christian]

From this we conclude, and the conclusion is inevitable, that just as being in the Roman unity does not make one a Christian, so being outside of that unity does not make one a heretic or unchristian. I should like to hear who would dispute this. For that which is essential must make a true Christian; but if it does not make a true Christian, it cannot be essential; just as it does not make me a true Christian to be at Wittenberg or to be at Leipzig. Now it is clear that external fellowship with the Roman communion[29] does not make men Christians, and so the lack of that fellowship certainly does not make a man a heretic or an apostate. Therefore it must also be false, that it is a divine command to be in connection with the Roman Church.[28] For whosoever keepeth one divine command, keepeth them all, and none can be kept without keeping the others[30]. Therefore it is an open and blasphemous lie against the Holy Ghost to say that the external unity under Roman authority is the fulfilment of a divine commandment, since there are so many in that unity who neither regard nor fulfil any of the Divine commandments. Hence, to be in this place or that, does not make a heretic: but to be without true faith makes a man a heretic.

Again, it is clear that to be a member of the Roman communion[31] does not mean to be in true faith, and to be outside of it does not mean to be in unbelief; otherwise those within it would all be believers and truly saved, for no one article of faith is believed without all the other articles.

Therefore all those who make the Christian communion[32] a material and outward thing, like other communities, are in reality Jews (for the Jews likewise wait for their Messiah to establish an external kingdom at a certain definite place, namely, Jerusalem), and thus sacrifice the faith, which alone makes the kingdom of Christ a thing spiritual and of the heart.

[Sidenote: The Head of the Church]

Again, if every temporal community is called after its head, and we say of this city, it is Electoral, and of that, it is Ducal, and of another, it is Frankish; then by right all Christendom should be called Roman, or Petrine, or Papal. But why, then, is it called Christendom? Why are we called Christians, if not from our head, although we are still upon earth? Hereby it is shown that for Christendom there is no other head, even upon earth, than Christ, for it has no other name than the name of Christ For this reason St. Luke tells us that the disciples were at first called Antiochians, but soon this was changed and they were called Christians. [Acts 11:26][33]

Furthermore, though a man consists of two natures, namely, body and soul, yet he is not reckoned a member of the Church according to his body, but according to his soul, nay, according to his faith. Otherwise it might be said that a man is a nobler Christian than a woman, because his physical structure is superior to that of a woman, or that a man is a greater Christian than a child, a healthy person a stronger Christian than an invalid; lords and ladies, the rich and powerful, better Christians than servants, maids, and the poor and lowly; whereas Paul writes, Galatians v, "In Christ is neither male nor female, neither lord nor servant, neither Jew nor Greek," [Gal. 3:28; 5:6] but as far as the body is concerned they are all equal. But he is the better Christian who is greater in faith, hope and love; so that it is plain that the Church[34] is a spiritual community, which can be classed with a temporal community as little as spirits with bodies, or faith with temporal possessions.

249

This, indeed, is true, that just as the body is a figure or image of the soul, so also the bodily community is a figure of this Christian, spiritual community, and as the bodily community has a bodily head, so the spiritual community has a spiritual head. But who would be so bereft of sense as to maintain that the soul must have a bodily head? That would be like saying that every live animal must have on its body a painted head. If this literalist (I should say, literary person) had really understood what the Church[34] is, without doubt he would have been ashamed even to contemplate such a book as his. What wonder, therefore, that from a darkened and wandering brain issues no light, but thick, black darkness St. Paul says, Colossians iii, "Our life is not on earth, but hid with Christ in God." [Col. 3:3] For if the Church were a bodily assembly, you could tell by looking at the body whether any one were Christian, Turk or Jew; just as you can tell by the body whether a person is a man, woman or child, or whether he is white or black. Again, I can tell whether one is gathered in temporal assembly with others in Leipzig, Wittenberg, or elsewhere; but I cannot tell at all whether he is a believer or not.

[Sidenote: The Church a Spiritual Thing]

Whosoever would not go astray should, therefore, hold fast to this, that the Church[34] is a spiritual assembly of souls in one faith, and that no one is reckoned a Christian for his body's sake; in order that he may know that the true, real, right, essential Church[34] is a spiritual thing, and not anything external or outward, by whatever name it may be called. For one who is not a Christian may have all those other things, and they will never make him a Christian without true faith, which alone makes Christians. For this reason we are called Christian believers, and on Pentecost we sing:

We beseech Thee, Holy Spirit[35],

Let true faith our portion be.

It is in this wise, and never in any other, that the Holy

Scriptures speak of the Holy Church and of Christendom.

[Sidneote: The External Church]

Beyond that, another way of speaking of Christendom has come into use. According to this, the name Church[36] is given to an assembly in a house or a parish, a bishopric, an archbishopric, or the papacy, in which assembly external rites are in use, such as chanting, reading, vestments. And primarily the name of "spiritual estate" is given to the bishops, priests and members of the holy orders; not on account of their faith, which they perhaps do not have, but because they have been consecrated with an external anointing, wear crowns, use a distinctive garb, make special prayers and do special works, say mass, have their places in the choir, and attend to all such external matters of worship. But violence is done to the word "spiritual," or "Church," when it is used for such external affairs, whereas it concerns faith alone, which, working in the soul, makes right and true spirituales and Christians; yet this maimer of using it has spread everywhere, to the great injury and perversion of many souls, who think that such outward show is the spiritual and only true estate in Christendom or the Church.

There is not one letter in the Holy Scriptures to show that such a purely external Church has been established by God; and I hereby challenge all those who have made this blasphemous, damnable, heretical book, or would defend it, together with all their followers, even if all the universities hold with them. If they can show me that even one letter of the Scriptures speaks of it, I am willing to recant. But I know that they cannot do it. The Canon Law and human statutes, indeed, give the name of Church or Christendom to such a thing, but that is not now before us. Therefore, for the sake of brevity and a better understanding, we shall call the two churches by different names. The first, which is the natural, essential, real and true one, let us call a spiritual, inner Christendom. The other, which is man-made and external, let us call a bodily, external Christendom: not as if we would part them asunder, but just as when I speak of a man, and call him, according to the soul, a spiritual, according to the body, a physical, man; or as the Apostle is wont to speak of the inner and of the outward man. [Rom. 7:22] Thus also the Christian assembly, according to the soul, is a communion[37] of one accord in one faith, although according to the body it cannot be assembled at one place, and yet every group is assembled in its own place. This Christendom is ruled by Canon Law and the prelates of the Church.[38] To this belong all the popes, cardinals, bishops, prelates, monks, nuns and all those who in these external things are taken to be Christians, whether they are truly Christians at heart or not. For though membership in this communion[37] does not make true Christians, because all the orders mentioned may exist without faith; nevertheless this communion is never without some who at the same time are true Christians, just as the body does not give the soul its life, and yet the soul lives in the body and, indeed, can live without the body. Those who are without faith and are outside of the first community, but are included in this second community, are dead in the sight of God, hypocrites, and but like wooden images of true Christians. And so the people of Israel were a type of the spiritual people, assembled in faith.

[Sidenote: The Church as a Building]

The third use of the term applies the word Church, not to Christendom, but to the edifices erected for purposes of worship. And the word "spiritual" is so stretched as to cover temporal possessions, not the possessions which are truly spiritual because of faith, but those which are in the second or external Church,[39] and such possessions are called "spiritual" or Church possessions.[40] Again, the possessions of the laity are called "worldly," although the laymen who are in the first or spiritual Church[39] are much better than the worldly clergy and are truly spiritual. After this fashion it now goes with almost all the works and the government of the Church;[39] and the name "spiritual possessions" has been so exclusively applied to worldly possessions that now no one understands it to mean anything else, and this has gone so far that men regard neither the spiritual nor the external

Church any more, and they squabble and quarrel about temporal possessions like the heathen, and say, they do it for the sake of the Church and of spiritual possessions. Such perversion and misuse of words and things has come from the Canon Law and human statutes, to the unspeakable corruption of Christendom.

[Sidneote: The Head of the Church: Christ]

Now let us consider the head of Christendom. From the foregoing it follows that the first-named Christendom, which alone is the true Church, may not and cannot have Church: a head upon earth, and that no one on earth, neither bishop nor pope, can rule over it; only Christ in heaven is the head, and He ruleth alone.

[Sidenote: Why the Church Cannot Have an Earthly Head]

This is proved, first of all, in this way: How can a man rule over anything which he does not know or understand? And who can know whether a man truly believes or not? Aye, if the power of the pope extended to this point, then he could take away a Christian's faith, or direct its progress, or increase it, or change it, according to his pleasure, just as Christ can do.

In the second place, it is proved by the nature of the head. For it is the nature of every head joined to a body to infuse into all its members life and feeling and activity. This will be found to be true of the heads in worldly affairs. For the ruler of a country instils into his subjects all the things which are in his own mind and will, and causes all his subjects to be of like mind and will with himself, and thus they do the work he wishes to have done, and this work is truly said to have been instilled into the subjects by the prince, for without him it would not have been done. Now no man can instil into the soul of another, nor into his own soul, true faith, and the mind, will and work of Christ, but this Christ Himself must do. For neither pope nor bishop can produce faith in a man's heart, nor anything else a Christian member should have. But a Christian must have the mind and will which Christ has in heaven, as the apostle says, I. Corinthians ii [1. Cor. 2:16; 3:23]. It may also happen that a Christian member has the faith which neither pope nor bishop has; how then can the pope be his head? And if the pope cannot give to himself the life of the spiritual church, how can he instil it into another? Who has ever seen a live animal with a lifeless head? The head must give life to the body, and therefore it is clear that on earth there is no other head of the spiritual Christendom but Christ alone. Moreover, if a man were its head here below, Christendom would perish as often as a pope dies. For the body cannot live when the head is dead.

It follows further, that in this Church Christ can have no vicar, and therefore neither pope nor bishop is Christ's vicar or regent in this Church, nor can he ever become such. And this is proved as follows: A regent, if obedient to his lord, labors with and urges on the subjects and instils into them the same work which his lord himself instils, just as we see in temporal government, where there is one mind and will in lord, regents, and subjects. And if he were more holy than St. Peter, the pope can never instill into or create in a Christian man the work of Christ his Lord, i. e., faith, hope, love, and every grace and virtue.

And if such illustration and proof were not without flaw, though founded on the Scriptures, yet St. Paul stands strong and immovable in Ephesians iv, giving to Christendom but one head and saying, "Let us be true (i. e., not external, but real and true Christians) and grow up into Him in all things, which is the head, even Christ, from Whom the whole body fitly joined together and compacted by that which every joint supplieth, according to the effectual working in the measure of every part, maketh increase of the body unto the edifying of itself in love." [Eph. 4:15,16] Here the apostle says clearly that the building up and increase of Christendom, which is the body of Christ, cometh alone from Christ, Who is its Head. And where can there be found another head on earth to whom such nature could be ascribed, especially since these "heads" in most cases have neither love nor faith? Besides, St. Paul referred in these words to himself, to St. Peter, and to every other Christian; and if another head were necessary he would have been utterly false in saying nothing about it.

I know very well that there are some who dare to say in reference to this and similar passages that though Paul was silent [1 Cor. 3:1], he did not thereby deny that St. Peter was also a head, but was feeding the unwise with milk. Just listen to this: they claim that it is necessary for salvation to have St. Peter for a head, and yet they have the effrontery to say that Paul concealed the things which are necessary to salvation. Thus these senseless goats would rather blaspheme Paul and the Word of God than be convinced of their error, and they call it "milk for babes" when Christ is proclaimed, and "strong meat" when St. Peter is proclaimed, just as if Peter were higher, greater, and more difficult to understand than Christ himself. And this is called explaining the Scriptures and overcoming Dr. Luther; this is the way to run out of the rain and fall into the trough. What could such babblers accomplish if we should have a disputation with the Bohemians[41] and the heretics? Truly nothing, except that we should be made a mockery for all, and give them due cause to look upon us all as blustering idiots, and they become more strongly entrenched in their own belief through the foolishness of our side.

[Sidenote: The Equality of Bishops]

But then you ask: If the prelates are neither heads nor regents of the spiritual Church, what are they?

Let the laymen answer this, when they say: St. Peter is a messenger[42] and the other apostles are messengers too. Why should the pope be ashamed to be a messenger, if St. Peter himself is no more? But beware, ye laymen, or the super-learned Romanists will burn you at the stake as heretics because ye would make the pope a messenger and letter-carrier. But ye have a strong argument, for the Greek Apostolos is in German "messenger," and thus are they called throughout the Gospel.

If, then, they are all messengers of the one Lord Christ, who would be so foolish as to say that so great a lord, in a matter of such great importance for the whole world, sends but one messenger, and he, in turn, sends other messengers of his own? Then St. Peter would have to be called, not a Zwölfbote (one of the twelve messengers), but an only-messenger, and none of the others would remain Zwölfboten, but they would all be St. Peter's Elfboten (i. e., his eleven messengers). But what is the custom at court? Is it not true that a lord has many messengers? Aye, when does it happen that many messengers are sent with the same message to one place, as now we have priest, bishop, archbishop and pope, all ruling over the same city, not to mention other tyrants, who shove in their rule somewhere between the rest? Christ sent all the apostles into the world with His Word and message with full, equal powers, as St. Paul says: "We are ambassadors for Christ." [1 Cor. 5:20] And in I. Corinthians iii. he says: "What is Peter? What is Paul? Servants through whom ye believed." [1 Cor. 3:5] This ambassadorship means to feed, to rule, to be bishop, and so forth. But that the pope makes all the messengers of God to be subject to himself, is the same as if one messenger of a prince detained all the other messengers, and then sent them out when it suited his pleasure, while he himself went nowhere. Would that be pleasing to the prince, if he found it out?

Should you say: True, but one messenger may be above another; I would reply: One may indeed be better and more skilful than another, as St. Paul was when compared with Peter; but since they bring one and the same message, one cannot be above another by reason of his office. But, put the other way, St. Peter is not a Zwölfbote at all, but a special messenger and lord over the Eleven. What can it be that one has above the others, if they all have one and the same message and commission from the one Lord?

Forasmuch then as all bishops are equal by divine right and sit in the Apostles' places, I may gladly concede that by human right one is above the other in the external Church. For here the pope instils what is in his own mind, as, for instance, his Canon Law and human inventions, whereby Christendom is ruled with outward show; but that does not make Christians, as I have said above[43]; neither are they heretics who are not under the same laws and ceremonies or human ordinances. For customs change with the country.

All this is confined by the article in the Creed: "I believe in the Holy Ghost, one Holy Christian Church, the Communion of Saints." No one says: "I believe in the Holy Ghost, one Holy Roman Church, a Communion of the Romans." Thus it is clear that the Holy

Church is not bound to Rome, but is as wide as the world, the assembly of those of one faith, a spiritual and not a bodily thing, for that which one believes is not bodily or visible. The external Roman Church we all see, therefore it cannot be the true Church, which is believed, and which is a community or assembly of the saints in faith, for no one can see who is a saint or a believer.

[Sidenote: The Marks of the Church]

The external marks, whereby one can perceive where this Church is on earth, are baptism, the Sacrament, and the Gospel; and not Rome, or this place, or that. For where baptism and the Gospel are, no one may doubt that there are saints, even if it were only the babes in their cradles. But neither Rome nor the papal power is a mark of the Church,[44] for that power cannot make Christians, as baptism and the Gospel do; and therefore it does not belong to the true Church[44] and is but a human ordinance.

Therefore I would advise this Romanist to go to school another year, and to learn what the Church or the head of the Church[44] really means, before he drives out the poor heretics with writings of such height, depth, breadth and length. It grieves me to the heart that we must suffer these mad saints to tear asunder and blaspheme the Holy Scriptures with such insolence, license, and shamelessness, and that they make bold to deal with the Scriptures, whereas they are not fit to care for a herd of swine. Heretofore I have held that where something was to be proved by the Scriptures, the Scriptures quoted must really refer to the point at issue. I learn now that it is enough to throw many passages together helter-skelter, whether they are fit or not. If this is to be the way, then I can easily prove from the Scriptures that beer is better than wine.[45]

Of the same character is his statement in both his Latin and his German treatise[46] that Christ is the head of the Turks, heathen, Christians, heretics, robbers, harlots and knaves. It would be no wonder if all the stone and timber in the cloister stared and hooted this miserable wretch to death for his horrible blasphemy. What shall I say? Has Christ become a keeper of all the houses of shame, a head of all the murderers, of all heretics, of all rogues? Woe unto thee, thou miserable wretch, that thou thus holdest up thy Lord for all the world to blaspheme! The poor man would write about the head of Christendom, and in utter madness imagines that "head" and "Lord" are one and the same. Christ is, indeed, Lord of all things, of all the good and the evil, of the angels and the devils, the virgins and the harlots; but He is not the head, except only of the good, believing Christians, assembled in the spirit. For a head must be united with its body, as I showed above from St. Paul in Ephesians iv,[47] and the members must cleave to the head and receive from it their activity and life. For this reason Christ cannot be the head of an evil community, although it is subject unto Him as Lord; even as His kingdom, namely Christendom, is not a bodily community or kingdom, yet all things are subject unto Him, be they spiritual or bodily, of hell or of heaven.

Thus in his first argument this reviler vilified and slandered me; in this second argument he reviled Christ much more than me. For even if he thinks much of his own holy prayers and fastings in contrast to a poor sinner like me, yet he has not called me a brothelkeeper and archknave, as he has Christ.

[Sidenote: III. The Argument from Scripture]

Now comes the third argument, in which the high majesty of God is made a target, and the Holy Spirit becomes a liar and a heretic, so that by all means the contention of the Romanists may be upheld.

The third argument is taken from the Scriptures, just as the second was taken from reason and the first from folly, so that everything may be done in proper order. It runs as follows: The Old Testament was a type of the New Testament, and because it had a bodily high-priest, the New Testament must have one likewise—how else shall the type be fulfilled? For has not Christ Himself said: "Not one jot or tittle of the law shall pass away; it shall all be fulfilled"? [Matt. 5:18]

A book more foolish, senseless, and blind I have never seen. Once before, another[48] wrote the same thing against me, so coarse and foolish that I could not but scorn it. But because they have not sharpened their wits, I must speak bluntly for the thickheads; I see that the ass does not appreciate a harp, I must offer him thistles.

[Sidenote: Type and Fulfillment]

In the first place, it is evident that a type is material and external, and the fulfilment of the type is spiritual and internal; what the type reveals to the bodily eye, its fulfilment must reveal to the eye of faith alone, or it is not really a fulfilment.

I must prove that by illustration. By many miracles the Jewish people came in a bodily manner out of the bodily land of Egypt, as is written in the book of Exodus [Ex. 13:18 ff.]. This type does not mean that we, too, shall in a bodily manner come out of Egypt, but that our souls by a right faith shall come forth from sins and the spiritual power of the devil; so that the bodily assembly of the Jewish people signifies the spiritual and internal assembly of the Christian people in faith. Thus, as they drank water from a bodily rock, and ate bodily manna with the bodily mouth, so with the mouth of the heart we drink and eat of the spiritual Rock, the Lord Christ, when we believe in Him [1 Cor. 10:3]. Again, Moses set a serpent on a pole, and whosoever looked upon it was made whole [Num. 21:8]. That signifies Christ on the Cross; whosoever believeth in Him, is saved. And so throughout the entire Old Testament, all the bodily, visible things in it signify in the New Testament spiritual and inward things, which one cannot see, but possesses only in faith. St. Augustine understood the types in this manner, when he says[49] on John iii, "This is the difference between the type and its fulfilment: the type gave temporal goods and life, but the fulfilment gives spiritual and eternal life." [John 3:14] Now the outward show of Roman power can give neither temporal nor eternal life, and therefore it is not only no fulfilment of the type of Aaron, but far less than the type, for that was established by divine direction. For if the papacy could give either eternal or temporal life, all the popes would be saved and be in good health. But he who has Christ and the spiritual Church, is truly saved and has the fulfilment of the type, yet only in faith. And since the pope's external show and the oneness of his Church can be seen with the eyes, and we all see it, it is not possible that he can be the fulfilment of any type. For the fulfilment of types must not be seen, but believed.

[Sidenote: The High-Priest Not a Type of the Pope]

Now see—are they not skilful masters who make the high-priest of the Old Testament to be a type of the pope, when the latter makes as much, nay more of an external show than the former, and thus a bodily thing is made to be the fulfilment of a bodily type! That would mean that type and fulfilment are exactly alike. But if this type is to stand, the new high-priest must be spiritual, and his graces and adornment likewise spiritual. The prophets also saw this when they said of us, Psalm cxxxii, "Thy priests shall be clothed with faith or righteousness, and Thine anointed ones shall be adorned with joy." [Ps. 132:9] As if he would say: Our priests are types, and are clothed externally with silks and purples, but your priests shall be clothed with grace inwardly. Thus is this miserable Romanist routed with his "type," and his jumbling together of much Scripture has been in vain. For the pope is an external priest, and they think of him in his external power and adornment. Therefore Aaron cannot have been a type of him; we must have another.

[Sidenote: Scriptural Types Interpreted in Scripture]

In the second place—in order that they may realize how far they are from the truth—even if they had been wise enough to give a spiritual fulfilment to the type, yet that would not stand the test, unless they had a clear passage from the Scriptures, which brought the type and its spiritual fulfilment together; otherwise every one could make out of it what he desired. For instance, that the serpent lifted up by Moses signifies Christ, is taught by John iii [John 3:14]. If it were not for that passage my reason might evolve very strange and weird fancies out of that type. Again, that Adam was a type of Christ, I learn not from myself, but from St. Paul in Romans v [Rom. 5:14]. Again, that the rock in the wilderness signifies Christ, is not so stated by my reason, but by St. Paul in I. Corinthians x. [1 Cor. 10:4] Therefore, let none other explain the type but the Holy Spirit Himself, Who has given the type and wrought the fulfilment, in order that both promise and performance, type and fulfilment, and the interpretation of both, may be God's own and not man's, and our faith be founded not on human, but on divine works and words.

What leads the Jews astray but that they interpret the types as they please, without the Scriptures? What has led so many heretics astray but the interpretation of the types without reference to the Scriptures? And though the pope were something spiritual, yet even then it would count for nothing if I made Aaron to be his type, unless I could point to a passage where it is explicitly stated: Behold, Aaron was a type of the pope. Otherwise who could prevent me from assuming that Aaron was a type of the bishop of Prague? St. Augustine has stated that types are not valid in controversy unless supported by the Scriptures.[50]

But now this poor chatterbox has neither: no spiritual, inward high-priest and no passage of the Scriptures; he goes at it blindly with his own dreams, and assumes as his basis that Aaron was the type of St. Peter, the very thing which is in greatest need of foundation and proof, and he just goes on prattling that the law must be fulfilled and not one iota omitted. My dear Romanist, who has ever doubted that the law of the Old Testament and its types must be fulfilled in the New? There was no need of your scholarship to establish that. But here you might make a great show and demonstrate by your ingenuity that this fulfilment occurs in Peter or in the pope. You are as mute as a stick when it is time to speak out, and a chatterbox when speech is unnecessary. Have you not learned your logic better than that? You argue your major premises, which no one questions, and assume the correctness of your minor premises, which every one questions, and then you draw the conclusion to suit yourself.

[Sidenote: A Lesson in Logic]

Listen to me, I will give you a better lesson in logic. I agree with you in saying: All that is typified by the high-priest in the Old Testament must be fulfilled in the New, as St. Paul says in I. Corinthians i. Thus far we agree. Now you continue: St. Peter, or the pope, was typified by Aaron. Here I say, Nay. And what can you do then? Now show your learning, and call the whole crowd of Romanists to assist you, bring just one jot or tittle from the Scriptures in defence, and I will call you a hero. On what foundation have you builded, however? On your own dreams; and yet you boast you will argue against me with the Scriptures. It was not necessary for you thus to play the fool against me, I should have had a fool to overcome at any rate.

[Sidenote: Aaron a Type of Christ]

258

Listen to me further: I say that Aaron was a type of Christ, and not of the pope. And when I say this, I do not utter my own invention, as you do; but I will prove it, so that neither you, nor the world, nor all the devils shall overthrow it. In the first place, Christ is a spiritual priest for the inner man; for He sitteth in heaven, and maketh intercession for us as a priest, teaches us inwardly in the heart, and does everything a priest should do in mediating between God and man, as St. Paul says, Romans iii, and the whole Epistle to the Hebrews. Aaron, the type, is bodily and external, but the fulfilment is spiritual and inward, and the two agree together. [Rom. 3:25]

Secondly, in order not to bring my own thoughts, I have the passage, Psalm cx, "The Lord hath sworn and will not repent: Thou art a priest forever after the order of Melchizedek." [Ps. 110:4] Can you also bring a passage like that about St. Peter or the pope? For I think that you will not deny that this passage refers to Christ, as St. Paul, in Hebrews v. [Heb. 5:6] and at many other places, and our Lord Christ Himself, in Matthew xxii, so explain it [Matt. 22:44]. Thus we can see how beautifully the Romanists treat the Scriptures and make out of them what they like, as if they were a nose of wax, to be pulled around at will.

Now we have proved by the Scriptures that Christ is the High-priest of the New Testament. Clearer still is Paul's comparison of Aaron and Christ in Hebrews ix, when he says: "Into the first tabernacle the priests went every day, to offer the sacrifices; but into the second went the high-priest alone once every year, not without blood, which he offered for himself and for the sin of the people. The Holy Ghost thus signifying that the way to the true, holy tabernacle was not yet made manifest, while the first tabernacle was yet standing, which was a type or figure needful for the time then present. But Christ being come, a high-priest of spiritual possessions to come, by a greater and more perfect tabernacle, not made with hands, that is to say, not of this temporal building: neither by the blood of goats and calves, but by His own blood He entered in once into the holy place, having obtained an eternal redemption." [Heb. 9:6 ff.]

What do you say to this, my super-learned Romanist? Paul says: The high-priest typified Christ; you say, St. Peter. Paul says, Christ entered not into a temporal building; you say, He is in the temporal building at Rome. Paul says, He entered in once, and hath obtained an eternal redemption, and makes the type to be altogether spiritual and heavenly, which you make to be earthly and external. What can you do now? My advice is this: Clench your fist, smite him on the jaw, and say he is a liar, a heretic, a poisoner, just as you do to me; and you will be like your father Zedekiah, who smote Micaiah on the cheek [1 Kings 22:24]. Do you not see, wretched blasphemer, whither your counsellors and your own madness have brought you? [John 5:43] Where are they now, those big-wigs, who interdicted my sermon on both kinds in the Sacrament?[51] It served them right. They would not tolerate nor hear the Gospel, and now they shall hear instead the lies and blasphemies of the Evil Spirit, even as Christ says to the Jews, "I am come in My Father's name, and ye receive Me not; another shall come in his own name, him ye will receive." [John 5:43]

But you might say, St. Peter too is typified by Aaron, along with Christ; and I answer, if you must keep on, you could also say that Aaron was a type of the Turk; and who could prevent you, since you delight in such senseless chatter. But you have given promise to argue from the Scriptures; now do it, and leave your dreams at home. Moreover, where faith is concerned, one must contend not with uncertain Scripture texts, but with those that refer to the issue in a way that is certain, clear, and simple; otherwise the Evil Spirit would toss us hither and yon, until at last we should not know at all where we were; just as has happened to many with these little words, Petros and Petra[52] in Matthew xvi [Matt. 16:18].

It would have been something less of a lie and a blasphemy for you to have said that Aaron was a type of Christ and also of St. Peter. But now you just scream with all your might that Aaron was not a type of Christ, but of St. Peter, and wantonly you strike St. Paul in the face. And in order that nothing may be lacking in this perfect piece of folly, you go on to say: Moses was a type of Christ. And you say this not only without any cause or indication in the Scriptures—just as if you were more than God, and everything which you emit must be taken for Gospel—but contrary to all the Scriptures, which make Moses a type of the Law, as St. Paul does in II. Corinthians iii. [2 Cor. 3:7] It is not necessary to go into this just now, else you might strike him on the jaw again in your wantonness and insolence. Such venom you have imbibed from that man Emser's heretical and blasphemous output,[53] which I will give the answer it deserves when Sir Knight Eck comes along with his flourish.[54] You cannot carry it off in that way, my dear Romanists. I cannot prevent it by force, but you shall not bring any Scripture in support of it. Praise God, I am not quite ready to bite the dust.

[Sidenote: Types of the Apostles]

Now it is clear, I take it, that the third argument of his Romanist is rank heresy and blasphemy, for it flatly contradicts God the Holy Ghost and makes Him a liar, and utterly demolishes St. Paul. For since Aaron is a type of Christ, he cannot be a type of St. Peter. For what the Scriptures ascribe to Christ must not be ascribed to any other, so that the Scriptures may ever have one simple, direct, indisputable meaning, on which our faith may rest without wavering [Exod. 28:17 ff.]. This I will grant, that Peter is one of the twelve precious stones in the breastplate of Aaron, whereby there may be signified that the twelve Apostles, chosen in Christ, and known from all eternity, are the highest and most precious jewels in Christendom, but I can never allow Peter to become Aaron. Again, I will admit that St. Peter is one of the twelve lions that stood beside Solomon's great throne [1 Kings 10:19], but Christ must remain for me the one King Solomon. I will let the twelve Apostles be the twelve wells of water in the wilderness of Elim [Exod. 15:27], on this condition, however, that the bright cloud and pillar shall be nothing other than Christ himself. And just as little as the power of any one of these twelve extends over the others, so little does Peter have power over the other apostles, and the pope over other bishops and priests, by divine right.

One thing more, my good, dear Romanists, and then I have done. I ask most graciously for a correct answer. If Aaron was a type of the pope in external authority, vestments and state, why was he not a type in all other external and bodily matters; if it holds in one thing, why not in all the others?

It is written that the high-priest shall not take a widow or a divorced woman, but shall wed a virgin [Lev. 21:14]; why do they not give the pope a virgin to wed, so that the type may be fulfilled? Nay, why does the pope forbid matrimony to the whole priesthood, not only contrary to the Old Testament type, but also in opposition to God, and against right, reason, and nature, a thing which he has no authority, nor power, nor right to do, and over which the Church has never exercised authority, nor should it ever do so. So by his own caprice, without need, he has caused Christendom to be filled with whores, sinners, and guilty consciences, as St. Paul says of him, I. Timothy iv: "In the latter times some shall depart from the faith, giving heed to seducing spirits and doctrines of devils, speaking lies in hypocrisy, having their conscience seared with a hot iron, forbidding to marry, and commanding to abstain from meats, which God hath created, etc." [1 Tim. 4:1 ff.]

Does Paul herein not hit the Roman laws, which forbid the priesthood to marry, and command all Christians to abstain from butter, eggs, milk, and meats on certain days, while God Himself has left it to the free choice of Christians in every estate to eat or to marry, as they desire? Where are you now, my Romanist of the observance, with all your ranting that not one detail of the Old Testament type shall be omitted, and that every iota must be fulfilled? Yea, where is the pope, the successor of St. Peter, who was married, as was St. Paul[55] and all the Apostles?

[Sidenote: The Tonsure]

Again, the Old Testament high-priest was not permitted to have his head shorn [Lev. 21:5]. But why does the pope have a tonsure, and all the other priests, too? Wherein is the type fulfilled here to the very dot? Again, the High-priest was forbidden to own any portion of Israel's land, but subsisted entirely on the offerings of the people. Pray, why is the occupant of the papal throne so furious to possess the whole world, and has not only stolen lands and cities, principalities and kingdoms,[56] but has arrogated to himself the power to make kings and princes, seat and unseat and change them according to his pleasure, as if he were Antichrist. Wherein is there here a fulfilment of the type?

[Sidenote: Worldly Pretensions]

Again, the Old Testament high-priest was a subject under the rule of the kings. Why then does the pope have men kiss his feet, and aspire to be king of kings, which Christ Himself did not? Wherein is the type fulfilled here? Again, the high-priest was circumcised. And, finally, if having the external things in the New Testament identical with those of the Old be the fulfilment of types, why do we not become Jews again and keep the whole law of Moses? If we must observe it in one particular, why not in all? If not in all, why in one?

If it be desired to elevate the New Testament above the Old in the matter of outward splendor, would it not be the reasonable to suppose that there should be more than one high-priest in the New Testament, to make it more splendid and glorious than the Old, which did not have more than one? If reason should judge in this case and follow its own bent, what do you suppose it would do? Again, in the time of the Old Testament high-priest there were many holy men who were not under him, such as Job and his family—for he was not alone. Likewise the king of Babylon, the queen of Sheba, the widow of Zarephath, the prince Naaman of Syria, and many others in Eastern lands, together with their families, who are all commended in the Scriptures. Why does not the type hold in these instances, even to the letter? And yet the pope will let no one be a Christian except he be subject to him, and buy his seals and parchments at any price his Romanists please to charge. Or do the Romanists have power to interpret types as they please and as far as they please, without any warrant of the Scriptures?

Do you not see, my good Romanist, how envy and hatred have blinded you and your kind? Would it not have been a more seemly thing for you to have remained in your cell praying your vigils until you had been called or urged into this case? You do not know what a type is or signifies, and yet you boast of being a teacher and master of all the Holy Scriptures.[57] Yea, verily, a master in corrupting the Scriptures, and blaspheming God, and libeling truth. Come again, my dear Romanist, and I will deck you with lilies and give you for a new year's present[58] to those who have sent you.

I, too, desire to say one thing that is not in the Scriptures. In all estates which God has appointed there are always some who are saved, and no estate is without living saints on earth, as Christ says, Luke xvii, "Two men shall be in one bed; the one shall be taken, and the other left," etc. [Luke 17:34] If the papacy were from God it would be impossible for a pope to be damned, because there is but one person at a time in that estate, and whoever became pope would thereby be assured of his salvation; which is contrary to all the Scriptures.

Now let us see how these pious people treat the holy words of Christ in this case. Christ says to St. Peter, Matthew xvi: "Thou art, or art called, Peter; and on the Petram (i. e., on the rock) I will build My Church. And I will give unto thee the keys of the kingdom of heaven, and whatsoever thou shalt bind on earth, shall be bound in heaven, and whatsoever thou shalt loose on earth, shall be loosed in heaven." [Matt 16:18] From these words they have claimed the keys for St. Peter alone; but the same Matthew has barred such erroneous interpretation in the xviii. chapter, where Christ says to all in common, "Verily, I say unto you, whatsoever ye shall bind on earth, shall be bound in heaven, and whatsoever ye shall loose on earth, shall be loosed in heaven." [Matt. 18:18] It is clear that Christ here interprets His own words, and in this xviii. chapter explains the former xvi.; namely, that the keys are given to St. Peter in the stead of the whole Church,[59] and not for his own person. Thus also John, in the last chapter, "He breathed on them and said, Receive ye the Holy Ghost; whosesoever sins ye remit, they are remitted unto them, and whosesoever sins ye retain, they are retained." To maintain the sole authority of St. Peter, when there are two texts against one, many men have labored in vain. But the Gospel is too clear, and they have had to admit until now that in the first passage nothing special was given to St. Peter for his own person.

Thus it was also understood by many of the ancient Church fathers. It is likewise proved by the words of Christ just before He gave the keys to St. Peter, where He asks not Peter only, but all of them: "What think ye of Me?" [Matt. 16:15] Then Peter answers for them all, "Thou art Christ, the Son of the living God." [Matt. 16:18] Therefore the words in Matthew xvi. must be understood in accordance with the words in chapter xviii. [Matt. 18:16] and in John xx [John 20:22], and one passage must not be explained in a manner contrary to two strong ones, but the one be properly explained by the two. The proof is all the stronger where there are two instead of only one, and it is but fair that one should follow the two, and not two the one.

[Sidenote: Equality Among the Apostles]

It is plain, therefore, that all the apostles were equal to Peter in all matters of authority. This is shown by their acts as well as by their words, for Peter never selected an apostle, nor made, confirmed, sent out, or ruled over one; although if he had been their superior by divine appointment this would have had to be, or all of them would have been heretics. Moreover, all of the apostles together could not make St. Matthias and St. Paul apostles, but this must needs be done from heaven, as it is written in Acts i. [Acts 1:23 ff.] and xiii. [Acts 13:2] How then could St. Peter alone be lord over them all? This little nut no one has been able to crack as yet, and I trust they will be so gracious, even against their will, to leave it uncracked a while longer.

[Sidenote: Roman Authority never Universal]

263

And just as this Romanist boasts that the papal chair survives in spite of repeated assaults on its authority,[60] so I, too, boast that the Roman See ofttimes, and to this very day, has striven in mad frenzy for such power, yet has never been able to attain it, and, God willing, shall never attain it. It is an utter farce when a man boasts that he has always kept what he has never had. Why does not our dear Romanist boast also that the city of Leipzig has never been taken away from him, in which he does not even have a house? It would be a boast of equal value with the other. So they chatter on incessantly; anything that comes to their tongues is blurted out. Therefore, I say, that though the Roman tyrants have striven hard against the Gospel, to take the common power of the Church and make it their own, yet the word of Christ still stands, "The powers of hell shall not prevail against it." [Matt. 16:18] Now if this power had been given to the pope by divine right, God would not have desisted; at some time it would have been fulfilled. For he says that "not a jot or letter shall remain unfulfilled." [Matt. 5:18] But in the extension of Roman power over all Christendom not one letter has ever been fulfilled.

And it does not help to say, it is not the fault of the Romans, but of the heretics, that it has not been fulfilled. Heretic here, heretic there! God's order and promise cannot be hindered or prevented by the gates of hell, much less by the heretics; surely He is strong enough to make true His own Word, without the help of heretics. And inasmuch as He has never done so, and leaves it unfulfilled to this day, regardless of all the zeal, diligence, toil and labor, and cunning and trickery besides, which the Romans have expended on it, I hope it is sufficiently established just what the pope's authority is, beyond that of other bishops and priests; namely, that it is of human and not of divine right. Christ's kingdom has been at all times in all the world, as is written in Psalms ii. [Ps. 2:8] and xix [Ps. 19:4], but never was it entirely under the pope, even for one hour, in spite of those who say otherwise.

[Sidenote: Two Passages versus One]

Although all this is well-established truth, we shall nevertheless proceed to demolish their idle fairy-tales still more, and say: Even if it were not valid that the two sayings in Matthew [Matt. 18:18] and John [John 20:22], which make the power of the keys a common possession, should explain the one saying of Matthew, which sounds as if the keys were given to Peter alone; yet the case cannot proceed any further than to establish a doubt, whether the one passage shall interpret the two, or the two the one, and I hold as tenaciously to the two, as they to the one. Furthermore, that doubt gives certainty to us, so that it is entirely for us to say whether we will have the pope for a head or not. For where a matter is in doubt, no one is a heretic, whether he hold to one view or to another; this they themselves admit. And thus their argument again is brought to naught, and they can produce nothing but uncertainty and doubt. Therefore they must either give up all three passages as inadequate to establish their case, since their meaning is obscure; or else they must cite others, which explicitly indicate that the two must be interpreted by the one. This they cannot do; I defy them to try it.

But I will cite passages by which I shall prove that the one passage must follow the two.

Thus saith the Law—and Christ quotes it in Matthew xviii—, "Every case shall be established through the mouth of two or three witnesses, but at the mouth of one witness shall no man be put to death." [Deut. 17:6] And once I have two witnesses against one, my case takes precedence, and the one passage must follow the two; namely, that Peter received the keys not as Peter, but in the stead of the Church,[61] as Matthew xviii. and John xx. clearly say, and not as Peter alone, as Matthew xvi. seems to say.

Moreover, I am astounded at the great arrogance by which they would make the power of the keys a ruling power, which really fits together as well as winter and summer. For a ruling power means far more than the power of the keys. The power of the keys extends only to the Sacrament of Penance,[62] to bind and loose the sins, as Matthew xviii. [Matt. 18:18] and John xx. [John 20:22] clearly state; but a ruling power extends likewise to those who are pious and have naught to be bound or loosed; its scope includes preaching, exhorting, consoling, saying mass, giving the Sacrament, etc. Therefore, none of the three passages fits the power of the pope over all Christendom, except he were made the one confessor, or penitentiary,[63] or anathematizer, to rule only over the wicked and the sinners, which is not their desire at all. And if these words should establish the papal power over all Christians, I should very much like to know who could absolve the pope when he sins. He must certainly remain in his sins; neither will it do for him to transfer his power to another for his own absolution, for that would make him a heretic in acting contrary to divine command.

[Sidenote: Person and Office]

Some have invented the fiction that the pope's person and office are two different things;[64] that the person can be made subject to another, but not the office. That glitters for a moment, but is, in truth, like all such wares. For in their own laws, with great ado and show, they have forbidden any bishop of a lower rank to confirm a pope, although this confirmation is not the institution of the office, but the induction of the person into the office. And if in this case the person is not subject to any one, surely the same is true in absolution. But in all their doings and glosses and interpretations, their minds are in a whirl, and they say now this and now that; and in their twisting of God's Word they lose its true sense, forget where they are, go completely astray, and yet they would rule the whole world.

[Sidenote: The Keys Given to the Whole Church]

Therefore let every Christian believe that in these passages Christ does not give either to St. Peter or to the other Apostles the power to rule, or to soar so high. What then does He give? I will tell you. These words of Christ are nothing but gracious promises, given to the whole Church,[65] as was said above,[66] in order that poor sinful consciences may find comfort when they are "loosed" or absolved by man; and the words apply only to sinful, timid, troubled consciences, and are intended to strength en them, if they but believe. When these comforting words of Christ, given for the benefit of all poor consciences in the whole Church,[65] are thus made to strengthen and establish papal power, I will tell you of what it reminds me.

[Sidenote: A Parable]

It reminds me of a rich, kind prince who threw open his treasure-house, and gave complete freedom to all the poor to come and take what they needed. Among the needy there came a rogue, who made use of the permission all by himself and allowed none to come in who did not bow completely to his will, and arbitrarily explained the words of the prince to mean that the permission was given to him alone. Can you imagine what the kind prince would think of this rogue? If you cannot imagine it, hear what St. Matthew says of that selfsame servant: "If that evil servant shall say in his heart. My lord delayeth his coming, and shall begin to smite his fellow-servants, and to eat and drink with the drunken; the lord of that servant shall come in a day when he looketh not for him, and in an hour that he is not aware of, and shall cut him asunder, and appoint him his portion with the hypocrites: there shall be weeping and gnashing of teeth." [Matt. 24:48 ff.]

And now see: in the same manner as this servant interprets the intention of his lord, so the Romanists interpret the words of God, and this is the very best that can be said of their interpretation. For when they go stark mad, they act as if yon servant had not only made barter of his lord's kindness for his own profit, but as if he actually changed the goods, and gave chaff and stubble for com, copper for gold, lead for silver, and poison for wine. And therefore it is still a matter of grace, that they claim the keys for the pope at least in such a manner that we may buy them by giving money and everything that we possess. But it is an utter calamity when they preach their laws, authority, bans, indulgences and the like, in place of the Gospel. That is what the Lord calls the smiting of the fellow servants by the evil servant, who should rather feed them.

[Sidenote: Herod and the Romanists]

I will use a plain illustration, so that any one may see the difference between the true and the false interpretation of these words of Christ. The high-priest of the Old Testament wore, by divine appointment, an official robe. When King Herod elevated himself over the people of Israel, he took that robe, and although he did not use it himself, yet he usurped the authority to regulate its use, and the people were forced to pay for that to which God had given them the right. The same is true now. The keys have been given to the whole Church[65] as has been proved above.[66] But along come the Romanists, and although they never use them themselves nor exercise their office, yet they take to themselves authority over the use of the keys, and we are forced to buy with money what is in reality our own, given by Christ. And, not satisfied with this, they apply the words of Christ concerning the keys, not to the keys nor to their use, but to their usurped power and authority over the keys, so that the power of the keys, freely given by Christ, is now captive in the hands of the Romanists; and both the power of the keys and the power over the keys are supposed to come from the one word of Christ, just as if Herod had said that it was his power of which Moses was speaking, when he spake of the robe of the high-priest.

In like manner, a tyrant could obtain possession of a last testament, and explain the words, wherein the property is bequeathed to the heir, to mean that authority is given him over this testament, to decide whether he will allow its provisions to come to the heir gratuitously or for a price. So it is also with the power of the keys and the authority of the pope, understood as coming from one and the same word [of Scripture], whereas the two things are not only different, but the authority claimed is more than the power of the keys; and yet they make of it one and the same thing.

[Sidenote: What is Meant by the Rock]

Their argument, that the external authority of the pope is conferred in the words of Christ, "On this rock I will build My Church," [Matt. 16:18] understanding the rock to mean St. Peter and his authority, I have refuted many times,[67] and now I will say only this: First, they must prove that the rock means authority. They will not do this, nor can they do it, so they just have voice to their own inventions, and all their drivel must be divine command. Secondly, the rock can mean neither St. Peter nor his authority, on account of the words of Christ which follow, "And the gates of hell shall not prevail against it." Now it is clear as day that no one is edified in the Church, nor withstands the gates of hell by the mere fact that he is under the external authority of the pope. For the majority of those who hold so strongly to the authority of the pope, and lean upon it, are themselves possessed by the powers of hell and are full of sins and rascality. Then, too, some of the popes were heretics themselves, and gave heretical laws; yet they remained in authority. Therefore, the rock does not signify authority, which can never withstand the gates of hell; but it signifies only Christ and the faith in Him, against which no power can ever prevail.

[Sidenote: Prevailing Against the Gates of Hell]

That this authority continues to exist despite those who battle against it, does not mean that it has withstood the gates of hell. For so the Greek Church has continued, and all the other

Christians in the world; the Moscovites[68] and Bohemians continue, yea, the kingdom of Persia has continued for more than two thousand years, and the Turk for well nigh a thousand years, in spite of various and repeated attacks against them. And to tell you some more things that really should bring astonishment to such an illustrious Romanist: The world in its wickedness has stood from the beginning, and shall stand until the Last Day, and forever, even if God Himself with all holy men and angels never cease to preach, write and work against it. If you think good of it, my dear Romanist, defy God and all the angels, because the world has stood even against all their words and work. Why did you not ascertain, you poor, blind Romanist, before rushing into print, what it means "to prevail against the gates of hell"? If every prevailing means just as much as prevailing against the gates of hell, then the devil's kingdom prevails with a larger following than God's kingdom. This is what it means to prevail against the gates of hell: Not to be in an external communion[69], authority, jurisdiction or assembly in a bodily manner, according to your way of babbling about the Roman communion[69] and its unity, but by a firm and true faith to be built upon Christ, the Rock which can never be suppressed by any power of the devil, even if he counts more followers and uses unceasing strife, cunning, and violence against it.

[Sidenote: Evil Results of Roman Authority]

Now the greater part of the Roman communion,[69] and even some of the popes themselves, have forsaken the faith wantonly and without struggle, and live under the power of Satan, as is plainly to be seen, and thus the papacy often has been under the dominion of the gates of hell. And should I speak quite openly, this same Roman authority, ever since the time it has presumed to soar over all Christendom, not only has never attained its purpose, but has become the cause of nearly all the apostasy, heresy, discord, sects, unbelief and misery in Christendom, and has never freed itself from the gates of hell. And if there were no other passage to prove that Roman authority was of human and not of divine right, this passage alone would be sufficient, where Christ says, the gates of hell shall not prevail against His building on the rock. Now the gates of hell ofttimes had the papacy in their power, at times the pope was not a pious man, and the office was occupied by a man without faith, without grace, without good works; which God would never have permitted if the papacy were meant in Christ's word concerning the rock. For then He would not be true to His promise, nor fulfil His own word; therefore the rock, and the building of Christ founded upon it, must be something entirely different from the papacy and its external Church.

Accordingly I say further, that the Roman bishop has often been deposed or appointed by other bishops. If, however, his authority were by divine appointment and promise, God would never have permitted this to happen, for it would be against His word and promise. And if God were found to be unfaithful in so much as even one word, then would perish faith, truth, the Scriptures, and God Himself. But if God's words stand firm, then my adversaries must prove to me that the pope was never subject, even once, to Satan or to man. I would much like to hear just what my good Romanists have to say to this. I trust they are slain with their own sword, like Goliath [1 Sam. 17:51]. For I can prove that the papacy has been subject not only to Satan, but to other bishops, yea, also to temporal powers, to the emperors. How did the rock prevail then against the gates of hell? I will leave the choice to them: either these words mean defeat for the papacy, or God is a liar. Let us see which they will choose.

Nor is it enough that you try to squirm out of the dilemma by saying that even if the papacy has been under Satan now and then, yet there have always been pious Christians under it. I reply: Under the rule of the Turk there are Christians, and likewise there are Christians in all the world, as there were aforetime under Nero and other tyrants. How does that help you? The papacy and the pope himself must at no time have been under Satan if Christ's word refers to them when He speaks of "a rock set against the gates of hell." See, thus do the Romanists interpret the Scriptures in accordance with their mad folly. Faith they turn into authority, spiritual edification into outward show, and yet they are not heretics—they make all others to be the heretics. Such are the Romanists.

Another passage which they cite in support of their contention is that in which the Lord says three times to Peter, "Feed My sheep." [John 21:15] Here they reach real eminence as theologians when they say: Since Christ said to Peter in particular, "Feed My sheep," He thereby conferred on him authority above all others.

[Sidenote: Feeding the Sheep and Roman Authority]

Now we shall see to what labor and pains they are put to bring about that result. In the first place, we must know what they mean by "feeding." "Feeding," in the Roman sense, means to burden Christendom with many human and hurtful laws, to sell the bishoprics at the highest possible price, to extract the annates[70] from all benefices, to usurp authority over all foundations, to force into servitude all the bishops with terrible oaths, to sell indulgences, to rob the whole world by means of letters, bulls, seals and wax, to prohibit the preaching of the Gospel, to appoint knaves from Rome to all the places, to bring all litigation to Rome, to increase quarrels and disputes—in short, to allow no one to come freely to the truth and to have peace.

But if they say that by "feeding" they do not understand such abuse of authority, but the authority itself, it is simply not true. And I prove it in this wise: Where one protests very mildly against such abuse, and with all deference to the authority, they rail and threaten thunder and lightning, they clamor that it is heresy and high treason, that it is a rending of the seamless garment of Christ, and they would burn up the heretics, rebels, apostates and everybody in the whole world. By all of which it is clear that they hold "feeding" to mean naught else but such preying and flaying. In the meanwhile, however, we think that feeding does not mean preying on others. Let us endeavor to see what it means.

They have a high-sounding, keen and subtile speech—as they imagine—when they say that person and office are not one and the same, and that the office remains, and remains good, though the person be evil. From this they conclude, and it must, indeed, follow, that the word of Christ, "Feed My sheep," means an office of external power, which even an evil man may have, for the office makes no one holy. Very well. This is acceptable to us, and we will ask the Romanists a question. Whoever keeps and fulfils the word of Christ, he is truly obedient and pious, and shall be saved, for His words are spirit and life [John 6:63]. If, therefore, "feeding" means to sit in the highest place and to have an office—even if the incumbent be a knave—it follows that he feeds who sits in the highest seat and is pope; and whoever does this work of feeding is obedient to Christ; and whoever is obedient in one particular is obedient in all and is a saint Therefore it must be true that whoever is pope and sits in the chief room is obedient to Christ and is a saint, though he be a knave, or a rogue, or what not. Have thanks, my dearest Romanists! Now I know, for the first time, why the pope is addressed as "your holiness." Thus must the word of Christ be explained, so that knaves and rogues are made out to be holy and obedient servants of Christ, just as in the previous pages you have made Christ an arch-knave and a brothel-keeper.[71]

[Sidenote: Being Fed in the Roman Sense]

Further, if "feeding" means to sit in the highest place, then "being fed" must mean to be subject, so that just as "feeding" means external governing, "being fed" must mean to be governed, and, as they say, to live in the Roman fellowship.[72] Then it must also be further true that all who are within the Roman fellowship,[72] be they good or evil, are saints, because they are obedient to Christ and are being fed. For none can be obedient to Christ in one thing, without being obedient in all, as St. James says [Jas. 2:10]. Now is that not a fine Church under the Roman authority, where there are no sinners at all and naught but saints! But what becomes of the poor indulgence, if no one needs it any more in the Roman fellowship?[72] What becomes of the father confessor? How shall the world be robbed, if penance disappears? Nay, what becomes of the keys if they are no longer needed? But if there are still sinners among them, they must go unfed and be disobedient to Christ.

What do you say to this, my good Romanists? Come now and pipe your lay. Do you not see that "feeding" must mean something else than having authority, and "being fed" something else than being externally subject to the Roman power, and how utterly senseless it is to cite the saying of Christ, "Feed My sheep," in order to strengthen Roman authority and its external unity or fellowship!

[Sidenote: Feeding and Loving]

270

Christ also says, "He that loveth Me, keepeth My word; he that loveth Me not, keepeth not My words." Prick up your ears at this, my dear Romanists. Ye boast that the word of Christ, "Feed My sheep," [John 14:23] is a command and word of Christ. Let us ask, then, where are they who keep it? You say, even the knaves and rogues keep it. Christ says no one keepeth it, except he love and be a righteous man. Now come to some agreement with Christ in this matter, so that we may know if you or He is to be charged with lying. Therefore, the pope who loves not, and is not righteous, does not "feed the sheep," and does not keep Christ's word: neither is he a pope, nor has he authority, nor anything at all that is included in the term "feeding the sheep." For Christ stands immovable, and says, "He that loveth Me not, keepeth not My word"; nor does such a one perform any "feeding of sheep," i. e., he is no pope at all, as they explain it. Thus it comes that the same passages which are cited in its favor are against the papacy; a just retribution for those who treat the holy Word of God in sheer madness, as though it were fool's talk, and who would make out of it what they please.

Perhaps you might reply, that a subject can be obedient to temporal authority even if that authority were not righteous; why should one not be obedient to the pope's authority? Therefore to "feed," or to "be fed," must not necessarily include the idea of obedience. Answer: The Scriptures do not call temporal authority "feeding," and in the New Testament there is no instance where God publicly appointed any one to temporal power, although no such power arises without His secret ordering. For this reason St. Peter calls such powers "ordinances of men," [1 Peter 2:13] because they rule not by God's word, but by God's governance, and it is not needful, therefore, that such rulers should be righteous. But inasmuch as we here have God's word, "Feed my sheep," neither the shepherd nor the sheep can fulfil this word except by obedience to God and righteousness of life. Therefore I let bishop, pope, priest be what they may; unless they love Christ and are righteous, this term, "feeding," is not for them, and they are something entirely different from the shepherds and feeders of sheep who alone are meant in this word. For this reason it cannot be tolerated that this word of Christ shall be made to cover external power, which has nothing to do with obedience or disobedience to Him; "feeding" can mean naught else but to be obedient.

And this is what Christ desired. For before saying three times to Peter: "Feed My sheep," He asked him thrice if he loved Him, and Peter thrice answered that he loved Him. [John 21:15 ff.] It is evident, therefore, that there is no "feeding" where there is no love. Therefore, the papacy either must be love, or it cannot be a feeding of the sheep, and if the word "Feed My sheep" establishes the papal chair, it follows that all are popes who love Christ and feed the sheep. And this is perfectly true: for aforetime all bishops were called popes, which title is now restricted to the one at Rome.

[Sidenote: A Distinction in Love]

But here look you what our Romanists do when they cannot overcome these words of Christ, and must admit, though with great reluctance, that no one can feed except he love Christ, as the clearly expressed words of Christ declare. Gladly they would give Him the lie, or deny Him; but now that they are hit squarely between the eyes, so that their heads swim, hear what they say. They say that Christ indeed demands love in the office of the pope, but not that high love, which, they say, is meritorious unto eternal life; but the ordinary love is quite sufficient, such as a servant has toward his master.[73] Now see, this lying explanation[74] of love they bring forth entirety out of their own heads, without warrant of the Scriptures, and yet they would have it appear that they are dealing with me in the Scriptures. Tell me, my dear Romanists, all of you melted together into one heap, where is there so much as one letter in the Scriptures concerning this love of which you dream? If your vile brew of Leipzig[75] could speak, it would easily overcome such feather-brains, and speak better than you do of love.

But let us follow this matter further. If there must needs be some sort of love in the papacy, what becomes of it when a pope does not love Christ at all, and seeks in it only his own gain and honor? And there have been many such, yea, almost all since the beginning of the papacy. You have not escaped me yet—you must confess that the papacy has not always existed, it has often perished, because it was ofttimes without love. But if it had been established by divine right, in these words of Christ, it would not have perished. Twist and turn as you will, these words will not yield a papacy; or else the papacy must cease in Christendom whenever the pope is without love. Now you have said yourself that the person may be evil, but the office remains; again you admit, and must admit, that the office is nothing if the person be evil—or you must let "feeding the sheep" be something else than the papacy. And this is true; let us see what you can bring against it.

[Sidenote: A Shepherd's Love]

But let every one beware of the poisoned tongues and devil-glosses which can invent a love of such description. Christ speaks of the highest, strongest, best love of which man is capable. He will not be loved with a false, divided love; here there must be whole-hearted and pure love, or none at all. And the meaning of Christ is that in St. Peter's person He is instructing all preachers how they must be equipped; as if He would say: "See, Peter, if you shall preach My word, and thereby feed My sheep, there shall rise against you the powers of hell, devil, world, and all that therein is, and you must be willing to venture body, life, goods, honor, friends, and everything which you have; and this you will not do if you do not love Me and cleave close to Me. And if you should begin to preach, and the sheep were being fed in the pastures, and the wolves would break in, and you would then flee as a hireling, and not venture your life, but leave the sheep without care, to the wolves [John 10:12 ff.], it would have been better that you had never begun to preach and feed the sheep." For if he falls, who preaches the Word and should stand at the head, offence is given to every one, the Word of God is brought to deepest disgrace, and more harm is done to the sheep than if they had no shepherd at all. Christ cares much for the feeding of the sheep; He cares nothing at all how many crowns the pope wears, and how in all his splendor he lifts himself far above the kings of the world.

Let any one tell if he can, whether the papacy has such love, or if Christ, in these words, has instituted such a worthless authority as the papacy is. Without doubt he is truly a pope who preaches with such love; but where can such a one be found? There is no passage that gives me as much sorrow in my preaching as this one does—of love I feel not much, of preaching I do more than enough. They accuse me of being rabid and revengeful; I fear that I have done too little. I should have pulled the wool[76] much harder for the ravening wolves, who never cease to rend the Scripture, to poison and pervert it to the great injury of the poor, forsaken sheep of Christ. If I had only loved them enough I should have dealt quite differently with the pope and his Romanists, who with their laws and their prattle, their letters of indulgence, and the rest of their foolery, bring to naught out faith and God's Word. They make for us what laws they will, only to capture us, and then sell them to us again for money;[77] with their mouths they weave snares for money, and yet boast that they are shepherds and keepers of sheep, whereas they are truly wolves, thieves, and murderers, as the Lord says in John x.

I know right well that this little word, "love," scares the pope and his Romanists and makes them weak and weary, nor are they willing that it should be pressed, for it overturns the whole papacy. It made Dr. Eck weary at Leipzig;[78] and whom would it not make weary, since Christ directly commands Peter not to feed the sheep except there be love? He must have love or there can be no "feeding." I shall wait a while now to see how they will parry this thrust. If they prick me with "feeding," I will prick them much harder with "loving," and we shall see who prevails. This is the reason why some of the popes in their Canon laws so neatly pass in silence this word "love," and make so much ado about "feeding," thinking that thereby they have preached only to drunken Germans, who will not notice how the hot porridge burns their tongue. This is the reason, too, why the pope and the Romanists cannot bear any questioning and investigating of the foundation of papal power, and every one is accused of doing a scandalous, presumptuous and heretical thing, who is not satisfied with their mere assertions, but seeks for its real basis. But that one should ask if God is God, and seek in frivolous presumption to penetrate all His mysteries, they suffer with equanimity, and it does not concern them. Whence this perverted game? From this, that, as Christ says, John iii, "He that doeth evil, feareth the light." [John 3:20] Where is the thief or robber who courts investigation? Thus the evil conscience cannot bear the light; but truth loveth the light, and is an enemy to darkness, even as Christ says in the same chapter, "He that doeth truth, cometh to the light." [John 3:21]

Now we see that the two sayings of Christ, spoken to Peter, on which they build the papacy, are stronger against the papacy than all others, and the Romanists can produce nothing that does not make them a laughing-stock. I shall let the matter rest here, and pass by whatever else this miserable Romanist spues out in his book; since I have controverted it all many times before, and now also some others have effectually done so in Latin.[79] I find nothing in it, except that he soils the Holy Scriptures like a sniveling child; in no place does he show a mastery of his words or an understanding of his subject.

[Sidenote: The Conclusion of the Matter]

On the subject of the papacy I have come to this conclusion: Since we observe that the pope has full authority over all our bishops, and has not attained it apart from the providence of God—although I do not believe that it is a gracious, but rather a wrathful providence which permits men, as a plague on the world, to exalt themselves and oppress others—therefore I do not desire that any one should resist the pope, but rather bow to the providence of God, honor this authority, and endure it with all patience, just as if the Turk ruled over us; in this wise it will do no harm.

I contend for but two things. First: I will not suffer any man to establish new articles of faith, and to abuse all other Christians in the world, and slander and brand them as heretics, apostates and unbelievers, simply because they are not under the pope. It is enough that we let the pope be pope, and it is not needful that, for his sake, God and His saints on earth should be blasphemed. Second: All that the pope decrees and does I will receive, on this condition, that I first test it by the Holy Scriptures. He must remain under Christ, and submit to be judged by the Holy Scriptures.

But these Roman knaves come along, place him above Christ, and make him a judge over the Scriptures; they say that he cannot err, and whatever is dreamed at Rome, nay, everything which they dare to come out with, they would prescribe for us as articles of faith. And as if that were not enough, they would introduce a new kind of faith, so that we are to believe what we can see with our bodily eyes; whereas faith, by its very nature, is of the things which no one sees or feels, as St. Paul says in Hebrews xi [Heb. 11:1]. Now the Roman authority and fellowship[80] is a bodily thing, and can be seen by any one. If the pope came to that—which may God forbid!—I would say right out that he is the real Antichrist, of whom all the Scriptures speak.

If they grant me these two things, I will let the pope remain, nay, help to exalt him as him as they please; if not, he shall be to me neither pope nor Christian. He that must do it may make an idol of him; I will not worship him.

Moreover, I would be truly glad if kings, princes, and all the nobles would take hold, and turn the knaves from Rome out of the country, and keep the appointments to bishoprics and benefices out of their hands. How has Roman avarice come to usurp all the foundations, bishoprics and benefices of our fathers? Who has ever read or heard of such monstrous robbery? Do we not also have the people who need them, while out of our poverty we must enrich the ass-drivers and stable-boys, nay, the harlots and knaves at Rome, who look upon us as nothing else but arrant fools, and make us the objects of their vile mockery?

It is a notorious fact that the Russians desired to come into the Roman fellowship, but then the holy shepherds of Rome "fed" those sheep of Christ in such a manner that they would not receive them unless they first bound themselves to a perpetual tax of I know not how many hundred thousands of ducats. Such "food" they would not eat, and so they remain as they are, saying, if they must buy Christ, they would rather save their money until they come to Christ Himself, in heaven. Thus thou doest, thou scarlet whore of Babylon [Rev. 17:4], as St. John calls thee—makest of our faith a mockery for all the world, and yet wouldest have the name of making every one a Christian.

Oh the pity, that kings and princes have so little reverence for Christ, and His honor concerns them so little that they allow such heinous abominations to gain the upper hand, and look on, while at Rome they think of nothing but to continue in their madness and to increase the abounding misery, until no hope is left on earth except in the temporal authorities. Of this I will say more anon,[81] if this Romanist comes again; let this suffice for a beginning. May God help us at length to open our eyes. Amen.

As for the slanders and evil names with which my person is assailed, although numerous enough, I will let my dear Romanist off without reply. They do not trouble me. It has never been my intention to avenge myself on those who rail at my person, my life, my work, my doings. That I am not worthy of praise, I myself know full well. But I will let no man reproach me that in defending the Scriptures I am more pointed and impetuous than some seem to like, neither will I be silenced. Whoever will, let him freely scold, slander, condemn my person and my life; it is already forgiven him. But let no one expect from me either grace or patience who would make my Lord Christ, Whom I preach, and the Holy Ghost, to be liars. I am nothing at all, but for the Word of Christ I give answer with joyful heart and vigorous courage, and without respect of persons. To this end God has given me a glad and fearless spirit, which they shall not embitter, I trust, not in all eternity.

That I have mentioned Leipzig, no one should consider an affront to the honorable city and University. I was forced to it by the vaunted, arrogant, fictitious title of this Romanist, who boasts that he is a public teacher of all the Holy Scriptures at Leipzig,[82] which titles have never before been used in Christendom, and by his dedication[83] to the city and its Council. If the jackanapes had not issued his book in German, in order to poison the defenceless laity, he would have been too small for me to bother with. For this clumsy ass cannot yet sing his hee-haw, and quite uncalled, he meddles in things which the Roman chair itself, together with all the bishops and scholars, has not been able to establish in a thousand years.

I should have thought, too, that Leipzig ought to have been too precious in his eyes, for him to smear his drivel and snivel on so honorable and famous a city; but in his own imagination he is no ordinary man. I perceive that if I permit the petulance of all these thick-heads, even the bath-maids will finally write against me.

But I pray that whoever would come at me arm himself with the

Scriptures. What helpeth it, that a poor frog puffeth himself up?

Even if he should burst, he is no ox.

I would gladly be out of this business, and they force themselves into it. May God grant both of us our prayers,—help me out of it, and let them stick in it Amen.

All glory be to God on high

And praise to all eternity. Amen.

FOOTNOTES

[1] Augustin Alveld, so named from the town of his birth, Alveld in Saxony, a Franciscan monk, Lector of his order at Leipzig. It is said of him that what he lacked in learning he made up for in scurrility, so that he himself complains that his own brother-monks wanted to forbid his writing. John Lonicerus, a friend of Luther, published a small book, Biblia nova Alveldensis, Wittenberg, 1520, in which he gathered a long list of Alveld's terms of reproach used against Luther. To him has been attributed the origin of the undignified style adopted by so many since 1520 on both sides of the controversy about Luther's teachings. Vid. H. A. Erhard, in Ersch und Gruber, Encyclopaedia, iii, 277; Algemeine Deutsche Biographi, I, 375.

[2] Cf., Augustine's Confessions, III, vii: "Just as if in armor, a man being ignorant what piece were appointed for what part, should clap a greave upon his head and draw a headpiece upon his leg…"

[3] The four chief literary opponents of Luther in the earlier years of the Reformation— Sylvester Mazolini, usually called Prierias, after the city of his birth, a papal official (Magister sacri palatii) who had published three books against Luther prior to 1520; Thomas of Gaëtano, Cardinal, and papal legate at the Diet of Augsburg, 1518; John Eck, professor in the University of Ingolstadt, who had been Luther's opponent at the Leipzig Disputation in 1519; Jerome Emser, also active at the Leipzig Disputation, whom Luther was to make the laughing-stock of Germany under the name of "the Leipzig goat," an appellation suggested by his coat-of-arms.

[4] The Theological Faculties of Cologne and Louvaine officially condemned Luther's writings; the former August 30th, the latter November 7th, 1519. The text of their resolutions was reprinted by Luther with a reply, Responsio ad condemnationem donctrinalem, etc. (1520); Weimar Ed., VI, 174 ff; Erl. Ed., op. var. arg., IV, 172 ff.

[5] Neidhart.

[6] The views which Luther expounds in this treatise had already been expressed in a Latin work, Resolutiones super Propositione XIII. de protestate Papae, 1519 (Erl. Ed., op. var. arg., III, 293 ff; Weimar Ed., II, 180 ff). The present work is written in German "for the laity."

[7] Christenheit. Luther carefully avoids the use of the word "Church" (Kirche). The reason will appear in the argument which follows. In many places, however, the word "Christendom" would not Luther's meaning, and there is, for the modern reader, no such technical restriction to the term "Church" as obtained among Luther's readers. Where the word Christenheit is rendered otherwise than "Christendom" it is so indicated in a footnote.

[8] The chief point argued at the Leipzig Disputation, whether the power of the pope is jure divino or jure humano.

[9] Das feine barfüssische Büchlein—i. e., a book written by a bare-footed friar. See below, p. 345.

[10] A comment explanatory of a passage of Scripture or of the Canon Law.

[11] Pallium, a scarf made of sheep's wool, which the pope is privileged to wear at all times, and others only on specified occasions; conferred by the pope on persons of the rank of archbishops; on its bestowal depended the assumption of the title and functions of the office. The granting of pallis became a rich source of revenue for the pope since each new incumbent of a prelacy had to apply for his own pallium in person, or by special representative, and to pay for the privilege of receiving it. At the appointment of Uriel as bishop of Mainz in 1508, even the emperor urged a reduction of one-half the usual fees, especially since the previous incumbent had paid the full price but four years previous. The request was denied. See Art Mainz in PRE 1, 2.

[12] Zur Halfte, so nicht mehr, geistlich. See below, page 356, No. 2.

[13] Is this an allusion to the papal title, servus servorum Dei, "the servant of the servants of God"?

[14] Alveld's German treatise described itself in the title as a "fruitful, useful little book."

[15] Alveld's Latin treatise especially abounds in these appellations.

[16] Alveld belonged to the branch of the Franciscan Order known as the "Observants" (fratres reglaris observatiae), from their strict observance of the Franciscan Rule. See the title of the Latin treatise in Weimar Ed., VI, 277.

[17] Christenheit.

[18] Gemeinde—the German equivalent for the Latin communio, communitas, or congregatio. In Luther's use of the term it means sometimes "community," sometimes "congregation," sometimes even "the Church" (Gemeinde der Heiligen). In this case it translates Alveld's civilitas (Weimar Ed., VI, 278).

[19] Christenheit.

[20] Luther quotes, in German, the reading of the Latin Vulgate.

[21] Christenheit.

[22] Gemeinde. A play on the word. On the second use of the term, compare the similar employment of the English word "parish."

[23] Christenheit.

[24] From Veni Sancte Spiritus, an antiphon for Whitsuntide dating from the eleventh century.

[25] Christenheit.

[26] Es ist erlogen und erstunken.

[27] Gemeinde.

[28] Christenheit.

[29] Versammlung.

[30] Gemeinde.

[31] Versammlung.

[32] Einigkeit oder Gemeinde.

[33] A quaint interpretation of the passage: "The disciples were called Christians first in Antioch."

[34] Christenheit.

[35] Nun bitten wir den heiligen Geist, a popular pre-Reformation hymn, of one stanza, for Whitsuntide, dating from the middle of the thirteenth century; quoted in a sermon by Berthold, the Franciscan, a celebrated German preacher in the Middle Ages, who died in Regesburg in 1272. Published by Luther, with three stanzas of his own added, in his hymn-book of 1524. Vid. Wackernage, Kirchenlied, ii, 44; Koca, Geachicte des Kirchenlieds, i, 185; Julian, Dict. of Hymnology, 821. Also Miss Winkworth's Christian Singers, 38.

[36] Christenheit.

[37] Gemeinde.

[38] Christenheit.

[39] Christenheit.

[40] All sources from which the Church or the clergy derived an income were called in the broader sense, "spiritual" possessions. A further distinction was drawn between two kinds of ecclesiastical income—the spiritualia in this sense being the fees, tithes, etc., and the temporalia the income from endowments of land and the like.

[41] The followers of John Huss.

[42] Zwölfbote, a popular appellation for the apostles, meaning one of the twelve messengers.

[43] See page 351.

[44] Christenheit.

[45] Literally, "Rastrume better than malvoisie." "Rastrum" was a Leipzig beer reported to be extraordinarily bad; "malvoisie," a highly prized, imported wine, known in England as "malmsey."

[46] In the German treatise Alveld says: "It is not enough to have Christ for a shepherd or a head; if that were sufficient, all the heathen, all the Jews, all the errorists, all the heretics would be true Christians. Christ is a lord, a guardian, a shepherd, a head of the whole world, whether we want him or not." (Weimar Ed., VI, 301) In the Latin he says: "No community or assembly (civilitars seu pluralitas) of men can be rightly administered except in the unity of the head, under the Head Jesus Christ." This proposition he develops in detail, saying that "No brothel (contubernium meretricum), no band of thieves, plunderers and robbers, no company of soldiers can be ruled or held together, or long exist without a governor, chief and lord, that is to say, without one head." (Weimar Ed., VI, 278).

[47] See above, p. 358.

[48] Jerome Emser, De disputatione Lipsicense and A venatione Luteriana aegocerotia assertio.

[49] Augustine, In Joannia Ev., 12, 3, 11. (Migne Ed., 35 149 ff.)

[50] Cf. Augustine, De unitate ecclesiae, 5, 8. (Migne Ed., 43, 396 f.)

[51] In his Sermon von Sacrament des Leichnams Christi of 1519 (Weimar Ed., II, 742 ff.) Luther had made a plea for the restoration of the cup to the laity. At the request of Duke George of Saxony, the bishop of Meissen (Jan. 20th, 1520) forbade the circulation of this tract in his diocese (Weimar Ed., VI, 76; Hauerbath, Luther, I, 316). The controversy, to which Luther contributed is Verklärung etlicher Artikel, etc. (Weimar Ed., VI, 78 ff.), was bitterest in the Leipzig circle to which Alved belonged.

[52] See pp. 373 and 380.

[53] A reference to Emser's De disputatione Lipsicense, and A ventione Luteriana aegocerotis assertio, see above, p. 363.

[54] Luther's greeting to a forthcoming and much heralded work of Eck's, which appeared under the title De primatu Petri.

[55] This statement cannot be substantiated. But see commentaries on Acts 26:10 f.

[56] The memory of the warlike and avaricious pope Julius II. was still fresh in the mind of Luther and his contemporaries.

[57] Alveld so announced himself in the title of his Latin treatise. In order go gain the necessary leisure for its composition he had obtained a dispensation from all the capel services of his monastery. See Weimar Ed., VI, 277.

[58] In a similar vein of satire Shakespeare uses this very phrase in "Merry Wives of Windsor," III, 5.

[59] Gemeinde.

[60] Alveld had stated that the attempt had been made "more than 23 times"; and again, "The assembly has existed more than 1486 under the chair of St. Peter which Christ has established." See Weimar Ed., VI.

[61] Gemeinde.

[62] Still the old terminology.

[63] Equivalent to father-confessor. The pope's own confessor is so called.

[64] Alveld makes this distinction in both of his treatises.

[65] Gemeinde.

[66] See page 373.

[67] See especially the Resolutiones super Propositione XIII.

[68] i. e., The Russians, who were in ecclesiastical fellowship with the Orthodox Greek Church. The metropolitan see of Moscow represented the opposition to union with Rome, which had been proposed in 1439; the second metropolitan see of Russia, that of Kief, was until 1519 favorable to the union. See A. Palmieri and W. J. Shipman, in The Catholic Encyclopedia, X, 594 ff; XIII, 255 f., and Adeney, Greek and Eastern Churches, 385 ff.

[69] Gemeinde.

[70] Annates (annatae, annalia), originally the income which a bishop received from the vacant benefices in his diocese, usually amounting to a year's income of the benefice. By a decree of John XXII, 1317 (Extrav. Jn. XXII, Lib. I, C. 2), the annates are fixed at one-half of one year's income of the benefice reckoned on the basis of the tithes, and payable on accession of the new incumbent. Two years later (1319) the same Pope set an important precedent by claiming for himself the annates from all benefices falling vacant in the next two years (Extrav. Comm. 3, 2, C. II). The right to receive annates subsequently became a regular claim of the popes. The term was extended after 1418 to include, beside the annates proper, the so-called servitia, payments made to the curia by bishops and abbots at the time of their accession. Luther discusses the subject at greater length in the Address to the Christian Nobility. (See Vol. II)

[71] See above, p. 362.

[72] Römische Einigkeit.

[73] This is Alveld's explanation in his German treatise.

[74] Comment, equivalent to "lie" or "invention."

[75] Rastrum, see above, note on p. 362.

[76] The sheeps' clothing in which they come.

[77] A reference to the sale of dispensations, more fully discussed in the Address to the Christian Nobility.

[78] At the well-known disputation in the previous year.

[79] John Lonicer in Contra romanistam fratrem, etc., and John Bernhardi in Confutatio inepti et impii libelli, etc.; both replies to Alveld's Latin treatise which appeared shortly before this treatise of Luther's.

[80] Gemeinde.

[81] A promise fulfilled in his Address to the Christian Nobility.

[82] In the title to his Latin treatise.

[83] Of the German treatise.

INDEX

SCRIPTURE REFERENCES

INDEX

Annates

Anthony, St.

Antichrist

Antilogistae

Apology

Apostate

Apostle

Apostles

Aristotle

Articles of faith

Assurance of salvation

Attrition

Augsburg Confession

    Diet of

Augustine

Augustine's Confessions

Auxiliatores

Ave Maria

Aven amal

Babylon, king of

Babylonian captivity

Baptism

    three parts of

    the sign of

    a flood of grace

    a covenant

    and penance

    significance of

    makes guiltless

Diseases, number known

Dishonesty

Disobedience

Dispensation from vows

Disputation

Doctors

Easter Day

Eck

Elevation of the host

Elmser

Endowments

Enemies, duties toward

Epicureans

Erasmus, Disider

Erasmus, St.

Estates, why instituted

Esther, Queen

Eternal punishment

Eucharistia

Eustachiua, St.

Evils, within us

    never fully known

    before us

    behind us

    beneath us

    on our left hand

    on our right hand

    above us

    to be loved

Lord's Prayer

   Supper

Louvaine

Love of God

   required in a bishop

Low Mass

Luther's coarse language

   inconsistency

   indifference to slander

   lack of love

   love of peace

   pride

   submission to pope

   zeal for Christ

Luther's zeal for the pope

   writings

   self-abasement

   sense of duty

   master of theology

   called a heretic

Luxury

Mainz, Boshopric

Malvoisie

Man, two natures

   three parts of

Manasseh, Payer of

   king

Margaret, St.

Mass

300

Zwölfbote

Note from the Editor

Odin's Library Classics strives to bring you unedited and unabridged works of classical literature. As such, this is the complete and unabridged version of the original English text unless noted. In some instances, obvious typographical errors have been corrected. This is done to preserve the original text as much as possible. The English language has evolved since the writing and some of the words appear in their original form, or at least the most commonly used form at the time. This is done to protect the original intent of the author. If at any time you are unsure of the meaning of a word, please do your research on the etymology of that word. It is important to preserve the history of the English language.

Taylor Anderson

Made in the USA
Las Vegas, NV
22 August 2023

76476063R00175